Heroines of the Medieval World

Heroines of the Medieval World

Sharon Bennett Connolly

AMBERLEY

For the two men in my life, my husband James and son Lewis, and my mum and dad. With love, always.

First published 2017

Amberley Publishing
The Hill, Stroud
Gloucestershire, GL5 4EP

www.amberley-books.com

British Library Cataloguing in Publication Data.
A catalogue record for this book is available from the British Library.

ISBN 978 1 4456 6264 0 (hardback)
ISBN 978 1 4456 6265 7 (ebook)

Typesetting and Origination by Amberley Publishing.
Printed in the UK.

Contents

Acknowledgements

Writing this book has been an incredible experience and I would like to thank everyone who has helped and encouraged me through the process. I would like to thank the staff at Amberley, especially Shaun Barrington and Cathy Stagg, for giving me the opportunity.

I would particularly like to thank Amy Licence, whose help, advice and friendship has been invaluable to me. I am very grateful to my fellow Amberley authors, Kristie Dean and Susan Higginbotham, who have offered advice and encouragement throughout.

I would also like to thank the readers of my blog, *History ... the Interesting Bits* for their wonderful support and feedback. A special thank you goes to my friends in the online community, whose amusing anecdotes and memes have given me that boost when I needed it, particularly Karrie Stone, Diana Milne, Tim Byard-Jones, Karen Clark, Geanine Teramani-Cruz, Anne Marie Bouchard, Harry Basnett, Derek Birks and every one of my Facebook friends and Twitter followers.

Particular thanks go to Kristie Dean, Karen Mercer and Tina Walker for their kind permission to use their wonderful photos. And to Sara Hanna-Black for her help with the Mortimer family's dates and details.

A thank you to my friends closer to home, for their wonderful support and for dragging me out for coffee when I needed a break.

I reserve a special thanks to my family. To my mum and dad for all their love and support, and for their own passion for history. A special thank you goes to my research assistant and son, Lewis Connolly, who has travelled to various wonderful places with me in the process of making this book a reality. And to my husband, James, thank you for putting up with all the history talks.

I couldn't have done it without all of you.

Introduction

Heroines come in many different forms, and it is no less true for medieval heroines. They can be found in all areas of medieval life; from the dutiful wife and daughter to religious devotees, warriors and rulers. What makes them different compared to those of today are the limitations placed on them by those who directed their lives – their fathers, husbands, priests and kings. Women have always been an integral part of history, although when reading through the chronicles of the medieval world, you would be forgiven if you did not know it. We find that the vast majority of written references are focussed on men. The chronicles were written by men and, more often than not, written for men. It was men who ruled countries, fought wars, made laws and treaties, dominated religion and guaranteed – or tried to guarantee – the continued survival of their world. It was usually the men, but not all of them, who could read, who were trained to rule and who were expected to fight, to defend their people and their country.

You would be forgiven for assuming that the only role for a noblewoman – or any woman – was to provide heirs and inheritances for the men, that medieval women were seen as property, as chattels. From the moment of their birth they were the property of their fathers, who would decide their future; whether they married – and to whom – or joined a convent. Their father dictated their level of education and his connections decided their position in life, and their future sphere of influence. Once they married, women became the property of their husbands. They were needed to carry on a family line and to run the home and estates while the husband was away fighting or attending to the king. The woman's sphere of influence would rarely extend beyond the domestic.

These men had aims and desires for their wives and daughters – for what advantages they could bring them. The father wanted an advantageous marriage, in which his daughter would bring allies, status and prestige to his family. The husband looked for a bride who could bring money, property and provide an heir (or die trying). Heiresses were used to improve the coffers of impoverished lords – a rich heiress was a great prize for any lord or prince wishing to increase the size of his fortune, or a younger son looking for a title of his own.

Although there were many women in the medieval era who did the extraordinary, who stood out in a world dominated by men, they are not easy to find. The chronicles of the times were predominantly written by monks, men who had little, if any, time for women and who viewed females as descendants of Eve and therefore likely to be the cause of the downfall of men. Priests advised men against falling prey to the lures of the daughters of Eve. The Church insisted that as God made Eve from Adam's rib, so women were subject to the rule of men. Chroniclers, often writing from the seclusion of their monasteries, were quick to detail the flaws of women, and highlight how female excesses caused crises in a kingdom. The mistress of Edward III in his declining years, Alice Perrers, was vilified by chroniclers for interfering in politics, benefiting herself and her friends and being an undue influence on the ageing, but much-loved, monarch. We do have some less critical chroniclers, such as Froissart who wrote in the times of Edward III, who tend to write about women while using high-flown language and an abundance of flattery. Women were also extolled as the inspiration for chivalry by writers such as Chaucer and Mallory. Geoffrey Chaucer, in particular, is known to have taken his inspiration from real-life people and the events of the royal court, to which he was closely related by marriage. His stories were designed (at least on the surface) to teach the morals and virtues of a good life.

A woman had to walk a fine line in the medieval world, and this applied throughout Europe, taking care not to be vilified as being too masculine; even a woman wearing men's clothing when riding was considered scandalous. However, women learned to survive – even flourish – in this male-dominated world, and to be subtle in order to get what they wanted out of life. Infrequently, a woman would astound people by going on Crusade, such as Eleanor of Aquitaine, or becoming queen regnant, such as Margaret, the little Maid of Norway, who almost became Scotland's first ruling queen.

These women did make it into the chronicles; they are there – even if the information on them is sparser than it would have been if they had been men. Throughout Europe, we have examples of women gaining power, even if only for a short time; women such as Jadwiga of Poland, a country that didn't have a queen regnant because they called their female rulers 'king'. Jadwiga is a rare woman in medieval Europe; she was a ruler in her own right. Many women have ruled, usually on behalf of their infant sons, holding their countries together until their children were old enough to take up the burden. Many such women were able to exert their influence even further into their son's reign and carve a position of authority for themselves, as advisers to their children, or by giving support and patronage to supplicants.

One place where women could achieve a certain level of autonomy was in the convents. Although overall their lives were still dictated by men, headed by the pope, within their own orders, in their own convents, nuns were ruled by women, by their prioresses and abbesses. Abbesses were often noblewomen who had sought a career in the Church, having been given to convents by their parents as children; they saw the Church as a place they could gain power and prestige, while doing something worthwhile with their lives. A convent was a place of education, where the wealthy would send their daughters to be taught languages and literature, and the essentials they would need in their adult lives. Many kings of England pledged daughters to convents that they patronised. Some young women would make their lives and careers in the Church, whereas others would leave when marriages were arranged for them. However, they would often return later in life, as a convent was also seen as a refuge and place of retirement for wealthy, older widows who had had enough of the outside world, or for younger widows who wanted to avoid the stresses of the marriage market.

Every now and then, if you read between the lines, you may see the women themselves – just a glimpse, a snippet only, of the women who made a difference or broke the mould. In picking out these sources, and connecting them like pieces of a jigsaw, we can see what women were capable of, what they managed to achieve even in the patriarchal world of medieval Europe. There are women such as Nicholaa de la Haye, who held Lincoln for King John against an invading French army when it looked as if the whole of England would soon be bowing to King Louis I. And Joan of Arc, who rallied the French to the banner of the dauphin and defeated the English, turning the tide of the Hundred Years War.

Women were the subjects of many laws, but very few women had the chance to influence them – such as Maud de Braose, who spoke out against King John's crimes and whose death (or murder) was the inspiration for a clause in Magna Carta. There are also the victims. Women whose position in life made them a threat to the men in power; such as Eleanor of Brittany, whose claim to the throne of England meant she spent her life in 'honourable' captivity, held by King John and subsequently his son Henry III. Her bloodline alone made her a threat to these kings – and a valuable prize to any man willing to take the chance to try to free her.

Only rarely, very rarely, do we find instances of true love. Often it develops within a marriage but there are examples where a lady has managed, against the odds, to obtain her heart's desire. The story of Joan of Kent and the Black Prince is one example. But the Black Prince's sister, Isabella of Woodstock, is a greater example of a woman – and a princess, no less – controlling her own life, refusing the husbands offered to her by her father and choosing to marry only in her thirties, when she believed she had found love. This was a truly remarkable feat, especially when you consider that a princess was a prized commodity on the international marriage market.

Other women were held as hostages against their families' ambitions, such as the relations of Robert the Bruce, or as guarantors for reparations, such as the daughters of Pedro the Cruel. It is true, however, there were also women who earned a place in the chronicles through their infamy, rather than fame, to be held up as warnings against the wiles of women, rather than as the ideals of womanhood. Women such as Eleanor Cobham, Duchess of Gloucester, and Alice Perrers, vilified for wanting to protect and advance their own ambitions.

It is interesting to note that only a tiny minority of women ever lived up to the male vision of the ideal woman; the model of medieval femininity was almost impossible to achieve. Women had their own methods of getting things done, of surviving. They tended to do things within the boundaries and restrictions of a male-dominated society, but they did find ways to circumvent the rules, to make a difference in the lives of not only their families, but of future generations of women.

What you discover, as you delve into the literature of the Middle Ages, and as you read the chronicles, look through records of the law courts, royal ordinances and wills, is that women were not as invisible or absent as you might assume. The evidence is there, if you look deeply enough, to piece together the lives of most of these remarkable women. There are gaps, of course. We often do not always know their parentage; sometimes we don't know the year they were born and have to heavily rely on estimates, based on their likely age when they married, or produced their first child. But we do know they were able to exert their influence on kings, princes and lords and what should not be surprising is that most of these men did not see their ladies as 'the little woman'; the clever ones used the talents of their wives as valued confidantes and trusted advisers. After all, the aims of a husband and wife are often one and the same. It is possible to discern their influence and to demonstrate the impact they had in societies throughout medieval Europe.

One point that should not be forgotten is that noblewomen (not the females of the lower classes of course) had *time*. They had time to learn on their own account, to explore art, sometimes even to produce it (in the form of tapestry work for example). Some of these women are far more cultured than their lords and masters.

From the decline of the Vikings to the dusk of the Middle Ages, and the centuries between, this book aims to paint a picture of the lives of these women by discussing the events that shaped their world so we can see the dangers and challenges they faced and overcame to survive and even flourish in the medieval era – but more than that, how they were seen in their own lifetimes by those who knew them, the chroniclers who recorded their stories, albeit briefly at times, and their contemporaries, who drew inspiration from their lives and actions.

While some of these women were something akin to the model of perfect womanhood espoused in the medieval world, the majority were not – yet they were all heroines in their own way. All of them showed intelligence, courage and fortitude in the face of overwhelming challenges. While some acted out of their own needs and desires, others shouldered the burdens of their own or often adopted countries. They acted as patronesses, guardians – and even rulers, when needed. Their stories deserve to be told.

A note on structure: this book can of course be read from beginning to end; it is not organised chronologically, however, but thematically, so it is possible (or should be) to read, for example, about female rulers independently of the other chapters.

1

The Medieval Ideal

The ideal medieval woman was more of a fantasy than a reality. Even those women later held up as examples of the medieval ideal, such as Matilda of Flanders, wife of William the Conqueror, were capable of more than was expected of them and, at times, followed their own initiatives to keep their family together. Noblewomen were expected to bring fortune and prestige to their families, both the one into which they were born and the family into which they would marry. Their primary function in a marriage was to produce children who would carry on the family line and the family name; but they were also expected to manage the household, to look after a husband's interests when he was away at war, and to supervise the education of children, at least in the early years.

Matilda of Flanders was the consummate duchess and queen. Born in the early to mid-1030s, possibly around 1032, Matilda was the daughter of Baldwin V, Count of Flanders, and his wife Adela, who was a daughter of Robert the Pious, King of France. Matilda had two brothers and each of them became Count of Flanders in his turn; Baldwin of Mons and Robert the Frisian. Matilda also had a sister, Judith, who married Tostig Godwinson, Earl of Northumberland, and younger brother of Harold, Earl of Wessex and, later, King of England as Harold II.

As is often the case with medieval women, we know very little of Matilda's early life and the first time she appears on the world stage is when her marriage is being discussed. There is a popular story of how Matilda refused to marry William, Duke of Normandy, stating that she was too highly born to marry a bastard. The story continues that on hearing this, William was so infuriated that he rode to Flanders and confronted Matilda; he is said to have assaulted her, throwing her to the ground, pulling her braids and cutting her with his spurs. Matilda, unlikely as it seems, then accepted his proposal and they were married. This story of rough wooing is probably a later invention, perhaps designed to highlight the masculinity of the Conqueror. It seems William was the one to propose the marriage and although he was a duke, his illegitimacy would have meant making a proposal to a niece of the King of France was audacious, to say the least.

The arrangements for the marriage of Matilda and William probably started in 1048, but it was a long, drawn out matter, marred by papal and political machinations. Indeed, the Synod of Reims, of 3 and 4 October 1349, issued a decree instructing Count Baldwin not to allow the marriage of his daughter to Duke William. Although no reason was given for the prohibition, historians have speculated this was possibly due to consanguinity – that the couple were related within the prohibited seven degrees. Historian Teresa Cole has done a detailed study of the lineage of the couple and has found no connections, except when William's aunt became the second wife of Matilda's grandfather, Baldwin IV; however, Matilda's father was the son of Baldwin IV's first wife, not his second.[1] Her research shows there was no consanguinity.

It seems more likely that the basis of the prohibition was politically motivated. Baldwin V had recently backed the failed Lotharingian rebellion, against the Holy Roman Emperor, and it may well be that the new pope, Leo IX, a German, was being loyal to his Imperial backers by forbidding a marriage that would strengthen an anti-German alliance. However, although the pope's decree probably delayed the marriage, it failed to prevent it, and it may have taken place as early as 1050, when Matilda first appeared as witness to a Norman charter, but had certainly happened at the latest by 1053. By then the pope was effectively a prisoner of those Normans who had established themselves in the southern Italian states. As he was in no position to continue his opposition to the marriage, there was an informal withdrawal of the prohibition, although it was only formally lifted by the new pope, Nicholas II, in 1059. A penance was imposed on the couple for their disobedience in marrying against papal prohibition. Each was to found an abbey; William founded the Abbaye-aux-Hommes, or St Stephen's

Abbey, in his Norman capital of Caen, while Matilda founded the Abbaye-aux-Dames, or Holy Trinity Abbey, in the same city. The two abbeys still stand to this day.

The marriage between Matilda and William proved to be a strong and trusting relationship; William is one of very few medieval kings believed to have been completely faithful to his wife, no known lovers or illegitimate children have ever been uncovered, although that did not stop the rumours. William of Malmesbury related one such story, of William having a mistress, the daughter of a priest, who Matilda ordered to be hamstrung and disinherited; in revenge, Matilda is said to have been beaten to death by a horse bridle. Malmesbury himself was sceptical of the story and, given that Matilda's death came after a short illness in 1083, it does seem rather far-fetched.[2]

William trusted Matilda to act as regent in Normandy during his many absences on campaign or in England. Their relationship was more of a partnership than most medieval marriages; she was witness to thirty-nine pre-conquest and sixty-one post-conquest charters. Matilda supported her husband's proposed invasion of England; she promised a great ship for William's personal use, called the *Mora*. The ship had a figurehead of a small boy, whose right hand pointed forward and left hand held a horn to his lips. Just before leaving for England in 1066, William accompanied Matilda to the consecration of her foundation, Holy Trinity Abbey – the Abbaye-aux-Dames – in Caen, arranging for his duchess to act as regent in his absence. The Conquest was a close-run thing and it was not until 1068 that William felt secure enough to bring his wife over to England. Matilda, six months pregnant with her son Henry, who would be born in September, was crowned Queen of England in Westminster Abbey, by Archbishop Ealdred of Canterbury, at Whitsun in the same year. However, further unrest soon saw her, with baby Henry, returned to the relative safety of Normandy, where she was acting as regent for her absent husband.

Matilda and William had a large family, with four boys and at least four daughters. Their eldest son, Robert Curthose, who inherited Normandy, was followed by Richard, who was killed during a hunting accident as a youth; William, known as Rufus, who became King William II; and the future Henry I. Of the four or five daughters, Adeliza became a nun following a series of failed marriage plans, Cecilia was given to the convent of Ste Trinité as a child, Constance married Alain Fergant, Duke of Brittany, and Adela married Stephen of Blois; their son, another Stephen, would succeed Henry I as King of England. There are suggestions of two further daughters, Matilda and Agatha, though evidence for their existence is limited. Queen Matilda was very close to her family, especially her eldest son, Robert, whose later actions were to cause problems between his parents. William and Robert, father and son, were often at loggerheads, with Robert in open rebellion against his father as a young adult. Matilda was constantly trying to play the peacemaker and was so upset by one quarrel that she was 'choked by tears and could not speak'.[3] Even during a period of exile imposed on Robert, Matilda still supported her son as best she could. He was not known for his careful spending, so Matilda would send Robert vast amounts of silver and gold through a Breton messenger, Samson. On discovering Samson's complicity, William threatened to blind the messenger and it was only through Matilda's intervention that the Breton escaped.

Matilda was one of the most active medieval queens, standing in as an able administrator during her husband's absences; hearing land pleas and corresponding with leaders such as the pope, who is known, on occasion, to have asked her to use her influence over her husband. Indeed, Pope Gregory VII encouraged her: 'Urge your husband, do not cease to suggest useful things to his soul. For it is certain that, if the infidel husband is saved by a believing wife, as the apostle says, a believing husband can be made better by a believing wife.'[4] She was also the driving force in holding together her family, keeping relations as cordial as possible, even with the rebellious Robert. And it may well have been due to her own strength of character, as the centre of the family, that none of her sons were married until after her death.

Although the problems with Robert, their eldest son, caused considerable tensions within the marriage, Matilda and William's relationship is one of the most successful of the medieval period. Their partnership as rulers, and as husband and wife, was strong and appeared to be one built on mutual respect. One contemporary remarked that 'The Queen adored the King and the King the Queen.'[5] Said to be a happy and loving marriage, their trust in each other was demonstrable and it was remarked upon when William fell seriously ill during a stay at Cherbourg between 1063 and 1066. Matilda prayed for his recovery at the altar; the monks remarking on her informal appearance as a sign of the distress her husband's illness was causing her. William addresses Matilda warmly in a letter he wrote to her:

> William, by the grace of God King of the English, to Queen Matilda, his dear spouse, perpetual health/greeting. I want you to know that I grant to St Martin at Marmontier the church of Ste Marie des Pieux and the lands that depend on it, free of all rents, as priest Hugh held them on the day of his death. Furthermore, I charge you to render, as is just, all the land in Normandy belonging to St Martin, free and secure from all those who would wish to burden it, as well as from the demands of the foresters; above all forbid Hugolin de Cherbourg to meddle further with the affairs of this house.[6]

Matilda's piety was renowned. Although founding the Abbayeaux-Dames in Caen was a penance for her irregular marriage to William, her constant and repeated donations to religious houses demonstrate her dedication to her faith. Among her many donations; she gave the monks of Marmoutier a new refectory and a cope, and to the monks of St Evroult she gave £100 for a refectory, a mark of gold, a chasuble decorated with gold and pearls, and a cope for the chanter. To St Corneille at Compiegne she gave a vase decorated with gold and precious stones and to the abbey of Cluny a chasuble 'that was so rigid because of the metal that it could not be folded'.[7] The nuns of her abbey at Ste Trinité, Caen, received a substantial bequest from Matilda's will, written the year before her death; as well as her crown and sceptre, they were given a chalice, a chasuble, a mantle of brocade, two golden chains with a cross, a chain decorated with emblems for hanging a lamp in front of the altar, several large candelabras, the draperies for her horse and all the vases 'which she had not yet handed out during her life'.[8] There is, however, one black mark against her name in that she is said to have demanded that the monks of Abingdon send her their abbey's most precious ornaments, so that she could choose those she would like; although the veracity of the story is questionable as it comes from an English source in the 1130s and is used as an example of post-Conquest Norman bullying tactics.

In July 1083, as the relationship between her husband and son soured once more, Matilda fell ill. She, William and Robert were together for the last time at Caen, on 18 July, and Robert left court shortly after.[9] Matilda had drawn up her will in the previous year, so it is possible that she was aware of her illness long before her last summer. The continuing worry over the rift between her husband and beloved son cannot have helped her health, and the arrival of winter saw her gravely ill. Matilda died on 2 November 1083, having 'confessed her sins with bitter tears and, after fully accomplishing all that Christian custom requires and being fortified by the saving sacrament'.[10] Her husband was with her throughout the final moments of her illness, and he '… showed many days of the deepest mourning how much he missed the love of her whom he had lost'.[11] She was buried at Ste Trinité, Caen, following a funeral that lasted two days and that was attended by a host of monks, abbots, bishops and nuns; and 'a great throng of people' came to pay homage to the late, 'respected duchess'.[12] There is no record of which of her children attended the funeral, although her daughter Cecilia was most likely in attendance, being a nun of the abbey. The original tombstone still survives; it has an inscription carved around the edge, emphasising her royal descent on her mother's side. Matilda's height has been discussed frequently by historians, with some claiming that she was a dwarf. The casket containing her bones was opened in 1961 revealing a woman of about 4ft 2in tall.[13]

Following her death, William became increasingly isolated; Robert deserted him, leaving his brother William to support his father. William the Conqueror followed his wife to the grave four years later, in 1087. In many aspects of her life, Matilda is clearly seen as the ideal medieval wife and mother. Ever supportive of her husband, he relied heavily on her to administer Normandy in his frequent absences, she was seen by many as a conduit to the king, as shown by the pope's letters encouraging her to be a good influence on her husband. Even when disobeying William, in her support of their eldest son Robert, she was still trying to be the embodiment of the good medieval woman, playing the peacemaker between warring members of her family. Her piety and steadfast support of her husband provided an example for future queens, and noble ladies, to follow.

One such was Isabel de Warenne, a young lady whose vast inheritance made her an attractive bride. Isabel was the only surviving child of William de Warenne, 3rd Earl of Surrey, and his wife Ela, or Ala. Ela was the daughter of William (III) Talvas, Count of Ponthieu. Isabel was probably in her mid- to late teens when her father was killed during the Second Crusade; in January 1148, he was fighting in the rearguard of France's king, Louis VII, when the force was destroyed in the defiles of Laodicea.[14] Ela would marry, for a second time, sometime before 1152; her second husband was Patrick, Earl of Salisbury, by whom she had four sons, William (Patrick's successor as earl), Patrick, Philip and Walter, before her death on 4 October 1174.

On the death of her father, Isabel became 4th Countess of Surrey, in her own right, and one of the most prized heiresses in England and Normandy. She had large estates in Yorkshire and Norfolk. Her father had been a strong supporter of King Stephen; he fought alongside the king during the Anarchy – Stephen's battles with his cousin, the Empress Matilda, to control England – and supported his wife, Queen Matilda, after King Stephen was captured at Lincoln. This affinity with Stephen's regime helps to explain why, in the same year that her father died, and as part of King Stephen's attempts to control the vast de Warenne lands, Isabel was married to Stephen's younger son, William of Blois, who became Earl of Surrey, by right of his wife. William, it seems, was about seven years younger than his wife, having been born in 1137. William was removed from the succession to the crown, by his own father when Stephen made a deal with Empress Matilda's son, Henry of Anjou, that the crown would go to him on Stephen's death.[15]

The agreement, sealed at Winchester in 1153, guaranteed William's position as the foremost magnate in the realm, with the lands from Isabel's earldom and the inheritance of his mother's county of Boulogne. William appears to have accepted this compromise, on the whole, although he was implicated in the 1154 plot to assassinate Henry of Anjou, most likely masterminded by William of Ypres. Unfortunately for William, his father's death, on 25 October in the same year, ended his chances of ousting Henry from the succession. Henry II reduced the threat William posed to his regime, in 1157, by stripping him of any lands that had been acquired by his father after the death of Henry I in 1135, and confiscating his castles at Pevensey and Norwich. In the following year, on 24 June, with the king's consent, William was knighted at Carlisle.

Isabel and William had been married for just over ten years when he died in October 1159, while he was returning home to England after the king's expedition to Toulouse. William was buried at the Abbey of Montmorel, in Poitou. Their marriage had been childless, and Isabel was again an important heiress so she had a little respite from the marriage market. By 1162 Henry II's youngest brother, William X, Count of Poitou, was seeking a dispensation to marry her. The dispensation was refused by Thomas Becket, Archbishop of Canterbury, on the grounds of consanguinity. The objection was not due to a blood relationship between Isabel and William, but between William and Isabel's first husband, William of Blois, who were second cousins. It has often been suggested that this was a love-match rather than an arranged marriage. We will, of course, never know how Isabel felt but William died shortly afterwards, at Rouen on 30 January 1164, supposedly of a broken heart. One of William's knights, Richard Brito, was among the quartet who murdered Thomas Becket in 1172, and is said to have cried as he struck his blow 'for the love of William, the King's brother'.[16]

Henry II was not to be thwarted, however, in his plan to bring the de Warenne lands into the royal family. His illegitimate half-brother, Hamelin, a son of Henry's father, Geoffrey of Anjou, by an unnamed woman, was married to Isabel in 1164. The couple wed in April 1164; Isabel's trousseau cost an impressive £41 10s 8d.[17] Hamelin became the 4th Earl of Surrey by right of his new wife and, in an unusual step, took his wife's surname. The marriage appears to have been highly successful. Hamelin was loyal to his brother, Henry II, and supported the king during the conflict with his sons in 1173. He was among the nobles chosen to escort Joanna, the king's daughter, to her marriage to William, King of Sicily; the nobles were ordered not to return home until they had seen 'the King of Sicily and Joanna crowned in wedlock'.[18]

Hamelin continued his support of the crown when his nephew Richard I succeeded in 1189. He played a prominent part in English politics while Richard was absent on the Third Crusade, supporting the chancellor during the chaos caused by the intrigues of the king's brother, John. He was one of the treasurers for the collection of the king's ransom, and carried one of the three swords at Richard I's second coronation on 17 April, 1194. He was also present at John's coronation on 27 May 1199. As Earl of Warenne and Surrey, Hamelin built the highly innovative, hexagonal keep at Conisbrough Castle in the 1170s and 1180s. King John visited Conisbrough on 5 March 1200 or 1201, from where he issued a charter, witnessed by William de Warenne (probably Hamelin's son and heir) and a letter to the dean and chapter of York.[19]

Isabel and Hamelin had four surviving children. Their son and heir, William, would become the 5th Earl of Surrey and married Maud, daughter of the great William Marshal, Earl of Pembroke and regent of England during the minority of Henry III. There were also three daughters, Ela, Isabel and Matilda, however it is possible Matilda was Hamelin's illegitimate daughter by an unknown woman. Ela married twice, firstly to a Robert de Newburn, of whom nothing else is known, and secondly to William Fitzwilliam of Sprotborough, a village just a few miles from Conisbrough. Isabel was married, firstly, to Robert de Lascy, who died in 1193, and secondly, no later than the spring of 1196, to Gilbert de Laigle, Lord of Pevensey. Matilda, or Maud, married Henry, Count of Eu, who died around 1190. She then married Henry d'Estouteville, a Norman lord. One of the daughters of Isabel and Hamelin – although it is not clear which – bore an illegitimate son, Richard Fitzroy, by her cousin, John (the future King John).

Although Isabel's story is one of those of which we know very little, and it is told through her husbands and children, rather her own actions, she was one of the foremost women in the realm, after the queen. As a young woman, and in her first widowhood, she probably attended Henry's queen, Eleanor of Aquitaine, at least on occasion. Isabel possessed her own seal, which is on display at Conisbrough Castle in South Yorkshire, and she witnessed a charter relating to Harthill, as Countess Warenne, during that first widowhood of 1159–64.[20] She would have been heavily involved in patronage, both secular and religious, throughout the vast Warenne estates. Her family's main religious interest was Lewes Priory, in Sussex, a Cluniac religious house founded by the first earl and his first wife, Gundrada, and the family mausoleum. Isabel and Hamelin gave generously to Lewes and several other religious institutions, such as West Dereham Abbey in Norfolk, St Katherine's Priory in Lincoln and also the chapel of St Philip and St James, which is within their keep at Conisbrough Castle.

Isabel was widowed for a second time when Hamelin died in 1202; in the same year, she granted sixty beasts to St Katherine's Priory at Lincoln, for the soul of her husband, 'namely 40 as of his gift and 20 as of hers'.[21] Isabel herself died the following year, at the grand age of seventy–three; she was buried in the chapterhouse at Lewes Priory, beside Hamelin. Although we know nothing about her personality, Isabel had been the consummate medieval countess, who was generous in her patronage, and whose marriages and children increased her family's prestige and influence. She had as little say in the direction of her life as any other medieval woman, but she appears to have made the most of it.

A princess of England, just a generation younger than Isabel, who not only found contentment in her marriage, but also love, was the daughter of the queen whom Isabel would have served. On 13 October 1162 (1161 has also been suggested, but most sources agree on 1162) the Queen of England gave birth to a daughter at Domfront Castle in Normandy; the little girl was named Eleanor, after her mother. She was the sixth child and second daughter of Europe's most glamorous and controversial couple, Henry II of England and Eleanor of Aquitaine. Baby Eleanor was baptised by Cardinal Henry of Pisa, with the chronicler Robert de Torigny standing as her godfather. Of Eleanor's four older brothers, three had survived infancy; Henry, the Young King; Richard the Lionheart, and Geoffrey, later Duke of Brittany. Geoffrey was nearest to Eleanor in age, but already four years old when she was born. Eleanor's older sister, Matilda, had been born in 1156 and would be married to Henry V 'the Lion', Duke of Saxony and Bavaria, when Eleanor was six years old. At the age of three Eleanor would be joined by a baby sister, Joanna, in the Plantagenet nursery and by a last brother, John, in 1166.

Eleanor's birth coincided with an awkward period in her parents' marriage. Eleanor of Aquitaine's vassals, unhappy with Henry's rule, were attempting to get her marriage to Henry annulled on the grounds of consanguinity. Although the plot was unsuccessful because the cardinals were unimpressed with the argument, it cannot have been an easy time for the king and queen. In her early childhood Eleanor often travelled with her parents, in her mother's entourage. Henry had been absent from England for five years when baby Eleanor first came to the country with her parents, in 1163. The royal family would spend the Christmas of 1164/5 at Marlborough, while in the midst of the crisis of Henry's disagreements with his Archbishop of Canterbury, Thomas a Becket. Eleanor of Aquitaine would then take her children to

Winchester, from where they visited Sherborne Castle in Dorset and the Isle of Wight before moving to Westminster.

In February 1165, three-year-old Eleanor was betrothed to the infant son of Frederick Barbarossa, also named Frederick, to cement a treaty with the emperor. And following the conclusion of the treaty, the Archbishop of Cologne was introduced to the future bride, Eleanor, and her sister, Matilda, who was to marry Henry the Lion. However, while Matilda departed for her new life in Germany in 1168, Eleanor's proposed marriage was still in the distant future. Some historians have speculated that Eleanor was educated for some time at Fontevrault Abbey, with her younger sister Joanna and her baby brother, John, who spent five years there after initially being intended for the Church. Even if this were so, by 1168 she was staying with her mother, who had settled in Aquitaine on an almost permanent basis, and was allowed, by Henry II, to have her children with her. By 1170 young Eleanor's marriage to the emperor's son was no longer a part of Henry II's plans, and he decided to look elsewhere for an alliance. Seeking to extend his influence beyond the French borders and to prevent a French alliance with Castile, Henry betrothed Eleanor to Alfonso VIII, the twelve-year-old King of Castile. Raoul de Faye, Seneschal of Poitou for Eleanor of Aquitaine, was influential in negotiating the marriage, arranging for the young princess to receive Gascony as her dowry, but only after the death of her mother.[22]

In September 1177 Eleanor set out for Castile, a month short of her fifteenth birthday; some historians suggest she was escorted as far as Bordeaux by her mother, but this is not supported by the contemporary chronicles.[23] Queen Eleanor was in high disgrace at this time. Having sided with her sons in their rebellion against her husband, Queen Eleanor was now more Henry II's prisoner than she was his wife. However, the young princess would have been given a suitable escort – as the daughter of a king and as a future queen herself – to see her safely delivered to her wedding at Burgos Cathedral. Eleanor and Alfonso appear to have had a very successful marriage and a close, trusting relationship. Known as Queen Leonore in her new country, she is renowned for introducing her mother's Poitevin culture into the Castilian court. The court encouraged the arts and architecture of Eleanor's youth, while blending it with the luxuries offered by the neighbouring Moorish culture. Castilian poet Ramon Vidal described Eleanor as

'Queen Leonore modestly clad in a mantle of rich stuff, red, with a silver border wrought with golden lions', while the troubadour Pierre Vidal described Eleanor as elegant and gracious.[24]

Eleanor and Alfonso had seven children who survived infancy. Their eldest daughter Berengaria would marry Alfonso IX, King of Leon, and would act as regent in Castile for her younger brother, Henry I, before succeeding him as queen regnant. Berengaria and Alfonso's marriage was dissolved by the papacy, on the grounds of consanguinity; but their children were declared legitimate. Shortly after succeeding to the throne of Castile, Berengaria abdicated in favour of her son, Ferdinand III, but continued to act as his closest adviser. One daughter, Eleanor, married James I, King of Aragon, but they divorced in 1229. Another daughter, Constance, was dedicated as a nun and eventually became abbess of the Abbey of Las Huelgas, founded by her parents in 1187. The abbey's nuns were drawn from the highest ranks of the Spanish nobility; they belonged to the Cistercian order, a closed community cut off from the world.[25]

Alfonso and Eleanor had two sons who would survive childhood. Their eldest, Ferdinand, predeceased his parents, dying of a fever in either 1209 or 1211. Henry I would succeed his father, but died tragically in 1217 when a loose roof tile fell on his head; he was thirteen years old. Two other daughters survived childhood. Eleanor's second eldest daughter, fourteen-year-old Urraca, was initially suggested as the bride for the future Louis VIII of France, son of Philip II Augustus. In 1200 the girls' grandmother, Eleanor of Aquitaine, Dowager Queen of England, was instrumental in arranging the marriage; her dowry was to be provided from the territories Richard I had won from France at the end of the 12th century. The elder Eleanor outlived all but two of her children; with the deaths of Richard I and his sister Joanna in 1199, only Eleanor in Castile and her baby brother John, now King of England, remained of the once large brood of four boys and three girls who had survived infancy. Such recent losses may have helped to persuade the seventy-seven-year-old Eleanor of Aquitaine to make the hazardous journey to Castile, in person and in the depths of winter, to collect the granddaughter who would be Louis' bride, and to spend some time with the daughter she hadn't seen in more than twenty years. The reunion of the two Eleanors must surely have been highly emotional.

England's Dowager Queen was received at Alfonso's court with all the pageantry and courtesies appropriate for the most remarkable woman of her time. Eleanor of Aquitaine stayed with the Castilian royal family for over two months, taking the opportunity to spend some time with her daughter and grandchildren, as the marriage would not be able to take place until after the Lenten season. In getting to know her granddaughters, Eleanor of Aquitaine seems to have decided that twelve-year-old Blanca would make a more suitable bride for Louis. It might have been because of the girls' temperaments or simply a matter of names, the excuse made at the time. Urraca was not a name easily translated into French, whereas Blanca, as Blanche, was easily recognisable. Urraca had been first choice, before Eleanor had met her granddaughters, but once she had, it was decided it would be twelve-year-old Blanche who travelled back to France with her grandmother to marry the dauphin, Louis; the same Louis who would be invited to become England's king by the barons rebelling against King John and besieging Lincoln Castle in 1216. Blanche and Louis were married in Normandy; as France was under papal interdict at the time; Blanche would be the mother and lifelong adviser of Louis IX (St Louis). In 1206 Urraca was married the heir to the throne of Portugal – the future King Alfonso II.[26]

Eleanor of England and Alfonso VIII appear to have had a happy, successful marriage, producing a family of four sons and eight daughters over a sixteen-year period. Eleanor enhanced the culture of the Castilian court and acted as a diplomatic conduit between her husband and her brothers Richard and John, in order to aid each other and keep the peace – most of the time. However, in 1204, following the death of Eleanor of Aquitaine, Alfonso had to resort to a show of military force to successfully claim his wife's dower rights over Gascony from John. Their marriage ended when Alfonso died in Burgos on 6 October 1214. He was buried in the Abbey of Las Huelgas, where their daughter Constance was now abbess, leaving Eleanor as regent for their ten-year-old son, Henry I. Broken-hearted Eleanor, however, only survived her husband by a little over three weeks. Overcome with grief, she died in Burgos on 31 October 1214, aged fifty-two and just over two weeks after her birthday. She was laid to rest beside her beloved husband; leaving their daughter Berengaria to take up the regency for Henry.[27] Of Eleanor's grandchildren two were to become saints,

Louis IX of France and Berengaria's son Ferdinand III, King of Castile; her great-granddaughter and namesake, Eleanor of Castile (Ferdinand's daughter), would become Queen of England as the wife of Edward I. Eleanor was the ideal medieval queen. She was a dutiful and supportive wife, who provided her husband with a large family – a son to inherit the throne and a number of daughters to make strategic marriage alliances within the Iberian Peninsula, and beyond. She was also one of those lucky, rare women in medieval history; she found love and happiness within her marriage.

Another young woman who appears to have found contentment, and maybe love, in her marriage, was Blanche of Lancaster. Blanche is another of those ladies in history whose fame derives from her children and the acts of her husband, rather than from her own actions. Blanche's life was pitifully short, but her legacy was dramatic. It would see the unravelling of peace in the 15th century, and the decades of civil war called the Wars of the Roses. Blanche of Lancaster was born around 25 March 1345, at Bolingbroke Castle in Lincolnshire. She was the second and youngest daughter of illustrious parents; Henry of Grosmont, Duke of Lancaster, and Isabella de Beaumont. Henry of Grosmont was the grandson of Edmund Crouchback and a great-grandson of Henry III. Isabella was the daughter of Henry, 1st Baron de Beaumont and Earl of Buchan by right of his wife, Scottish heiress Alice Comyn; she was the granddaughter of John of Brienne, King of Jerusalem.

Blanche had only one sibling, her older sister, Matilda (or Maud), who married twice. As a child she was married to Ralph de Stafford, who died when Matilda was still only seven or eight years old. In February 1352, she was married, in the King's Chapel at Westminster, to William V, Duke of Bavaria, Count of Holland, Hainault and Zeeland, nephew of Edward III's queen, Philippa of Hainault. Blanche herself was betrothed to John de Segrave as a child, the agreement being made on 4 May 1347, but this seems to have been set aside soon afterwards.[28] As part of their education Matilda and Blanche joined the household of Queen Philippa; they would have been given lessons in deportment, dancing, needlework and the scriptures, in preparation for their futures as wives and mothers.

By the late 1350s Blanche was a part of King Edward III's plans to provide for his growing number of sons. As one of the country's richest heiresses, Blanche was chosen as the bride for Edward's third surviving son, John of Gaunt. Blanche and John were third cousins, being great-great-grandchildren of Henry III. John of Gaunt was already a seasoned soldier at the time of the wedding. He had served in the household of his older brother Edward, the Black Prince, for several years and had joined his brother on campaign in France, culminating in the Battle of Poitiers, when he was fifteen years old. He was already the father of an illegitimate child, also named Blanche, by one of his mother's ladies-in-waiting.[29]

The couple married on 19 May 1359 at Reading Abbey in Berkshire; Blanche was about fourteen and John was nineteen years old. The wedding was a lavish affair, conducted by Thomas de Chynham, clerk of the Queen's Chapel, with the whole royal family present as witnesses. Blanche was given a diamond ring by her new husband, while her father-in-law showered presents amounting to the grand total of £389 11s 6d on her consisting of jewels, belts and buckles; one ruby alone cost £20. Other family members gave gifts amounting to a total of £300.[30] The ceremony was followed by three days of celebrations at Reading, including a joust in Blanche's honour and three further days when the royal party returned to London.

The first year of a marriage must have been a whirlwind for Blanche. Within weeks she was pregnant with her first child, and within five months, in October 1359, her husband left on campaign as part of Edward III's invasion of France; Blanche's father was also part of the invasion force. Blanche stayed in Philippa's household while her husband was away. A letter from the king to Philippa of Hainault suggested that the pregnant Blanche stay with the queen 'because of the concern we feel for her condition'.[31]

In 1361 Blanche suffered a double tragedy. Her father, Henry of Grosmont, Duke of Lancaster, had returned from France in November 1360, triumphant after his successful conclusion of the Reims campaign and negotiation of the Treaty of Brétigny. However, in early 1361 he succumbed to the latest outbreak of bubonic plague, dying at Leicester Castle on 23 March. He was laid to rest beside the high altar in the Church of the Annunciation of the Blessed Virgin Mary at the Newarke in Leicester. Blanche's mother was buried beside him after falling victim to the same dreaded disease; she died on 6 July, just over three months after her husband. While Blanche's sister inherited the earldoms of Leicester and Lincoln, through Blanche, John of Gaunt inherited those of Derby and Lancaster; however, the title of Duke of Lancaster fell into abeyance with Henry of Grosmont's death. By mid-1362 Blanche's immediate family were all gone, her sister had returned to England from Bavaria to claim her inheritance of the earldom of Leicester, but fell victim to the same disease that had claimed her parents, and died on 10 April; there were some rumours of poison, but this seems unlikely. Matilda's remains were returned to Bavaria, where she was laid to rest at Rijnsburg Abbey. As Matilda had died childless, Blanche now inherited the remainder of her father's estates, adding the earldoms of Leicester and Lincoln to their vast holdings. John of Gaunt was soon invested with the title of Duke of Lancaster and became the most powerful magnate in England; holding more than thirty castles, his lands and possessions were second only to those of the king.

Blanche was pregnant for most of her married life, giving birth to seven children between 1360 and 1368. Three sons, John, Edward and a second John, and a daughter, Isabella, died young. Two daughters and a son did, however, survive into adulthood. The eldest daughter, Philippa, who will be discussed shortly, was born on 31 March 1360 and would marry King John I of Portugal. A second daughter, Elizabeth, was born in February 1364, at Kenilworth Castle. Her first marriage to John Hastings, 3rd Earl of Pembroke, was annulled; her second marriage to John Holland, 1st Duke of Exeter, would end with his execution for treason in 1400. They had five children. Elizabeth would marry for a third time to John Cornwall, 1st Baron Fanhope, with whom she had a daughter before she died in 1426. Blanche and John's last surviving child, Henry of Bolingbroke, was born at Bolingbroke Castle, Lincolnshire, in 1367, probably on 15 April. Having been exiled in the later years of the reign of his cousin, Richard II, Henry would return to England following the death of his father and the confiscation of his inheritance by the king. Richard was forced to abdicate and Henry succeeded to the throne as Henry IV. Henry's first marriage, to Mary de Bohun, produced seven children, including the future king, Henry V; his second marriage was to Joanna of Navarre, Duchess of Brittany, but would remain childless, probably due to Henry's declining health. Henry IV died on 20 March 1413 and was buried at Canterbury Cathedral; Joanna would be buried beside him following her own death in 1437.

By 1365 Blanche had taken Katherine Swynford into her household; Katherine was the wife of one of John of Gaunt's Lincolnshire knights. Moreover, John was godfather to their daughter, Blanche, who was named after the duchess. Young Blanche Swynford was lodged in the same chambers as the duchess's daughters, Philippa and Elizabeth, and accorded the same luxuries as the princesses. Having lost her parents and sister to the Black Death, it is not surprising that Blanche was fearful of the disease. In the summer of 1368 she is said to have moved her family away from the city, to Bolingbroke Castle, to escape the pestilence. There seems to be some confusion over the year of her death – some sources say 1368 – and even the nature of it. One theory is that Blanche succumbed to the bubonic plague, the disease she most feared, in 1369. As a daughter, Isabella, who died young, was born in 1368 some have suggested Blanche died in childbirth. Recent research by historian Amy Licence has revealed that Blanche died at Tutbury on 12 September 1368, more likely from the complications of childbirth than from the plague.[32] Her husband was by her side when she died and arranged to have prayers said for the soul of his lost duchess. Blanche was buried in Old St Paul's Cathedral, London; where John of Gaunt arranged for a splendid alabaster tomb and annual commemorations for the rest of his life. And despite two subsequent marriages, John of Gaunt would be interred next to Blanche following his own death in 1399. The tomb was lost when the cathedral was destroyed during the Great Fire of London in 1666.

Blanche is one of the few ladies of the 14th century of whom we have several descriptions. The chronicler Froissart noted that she was '*jone et jolie*' – young and pretty.[33] The best description, however, is from Geoffrey Chaucer, Katherine Swynford's brother-in-law, who was commissioned by John of Gaunt to write *The Book of the Duchess*, also known as *The Deth of Blaunche*. The poem is said to depict Gaunt's mourning for his wife, in the tale of a knight grieving for his lost love. Chaucer describes Blanche's neck (yes, her neck) as 'whyt, smothe, streght and flat'. Naming the heroine 'White', he goes on to say she is 'rody, fresh and lyvely hewed'. Blanche (White) was 'bothe fair and bright' and Nature's 'cheef patron of beautee'.[34] Despite John of Gaunt marrying Constance of Castile just two years later; as well as his eventual marriage to his mistress, Katherine Swynford, being singled out as one of the great love affairs of the age, it was said that Blanche was the love of his life. Chaucer's poem and the lavish tomb and commemorations are believed to highlight Gaunt's love for his first wife; the fact he was eventually buried beside her has been seen, by many, as the final proof of this love.

Although only twenty-three years old when she died, Blanche will forever be remembered as the mother of the Lancastrian dynasty, through her son, Henry IV. She was also, moreover, grandmother to the Portuguese Illustrious Generation through her daughter, Philippa. Like her mother, Philippa of Lancaster was the image of the ideal medieval lady. Born at Leicester on 31 March 1360, she was the eldest daughter of John and Blanche. Through her father, she was a granddaughter of Edward III and through her mother she was great-great-great-granddaughter of Henry III. Her father, as Duke of Lancaster, was one of the richest men in the country, and one of the most powerful. Philippa's life as a child would have been one of luxury and privilege, with a glorious dynastic marriage awaiting her in the future. She was raised with her younger sister, Elizabeth, who was born in 1363, and her baby brother, Henry of Bolingbroke, born in 1367. The children shared a household for some of their childhood and were given the best education available. Philippa was very well educated, studying poetry under Jean Froissart and philosophy and theology under John Wycliffe, the theologian who first translated the Bible into English. As we have seen, they lost their mother when Blanche died at Tutbury Castle on 12 September 1368; giving birth to her daughter, Isabella, who did not survive. The children's father, although he was with Blanche when she died, departed on campaign to France soon afterwards; however, it is doubtful that the children's care was interrupted by such tragedy and upheaval. The Lancaster household was well-organised and by 1376 the girls had been appointed a new governess, Katherine Swynford, who was by this time also mistress to their father, John of Gaunt.

As with most high-born women of the time, Philippa's marriage was in the hands of her father. John of Gaunt was keen to find a dynastic match, which would benefit and complement his own dynastic ambitions, although several early plans came to nothing. In 1374, Philippa was betrothed to Gaston, Count of Foix, but nothing came of it. In 1381/2 she was offered in marriage to Jean de Blois, claimant to the Duchy of Brittany; and in 1383 her prospective husband was Count William of Ostrevant, the heir to Hainault, Holland and Zeeland. By 1385 and now twenty-five years old, Philippa was still unmarried, an unusual situation for a princess. However, in the following year her father took her on his military expedition to Spain, hoping to claim the kingdom of Castile in right of his second wife, Constance of Castile.

Philippa's marriage to John (or João) I of Portugal was agreed as part of an alliance made between John and Philippa's father at Ponte do Mouro in November 1386. Philippa was married to King John at Oporto on 2 February 1387, before they had received the required papal dispensation; indeed, the couple had not even met as the marriage was conducted by proxy.[35] The British Museum has a beautifully illuminated manuscript that depicts the wedding; Philippa wearing a tall, pointed headdress and attended by three maids of honour, with John of Gaunt and his wife, Constance, looking on.[36] Philippa was twenty-six, about ten years older than the average age for a princess to marry; John was three years her senior and had been king for just short of two years.

Philippa became known as *Dona Fillipa* in Portugal and would be one of the country's best-loved queens because her natural predisposition to austerity and piety endeared her to the Portuguese people. Philippa reformed the court and encouraged games among her ladies. French poet Eustace Deschamps characterised her as the chief patron of the order of The Flower of England, casting her at the centre of the court and the May Day celebrations. A patron of literature, Philippa was sent a copy of John Gower's poem *Confessio amantis*, which was translated into Portuguese by Robert Payn, an English canon of Lisbon Cathedral.

Philippa had been made a Lady of the Garter in 1378 and was instrumental in fostering links between England and Portugal, helped by the mixture of English and Portuguese servants in her household. She was on good terms with both Richard II and his successor – her brother, Henry IV. In 1399 she wrote to the Archbishop of Canterbury, Thomas Arundel, asking him to intervene with Henry on behalf of her friend, Bishop Henry Despenser of Norwich, who had angered the new king by defending Richard II at the time of Henry's invasion of England and seizure of the throne. Philippa also had a hand in persuading Henry to arrange the marriage of her stepdaughter, Beatriz (her husband's illegitimate daughter) to the Earl of Arundel in 1405.

Almost immediately after the wedding John I returned to the war, accompanied by his new father-in-law, John of Gaunt, as well as Gaunt's wife and two unmarried daughters, Elizabeth and Catherine (or Catalina) of Lancaster. In July 1387 Philippa miscarried their first child while visiting John at Curval, where he lay seriously ill, to the extent that his life was despaired of.[37] However, with the war coming to a close in 1388 with the Treaty of Bayonne, and after what appears to have been a bumpy start, the couple seem to have been well-matched. John had had two illegitimate children before his marriage, but was demonstrably faithful to Philippa after the wedding. In fact, when court gossip reached the queen that he had been unfaithful, John went to great lengths to convince Philippa of his innocence. He even went so far as to commemorate the event by having a room in the royal apartments at Cintra decorated with chattering magpies – he must have had a great sense of humour, and confidence in his relationship to be so bold.[38]

Philippa and John had a large family, which they brought up with great care, both parents being involved in their children's education. Of their nine children, five sons and a daughter survived infancy and would later be known in Portugal as 'the Illustrious Generation'. Their son and heir, Alfonso, died at the age of ten, in 1400. Their eldest surviving son, Edward, was born in 1391 and would succeed his father as King of Portugal in 1433. Peter, Duke of Coimbra, was born in 1392 and would act as regent for his nephew, Afonso V, following Edward's death in 1438. Their most famous son was Prince Henry 'the Navigator', Duke of Viseu, who was renowned for researching and financing great explorations – although he never actually undertook expeditions himself. Their next youngest son was John, Duke of Beja and Constable of Portugal, who married Isabella, the daughter of Alfonso I, Duke of Braganza. The baby of the family was Ferdinand, Grand Master of Aviz; he was born in 1402 and was later known as 'the Saint Prince' following his death as a prisoner of the Moors. Ferdinand had been held as a hostage for the return of Ceuta following the Disaster of Tangier, a siege led by his brother Henry. Ferdinand was held in increasingly severe confinement when it became apparent no ransom would be forthcoming, until he finally died in 1443.

Two daughters, both named Blanche, died in infancy, but John and Philippa had one surviving daughter, Isabella, who was born in 1397 and would go on to marry Philip III the Good, Duke of Burgundy; she was the mother of Charles the Bold, Duke of Burgundy. By 1415, Philippa's oldest sons were itching to prove their martial prowess. Scorning their father's offer to hold a magnificent tournament for them, and with Philippa's encouragement, they persuaded him to mount an attack on the port of Ceuta in North Africa instead. As they were about to set sail, Philippa fell ill. She had contracted plague and died at Odivelas, near Lisbon, on 18 or 19 July 1415. She was fifty-five. On her deathbed, she gave each of her three eldest sons a jewel-encrusted sword, in anticipation of their impending knighthoods, and a piece of the true cross. She gave them her blessing for the forthcoming military expedition and exhorted them to preserve their faith and to fulfil the duties of their rank. The expedition sailed just five days after her death and Ceuta fell after only one day of siege, becoming Portugal's first African possession.

Described as pious, charitable, affable and obedient to her husband, Portuguese historian Fernao Lopes, secretary to Philippa's son, Fernando, held up Philippa as a model queen. Her piety was renowned; in later life, she was said to read the *Book of Psalms* regularly. Queen Philippa was buried in the Dominican Priory at Batalha Abbey, which had been founded by her husband. King John arranged for a magnificent tomb to be built in the Capela do Fundador. Constructed between 1426 and 1434, it is topped by their effigies, clasping each other's hands. King John himself was laid beside her after his death in August 1433. Their sons, Ferdinand, John, Henry and Peter, were laid to rest along the south side of the same chapel.

Philippa, as with all the ladies in this chapter, had fulfilled her role as the epitome of the admirable medieval woman. She had made a great marriage, forging an alliance between her husband and father that was beneficial to both. Her children were carefully educated and gained renown as soldiers, explorers – and a saint. However, Philippa, as with Matilda, Isabel de Warenne, Eleanor of England and her own mother, Blanche, before her, was so much more than the ideal that was held up as an example to others. These women supported their families, brought alliances and opportunities through their marriages and raised their children with care. Matilda was an able regent for her husband, William, while he was away in England, and a peacemaker between William and their eldest son, Robert. Isabel de Warenne also seems to have had a close relationship with her husband; she and Hamelin issued a number of charters together, particularly to benefit the religious houses of which they were patrons. Poor Blanche was pregnant for almost her entire marriage and died giving birth to her last child, at the age of only twenty-three. These women attained the medieval ideal of womanhood, but were heroines in that, although they followed the rules, they still stood behind their principles and used their influence to make a difference. Each of them made their own mark on the world, in their own way.

2

Heroines in Religion

Religion of course played a large role in the lives of medieval people, rich and poor alike. For women, entering a religious order could provide a modicum of self-determination in their lives, and for noble women it could provide an alternative to being a wife and mother. The age at which a young woman could profess a nun's vows was sixteen, although it was not unknown, especially among the aristocracy, for girls to enter the cloister at a much younger age. Indeed, Edward I's daughter, Mary, was just seven years old when she was veiled as a nun at Amesbury Priory, Wiltshire, the abbey to which her grandmother, Eleanor of Provence, Queen of Henry III, had retired several years earlier. In the years between 1216 and 1230 there were about 256 convents, housing more than 3,000 nuns and canonesses.[1] Most nunneries were small priories, comprising a mixture of women; those seeking the Church as a vocation and those, such as widows, seeking a place of retirement and security. However, not all women of religion were cloistered, or allowed to be cloistered. Aristocratic women, in particular, were valuable on the marriage market and no matter their religious leanings they were too politically and financially valuable to be allowed to live a life of seclusion and prayer.

St Margaret was one such lady. Her valuable royal blood meant she would never be allowed to pursue a life of seclusion in a convent. Margaret had an impeccable Saxon pedigree – she was the daughter of Edward the Exile and his wife, Agatha. Edward was the son of Edmund II, usually known as Ironside, King of England in 1016; Edward's grandfather was, therefore, Æthelred II (the Unready) and his uncle was Edward the Confessor, England's king from 1042 until 1066. When his father, Edmund II, was murdered in 1016, Edward and his younger brother Edmund were sent into exile on the Continent by England's new king, Cnut. It is thought that Cnut intended that they would be killed, but the boys were protected by the King of Sweden and sent on to safety in Kiev, at the court of its prince, Jaroslav. Around 1043 Edward married Agatha, probably the daughter of Luidolf, Margrave of West Friesland and a relative of Emperor Heinrich III. Margaret, the eldest of three children, was born in either 1045 or 1046; her sister, Christina, was born around 1050 and her brother Edgar, the Ætheling, was born sometime between 1052 and 1056.

The family might have spent their whole lives in European exile, were it not for Edward the Confessor lacking an heir to the English throne; although Edward was married to Edith Godwinson, the couple remained childless. Sometime in 1054 King Edward sent an embassy to Edward the Exile, to bring him back to England as ætheling, the heir to the throne. The family could not travel immediately, possibly because Agatha was pregnant with Edgar, and only arrived in England in 1057, having journeyed in a ship provided by Emperor Heinrich III. Just days after their return, Edward the Exile was dead, whether by nefarious means or a simple twist of fate is uncertain. The suspicion has been raised that Edward's rival for the throne, Harold Godwinson – the future Harold II – may have taken the opportunity to remove his rival; although it was Harold who accompanied Edward back to England, so surely, had he intended murder, he would have done it sooner.

Whatever the circumstances, the death of Edward the Exile was a blow for Edward the Confessor's dynastic hopes. Little Edgar, now the ætheling, was much too young to assume a political role. He and his sisters, with their mother, were now under the protection of King Edward. They continued to live at court and by January 1066, when Edward the Confessor died, Margaret was approaching her twentieth birthday, while Edgar could have been as young as ten and was probably no older than fourteen. Due to his tender years, Edgar was passed over as candidate for the throne in preference for the older and more experienced Harold Godwinson, who was crowned as Harold II. Following Harold's death at the Battle of Hastings in October 1066, Edgar was proclaimed king by some of his supporters, but was incapable of mounting any real challenge to William the Conqueror and his army of Normans; he had no option but to come to terms with him.

By 1068 Edgar the Ætheling had become involved in the opposition to Norman rule, which had been festering in northern England. However, when events turned against him he fled to Scotland, taking his mother and sisters with him. The family were warmly received at Dunfermline by Scotland's king, Malcolm III Canmore. In 1057, King Malcolm had defeated King Macbeth in battle, at Lumphanan, to take the throne. By 1069 he was well established as king and married to Ingebiorg; the couple had at least two sons, Duncan and Donald. Whether Ingebiorg died or was put aside seems uncertain, although her death seems most likely, leaving Malcolm free to find another wife. In 1069 Malcolm asked Edgar and his mother for Margaret's hand in marriage. Margaret was reluctant to agree to the marriage as she was more inclined to a religious life and had hoped to become a nun. Nonetheless, with pressure from Malcolm and, possibly, her own sense of obligation to the king who was sheltering her family, she eventually accepted his proposal. They were married at Dunfermline sometime in 1069 or 1070 and, by all accounts, it seems to have been a happy and successful marriage and partnership.

Margaret's life as Queen of Scotland did not prevent her pursuing an active religious life; indeed, her position gave her a unique opportunity to influence the practice of Christianity in Scotland. Margaret strived to bring the Church of Scotland into conformity with the practices of Western Catholicism, and away from the tenets of the Celtic Church, which had a lot of influence in the country. She encouraged the Scottish clergy, and its people, to receive communion more than once a year at Easter, to refrain from working on a Sunday and to observe the Lenten fast from Ash Wednesday, rather than the following Monday. Margaret also urged the clergy to celebrate Mass with a common ritual and sought to forbid marriage between a man and his stepmother or sister-in-law.

Margaret was supported in all her reforms by her husband; indeed, if Malcolm III had not given his support it is doubtful that Margaret's influence would have achieved much, if anything at all. His role in her attempts at religious reform is vague, although Malcolm did arrange a conference for the clergy to introduce a number of reforms. Margaret was present, and embarrassed some of the clerics by knowing more about the proper procedures of the Church than they did. She even had the papal manuals to quote from. The queen founded a monastic community at Dunfermline, building the first major stone church in Scotland; and arranged with Lanfranc, Archbishop of Canterbury, to send monks from the cathedral monastery at Canterbury to become its first community. Although it started as a priory, it was elevated to an independent abbey in 1128, at the instigation of Margaret's son, David I.[2]

Margaret was a strong figure; she was pious but also worldly-wise. Having grown up on the Continent, she was familiar with many of the courts of Europe and had met some of its leading churchmen. A modernising queen, Margaret brought luxury to the Scottish court and into the lives of the nobles of her new country. A *Life of St Margaret* was commissioned by her daughter, Matilda, when she became Queen of England. It was written sometime between 1100 and 1107 by Turgot, Margaret's former chaplain and the prior of Durham. The biography emphasises the queen's compassion for children and the poor and stresses her piety, pointing to the severity of her self-denial and her frequent fasting. However, it also tells us that she had a love of etiquette and formality, and had a fondness for fine clothes and jewellery.[3] Margaret enjoyed a high reputation in the Anglo-Norman world, even in her own lifetime; Orderic Vitalis described her as 'eminent from her high birth, but even more renowned for her virtue and holy life'.[4]

Margaret and Malcolm would have a large family, with six sons and two daughters growing to adulthood. Margaret took great care in educating them, ensuring they were given the essentials for their future royal careers. Her second son, Edmund, became king in November 1094, ruling jointly with his uncle – Malcolm's brother – Donald III, following the death of his half-brother, Duncan II. Edmund ruled south of the Forth/Clyde boundary, while Donald ruled the north, although there is no indication that he was ever crowned. In 1097, the co-kings were deposed in favour of Edmund's younger brother, Edgar; Edmund became a monk at Montacute Abbey, Somerset, and died there, having never married. Edgar himself died on 8 January 1107. Unmarried and childless, he was succeeded by his brother, Alexander I, who died in April 1124. David I succeeded Alexander; he reigned until 1153 and was succeeded, in turn, by his grandson, Malcolm IV the

Maiden. Another son, Æthelred, styled Earl of Fife, became Lay Abbot at Dunkeld and died around 1097. Malcolm and Margaret also had two daughters: Edith, who changed her name to Matilda on marrying King Henry I of England; and Mary, who married Eustace III, Count of Boulogne, and was the mother of Matilda of Boulogne, wife of Stephen, King of England.[5] Edith (Matilda) and Mary were educated at Romsey Abbey, where Margaret's sister, Christina was abbess.

As King of Scots, Malcolm also had claims to Cumbria and Northumbria and in 1069/70, he made raids into Northumberland. William I responded by sending an army north and the eventual peace treaty saw Malcolm's oldest son by Ingebiorg, Duncan, being sent south as a hostage and guarantee of his good faith. Duncan would eventually reign, briefly, as Duncan II but was killed at the Battle of Monthechin in 1094. Malcolm made frequent raids into Northumberland, notably in 1079 and 1091, in attempts to gain control over the county. When a diplomatic mission in 1092 failed, he attacked again in 1093, taking his eldest son by Margaret, Edward, with him. Edward died near Jedburgh, from wounds received at the Siege of Alnwick, the same battle in which his father was killed. Margaret died three days after the battle, possibly on receiving the news of the deaths of her husband and eldest son, although the fact her body was weakened by her frequent fasting may have hastened her death. She was buried in the abbey she had founded at Dunfermline. Malcolm was initially buried at Tynemouth, but was later moved to join his wife at Dunfermline.

Margaret's sons honoured their mother's memory, encouraging the popular cult of St Margaret that developed soon after the queen's death, to foster the idea that she should be made a saint. Such an honour would serve to enhance the political and religious status of their family. One of the miracles attributed to her was that in 1199 Scotland's king, William the Lion, was persuaded against launching an invasion of England after experiencing a vision while holding a vigil at Margaret's tomb at Dunfermline. Her canonisation came in 1250, and in 1673 Pope Clement X named her Patroness of Scotland. Following the Reformation, the remains of both Margaret and Malcolm were removed to Spain by Philip II and reinterred in a chapel at the Escorial in Madrid.[6]

Margaret was a direct descendant of King Alfred the Great of Wessex; her Saxon royal blood guaranteed she would not be allowed to enter a convent, she was too valuable on the marriage market. However, through her efforts to reform the Scottish Church, it could be said that she found a better way to worship God. Her legacy was cemented through the work of her son, David I, who continued in her policy of Church reform; while her Saxon blood found its way back into the English royal family through her daughter, Matilda, and her marriage to Henry I.

Saint Margaret's royal lineage ensured that she would not be allowed to devote her entire life to God, but her position as Queen of Scotland gave her the opportunity to direct her devotional tendencies into Church reform, making her a heroine to generations of Scots. Her great-granddaughter, Mary of Blois, would be allowed to enter a convent at a young age; however, it was the royal blood that she carried, thanks to St Margaret, which meant a convent life would be cruelly denied her.

Mary was the daughter of Stephen of Blois and his wife, Matilda of Boulogne, herself the granddaughter of St Margaret. The couple had three children who survived infancy, and yet – on his death – Stephen left his throne to Henry, Count of Anjou and son of Stephen's bitter enemy, Empress Matilda. The empress was Henry I's only surviving legitimate child and designated heir – but England's nobles were reluctant to be ruled by a woman. Stephen was Henry I's nephew, one of his closest male relatives and in the confusion following Henry's death it was Stephen who acted quickly and decisively, and took the crown. What followed was a period known as the Anarchy, almost 20 years of conflict and bloodshed as Stephen and Empress Matilda battled for supremacy. Ultimately, Stephen managed to retain control of England but the empress's eldest son, Henry, was eager to win back his birthright. Following several incursions by Henry – while still in his teens – he and Stephen came to an agreement: Stephen would hold the throne until his death, but Henry would succeed him.

Of Stephen and Matilda of Boulogne's three children, Eustace IV, Count of Boulogne, was the eldest to survive into adulthood. Eustace was an unpleasant character, by all accounts. The *Anglo-Saxon Chronicle* called him 'an evil man' who 'robbed the lands and laid heavy taxes upon them'.[7] Eustace was married in Paris, in 1140, to Constance, the only daughter of Louis VI of France and his second wife, Adelaide of Savoy. Constance 'was a good woman but enjoyed little happiness with him';[8] following their marriage, she was kept as a virtual prisoner at Canterbury Castle. Stephen made attempts to have Eustace crowned, in his own lifetime, as heir-designate, but this was blocked by the papacy, which backed Henry's claim to the crown. Although Eustace had been recognised as Stephen's heir by the secular baronage, I can't help thinking that it was a real stroke of luck for England when Eustace died of a seizure or 'in a fit of madness' in August 1153.[9] Rumours of poisoning are not surprising; Eustace's death paved the way for an understanding over the succession between Stephen and Henry of Anjou.

Stephen's youngest son was William, born around 1134. In 1149 he was married to Isabel de Warenne, sole heiress to William de Warenne, 3rd Earl of Surrey, to bring the vast de Warenne lands within the influence of the Crown. William would succeed to the County of Boulogne in 1153, on the death of Eustace. Shortly after his brother's death, and with the help of the clergy, William made an agreement with Henry of Anjou, whereby he waived his own rights to the crown in return for assurances explicitly recognising his rights to his lands, as Count of Boulogne and Earl of Surrey. Although, it is not known whether he did this willingly, or was pressured, the agreement was an essential tool for the peaceful accession of Henry. William was implicated in a plot against Henry in early 1154 – or he at least knew about it – and there may have been a tit-for-tat attempt as William's leg was broken in an 'accident' at about the same time. However, when his father died, he made no attempt to oppose Henry's accession and even accepted a knighthood from the new king. William died, without issue, in 1159, while returning home from the Siege of Toulouse and was buried in the Hospital of Montmorillon in Poitou, France.

William was succeeded in the County of Boulogne by his sister, Mary. Mary was the youngest daughter of Stephen and Matilda of Boulogne; she was born in Blois, France around 1136. She was destined for the cloister from an early age and was placed in a convent at Stratford, Middlesex, with some nuns from St Sulpice in Rennes. However, there seems to have been some discord in the nunnery and between 1150 and 1152, Mary was moved and her parents founded a new convent for her at Lillechurch (Higham) in Kent, making it a sister convent with St Sulpice. Mary does not appear to have been given the title of prioress, however, a charter of Henry II's, dated around 1155–58, confirmed Lillechurch to Mary and her nuns, suggesting she held some position of authority.[10] By 1160 Mary had become abbess of the great abbey at Romsey, an older and much more prestigious institution than her little foundation at Lillechurch.

However, in 1160 Mary's life was turned upside down with the death of her youngest brother, William. Mary was suddenly a great heiress, Countess of Boulogne in her own right, and too great a marriage prize to be allowed to remain secluded in the cloisters. She was abducted from Romsey by Matthew of Alsace, second son of the Count of Flanders, and forced to marry him. This may well have been a political move; although there does not appear to be any proof that Henry II sanctioned it, most sources imply that the marriage was forced on Mary at the behest of the king and he certainly benefited from her being safely married to a loyal vassal. She was, after all, not only a great heiress but, through her father, she had a strong rival claim to the throne of England.

There was great outrage among the clergy; marriage with a nun was a breach of canon law and opposed by the leading ecclesiastical figures of the day. One source suggested the pope had granted a dispensation for the marriage.[11] However, given that Pope Alexander III expressed great disapproval of the marriage in a letter to the Archbishop of Reims, his consent seems highly unlikely. The pope imposed an interdict on Matthew of Alsace and pressed the claims of the wife of Mary's brother, Eustace, to the Boulogne estates, even though Constance had died some fourteen years before. The furore seems to have eventually died down, and the marriage was allowed to stand. Unfortunately for Henry II, Matthew turned out to be a not-so-loyal vassal and rebelled at least twice. The first occasion arose when Matthew tried to press his claims to Mortain, land that should have been part of Mary's inheritance but was now held by Henry II. The king was not too accommodating. An agreement was eventually reached whereby, in return for £1,000, Matthew would renounce all claims to those parts of his wife's estates that were still in royal hands.

Mary seems to have had little love for Henry II, possibly due to his involvement in her abduction and marriage, or simply because of the fact their respective families had spent many years at war. With so much bad history, you wouldn't expect them to have an affectionate relationship, but Mary appears to have actively worked against Henry. Following a meeting with the ambassadors of the emperor, Frederick Barbarossa, she wrote to King Louis of France. In the document, she describes Henry II as 'the fraudulent king', while informing Louis of Henry's manoeuvring against him; Henry was proposing to marry his daughter to the emperor's son.[12]

Mary and Matthew had two children, daughters Ida and Mathilde; and it was after the birth of Mathilde that the couple were divorced, in 1170. There is some suggestion that Matthew was pressured to agree to the divorce by his dying father and the emperor, Frederick Barbarossa, probably in the hope of having the interdict – placed on Matthew on his marriage to Mary – lifted. Matthew would continue to rule Boulogne and be succeeded by Ida on his death in 1173. Ida married three times; her first husband, Gerard III, Count of Gueldres, died in 1183, while her short marriage to her second husband, Berthold IV, Duke of Zehringen, ended in his death in 1186. Her last marriage was to Renaud, Count of Dammartin, who was a childhood friend of France's king, Philip Augustus; he died in 1127, outliving Ida, who died in 1216, by eleven years. It was Matilda, the daughter of Ida and Renaud, who inherited Boulogne from Ida, and would also become Queen of Portugal through her marriage to Alfonso III of Portugal, although they eventually divorced. Ida's younger sister, Mathilde, married Henry I, Duke of Louvain and Brabant, when she was nine years old. She would have seven children before her death sometime in 1210 or 1211; she was buried in St Peter's Church, Leuven.

The interdict, which had been placed on Matthew on his marriage to Mary, was finally lifted when she returned to convent life, becoming a simple Benedictine nun at St Austrebert, Montreuil. She died there in July 1182, aged about forty-six, and was buried in the convent. A woman who obviously believed that her life should be devoted to God, she is remarkable in that she managed to fulfil her dynastic duties in a forced marriage, and yet asserted herself so that she was able to return to the secluded life she so obviously craved.

To many noble women, the religious life was a career that had been decided for them by their parents when they were still children, as with Mary of Blois; however, they did not necessarily spend their entire lives in the seclusion of the convent. This was the case with Princess Mary, daughter of Edward I and Eleanor of Castile. Mary of Woodstock was born in March 1279, the sixth daughter of Edward and Eleanor. Edward and Eleanor were quite a nomadic couple, travelling among their domains, so their children were raised in the royal nursery, based largely at the royal palaces of Woodstock and Windsor; visits from their parents were infrequent and from Edward, their father, even less frequent. Eleanor endured a remarkable number of pregnancies, the first was when she was about thirteen or fourteen, resulting in a child who was stillborn or died shortly after birth. The fact that several children died before they reached adulthood has been suggested as a reason for her keeping her distance from her children when they were young; however, it is just as likely that the simple fact Edward and Eleanor ruled a vast kingdom, including lands in France, meant their responsibilities necessitated long absences.[13]

Eleanor's almost-constant pregnancies, resulting in a total of sixteen children, meant there were regular additions to the nursery, which also housed a number of children from noble families, sent to be raised alongside the king's children. Mary would have had many companions, including her brother Alphonso, who was heir to the throne and five years her senior, and her sister Margaret, who was four years older than she was. She would be joined by another sister, Elizabeth of Rhuddlan, three years later. In 1285, a year after the death of Prince Alphonso, the king took his family on a progress into Kent. Edward went on pilgrimage to the shrine of St Thomas Becket, at Canterbury, before spending a week at Leeds Castle with his family, followed by some hunting in Hampshire. It was at the end of this family holiday that they arrived at Amesbury in Wiltshire, where little Mary, still only six years old, was veiled as a nun; much to the delight of her grandmother, Eleanor of Provence, but to the consternation of her mother, the queen. Indeed, the *Chronicle of Nicholas Trivet* emphasises that Mary's veiling was done by her father, at the request of her grandmother, but only with the 'assent' of her mother.[14] It may well be that Eleanor had reservations about her daughter's vocation being decided at such a young age, or that she feared it was only being done so Mary's grandmother, Eleanor of Provence, would have a companion in the abbey.

After a long and eventful life, and with her health failing, the dowager queen took her own vows at around the same time and retired to Amesbury Abbey for her final years, dying there in June 1291. Mary's veiling had been in the planning for some years; Edward I had been in correspondence with the abbey at Fontevrault, the mother house of Amesbury, since 1282. Eleanor's reluctance, therefore, was probably more to do with when Mary was to become a nun, rather than the vocation itself; after all, the conventual life was considered a good career for a noble lady. The timing of her veiling may have been advanced not only by the failing health of Eleanor of Provence, but also by the imminent departure of Mary's parents. Edward and Eleanor were about to embark for the Continent and were expecting to be in France for a considerable time, years rather than months. The actual ceremony must have been very moving. It took place at Amesbury Abbey on 15 August 1285, where Mary was one of fourteen high-born girls who took their vows. It may well be that her cousin, Eleanor of Brittany, took her vows at the same time; Eleanor would later demonstrate a great dedication to the religious life and, eventually, become Abbess of Fontevrault.

Mary's life at the abbey was probably a very comfortable existence; in the year she was veiled, Mary was awarded an annual income of £100, rising to £200 a year in 1292, following the death of Eleanor of Provence. As she was still only a child, the nuns at Amesbury would have been responsible not only for Mary's spiritual life, but also for her education. However, the cloistered life by no means meant that Mary was confined and separated from her family for any length of time. She made frequent visits to court throughout her life, and was present for most family occasions. Having taken the veil in August 1285, Mary returned to be with her family in the autumn, to see the unveiling of the newly created Winchester Round Table and the creation of forty-four new knights by her father, the king. She visited her family again in March and May of 1286, each visit lasting about a month. These visits also meant Mary had the chance to bid farewell to her parents, who departed for an extended stay in France in 1286. On 13 August 1289, Mary, her four sisters and little brother Edward were at Dover to welcome their parents home, after a three-year absence. Mary visited court again in 1290 and stayed for the wedding of her older sister, Joan of Acre, to Gilbert de Clare, Earl of Gloucester and Hertford; Joan and Gilbert were married in a private ceremony at Westminster on 30 April. It's likely that she was back at court later in the year for another wedding, this one at Westminster Abbey in July when her sister, Margaret, married John, the future Duke of Brabant.

Mary would have seen quite a lot of her parents in the spring of 1290 as her father chose Amesbury as the location for a special meeting, convened to settle the arrangements for the English succession. Edward may have chosen the abbey so that his ailing mother could be present for the discussions. The Archbishop of Canterbury and five other bishops, in addition to Edward, Eleanor of Castile and Eleanor of Provence, were all present to formalise the settling of the succession on Edward's only surviving son, six-year-old Edward of Caernarvon. Should Edward of Caernarvon die without heirs, it was decided that the succession would then pass to Edward I's eldest daughter, the newly married Countess of Gloucester and Hereford, Joan of Acre. Eleanor of Castile was a distant mother when her children were young, but she seems to have developed closer relationships as they grew older, so it is not hard to imagine her taking the opportunity to spend time with twelve-year-old Mary while they were staying at the abbey.

It was probably one of the last times that Mary spent any real time with her mother, who died at Harby, near Lincoln, on 28 November 1290. Indeed, it may well have been one of the last times they saw each other; Eleanor was at the king's palace of Clipstone in Nottinghamshire when it was realised that her illness was probably fatal. Some of her children, Joan, Edward and Elizabeth, were summoned to the queen's bedside; although Mary is not mentioned, it does not mean that she did not visit her mother one last time.[15] Mary's deep affection for her mother was demonstrated in 1297 when she and her younger sister, Elizabeth, jointly paid for a special Mass in their mother's honour.[16]

Mary's career in the Church was far from spectacular; although her high birth gave her some influence, she never made high office and was never given a priory or abbey of her own. However, she was given custody of several aristocratic nuns at Amesbury, trusted to oversee their education and spiritual training. Abbey life seems to have held few restrictions for her. Mary was regularly away from the cloister. She was frequently at court, or with various members of her family. In 1293 Mary spent time with her brother, Edward, and in 1297 she spent five weeks at court, taking the opportunity to spend some time with her sister, Elizabeth, who had been recently married to John, Count of Holland, and was preparing to join him there. In the event, news of John's death arrived before her departure and Elizabeth never left England.

Mary had many cultural interests and was a patron of Nicholas Trivet, who dedicated his chronicle, *Annales Sex Regum Angliae*, to her. Mary was probably Trivet's source for many of the details of Edward I's family and the inclusion of several anecdotes that demonstrated Edward's luck, such as the story of the king's miraculous escape from a falling stone while sitting and playing chess. He had stood up to stretch his legs when the stone from the vaulted ceiling landed on the chair he had just vacated.[17] The stories that Mary passed on to Trivet also serve to demonstrate that she was at court on a regular basis.

The financial provisions settled on her by Edward I meant that Mary didn't have to suffer from her vows of poverty. In addition to the £200 a year she received from 1292, Mary was also granted forty cocks a year from the royal forests and twenty tuns of wine from Southampton. In 1302, the provision was changed and she was given a number of manors and the borough of Wilton in lieu of the £200, but only for as long as she remained in England. Given that a proposed move to Fontevrault had been dropped shortly after the death of Eleanor of Provence, the likelihood of Mary leaving England seems to have been only a remote possibility. Mary had a penchant for high living; she travelled to court with an entourage big enough to require twenty-four horses. By 1305, despite her income, she was substantially in debt, with the escheator south of the Trent being ordered to provide her with £200 in order to satisfy her creditors. Mary also had a taste for gambling, mainly at dice, and her father is known to have paid off at least one gambling debt.[18] Following her father's death in 1307, her younger brother, now King Edward II, continued to support Mary financially and she continued to make regular visits to court.

Mary died sometime around 1322 and was buried where she had lived, at Amesbury Abbey. She was a princess whose future was decided for her at a very young age. She doesn't seem to have excelled at the religious life in terms of unreligious wordly power, in that she never achieved significant office, but she did make the most of the life chosen for her, making frequent pilgrimages and taking charge of the young, aristocratic ladies who joined the convent. Despite her dedication to the Church, she found her own path within it and seems to have achieved a healthy (for her) balance between the cloister and the court. There was, however, one moment of scandal; although it didn't arise until more than twenty years after Mary's death. In 1345, in an attempt to escape an unhappy marriage John de Warenne, Earl of Surrey, claimed that he had had an affair with Mary and that, therefore, his marriage to her niece was invalid due to their close blood relationship. Although it is highly unlikely that the claim was anything more than Surrey's desperate attempt to find a way out of his marriage, it cannot be ignored that Mary was frequently at court and such an opportunity may have arisen. The court, however, refused to believe him and Mary's reputation remains intact.

The religious life was not the exclusive domain of royal and noble ladies. It also provided a refuge for widows and elderly women in search of calm and peace at the end of their lives. It was an alternative to marriage, and childbearing, for women and girls from diverse backgrounds. Moreover, the cloistered life was not the only path for a woman who wanted to devote her life to God. One such devotee was Saint Julian of Norwich, an anchorite and mystic who lived in a cell at the parish church of St Julian at Conisford in Norwich. Her life was remarkable in its simplicity, devotion and spirituality, and because of her writing. Having survived 600 years, her book, *Revelations of Divine Love*, is the earliest surviving of its kind – a book written in English, by a woman. She is renowned for her words 'all shall be well, all shall be well, and all manner of things shall be well,' which still offers hope and encourages positivity today.[19]

Julian's true identity and origins remain obscured. It is possible that Julian took her name from the church in which she lived, St Julian's, however, it may have been hers from birth. Although Julian was not a common name for a woman at the time, it was not unknown. It may even be a derivative of Juliana, a more familiar woman's name. However, there was a contemporary of the same name, Julian of Erpingham, who was from one of the foremost noble families of Norwich in the 14th century. Julian of Erpingham has been suggested by Father John Julian as a possible candidate for the identity of Julian of Norwich.[20] She was the sister of Sir Thomas of Erpingham, who had been a friend of Edward III and later fought at Agincourt in 1415. Julian of Erpingham was married twice; her first husband died in 1373, and her second was dead by 1393. She had at least three children, with a daughter already married and the youngest possibly fostered out by the time Julian entered the Church. If Julian of Erpingham and Julian of Norwich are one and the same person – and this is far from certain – the legacies from her two husbands would have helped to pay for Julian's upkeep once she had dedicated herself to God.

It is also possible that Julian had been a nun at the Benedictine priory of Carrow, which was close by and had an affinity with St Julian's Church. She was probably from a well-to-do, if not noble, family as she seems to have had some level of education; given that she could, at least, read before she became an anchorite. However, we simply do not know enough about Julian's early life to positively identify her origins. Although *Revelations of Divine Love* is considered autobiographical, it concentrates on her spiritual journey, as opposed to her physical life. We can glean some insight, if not a great deal, from the information she gives at various points in her text. For example, we know that Julian was born in the second half of the year 1342, as she mentions in her writing that she received her visions in May 1373, when she was aged thirty-and-a-half.

In that month Julian suffered an illness so serious that her life was despaired of. Whether it was the Black Death, prevalent in England since its first major outbreak in 1348–9, or some other disease, as her illness progressed she was paralysed to the extent that she could barely even move her eyelids. She was given the last rites and she wrote of how the priest '…set the cross before my face and said, "I have brought you the image of your maker and saviour. Look at it and take comfort from it."'[21] Julian wrote in *Revelations of Divine Love* that she had wanted to have a life-threatening illness, which would bring her close to death, but from which she would be saved.[22] Maybe she believed it would bring her closer to God? Whatever the reason, her illness brought on a series of visions in which she encountered Jesus Christ and his mother the Virgin Mary. The sixteen visions were to form the basis for the direction of her spiritual life and for her book, charting her struggle to understand the divine. Julian wrote two versions of *Revelations of Divine Love*; the Short Text is believed to have been written soon after experiencing her visions, though it took several years to complete. The Long Text – which is six times as long – is more contemplative and appears to have been a constant work-in-progress in her later years.

Although her near-death experience directed her later life, it was only many years after her illness that Julian entered her cell as an anchorite. The exact date is uncertain, but it is believed to have been in the 1390s that her enclosure may have come, possibly after the death of her husband or family members. The life of an anchorite was a strange, solitary existence in which the person was physically cut off from the world, while still being a part of it. It was a life that could be followed by a man or woman, but was one which could not be lightly taken on by the anchorite themselves, or by the Church at large. Not all were suited to the life and a person wanting to profess themselves as an anchorite had to go through a rigorous process to assess that suitability. This even included an interview with the bishop. In Julian's case, it was probably Henry Despenser, Bishop of Norwich, in the late 14th century. Of particular concern was the anchorite's mental capacity to deal with the solitude and limitation on human contact. Once the Church had endorsed a person's suitability to become an anchorite, there was a specific ceremony to signify the end of the life they had previously known. An anchorite was, effectively, dead to the world. They would live in a small cell, attached to the church. As they were led to this cell, a requiem Mass would be sung for them and they would receive extreme unction, normally reserved for the dying. They would be sprinkled with dust, to signify their burial, and then the door to the cell bolted from the outside. In some cases, the cell was walled up. The only access to the outside world was a small, curtained window.[23]

Once they had taken their vows, anchorites were forbidden to leave their cell, on pain of excommunication from the Church. As an anchoress, Julian had to adhere to vows of poverty and chastity and to remain in her cell for the rest of her life. She was not allowed to teach young girls, or possess valuables. Conversations with men in private were strictly forbidden and communication with the outside world was done from behind a black curtain, through which she could also hear the daily church offices, even if she couldn't interact with them. She would have had a servant to see to her daily needs, such as food, laundry, and clearing away waste. However, her daily interactions with her servant would have been restricted to dealing with her physical needs, rather than friendship and companionship. She was also allowed to keep a cat, to control the mice and rats; many images of Julian show her dressed in the habit of a nun, with a cat sat at her feet as she studies her books.

Anchorites were expected to devote their lives to prayers and contemplation, to be a benefit to their community and to work for it by praying for their souls. They were an integral part of the Church, and the parish in which they lived;

> True anchoresses are indeed birds of heaven which fly up high and sit singing merrily on the green boughs – that is, direct their thoughts upwards at the bliss of heaven.'[24]

Once Julian entered her cell, her time was her own. She could manage her own daily routine, although she probably followed the canonical hours and prayed seven times daily. Julian probably read a great deal, she would have had access to books brought by well-wishers and the large selection available at the library of the cathedral priory in Norwich; a collection that was added to in 1407 by a substantial bequest of more than 200 books from Cardinal Adam Easton, a supporter of Bridget of Sweden, who was later canonised.[25] Julian spent many hours in contemplation, reading and writing. *Revelations of Divine Love* was written in the English vernacular, in beautiful, poetic prose; remarkably, it was written by Julian herself, rather than dictated to a scribe. The text's near-miraculous survival, through 600 years and the Reformation, is due to three Long Text manuscripts, which were copied in the 17th century by English nuns at Cambrai and Paris.[26] The book describes the sixteen visions of Christ that she had received during her illness, and her subsequent reflections on their meaning.

Not only does Julian describe her visions in the book, but she also describes the physical experience of the visions, saying, 'All this was shown in three ways: that is to say, by bodily sight, and by words formed in my understanding, and by spiritual visions. But I neither can nor know how to disclose the spiritual vision as openly or as fully as I would wish'.[27] *Revelations of Divine Love* is a spiritual autobiography, contemplating the relationship between love, sin, suffering and God. It is heavily imbued with mysticism, where the author attempts to move beyond normal human thought, exploring sensations and feelings and the relationship with God. Its message of love and peace still gives it relevance today, and her thoughts are possibly more widely respected now than at any time in the past.

Though Julian was appreciated in her own time. People visited to talk with her, and she was the recipient of several legacies, which helped to pay for her keep. In his will, Richard Reed left 2*s* to

'Julian anchorite', while Thomas Edmund, in 1404, bequeathed a legacy of 12*d* to Julian and 8*d* to Sara, her maid.[28] Julian died in, or shortly after, 1416; she was around seventy-three years old. She had pursued her calling with quiet dignity and spirituality, ensuring her place in history as a heroine to women on many levels, not only for her piety but also as a writer, a mystic and a visionary, whose approach to God is arguably more relevant today than it was in her own day.

A few years before Julian's death, she was visited by fellow mystic Margery Kempe. Margery's approach to her religion was a direct contrast to the path followed by Julian, but the meeting between the two women strikes me as extraordinary.

Margery Kempe was about thirty years younger than Julian of Norwich, born around 1373, possibly even in the same year that Julian experienced her visions. She was the daughter of a prominent merchant and dignitary from Bishop's Lynn. Although her mother's identity is unknown, her father, John Burnham, had acted both as a Member of Parliament and mayor of Lynn several times between 1364 and 1391. At around the age of twenty she was married to John Kempe, the younger son of a skinner from Lynn. As the wife of a prominent merchant, Margery enjoyed a comfortable life; she later admitted to pride in her sumptuous wardrobe, saying she would walk through Lynn 'wearing gold pipes on her head, and her hoods with the tippets were fashionably slashed, her cloaks modishly slashed and under laid with various colours between the slashes.'[29] She 'was enormously envious of her neighbours if they were dressed as well as she was. Her whole desire was to be respected by people.'[30]

Margery had her first child about a year after her marriage, and suffered from severe post-natal depression for eight months after that. She only recovered after having a vision of Jesus sitting on her sickbed, talking to her and comforting her. This was, apparently, the start of her spiritual journey, although she would continue in her lavish lifestyle for several more years. It was only after thirteen more children that she persuaded her husband, in about 1413, to agree to a celibate marriage. Furthermore, thinking her business failures were punishment for her sinfulness, she decided to pursue a life of penance. She went so far as to imagine herself married to Christ; this, combined with her visions, her tendency to excessive crying and collapsing in public, must have been interpreted by others as mysticism. A lot of the information on Margery comes from her own book, *The Book of Margery Kempe,* which was written, to her dictation, by a scribe; although she is mentioned in other sources, especially when she came into contact with the authorities. We know, for example, that she went to the Bishop of Lincoln, Philip Repyndon, to ask permission to become a vowess, asking that she could wear white clothes to signify her spiritual purity. She was sent on to Thomas Arundel, Archbishop of Canterbury, although it is unclear whether she ever did take her vows.

Unlike Julian, Margery's religious life was lived very much within the wider world. She travelled frequently, including a pilgrimage to the Holy Land in 1414, travelling through Venice and living on alms donated on her journey. She travelled throughout the Holy Land, visiting Jerusalem and Calvary; and it was at the Church of the Holy Sepulchre, where Christ's body was laid to rest after the Crucifixion, that she first experienced the uncontrollable crying, which was viewed as a mark of her devotion. On her return home, Margery visited various places in Italy, including Rome and Assisi. It seems her white clothing and loud, uncontrollable weeping caused much hostility, not just in Italy, but also in Lynn when she arrived home in 1415. In 1417, Margery undertook a second pilgrimage, this time to Santiago de Compostela in Spain. She was welcomed into many houses on her journeys and treated like a celebrity by many people; her supporters even paid her to pray for them. However, she was often abused by fellow travellers and her actions resulted in her being suspected of holding Lollard sympathies on a number of occasions. The Lollards were considered heretics by the established Church. An early Protestant movement, they were followers of John Wycliffe, who had translated the Bible into English, and they criticised the luxury of the priesthood and questioned the sale of indulgences. Despite her veneration of the saints and frequent pilgrimages, it was Margery's tendency to preach as she travelled that meant she was susceptible to accusations of Lollardy.[31] She was eventually questioned by the Archbishop of York, Henry Bowet, at his residence at Cawood, just outside York, who declared her to be orthodox; although she eventually had to obtain a letter from Henry Chichele, Archbishop of Canterbury, certifying her orthodoxy to prevent the continual arrests for heresy, and to ensure she was allowed access to confession and communion.[32] From 1418 onwards, Margery succumbed to a painful illness, which restricted her travelling. However, she was still experiencing visions, conversations with Jesus and the fits of tears. A priest read to her over the years, including passages from the Bible and works by St Bridget and Richard Rolle.

In the 1420s, although living apart from her husband, Margery nursed him following an accident and during his decline into senility, until his death in 1431. Without seeking permission to travel from her confessor, a requirement for a vowess, Margery travelled to Germany in 1433 with her daughter-in-law, and saw the miraculous Holy Blood at Wilsnack in Brandenburg and the holy relics at Aachen Cathedral, before returning to England. *The Book of Margery Kempe* was completed in 1438; it is a colourful narrative of life in Norfolk. Lacking the subtlety of Julian's *Revelations of Divine Love*, it is, nevertheless, a passionate text dealing with sin and forgiveness and the rejection of earthly worries. It also demonstrates Margery's concerns and insecurities; she worries that the source of her visions may be the devil, rather than God.

The Book of Margery Kempe also tells us of Margery's meeting with Julian of Norwich, at least from Margery's point of view. She visited Julian in 1413, just three years before the anchoress's death. Margery told Julian of her experiences, the conversations she had had with Jesus and the 'many wonderful revelations'.[33] Although delighted with Margery's visions, Julian cautioned her about the source of them, saying, 'As long as it is not contrary to the worship of God and the benefit of her fellow-Christians; for if it was, then it was not the inspiration of a good spirit but of an evil spirit.'[34] The meeting was an incredible moment in history; the meeting of two spiritual minds, one nearing the end of her journey as the other had far to go. Julian was around seventy, while Margery was turning forty, but it may have had a deep effect on Margery, who departed for her pilgrimage to the Holy Land at the end of that year.

Does *The Book* exhibit evidence of psychiatric disorder, bipolar disorder perhaps, or some kind of psychosis? Some have seen the work in this light. It nevertheless provides us with one of the first, if not *the* first, autobiography of a woman.

The Book of Margery Kempe and *Revelations of Divine Love* are two remarkable demonstrations of female spirituality in the 15th century. We are lucky that they have survived the centuries, through war and the Reformation, to give witness to the incredible lives of these two women of the religious world. The books also serve to demonstrate the progress in the way women were able to create a life for themselves in a Church that was dominated by the male clergy, and within the restrictions of their sex. Where St Margaret used her position as the queen in Scotland to initiate the reform of the Church, Julian and Margery used their books to promulgate the idea of a loving, forgiving God, standing up for what they believed in through their own personal, spiritual experiences and visions.

3

The Medieval Mistress

You wouldn't, ordinarily, think of mistresses of kings and lords being considered heroines in any sense. They were, after all, by definition, 'the other woman'. However, these women stood by their men, despite the fact they did not have the protection guaranteed to a traditional wife. They were exposed to slander and vilification, their children (sometimes) unable to inherit, and their own status always in question, in a sort of limbo, and always subject to the whim of their royal or noble lover.

Harold Godwinson was born around 1022 and received the earldom of East Anglia in 1044 and, as the oldest surviving son of Godwin, Earl of Wessex, succeeded to his father's earldom in 1053. Harold's sister, Edith, was the wife of King Edward the Confessor, while his three surviving brothers, Tostig, Gyrth and Leofwine, were all earls. Harold, himself, was not only one of the king's foremost earls but also one of his most respected advisors. In short, the Godwinsons were the most powerful family in the kingdom, after the king himself. At one point Harold, with his father and brothers, had been exiled from England after quarrelling with the king. He is even said to have sworn an oath to back William of Normandy's claim to the English throne in the likely event that Edward the Confessor died without an heir; a claim that William used to the full in order to secure papal approval for his invasion of England. However, when it came to the moment of truth, when Edward the Confessor died, it was Harold who took the throne and prepared to defend England against the rival claimants of Norway and Normandy.

Harold met Edith the Swan-neck at about the same time as he became Earl of East Anglia, in 1044, which makes it possible that Edith the Swan-neck and the East Anglian magnate, Eadgifu the Fair, are one and the same. Eadgifu the Fair held over 270 hides of land and was one of the richest magnates in England. The majority of her estates lay in Cambridgeshire, but she also held land in Buckinghamshire, Hertfordshire, Essex and Suffolk; in the Domesday Book Eadgifu held the manor at Harkstead in Suffolk, which was attached to Harold's manor of Brightlingsea in Essex and some of her Suffolk lands were tributary to Harold's manor of East Bergholt. While it is by no means certain that Eadgifu is Edith the Swan-neck, several historians – including Ann Williams in the *Oxford Database of National Biography* – make convincing arguments that she was. Even their names, Eadgifu and Eadgyth, are so similar that the difference could be merely a matter of spelling or mistranslation; indeed, the Abbey of St Benet of Hulme, Norfolk, remembers an Eadgifu Swanneshals among its patrons.[1]

What we do know is that by 1065 Harold had been living with the wonderfully-named Eadgyth Swanneshals (Edith the Swan-neck) for twenty years. History books label her as Harold's concubine, but Edith was, obviously, no weak and powerless peasant, so it's highly likely they went through a hand-fasting ceremony – or 'Danish marriage' – a marriage, but not one recognised by the Church, thus allowing Harold to take a second 'wife' should he need to. Harold and Edith had at least six children – including four sons, Godwin, Edmund, Magnus and Ulf, and two daughters, Gytha, who married Vladimir Monomakh, Great Prince of Kiev, and Gunnhild, who it was intended would become a nun at Wilton Abbey in Wiltshire, but eloped before taking her vows.

However, despite their twenty years and many children, with the health of the king, Edward the Confessor, deteriorating, it became politically expedient for Harold to marry to strengthen his position as England's premier earl and, possibly, next king. Ealdgyth of Mercia was the daughter of Alfgar, Earl of Mercia, and, according to William of Jumieges, very beautiful. She was the widow of Gruffuddd ap Llywelyn, King of Gwynedd from 1039 and ruler of all Wales after 1055, with whom she had had at least one child, a daughter, Nest. Gruffuddd had been murdered in 1063, following an expedition into Wales; some sources suggest it was by Harold himself, however, Gruffuddd's own men are also suspects. Harold's subsequent marriage to Ealdgyth not only secured the support of the earls of Northumbria and Mercia – Ealdgyth's brothers – but also weakened the political ties of the same earls with the new rulers of north Wales.

As Harold's wife, Ealdgyth was, therefore, for a short time, Queen of England. However, with Harold having to defend his realm, first against Harold Hardrada and his own brother, Tostig, at Stamford Bridge in September of 1066 and, subsequently, against William of Normandy at Hastings, it is unlikely Ealdgyth had time to enjoy her exalted status. At the time of the Battle of Hastings, on 14 October 1066, Ealdgyth was in London, but her brothers took her north to Chester soon after. Although sources are contradictory, it seems possible Ealdgyth was heavily pregnant and gave birth to a son, Harold Haroldson, within months of the battle. Unfortunately, that is the last we hear of Ealdgyth; her fate remains unknown. Young Harold is said to have grown up in exile on the Continent and died in 1098.

Despite his marriage to Ealdgyth of Mercia it seems Edith the Swan-neck remained close to Harold and it was she who was waiting close by when the king faced William of Normandy at Senlac Hill near Hastings in October 1066. She awaited the outcome alongside Harold's mother, Gytha. Having lost a son, Tostig, just two weeks before, fighting against his brother and with the Norwegians at the Battle of Stamford Bridge, Gytha lost three more sons – Harold, Gyrth and Leofwine as well as her grandson, Haakon, on that fateful October day. It is heart-wrenching, even now, to think of Edith and the elderly Gytha, wandering the blood-soaked field after the battle, in search of the fallen king. Sources say that Gytha was unable to identify her sons amid the mangled and mutilated bodies. It fell to Edith to find Harold, by undoing the chain mail of the victims, in order to recognise certain identifying marks on the king's body – probably tattoos. There is a tradition from the monks of Waltham Abbey of Edith bringing Harold's body to them for burial soon after the battle. Although other sources suggest Harold was buried close to the battlefield, and without ceremony, it is hard not to hope that Edith was able to perform this last service for the king. However, any trace of Harold's remains was swept away by Henry VIII's dissolution of the monasteries, so the grave of England's last Anglo-Saxon king is lost to history.

Harold's mother, Gytha, eventually fled into exile on the Continent, taking Harold and Edith's daughter, another Gytha, with her, possibly arranging her marriage to the prince of Smolensk and – later – Kiev. Edith and Harold's sons fled to Ireland with all but one living into the 1080s, though the dates of their eventual deaths remain uncertain. Gunnhild remained in her nunnery at Wilton until sometime before 1093, when she became the wife or concubine of Alan the Red, a Norman magnate. Whether or not she was kidnapped seems to be in question but when Alan died in 1093, instead of returning to the convent, Gunnhild became the mistress of Alan's brother and heir, Alan Niger. Alan the Red (Rufus) held vast lands in East Anglia – lands that had once belonged to Eadgifu the Fair and, if Eadgifu was Edith the Swan-neck, it's possible that Alan married Gunnhild to strengthen his claims to her mother's lands. After 1066 Edith's lands had passed to Ralph de Gael before eventually falling into the hands of Alan the Red. Of Edith the Swan-neck, there is no trace after Harold is interred at Waltham Abbey, she simply disappears from the pages of history. Overall, history has treated Edith kindly; empathising with a woman who remained loyal to her man to the end, despite the fact her official status was questionable.

One of the most fascinating and colourful of medieval mistresses has to be Princess Nest of Wales. I came across Nest by accident, and knew very little of her, but her life was nothing if not eventful. Nest was born sometime before 1092, probably around 1085; she was the daughter of Rhys ap Tewdwr, king of the Welsh land of Deheubarth, and his wife Gwladus, a daughter of Rhiwallon ap Cynfyn of Powys. King Rhys had come to the throne in 1079, a year after the death of the former king, his second cousin Rhys ap Owain. Nest had at least two brothers, Gruffuddd – who succeeded their father as king – and Hywel. When Nest was probably still a child, the Normans who had invaded England in 1066 started pushing into Wales; her father was killed while campaigning against the Norman settlers of Brycheiniog in 1093.

After his death, Normans overran his kingdom and his family seems to have been separated, with Gruffuddd escaping to Ireland and Nest being taken as a hostage. Despite the fact a woman had few legal rights and could not inherit in Wales, she was still a valuable prisoner as far as the English were concerned. Although initially a prisoner of the Earl of Shrewsbury and his son Arnulf, the new Earl of Pembroke, she eventually arrived at the English royal court. It was probably during her stay at the English court that Nest, still a teenager but said to be a great beauty, was seduced by Henry, brother of King William II Rufus, and soon to become king himself. Nest was not an attractive enough prospect, politically, to become Henry's wife, but she did become his mistress. Their son, Henry FitzHenry, was born around 1103–1105.

There are discrepancies in her story, and other sources suggest she probably made her first marriage shortly after 1097; this was to Gerald of Windsor, a Norman knight who was castellan of Pembroke Castle and steward of Pembrokeshire for Count Arnulf de Montgomery. Her relationship with Henry is not in question, just the timing of it.

Some have suggested that Nest and Henry's affair happened during his campaigns in Wales in 1114. However, it seems likely that Nest and Henry were lovers at around the turn of the century, just as he became king and that Nest was married to Gerald later, shortly after the birth of her son by the king; their marriage was probably a way of securing Nest's future, while getting her away from the king, who now had a royal, politically acceptable, wife in Matilda of Scotland. Nest and Gerald seem to have had a successful marriage; they each brought mutual benefits, with Gerald giving Nest status among the Anglo-Norman lords, while Nest gave Gerald legitimacy in his Welsh lands.

Nest's son by Henry went with his mother and was raised in Gerald's household.[2] By 1109 Gerald and Nest already had at least two sons and a daughter when they were staying, for safety, at Gerald's castle of Cenarth Bychan (Cilgerran). It was at a Christmas feast at the castle that Nest's cousin, Owain ap Cadwgan, is said to have become obsessed with her. The *Chronicle of the Princes* tells the story:

> Owain had heard that Nest was in the castle. He went with but a few men in his company to visit her as a kinswoman. And after that he came of a night to the castle and but a few men with him, about fourteen, unknown to the keepers of the castle. And then he came to the chamber in which Gerald and Nest were sleeping. And they raised a shout around and about the chamber in which Gerald was, and kindled tapers and set fire to the buildings to burn them. And when he heard the shout, Gerald awoke,

not knowing what to do. And then Nest said to him, 'Go not out to the door, for thine enemies await thee, but follow me'.

And that he did. And she led him to the privy which adjoined the chamber. And there, as is said, he escaped by way of the privy hole. And when Nest knew that he had escaped, she cried out from within and said to the men who were outside, 'Why do you cry out in vain? He whom you seek is not here. He has escaped.' And when they did not find him, they seized Nest and her two sons and her daughter and another son of his by a concubine, and they sacked and plundered the castle.[3]

Nest is said to have offered to stay with Owain, so long as he returned her children to their father. From the distance of 900 years, it is hard to say exactly what happened, whether Nest allowed herself to be seduced by Owain, or whether she was raped. Whether the abduction of Nest was a result of Owain's infatuation with his cousin, or a more calculated political move and the signal to start a Welsh uprising, cannot be said for certain. Her kidnapping, however, did incense the Normans.

Henry I, Nest's former lover, sent a punitive expedition into Wales, whether out of opportunism or anger at Nest's treatment is, again, open to interpretation. A civil war started when Owain's Welsh enemies were then bribed to attack him and his father. Owain fled to Ireland and Nest was returned to Gerald. Nest and Gerald had three sons, William, Maurice and David – David was born after Nest's abduction by Owain and later became Bishop of St David's – and a daughter, Angharad. The family settled in Pembroke, where Nest's brother, Gruffuddd, sought refuge when things were going against him.

Following their father's death, Gruffuddd had grown up in Ireland but returned to try to recover his kingdom of Deheubarth, pursuing a guerrilla war between 1115 and 1117. Gruffuddd's actions would cause family strife for Nest; he took up open rebellion against the English king, to whom Gerald was wholly loyal. The ensuing years were turbulent, with Welsh prince against Welsh prince, and the Normans trying to take advantage of the opportunities that the unrest and uncertainty presented. Henry was campaigning in Powys in 1114, which provides us with the second possible date for Nest's affair with the Norman king, although it does seem less likely. By 1116 Owain had returned to Wales, and was working alongside King Henry's Norman forces in south Wales when he and his men were ambushed by Flemish mercenaries led by Gerald of Windsor. According to the Welsh chroniclers:

> ... the Flemings were fired with the old hate that formerly existed between them and Owain; for many a time had Owain done them hurt. Instigated also by Gerald, the man from whom Owain had carried off his wife ... they thought to pursue Owain ... and with shooting on either side, Owain was wounded until he was slain.[4]

Gerald of Windsor disappears from the historical record in the following year; although we cannot be certain he died in 1117, or soon after, it does seem probable. Nest's life gets a little confusing after Gerald's death. She does not seem to have settled down into respectable widowhood with her young family. Probably still only in her late twenties or early thirties, Nest was still a very attractive woman – physically, financially and politically – and was faced with two options; to remarry or enter a convent. At some point, she married Hait, a Fleming who was the sheriff of Pembroke, with whom she had a son, William. The marriage appears to have been short-lived for it was not long before Nest was married to Stephen, the Constable of Cardigan castle, with whom she had at least one son, Robert. Nest had a further three children by unknown fathers. One of these, Hywel, could have been a second son by her third husband, Stephen. A daughter, Gwladus, who was later married to a Welsh baron, and a son, Walter, have both been identified as Nest's children, although their fathers remain a mystery.[5]

In total, Princess Nest was the mother of at least nine children by no less than five different men. Her daughter by Gerald, Angharad, was the mother of the renowned cleric and chronicler Gerald of Wales, also known as Giraldus Cambrensis, who chronicled many of the exploits of his cousins, Nest's grandchildren. Nest's eldest son by Gerald, William, became Lord of Carew, while Maurice Fitzgerald campaigned in Ireland and settled there. Nest's son Robert FitzStephen also became one of the Norman conquerors of Ireland. The large number of grandchildren would mean that Nest was related to most of the noble families in Wales and is an ancestor of the Tudor and Stuart royal houses. The princess lived through the most tumultuous of times so how much control she had over her own life is open to question. A remarkable woman who, at various times, suffered life as a hostage, a kidnap victim and widow, her exploits earned her the nickname of 'Helen of Wales'. Whether the name refers largely to her looks, her abduction or the fact that her abduction started a war remains unclear; maybe it was a combination of all three. Unfortunately, despite her chronicler grandson, Nest's death and final resting place are unrecorded. She was still living in 1136, but that is all we know.

While other medieval women struggled with the status of mistress, their eventual fates varied greatly. Ida de Tosny, one-time lover of Henry II and mother of his son, William Longspée, Earl of Salisbury, was married to Roger Bigod, 2nd Earl of Norfolk, after her relationship with the king ended. She was able to overcome the stigma of royal mistress and raise a new family with her noble husband.

The most successful of mistresses must be Katherine Swynford, the one mistress who defied the odds and eventually married her man, thus spawning a multitude of novels and love stories. Katherine was born around 1350; she was the younger daughter of Sir Payn Roelt, a Hainault knight in the service of Edward III's queen, Philippa of Hainault, who eventually rose to be Guyenne King of Arms. Unfortunately, the identity of her mother has never been established, not an unusual situation when you think Katherine was born to an obscure knight and her significance only became evident later in life. Katherine and her older sister, Philippa, appear to have been spent their early years in Queen Philippa's household. Philippa de Roelt (or Rouet) joined the household of Elizabeth de Burgh, wife of Lionel of Antwerp, where she met her future husband, the literary giant of his age, Geoffrey Chaucer. By 1365 Katherine was serving Blanche, Duchess of Lancaster, the first wife of John of Gaunt. John was the third surviving son of Edward III and Queen Philippa, and had married Blanche, co-heiress of Henry of Grosmont, Duke of Lancaster, in 1359. Soon after joining Blanche's household, Katherine was married to Sir Hugh Swynford of Coleby and Kettlethorpe, Lincolnshire. Sir Hugh was a knight and tenant of John of Gaunt, who would serve with his lord on campaigns in 1366 and 1370. The couple had two children, Thomas and Blanche, who was named after the duchess. John of Gaunt stood as little Blanche's godfather and she was raised alongside his own daughters by Duchess Blanche. Following the duchess's death in September 1368, Katherine became governess to the duke's three children: Elizabeth, Philippa and Henry. Three years after the death of Blanche, in September 1371, John married again, this time to a Spanish princess, Constance of Castile, the daughter of Pedro the Cruel, King of Castile, and Maria de Padilla, the king's concubine-turned-wife. The marriage was a dynastic move, with Constance being heiress to the kingdom of Castile there was a distinct chance of John becoming King of Castile, if only John could wrest it from her father's killer and illegitimate brother, Henry of Trastámara. From January 1372, he assumed the title of King of Castile and Leon, though in name only as he was never able to consolidate his position.

Shortly after the marriage of John and Constance, in November 1371, Sir Hugh Swynford died while serving overseas, leaving Katherine a widow with two very young children; the youngest was probably less than two years old. It was not long after Sir Hugh's death that Katherine became John of Gaunt's mistress; although some sources suggest the couple were lovers even before Sir Hugh's death, which has brought into question the paternity of Katherine's eldest son by John of Gaunt. However, the majority of historians agree the relationship between John and Katherine started in late 1371 or early 1372 and was developing well in the spring of that year, when Katherine received rewards and a significant increase in her status within Gaunt's household.

Between 1373 and 1377 Katherine continued her role as governess to John of Gaunt's two daughters, while also giving birth to the couple's four children; John, Henry, Thomas and Joan. The children were given the surname Beaufort, the origin of which is obscured by time, though most suggest it is in reference to the lost Beaufort lands in France, which had previously been part of John of Gaunt's domains. John's wife Constance also had children during this time – she gave birth to a daughter, Catherine, (Catalina) in 1373 and a son, John, in 1374. Although little John died shortly after birth, Catherine would grow up to marry Henry III of Castile, becoming Queen Consort of Castile and Leon. Nothing is recorded of Constance's reaction to her husband's relationship with Katherine, but she can't have been too happy about it and her marriage does appear to have been strained in the late 1370s, early 1380s.

In 1377 John granted to Katherine the manors of Wheatley and Gringley, in Nottinghamshire, with an annual income of more than £150. The gift was seen as a public acknowledgement of Katherine's position and a slight to Gaunt's wife, Duchess Constance. Contemporary chroniclers denounced Katherine as *une deblesce et enchauntresce.*[6] As political unrest culminated in the Peasants' Revolt in 1381 so, it seems, did the pressure on John of Gaunt to normalise his personal life. The revolt blamed 13-year-old King Richard II's counsellors as the cause of the country's problems. John of Gaunt was one of the main targets of the rebels' anger and his Savoy Palace on the Strand was burned to the ground, despite Gaunt's absence from the centre of proceedings – he was on his way to Scotland at the time. In June 1381, possibly as a way to recover some popularity, John renounced his relationship with Katherine and reconciled with his wife, Constance. Katherine gave up her position as governess in September and left court, with a further pension of 200 marks a year. She settled at her late husband's manor at Kettlethorpe, before moving to a rented townhouse in Minster Yard in Lincoln. The renunciation appears to have been a formal process because John of Gaunt visited Katherine regularly throughout the 1380s, although now it was done discreetly. Katherine was frequently at the Duke's court, where a stable of twelve horses was kept for her use. Her relationship with John of Gaunt and, indeed, his family, remained cordial. She is known to have lent him money for his Castilian expedition of 1386 and in 1387 received a New Year's gift from the Countess of Derby, the wife of John's eldest son, Henry.[7] In 1388 she received a most prestigious order for a lady whose social position was ambiguous to say the least – Katherine was made a Lady of the Garter, an honour awarded to the highest ladies in the land.

When Duchess Constance died in 1394, Katherine's situation changed again. John and Katherine were finally married at Lincoln Cathedral in January 1396. Although it undoubtedly caused surprise and upset among members of the royal court, the marriage had a very practical outcome. John was able to petition the pope for the legitimisation of his four children by Katherine. This was achieved by papal bull in September 1396 and by Richard II's royal patent in the following February, thus exalting the children in court society and vastly improving their marriage and career prospects. However, their older half-brother, Henry, once he became King Henry IV, would later issue a charter that excluded the Beauforts from the succession.

Katherine had finally got her prince and was now Duchess of Lancaster. She was even, briefly, the first lady in the land, following the death of Richard II's queen, Anne of Bohemia. Unfortunately, married life was far from blissful, with the country in turmoil. John's eldest son, Henry, was exiled for 10 years in 1398 by Richard II, following a quarrel with Thomas de Mowbray, 1st Duke of Norfolk. John of Gaunt died in the following year, in February 1399, at Leicester Castle. He was buried beside his first wife, Blanche, in a now-lost elaborate tomb in St Paul's Cathedral in London. Immediately following John's death, Henry's exile was extended to life and the Lancaster lands were confiscated by the Crown – but the king's actions led to his deposition and Henry's accession as King Henry IV.

After John's death, Katherine retired to Lincoln to live in a house close to the east end of the cathedral. Her son, Henry Beaufort, was now Bishop of Lincoln, following his legitimisation. Katherine died in Lincoln on 10 May 1403. She was buried, close to the high altar, in the cathedral in which she had married her prince just seven years earlier. Her daughter Joan, Countess of Westmoreland, was laid to rest beside her, following her death in 1440, in a slightly smaller tomb. Although they can still be seen today, the tombs themselves are empty, with Katherine and Joan buried beneath the floor of the cathedral. Henry IV referred to her in her widowhood as 'The King's Mother'; as Henry was born only a year before his own mother Blanche of Lancaster died, Katherine had been the ever-present mother figure in his life.

It is through her four children with John of Gaunt that Katherine is the ancestress to the Yorkist, Tudor and Stewart kings. Their daughter Joan had married Sir Robert Ferrers of Overley, one of John of Gaunt's retainers, in 1392. However, his death, sometime between May 1395 and November 1396 and Joan's legitimisation by the pope, led to a more exalted second marriage, with Ralph Neville, 6th Baron Neville of Raby and later Earl of Westmorland. Among her fifteen children with Ralph Neville was Cecily Neville, Duchess of York and grandmother of the Yorkist kings Edward IV and Richard III. Katherine and John's eldest son John, Earl of Somerset, was the grandfather of Margaret Beaufort and great-grandfather of Henry VII, the first Tudor monarch. John's daughter, another Joan Beaufort, married James I, King of Scotland, in a famous love-match and was the mother of James II. Gaunt and

Katherine's second son, Henry, as Bishop of Lincoln and, later, Cardinal Beaufort, enjoyed an active and influential political career under the three Lancastrian kings: Henry IV, Henry V and Henry VI. The youngest Beaufort brother, Thomas, Duke of Exeter, was an accomplished soldier for Henry IV and Henry V, and was appointed as guardian to the infant Henry VI.

Katherine's legacy, and perhaps the reason she has suffered less at the hands of history than other royal mistresses, is in her children and her relationship with her stepchildren. Whereas her contemporary counterpart, Alice Perrers, had no such legacy to protect her reputation and has, as a result, suffered at the hands of chroniclers and historians, past and present.

The origins of Alice Perrers are far more obscure than those of Katherine Swynford. Whereas we know for certain that Katherine was the daughter of the Hainault knight Sir Payn Roet, Alice's parentage is open to question. It has long been thought that she was probably the daughter of Sir Richard Perrers of Hertfordshire, a knight who fell foul of the Abbey of St Albans and was imprisoned in 1350 and outlawed in 1359 over a land dispute. The story also provided the origin for the later enmity of Thomas of Walsingham, the chronicler of St Albans, towards Alice; it was Walsingham who claimed she was the daughter of a thatcher and that her hold over the king was through sorcery and the 'blandishments of her tongue', rather than any natural beauty.[8] Another theory was that she was the daughter of a Devon weaver. However, work by W.M. Ormrod has suggested an alternative. In a recent article, Ormrod argued that Alice may have been older than was previously believed and Perrers was a married name rather than her maiden name. According to Ormrod, Alice had a brother named John Salisbury, meaning she was not the daughter of the Hertfordshire knight but more likely from a family of London goldsmiths – the Salisburys – providing jewels to the royal court, and married to another London goldsmith – Perrers. This would have given Alice connections to court circles and would also explain her familiarity with the affairs of the city and litigation, as well as explaining her well-known fondness for jewellery.[9]

As a result of her uncertain origins, nothing is known of Alice's early life and neither is it known how Alice came to the attention of the king. She may have been a maid of honour in the household of Queen Philippa of Hainault, however, it is unclear whether this was before or after her relationship with Edward III had started. The liaison with Edward appears to have begun in 1364 as in that year a merchant and courtier, Richard Lyons, was ordered not to interfere with Alice's movements when she was on the king's business or her own.[10] We know Alice had been installed as a maid of the Queen's bedchamber by October 1366. Indeed, it was probably in 1365 or 1366 that Alice's first son by the king, John de Southeray (or Surrey), was born; as by 1377 he was old enough to be married and in 1381–2 he accompanied the Earl of Cambridge on his Portuguese campaign. Alice had a further two children by the king, daughters named Joan and Jane. Alice's relationship with the king remained a closely guarded secret during the queen's lifetime, and only became public after Philippa's death in 1369. The king appears to have relied heavily on Alice during his grieving for his queen and it was from this period onwards that Alice was given numerous and varied gifts, from wardships to lands and jewels. In 1371 she was permitted to purchase the valuable royal manor of Wendover for just £500.[11] In 1373 she was said to have been given a selection of Queen Philippa's jewels, although the jewels were in fact items that had been given, by the queen, to Euphemia, wife of Walter Hasleworth, rather than the queen's own jewellery. The gifts were recorded in the patent rolls, suggesting they were made on Edward's personal orders, rather than as an avaricious acquisition by Alice. However, the more secure she was in her position, it seems, the more grasping Alice became. She received gifts from courtiers and those eager to use her influence over the king to advance their own positions. Alice undertook land acquisitions and made moves to protect them in the event of Edward III's death, fully aware that her position was secure only while the king lived.

In 1374 Alice's power was at its height; the Abbot of St Albans, in the midst of a property dispute with Alice, was advised that 'she had such power and eminence in those days that no one dared to prosecute a claim against her.'[12] Thus advised, the abbot abandoned his suit, preferring to await more favourable circumstances. The chronicler of the Abbey of St Albans, Thomas of Walsingham, as already mentioned, was not an admirer of Alice Perrers. He described her as extremely ugly and said she ruled the king through her clever tongue.[13] The 'clever tongue' was probably true, as Edward was known to like intelligent women; however, he also liked attractive women, so Alice's looks were likely to be anything but ugly. Given her litigation against the Abbey of St Albans, combined with the fact Alice was the king's mistress and, therefore, a fallen woman in the eyes of the Church, probably goes some way to explaining Walsingham's animosity towards her.

Edward appears to have been besotted with Alice Perrers throughout the last decade of his life. Although the king had not been faithful to his queen throughout his marriage, Alice was his first open liaison and he denied her nothing. Not only did Alice control access to the king, but she also exerted considerable influence over the courts of justice and government itself; she is said to have sat on the bench in court and bullied the judges. Alice became Edward's chief counsellor, using her position to advance the interests of her friends and paving the way for increased corruption within the royal household. In 1375 the king held a tournament at Smithfield in which Alice was presented as the Lady of the Sun; a lack of conventional discretion that was always likely to be denigrated. Whereas Katherine Swynford was reasonably invisible in her relationship with John of Gaunt and mostly remained in the domestic sphere, Alice was flaunting her position for all the world to see – and criticise. The venal character of Lady Mead in Langland's *Piers Plowman* is thought to have been based on Alice, as is Geoffrey Chaucer's *Wife of Bath*. Things came to a head in the Good Parliament of 1376 when the Speaker of the Commons, Peter de la Mare, openly accused Alice of 'relieving the exchequer of £2,000 or £3,000 a year without profit to the realm'.[14] According to Walsingham, the parliament also arrested a Dominican friar, accused of weaving spells over the king. However, the parliament rolls only record that an ordinance was issued prohibiting women from pursuing their quarrels within the royal courts 'by way of maintenance'.[15] Walsingham reported:

... the Parliamentary knights complained bitterly about one Alice Perrers, a wanton woman who was all too familiar with Edward III. They accused her of numerous misdeeds, performed by her and her friends in the realm. She far overstepped the bounds of feminine conduct: forgetful of her sex and her weakness, now besieging the king's justices, now stationing herself among the doctors in the ecclesiastical courts, she did not fear to plead in defence of her cause and even to make illegal demands. As a result of the scandal and great shame which this brought on King Edward, not only in this kingdom but also in foreign lands, the knights sought her banishment from his side.[16]

The one thing Katherine Swynford and Edith Swan-neck had in common was their constancy; they spent decades by the side of their men, despite the lack of a wedding ring. They were faithful, with no rumours that they had strayed from their lovers' beds. By contrast, it emerged during the proceedings of the Good Parliament that despite her relationship with the king, Alice was, in fact, married to Sir William Windsor. Windsor was a knight from the county of Westmoreland, in northern England. He had been appointed Royal Lieutenant of Ireland in 1369 but was recalled in 1373 due to accusations of extortion and maladministration of taxation. Alice appears to have married him secretly, soon after his return to England, and it seems likely that his reappointment to Ireland in 1374 was due to Alice's influence on the king.

The outcome of the parliament saw Alice banished from court and ordered to refrain from instigating legal proceedings, or to face forfeiture of her goods and property and exile from England. In the end, Alice was allowed to stay in England without further prosecution, on condition that she stayed away from the king. Should she break the restrictions placed on her, the punishment would be perpetual exile. Alice's marriage had meant the king had been committing adultery and he is said to have sworn an oath by the Virgin Mary that he did not know she was married. King Edward was devastated on hearing about the marriage, but even more so by the banishment of his mistress. Bereft of his wife, with the death of his eldest son and heir, Edward the Black Prince, on 8 June 1376, and with the rest of his family spread far and wide, the king probably saw Alice as the comfort and companion of his old age.

However, if the banishment was implemented at all it was of short duration and Alice was back at the king's side within months. John of Gaunt had returned from his duties as the king's lieutenant on the Continent and was practically ruling the kingdom, allowing the recall of those banished by the Good Parliament. Edward 'recalled his mistress, Alice Perrers, to his company; she had been legally banished from his presence, on account of the scandal and shame which came from her wantonness. This was against the oath by which Alice had bound herself and which the king himself had ratified; namely that she would not come near the king in any way. She stayed with him until his death.'[17] On 22 October 1376, Alice was pardoned by the king and remained at his side from that moment until his death in the following year. In January 1377, their son, Sir John de Southeray, married Maud Percy, a half-sister of Henry, Lord Percy, the future Earl of Northumberland; and on 17 June of the same year, just four days before his father's death, the king granted him a satin coat of arms. As his sisters were still children when their father the king died, their marriages would prove to be less prestigious than that of their brother; Jane would marry Richard Northland and Joan would be married to Robert Skerne, a lawyer from Kingston, Surrey.

Alice remained at the king's side to the very end, which came on 21 June after a final stroke; although this was not seen as loyalty to her aged and dying lover by the chronicler, Foissant, who reported:

> Shameful to relate, during the whole time that he was bedridden, King Edward had been attended by that infamous whore Alice Perrers, who always reminded him of things of the flesh. She never discussed nor permitted discussion about the safety of his soul, but continually promised him a healthy body, until she saw a sure sign of his death with the failing of his voice. When she realised that he had lost the power of speech and that his eyes had dulled, and that the natural warmth had left his body, quickly that shameless doxy dragged the rings from his fingers and left.[18]

Even if she had wanted to slip into obscurity after the king's death, Alice was not allowed just to drift away. The Lords and Commons, who had resented her power and influence over the king, wasted no time in exacting their revenge. In November 1377 people were encouraged to bring their petitions before parliament, to sue her for her offences against the king and people. The king's oldest surviving son, John of Gaunt, who was now uncle and chief advisor to the new king, Richard II, presided over the subsequent trial. Alice was charged on two counts. The first was that in November 1376 she persuaded the king to countermand the council's order to send Sir Nicholas Dagworth to Ireland to investigate the corruption charges against William Windsor, Alice's husband, on the grounds that Windsor and Dagworth were enemies. The second charge was that in May 1377 she persuaded Edward III to grant a full pardon and a gift of 100 marks to Richard Lyons, a friend of Alice's who had been, like her, denounced in the Good Parliament.

Although Alice vehemently maintained her innocence on both charges, she was convicted and sentenced to banishment from England and forfeiture of all her goods and lands. Unusually, the forfeiture included all lands which she had enfeoffed others to her use. Such lands were normally exempt from confiscation and a clause in the sentence specifically stated that it should not be used as a precedent in other cases, but was imposed only 'for such an odious thing in this special case'.[19] On 3 December 1377 the orders to seize Alice's lands were issued. The inventory from the resulting inquisitions included properties in at least fifteen counties. It was also claimed that she had hidden £20,000 worth of jewels with Windsor, to prevent their seizure; this may be an exaggeration but at least £3,000 was recovered from Alice following her arrest.[20] Alice would spend the remainder of her life in almost endless litigation, in repeated attempts to recover her goods and property. Windsor helped in the early years following the king's death; in October 1378, Alice had still not left England when Windsor petitioned parliament to reverse the judgement against her, for which he was given leave to pursue his suit. A further petition saw the sentence of banishment revoked on 14 December 1379; at the same time, she was pardoned for having not left England and Windsor was pardoned for harbouring her. The recovery of lands was a slow, drawn-out process, and not without setbacks. Although Windsor was granted some of those lands confiscated from Alice in March 1380, in return for military service to the Crown, his death on 15 September 1384 caused new problems. Not only had he died in debt to the Crown, but the lands that had once belonged to Alice had been enfeoffed to a group of trustees who were to dispose of them according to Windsor's final wishes. Even though Alice claimed that Windsor had intended to leave the lands to her, the trustees insisted he had nominated his nephew, John Windsor, as beneficiary. Alice spent the remaining years of her life in the struggle to recover her lands from John Windsor. Numerous petitions to parliament resulted in John Windsor being imprisoned in Newgate gaol for a very brief time and the recovery of only a small number of properties, including her manor at Gaines in Upminster, where she lived in her final years.

Alice's will, dated 15 August 1400, shows that her bitterness lasted to the very end; it bequeathed all the lands, which John Windsor had 'usurped', to her daughters, Joan and Jane, 'for that I say, on pain of my soul, he hath no right to these, nor never had'.[21] She asked to be buried in Upminster Church, Essex, and left her manor at Gaines to her youngest daughter Joan, with the remainder of her property to be divided equally between the two daughters. The fate of her son John is far from clear. His marriage to Mary Percy was annulled in 1380 after Mary claimed she had never consented to the marriage. John fought in the Portuguese campaigns of 1381–2, but nothing is heard of him afterwards, and given that he is not mentioned in his mother's will he probably died shortly after the campaign's end. Alice Perrers herself died in the winter of 1400–01; her will was proved on 3 February 1401.

Her reputation has come down through history as that of a greedy, grasping, but intelligent woman, who made an ageing king's final years lonely and miserable. If Thomas of Walsingham is to be believed, she had no redeeming qualities. However, she was a strong, intelligent woman who tried to hold her own in the world of men, fighting her corner in parliament and the courts, even though her eventual victories were fleeting and limited. Knowing that her power and influence was limited to the king's lifetime, and knowing that time was very short, was it really so heinous of her to try to ensure her future financial security while she could?

Of course, being a royal mistress did not guarantee a happy ending. These women risked all to be with their men, knowing that their very position as mistress meant countless insecurities – in position, affection, and the future. And only in one instance, Katherine Swynford, was marriage and a 'happily ever after' – however brief – the result of years of patience and silent support. These women were vilified as outcasts because the men they wanted were not their husbands. However, not one of them would have been in a position to say no to the powerful men who chose to bed them. They made the most of a life that was decided for them, whether by marrying elsewhere, as in Nest's case, or by grasping the opportunities their situation presented to them, as with Alice. The one characteristic in each of them was their loyalty to a man who was not their husband, and they should be lauded for making a life for themselves out of such desperate, uncertain relationships.

4

Scandalous Heroines

It may seem odd to think of women who were mired in scandal as heroines; however, many of them were victims of the political machinations of powerful men, their actions portrayed as criminal or suspicious to suit the ends of those who sought more power and control. And for some, the scandal was caused, simply, by their search for love, for a connection outside their arranged and controlled lives.

It may be that an affair was the only way for a woman to take back some control of her own life. Many daughters, especially those of kings, had little or no say in who they would marry; they were bargaining pieces in the search for alliances. Even their legitimacy mattered little compared to what they could bring to the table, if their fathers were powerful enough. Joan, or Joanna, the illegitimate daughter of King John, was one such young lady. Very little is known of Joan until her appearance on the international stage in 1203, aged twelve or thirteen. It was that year mention is made of a ship, chartered in Normandy, 'to carry the king's daughter and the king's accoutrements to England'.[1] The daughter in question appears to be Joan, born around 1191 to an unknown mother, possibly a lady by the name of Clemencia or Clementina. Nothing is known of Joan's childhood, which appears to have been spent in Normandy. However, although she grew up in obscurity, Joan must have received an education suitable to her rank as the daughter of a prince and, later, king; after all, her father intended to marry her to a prince and so would need her to be able to act the part of a princess.

By 15 October 1204 Joan was betrothed to the foremost prince in Wales; Llywelyn ab Iorweth, prince of Gwynedd, also known as Llywelyn Fawr, or Llywelyn the Great. In the summer of 1204, he had paid homage to King John for his Welsh lands, having recognised the English king as overlord by treaty in July 1201; allowing him to marry Joan was a sign of John's favour. By the time of his marriage, Llywelyn was already an accomplished warrior and experienced statesman; and was the father of at least two children, a son and daughter, Gruffuddd ab Llywelyn and Gwenllian. Their mother was Tangwystl, but her union with Llywelyn was not recognised by the Church and the children were considered illegitimate under Church law. Joan and Llywelyn were probably married in the spring of 1205; part of Joan's dowry, the castle and manor of Ellesmere, were granted to Llywelyn on 16 April 1205, suggesting the wedding took place around that time.[3] Joan was fourteen or fifteen at the time; at thirty-two, Llywelyn was about eighteen years her senior. Having been uprooted from her home in Normandy, she had probably spent a year at the English court before moving to her new home in Wales. The language and traditions of her new homeland would have been completely alien to the young woman. Even her name was not the same, in Welsh, she was known as Siwan. For someone barely into her teenage years, all these changes must have been daunting. Not only was she expected to become a wife and a princess to a nation that was totally alien to her, but her responsibilities also included the role of peacemaker. In a prestigious marriage for an illegitimate daughter, Joan was thrown into the heart of Anglo-Welsh relations. She was to become an important diplomatic tool for her father and, later, her half-brother, Henry III; acting as negotiator and peacemaker between the English crown and her husband, almost from the first day of her marriage.

Despite the marriage of Joan and Llywelyn, relations between England and Wales were rarely cordial. Following a devastating defeat by the English in 1211, in which the invading army had swept into Gwynedd, capturing the Bishop of Bangor in his own cathedral, Joan's skills were sorely needed and 'Llywelyn, being unable to suffer the King's rage, sent his wife, the King's daughter, to him by the counsel of his leading men to seek to make peace with the King on whatever terms he could.'[4] Joan managed to negotiate peace, but at a high price, including the loss of the Four

Cantrefs (the land between the Conwy and the Dee rivers), a heavy tribute of cattle and horses and the surrender of hostages, including Llywelyn's son, Gruffudd.[5] Following a deterioration of Anglo-Welsh relations, twenty-eight of the Welsh hostages were hanged in 1212. John was preparing for a campaign in Wales, and had hanged the hostages as a precursor to his invasion. However, the attack was called off when he received word from Joan that his barons were planning treason closer to home. Joan's warning was one of several from disparate sources, and persuaded John to disband his army. The last years of John's reign were taken up with conflict with his barons, leading to the issuing of Magna Carta in 1215 and a French invasion by Louis, eldest son of Philip II Augustus. The last thing John needed, if he was to save his kingdom, was to be distracted by discontent in Wales. In 1214 Joan successfully negotiated with her father for the release of the Welsh hostages still in English hands, including Llywelyn's son, Gruffudd; they were released the following year.

Following her father's death in October 1216, Joan continued to work towards peace between Wales and England. She visited Henry in person in September 1224, meeting him in Worcester; Joan seems to have had a good relationship with her half-brother, evidenced by his gifts to her of the manor of Rothley in Leicestershire, in 1225, followed by that of Condover in Shropshire, in 1226.[6] An extant letter to Henry III, addressed to her 'most excellent lord and dearest brother' is a plea for him to come to an understanding with Llywelyn. In the letter, Joan uses her relationship with Henry to try to ease the mounting tensions between the two men. She describes her grief 'beyond measure' that discord between her husband and brother had arisen out of the machinations of their enemies, and reassures her brother of Llywelyn's affection for him.[7] In the mid-1220s, Henry acted as a sponsor, with Llywelyn, in Joan's appeal to Pope Honorius III to be declared legitimate; in 1226 her appeal was allowed on the grounds that neither of Joan's parents had been married to others when she was born.

Joan and Llywelyn's marriage appears to have been, for the most part, a successful one. Joan's high-born status, as the daughter of a king, brought great prestige to Gwynedd. As a consequence, her household was doubled from four to eight staff, including a cook who could prepare Joan's favourite dishes. Llywelyn seems to have valued his wife's opinion; as we have seen, he often made use of her diplomatic skills and relationship with the English court and he often consulted her on other matters. Her influence extended to Welsh legal texts, which, from this period onwards, included French words. Joan's position was strengthened even further by the arrival of her children. Sometime between 1212 and 1215, her son, Dafydd, was born; in 1220 he was recognised as Llywelyn's heir by Henry III, officially supplanting his older, illegitimate, half-brother, Gruffudd, who was entitled to his father's lands under Welsh law. The move received papal approval in 1222. As a result, in 1229 Dafydd performed homage to Henry III, as his father's heir. A daughter, Elen, was probably born around 1210, as she was first married in 1222, to John the Scot, Earl of Chester. Her second marriage, in 1237 or 1238, was to Robert de Quincy. Joan may have been the mother to two more of Llywelyn's daughters, Gwladus and Margaret, although they may have been the daughters of a mistress. Gwladus was married to Reginald de Braose. Her stepson, William (V) de Braose, was to play a big part in Joan's scandalous downfall in 1230.

Joan's life in the first quarter of the 13th century had been exemplary; she was the ideal medieval woman, a dutiful daughter and wife, whose marriage helped to broker peace, if an uneasy one, between two countries. She had fulfilled her wifely duties, both by providing a son and heir and being supportive of her husband to the extent that she should not be included in the roll call of scandalous women – however, in 1230, everything changed. William de Braose was a wealthy Norman baron with estates along the Welsh Marches. Hated by the Welsh, who had given him the nickname Gwilym Ddu, or Black William, he had been taken prisoner by Llywelyn in 1228, near Montgomery. Although he had been released after paying a ransom, de Braose had returned to Llywelyn's court to arrange a marriage between his daughter, Isabella, and Llywelyn's son and heir, Dafydd. During this stay, William de Braose was 'caught in Llywelyn's chamber with the King of England's daughter, Llywelyn's wife'.[8]

William de Braose was publicly hanged, either at Crogan near Balsa, or possibly near Garth Celyn, on 2 May 1230. Joan, however, escaped with her life and was imprisoned in a tower at Llywelyn's palace of Garth Celyn.[9] We cannot say how long the affair had lasted, whether it was a brief fling in 1230, or had started when de Braose was a prisoner of Llywelyn in 1228. Joan's position in the

1220s had appeared unassailable but this scandal rocked Wales, and England, to the core. She was no young girl struggling to come to terms with her position in life; she was about forty years old, had been Llywelyn's consort for twenty-five years and had borne him at least two children when the affair was discovered. Contemporaries were deeply shocked at Joan's betrayal of her husband; indeed, following this scandal, Welsh law identified the sexual misconduct of the wife of a ruler as 'the greatest disgrace'.[10] However, there was no question over the legitimacy of her children, who had been born at least fifteen years before. The most surprising thing about the whole affair, moreover, is Llywelyn's response. His initial anger saw William de Braose hanged from the nearest tree, and Joan imprisoned in a tower. This rage, however vicious, was remarkably brief.

Maybe it was due to the strength of the previous relationship between Llywelyn and Joan, or maybe it was the high value placed on Joan's diplomatic skills and her links with the English court; but within a year the terms of Joan's imprisonment had been relaxed and just months after that, she was back on the political stage. Llywelyn appears to have forgiven her; the couple were reconciled and Joan returned to her life and position as Lady of Wales. Indeed, Joan soon reprised her diplomatic duties. She attended a conference between her husband, son and her brother, Henry III at Shrewsbury, in 1232. Despite William de Braose's betrayal of Llywelyn, and subsequent violent death, the wedding between his daughter, Isabella, and Llywelyn's son, Dafydd, was not derailed and by 1232 they were married.

Joan's indiscretion was forgiven by Llywelyn, maybe even forgotten, and when she died in February 1237, the Welsh prince was deeply affected by grief. Joan died at Garth Celyn, Abergwyngregyn, on the north coast of Gwynedd. She was buried close to the shore of Llanfaes, in the Franciscan friary that Llywelyn founded in her memory – a testament to his love for her. The friary was consecrated in 1240, just a few months before Llywelyn's own death in April of that year. The friary was destroyed in 1537, during Henry VIII's dissolution of the monasteries. Joan's remains were lost, but her coffin was eventually found, being used as a horse trough in the town of Beaumaris, on Anglesey. The effigy on the large stone coffin depicts Joan wearing a wimple and coronet, with her hands clasped in prayer, and now rests in the porch of

Beaumaris Church. It is a testament to Joan's personality, and the strength of her relationship with Llywelyn, that her affair with de Braose had few lasting consequences for her. Had she been younger, when the legitimacy of her children could have been called into question, her punishment could have been much harsher and the consequences more far-reaching.

In the early years of the 14th century, scandal rocked the French monarchy to its core and inadvertently contributed to the end of the Capetian dynasty. The year 1314 was a tumultuous year for France; the final act in the destruction of the Knights Templars was played out when the Grand Master, Jacques de Molay, and the Preceptor of Normandy, Geoffrey de Charney, were burned to death on the *Île de la Cité*. De Molay cursed Philip IV, King of France, and his descendants, from the flames. Philip IV would be dead within a year and his dynasty's rule over France would end with the death of his youngest son, Charles IV, in 1328.

Philip's eldest son and heir, Louis, was married to Marguerite de Burgundy. Louis seems to have been a hard person to live with – he had a number of nicknames, including the Quarreller, the Headstrong and Louis the Stubborn. If the nicknames really did reflect his personality, it is no surprise that the marriage was said to be unhappy. The couple had been married in 1305 but only one child, a daughter, Jeanne, would survive childhood to eventually become Queen of Navarre. The second son, Philip, was married to Marguerite's cousin, Jeanne d'Artois; they were married in 1307 and appear to have been content with each other, producing several children in a few short years. The youngest son, Charles, was married to Jeanne's younger sister, Blanche d'Artois. They were married in January 1308, and their first child, a son, Philip, was born on 5 January 1314.[11]

With all three sons married, Philip must have thought his dynasty's future secure. However, in 1314 the French king's only daughter, Isabella, unearthed a secret that threatened this security. Isabella, on a visit to Paris in 1313, had given a gift of silk purses to her sisters-in-law as souvenirs of the knighting of her three brothers, Louis, Philip and Charles, the sons of Philip IV. When she and her husband, King Edward II of England, visited Paris again in 1314, Isabella saw those same silk purses now adorning the belts of two knights of the French court, two brothers, Gautier and Philip d'Aunay.[12] Isabella could only wonder at how the purses came to be in the knights' possession and when she told her father of her suspicions the matter was investigated, and the brothers were put under surveillance. The d'Aunay brothers, it seems, were meeting with two of the princesses in secret. The whole scandal became known as the Tour de Neslé Affair, as the clandestine meetings were supposed to have taken place in this small palace on the outskirts of Paris (although some sources suggest that events happened at Philip IV's country retreat of Maubuisson Abbey).

Whatever the location, the affair was discovered; all three princesses were arrested and questioned. The unfortunate knights were arrested and, after being questioned and tortured, they confessed to the adultery and were condemned to death for the crime of *lèse majesté*. The brothers suffered a horrific execution; they were sentenced to castration and to be 'broken on the wheel' – they were strapped to large wheels, which were spun while their limbs were shattered with iron bars. The pain must have been beyond description, until, finally, they were beheaded by the executioner. When confronted in a secret court, Marguerite and Blanche confessed to adultery with the two brothers. Their heads were shaved and they were sent to life imprisonment in Chateau Gaillard. Blanche's sister, Jeanne, fared better; she was also arrested, and placed under guard at the Chateau Dourdan. Her marriage with Philip was a very happy one, and it seems she was only guilty of knowing of the affairs. Philip defended his wife before the Paris Parlement and, with Philip's support, Jeanne pleaded her innocence to the king, and was eventually allowed to return to her husband and the court.

Marguerite's imprisonment was the most severe. Some sources suggest she was held in a cell at the top of the donjon, open to the elements. On his accession to the throne in November 1314, Louis X applied to the pope for an annulment of the marriage. However, Pope Clement V died before he could grant the divorce and no new pope would be elected until 1316. Shortly after Clement's death, however, Marguerite died – probably strangled on the orders of Louis. Louis married Clemence of Hungary, but died in June 1316, while Clemence was pregnant with their son. Jean I the Posthumous, was born and died in November of the same year and the crown passed to Louis' brother, Philip V – with Jeanne d'Artois (by then Countess of Burgundy) at his side.

Unfortunately, Philip died in 1322, leaving only daughters, and the crown passed to his youngest brother. On his accession, Charles divorced Blanche – still in an underground cell in Chateau Gaillard – and transferred her to a monastery at Gavray, in Normandy, where she became a nun, and died there the following year. Charles IV died in February 1328, leaving his third wife, Jeanne d'Evreux, pregnant with what was hoped would be a son. However, in April 1328, she gave birth to a daughter, Blanche, and a power struggle followed. Charles' cousin, Philip de Valois, a grandson of Philip III, had been regent during Jeanne's pregnancy and used Salic law to advance his claim to the throne, and disinherit little Blanche. Salic law had never been applied to the French crown but was in practice throughout the French domains, dictating that the inheritance of land and titles went to the oldest living male relative. Valois' arguments won the day and he inherited the throne as Philip VI. Salic law, however, was not in force in Navarre, a kingdom that had come to the French crown when Jeanne I of Navarre had married Philip IV and to which the new king had no claim. Louis X's daughter, Jeanne, therefore inherited Navarre and reigned as Jeanne II, despite the questions that the scandal had raised over her parentage.[13]

The scandal cast a long shadow on the last years of the Capetian dynasty, with none of the three brothers producing a son to carry on their line. The harsh punishments reflected the need for queens and princesses to be above reproach, and the parentage of their children to be beyond question. However, who can say what they would not risk for love? These women were young, living in arranged, unhappy marriages and paid a terrible price for a few moments of freedom and passion; and the men they loved suffered horrendous agonies before finding relief in death. Maybe they deserve to be heroes and heroines, simply because they dared to risk all to be happy?

Joan of Kent was another woman who caused scandal and risked everything for the sake of love. She obviously had a strong sense of self because she managed to forge her own path, despite being embroiled in one of the most remarkable scandals of the Middle Ages. Joan was the daughter of Edmund of Woodstock, Earl of Kent and half-brother of Edward II. Edmund was a younger son of Edward I by his second wife, Margaret of France; he married Margaret Wake, Baroness Wake of Liddell, in 1325.

Their daughter Joan was the third of four children, and was born on 28 or 29 September 1328 at the Royal Palace of Woodstock, in Oxfordshire. When she was just eighteen months old, on 19 March 1430, Joan's father was beheaded for treason on the orders of the regent, Roger Mortimer and his lover, Queen Isabella. Being convinced that his brother, Edward II, was still alive after having been deposed in 1327, Edmund had become involved in a failed plot to free the erstwhile king. Whether he was the victim of a conspiracy to weed out Mortimer's enemies, or whether Edward II really did survive after his supposed murder in Berkeley Castle, is still debated by historians. Either way, the result of the plot was Edmund's execution. Joan's mother, Margaret Wake, was held under house arrest at Arundel Castle, with all four of her children; she gave birth to Joan's baby brother, John, just a month after their father's execution. A few months later, Edward III escaped Mortimer's control and assumed power; he took over responsibility for the family and Joan, a favourite of Edward's queen, Philippa of Hainault, was raised at court.[14]

The leading beauty of her day, Joan had little to offer a potential suitor beyond her looks and keen intelligence; Froissart called her 'the most beautiful woman in all the realm of England and the most loving'.[15] She had grown up in the same household as Edward III's eldest children – his son and heir Edward and his daughters Isabella and Joan. Around the age of eleven or twelve, it seems Joan of Kent secretly married, or promised to marry, Thomas Holland. Holland was a knight of the royal household, a soldier of some renown and, at twenty-four, twice Joan's age. Modern sensibilities make us cringe at Joan's tender age but, although it was young even for the period, an eleven-year-old bride was not unheard of. Their relationship remained a secret, however, and the couple had never obtained the king's consent.

Just a few short months later, Holland left to go on Crusade. In 1341, while Holland was away crusading in Prussia, Joan's mother, Margaret Wake, arranged an advantageous marriage for her daughter to William Montagu, 2nd Earl of Salisbury. Whether Margaret knew about the extent of Joan's relationship with Holland is uncertain – it may be that she believed Joan was infatuated with the landless knight and hoped that marrying her to Montagu would cure the pre-teen of puppy love.

By 1341 Joan and Montagu were married. Thomas Holland, however, didn't appear to be in a rush to return to claim his wife; once his crusading duties were done, he spent the next few years campaigning in Europe. In 1342–3 he fought in Brittany with the king, and was probably in Granada with the Earl of Derby by 1343. In 1345 he was back in Brittany, and was at the Siege of Caen in 1346; a battle in which Joan's other 'husband', Montagu, may also have taken part. Holland not only gained a reputation as a soldier but also made his fortune when he sold his prisoner, the Count of Eu, Constable of France, to Edward III for 80,000 florins.[16]

When he returned to England, Thomas Holland joined the Earl of Salisbury's household as his steward, and found himself in the strange position of working for the man who was married to his wife. In May 1348, Holland petitioned the pope, stating that Joan had been forced into her marriage with Salisbury. He went on to say that Joan had previously agreed to marry him and their relationship had been consummated. William contested the annulment; however, when it came time for Joan to testify, she supported Holland's claims.

It took eighteen months for Joan's marital status to be resolved. In the meantime, England was in the grip of the Black Death, the bubonic plague. To lift the country's spirits, Edward III arranged a grand tournament to be held at Windsor, on St George's Day, 23 April 1349. The knights in contention were the founder members of the Order of the Garter; England's greatest chivalric order, consisting of the king and twenty-five founder knights. The order was probably founded in 1348, though the date is uncertain. This tournament included William Montagu and Thomas Holland, both Joan's husbands. Joan herself is a part of the legend of the foundation of the Order of the Garter. She is said to be the lady who lost her garter during a ball celebrating the fall of Calais. Edward III is said to have returned the item to the twenty-year-old damsel with the words *'honi soit qui mal y pense'* ('evil to him who evil thinks'). Although the story is probably apocryphal, Joan's connection with the inaugural tournament is all too true; she brought an added spice to the St George's Day tournament of 1349. Her current husband, the Earl of Salisbury, fought on the king's team, while Sir Thomas Holland was on the side of Prince Edward. Joan's two husbands faced each other across the tournament field, with the object of their affection watching from the stands.

Although the results of the tournament are obscure, Joan's marital status was decided by Papal Bull, on 13 November 1349, when the pope ordered her to divorce Salisbury and return to Holland, a ruling she seems to have been happy to comply with.

Montagu wasted little time in finding himself another wife and married Elizabeth de Mohun shortly after the annulment had been granted. Elizabeth was the daughter of John, Lord Mohun of Dunster, and, given that she was born around 1343, was only six or seven at the time of the marriage. Several years later, they would have one child, a son, William, born in 1361. William was married in 1378, to Elizabeth FitzAlan, daughter of his father's companion-in-arms Richard, Earl of Arundel. Their happiness was short-lived, however, when William died after only four years of marriage, in a tragedy that must have rocked Montagu to the core – on 6 August 1382, young William was killed by his own father, the earl, in a tilting match at Windsor.

Joan succeeded her brother, John, as Baroness Wake of Liddell and Countess of Kent in December 1352 and was confirmed in her new titles in February 1353. Sir Thomas Holland, therefore, became Earl of Kent by right of his wife. Joan and Sir Thomas had five children – three sons and two daughters. Edmund was born in 1352 but died young. Thomas, Earl of Kent, married Alice, the daughter of Richard FitzAlan, 10th Earl of Arundel; he died in 1397. Their third son, John, was created Duke of Exeter in 1397 by his younger half-brother, Richard II (who was Joan's son by her later third marriage to Edward, the Black Prince). John married Elizabeth of Lancaster, daughter of John of Gaunt and Blanche of Lancaster, but was executed in 1400 for his involvement in a plot to assassinate Henry IV and return his brother to the throne. Of their daughters, Joan married John V, Duke of Brittany (who would marry Joanna of Navarre, the future queen-consort of Henry IV, as his second wife), but died in 1384. Their youngest child, Matilda, was born in 1359 and married twice; first to Sir Hugh de Courtenay, who died in 1377, and then to Waleran of Luxembourg, Count of St Pol and Ligny. Matilda died in 1391.

At the end of 1360, Sir Thomas Holland, the veteran soldier who had fought in the Crecy campaign, died so Joan was left a widow. Edward, Prince of Wales, the Black Prince, may have offered comfort to the Lady Joan, his friend from childhood, whom he used to call his 'Jeanette'.[17] Although a widow with five children, and bringing no beneficial foreign alliance to the marriage table, Joan and Edward appear to have fallen in love. It was not the political match his father had wanted for the heir to the throne, but all attempts at a marriage alliance with a princess from the Low Countries had come to nought, so it seems the king was quite happy to accept his son's choice of wife. It must have caused quite a scandal at the time. Although a beauty, Joan's bigamous marriage to William Montague was well-known – and he was still alive. She had five children by her first husband, Thomas Holland. Moreover, she was thirty-three years of age, two years older than her prince, and his father's first cousin. She must have hardly appeared to be 'queen material'. However, according to the Chandos Herald, one of the commentators of the period, Joan was 'a lady of great worth … very beautiful, pleasing and wise'.[18] Edward III sent one of his own people to the pope to ask permission for the marriage, which was swiftly granted. With great ceremony Edward and Joan had a second, official, wedding celebration at Windsor on 10 October 1361, officiated over by the Archbishop of Canterbury. Shortly after the wedding, the couple moved to Berkhamsted, where the king visited them after Christmas. In 1363 they moved their entire household to Bordeaux, after the prince was given the Duchy of Aquitaine by his father. Their court there was lavish, exceeding the king's own in brilliance. In 1365 their first child a son, Edward of Angoulême, was born and in April, following Joan's churching, Edward held a magnificent tournament to celebrate the birth. The next son, Richard of Bordeaux, followed on 6 January 1367.

The chronicler, Froissart, tells the story:

> In due course Joan, the princess, went into labour and by God's grace was delivered of her child. It was a fine son, Richard of Bordeaux, born at Epiphany, 6 January, which that year fell on a Wednesday.
>
> The child came into the world early in the morning to the great joy of the prince and the whole household, and was baptised the following Friday in the early afternoon on the holy font of St Andrew's Church in the city of Bordeaux. The child was named Richard and he afterwards became king of England.[19]

Richard's baptism was attended by three kings; Pedro of Castile, James IV of Majorca and Richard of Armenia. William Thorne, the Canterbury chronicler, described them as the three *magi* (or wise men), as Richard had been born on Epiphany, Twelfth Night – an auspicious sign for a bright future. The Black Prince wrote fondly to his wife while campaigning in Spain: 'Be assured, dearest companion, that we, our brother of Lancaster and all the great men of our army are, thank God, in good form.'[20] Froissart wrote of the Black Prince's return from Spain, and his arrival in Bordeaux; 'Where he was received with great celebrations. Princess Joan came to meet him and had Edward, her eldest son, carried with her; he was then about three years old.'[21] The Chandos Herald goes on to say that 'they walked together holding hands.'[22]

The Spanish campaign had been aimed at supporting Pedro of Castile's claim to the throne against that of his illegitimate half-brother, Henry of Trastámara. Although the Black Prince managed to re-establish Pedro's rule, the Castilian king could not pay the English army and Edward, already with a reputation for heavy-handedness in Aquitaine, taxed the duchy to raise funds; several of the lords appealed to France for aid. In 1370, Limoges rebelled against him and the Black Prince destroyed it completely, not a building was left undamaged, almost the entire population killed. Sometime in late 1370 or early 1371 the young family suffered a heartbreaking tragedy. Little Edward of Angoulême died of bubonic plague. He was buried in Bordeaux, his funeral arranged by John of Gaunt and attended by all the great lords of Gascony. The chronicler, Walsingham, describes the Black Prince's actions following the sack of Limoges: 'When he had done this, Prince Edward hurried to return to England, as much because of the infirmities which troubled him, as because of lack of money. Therefore, at the beginning of January [1371], with his wife and small son Richard, and with his household following behind, he reached Plymouth.'[23]

The Black Prince's health had been destroyed by a lifetime of campaigning. He returned to England a virtual invalid and died in 1376. Left a widow for a second time, Joan still had custody of her young son and was in charge of Richard's education until his accession to the throne on Edward III's death in 1377, aged only ten. In his will, Edward III gave to Joan, Princess of Wales, 1,000 marks and the free restitution of jewels she had pledged to him. Despite her marital history, and a reputation for extravagance – she was said to have spent £200 on a set of jewelled buttons – Joan was loved by the English people. It was with her that John of Gaunt sought refuge following the sacking of his Savoy Palace in 1376, when the people were discontented with his rule. Joan was seen as a calming influence on her son, Richard II, and was by his side during the dangerous days of the Peasant's Revolt of 1381; she sheltered in the Tower of London and rode in a carriage to accompany her thirteen-year-old son to meet with the rebels at Mile End.

In 1385 Joan's son, John Holland, while campaigning in Scotland, killed Ralph Stafford, son of the 2nd Earl of Stafford, in a quarrel. He fled to sanctuary at the shrine of St John of Beverley, but was condemned to death. Joan pleaded with her son, Richard, for days, begging him to pardon his brother. She died at Wallingford Castle, sometime in August 1385. The king pardoned his half-brother the following day. Although the Black Prince had built a chantry chapel for his wife, at Canterbury Cathedral, with ceiling bosses of her face, Joan was not buried at Canterbury with the Black Prince, but at the Greyfriars at Stamford in Lincolnshire, beside her first husband, Sir Thomas Holland.

It is difficult not to admire Joan of Kent. In a time when women had little say over their lives and marriages, she managed to choose two of her three husbands; and divorced the one husband who was not of her own choosing. She was probably a little selfish and traded on her good looks and inheritance, but she knew what she wanted and did everything she could to achieve it, a true heroine. She was not, however, the only princess of her time to search for love and be mired in scandal.

Another princess with a fascinating story is Isabella of Castile, the third daughter of Peter the Cruel of Castile (ironically, he was also known as Peter the Just) and his long-term mistress (and sometime wife, possibly, though the evidence is sketchy) Maria of Padilla. Isabella's childhood was marred by her father's battles to hold onto his throne and almost constant warfare with Aragon. Peter received support from Edward III's son the Black Prince, but his failure to pay the costs of the campaign, his faithlessness, and the failing health of the Black Prince, meant he was left to his own devices by 1367. Peter's own nobles backed his illegitimate brother, Henry of Trastámara, who eventually defeated and killed Peter in March 1369. Isabella's mother died in 1361 and her three-year-old brother, Alfonso, in 1362. On Peter's death in 1369, Isabella's older sister, Constance, inherited her father's claim to the crown of Castile and, taking Isabella with her, took refuge in the English territory of Guyenne. Constance married John of Gaunt (third son of Edward III) at Roquefort in September 1371; Gaunt saw the marriage as an opportunity to gain a kingdom of his own. It was not long after Constance's official entry into London, that, in 1372, Isabella married John's younger brother, Edmund of Langley, the fifth son of Edward III who would later become the 1st Duke of York. Their first son, Edward, was born the following year; he would succeed his father as the 2nd Duke of York, and played a prominent role in the reign of Richard II, but was killed at Agincourt in 1415. Their second child was a daughter, Constance, born in 1374.

Chroniclers of the time reported that Isabella and Edmund were an ill-matched pair; Thomas of Walsingham, in particular, commented on Isabella's 'loose morals', probably referring to her affair with John Holland, Duke of Exeter and half-brother to the king, Richard II.[24] The affair seems to have been an open secret and is believed to have started as early as 1374. It has cast doubt on the legitimacy of Edmund and Isabella's third child Richard of Conisbrough, grandfather of Edward IV and Richard III, thought to have been born in 1375. Isabella died on 23 December 1392 and is buried at King's Langley. In her will, she made Richard II her heir and asked that he provide a pension for her youngest son and Richard II's godson, Richard. Richard was given an allowance of £500 by the king, but this was only paid sporadically following Richard II's deposition by Henry IV. Richard was not even mentioned in the wills of his father and brother, causing speculation that this omission could be proof that Richard was not the son of the Duke of York.[25]

The surprising part of Isabella's story is to do with her daughter. The two women seem to have been very much alike, and neither was immune to scandal. Constance of York had been born around 1374, possibly at Conisbrough Castle in Yorkshire (although that is far from certain). She was the second of the three children born to Edmund and Isabella. At the age of four, in April 1378, Constance was betrothed to Edward le Despenser. However, young Edward appears to have died shortly after the betrothal as by November 1379, Constance was married to his only surviving, younger brother, Thomas, who was about six years of age at the time. It is highly likely that four-year-old Constance remained in her parents' household for several years after her marriage, although she may have also spent time in the household of her mother-in-law, who retained wardship of young Thomas despite her husband's death. (Thomas le Despenser was a great-grandson of the infamous Hugh le Despenser the Younger, despised favourite and alleged lover of Edward II, who was executed on 50-foot high gallows in 1326.) The marriage was seen as a good match on both sides: the Despenser family had a considerable fortune, they were among the twelve richest families in the country, while Constance was a granddaughter of Edward III and her hand in marriage completed the rehabilitation of the Despenser family.

In 1386, at just twelve years old Constance was made a Lady of the Garter by her cousin, Richard II; she was one of the youngest-ever recipients. In 1392 Constance's mother died and the following year, her father re-married. His new bride was about six years younger than Constance and was a niece to Richard II; Joan Holland was the daughter of Thomas Holland, 2nd Earl of Kent and granddaughter of Joan of Kent, Princess of Wales. In a bizarre twist, she was also the niece of John Holland, 1st Duke of Exeter, the late Duchess of York's alleged lover. During this time, Constance's husband, Thomas, was learning his trade as a soldier. He served with Richard II in Scotland in 1385, probably as a page or squire, given his tender years. In 1388 he was knighted by the Earl of Arundel, following his involvement in a naval expedition against the French. In 1391 Thomas travelled to Prussia to join the Crusade against the Lithuanians. However, it seems likely that, by 1394 when Thomas was back in England, Thomas and Constance were finally living together as a couple. In March of that year, Thomas had been granted full possession of his lands; he had been a ward of his mother, Elizabeth de Burghersh, since the death of his father, Edward, in 1375.

It is possible the couple had as many as five children, but only two survived infancy. A son, Edward, died young, Hugh died around 1401 and a daughter, Elizabeth, born around 1398, also died young. The first definite date of birth of a child is Richard, possibly their second son but the first to survive childhood, who was born on 30 November 1396. Richard would inherit his grandmother's title of Baron Burghersh on her death in about 1402. He married his second cousin Eleanor, daughter of Ralph Neville, 1st Earl of Westmoreland, and Joan Beaufort, herself the daughter of John of Gaunt and Katherine Swynford. Unfortunately, Richard and Eleanor had no children before Richard died, still only in his twenties. His title passed to his younger sister, Isabella, who had been born around 1400 and was successively married to two men, cousins, who had the same name; she initially married Richard de Beauchamp, Earl of Worcester, then later, Richard de Beauchamp, Earl of Warwick. Isabella's daughter by Warwick, Anne, would later marry Richard Neville, a prominent noble during the Wars of the Roses and known as the kingmaker. This marriage would produce two daughters, one of whom was Richard III's queen, Anne Neville.

Thomas le Despenser was a great supporter of Richard II; in 1397 he was involved in the arrest and prosecution of the Lords Appellant who had tried to put limits on the king's powers, the Duke of Gloucester and the Earl of Arundel; in return for which he received a share of their lands. On the 29 September 1397, le Despenser was created Earl of Gloucester. Despite his close links with Richard II, le Despenser initially supported the accession of Henry Bolingbroke as Henry IV, after usurping Richard's throne. However, after he was attainted for his role in the death of Thomas of Woodstock, Duke of Gloucester, and deprived of his earldom, he became disillusioned with the new regime. Fearful of losing his estates, and possibly his life, in January 1400 he joined in a conspiracy with the Earls of Kent, Salisbury and Huntingdon. Known as the Epiphany Rising, the earls planned to seize the king during a tournament at Windsor, intending to kill Henry IV and replace him with Richard II – still imprisoned at Pontefract Castle. The conspiracy was betrayed to the king by Edward of Norwich, Constance's older brother, and the conspirators were arrested and executed. Richard II himself became the prime victim of the plot, which led Henry IV to believe it was too dangerous to keep the erstwhile king alive; he died shortly afterwards, still in custody at Pontefract Castle, probably from starvation.

Thomas le Despenser was executed on 13 January 1400. It is tempting to feel sorry for Constance of York, former Countess of Gloucester, mother of several infants – it must have been difficult for her as a young, pregnant widow of a convicted traitor. With her husband's lands forfeited, she could well have wondered what was going to happen to her and her children, especially following the death of her father in 1402. However, Constance herself was not beyond plotting. In February 1405, during Owain Glyn

Dwr's rebellion, Constance became involved in the plot to abduct Edmund Mortimer, 5th Earl of March, from Windsor Castle. March had the greatest claim to the throne of all Henry IV's rivals, being descended from Edward III's second surviving son, Lionel of Antwerp. The plan was to deliver March and his younger brother, Roger, to their uncle, Sir Edmund Mortimer, who was married to Glyn Dwr's daughter. The boys were successfully released from Windsor, but recaptured before entering Wales. Although Constance does not seem to have suffered retribution for her part in the plot, she did implicate her brother Edward of Norwich, Duke of York, who, as a consequence, was imprisoned in Pevensey Castle for seventeen weeks.

Constance was also to cause scandal in her love life. As a young widow, she started a liaison with Edmund Holland, 4th Earl of Kent and the brother of Constance's step-mother, Joan. A daughter, Eleanor, was born to the couple at Kenilworth around 1405. She would later marry James Touchet, Lord Audley. Whether or not Eleanor's parents married became a bone of contention for the young woman when she attempted to lay claim to her father's lands and titles in 1430. Although she produced witnesses to prove the marriage of her parents in about 1404, on the petition of Edmund's sisters, Joan Duchess of York (Eleanor's step-grandmother) and Margaret Holland, Duchess of Clarence, Eleanor was adjudged illegitimate and was unable to inherit from her father. Edmund was killed at the Battle of Ile-de-Brehat in September 1408 and buried on the island of Lavrec.

Constance outlived her lover by eight years, the last survivor of the three York children. Her younger brother, Richard, had been executed in August 1415, for his part in the Southampton Plot to assassinate Henry V; and older brother Edward of Norwich, 2nd Duke of York, was killed at Agincourt in October of the same year.

Constance of York, Countess of Gloucester, died on 28 November 1416, and was buried at Reading Abbey in Berkshire. At first sight, it appears strange how most scandals, even in the medieval period, revolved around affairs of the heart; however, very few women were allowed to decide their own futures and husbands. The practice of arranged marriages, to an extent, explains why some women would look beyond wedlock to find affection.

However, not all scandals involved women looking for love. Although Eleanor Cobham had been involved in a love triangle, the scandal that would bring about her downfall was far more sinister. Born around 1400 and probably at the Castle of Sterborough in Kent, Eleanor Cobham was the daughter of Sir Reginald Cobham of Sterborough and his wife Eleanor, daughter of Sir Thomas Culpeper of Rayal. As is often the case with medieval women, nothing is known of Eleanor's early life. She appeared at court in her early twenties, when she was appointed lady-in-waiting to Jacqueline of Hainault, Duchess of Gloucester. Jacqueline had come to England to escape her second husband, the abusive John IV, Duke of Brabant. She obtained an annulment of the marriage from the Antipope, Benedict XIII, and married Humphrey, Duke of Gloucester, in 1423. He would spend a large part of their marriage trying to recover Jacqueline's lands from the Dukes of Brabant and Burgundy.

Humphrey was a younger brother of King Henry V and of John, Duke of Bedford. He had fought at the Battle of Shrewsbury at the age of twelve years and nine months, and would go on to fight at Agincourt in 1415. On Henry V's death, Humphrey acted as regent for his young nephew, Henry VI, whenever his older brother, the Duke of Bedford, was away fighting in France. However, he seems to have been little liked and was never trusted with full regency powers. In 1428 Pope Martin V refused to recognise the annulment of Jacqueline's previous marriage to John of Brabant and declared her marriage to Gloucester null and void. This should not have caused a problem for the couple as John of Brabant had died in 1426 so Humphrey and Jacqueline were free to remarry. However, in the meantime, Humphrey's attention had turned to Eleanor Cobham and he made no attempt to keep Jacqueline by his side.

This did not go down too well with the good ladies of London, who petitioned parliament between Christmas 1427 and Easter 1428. According to the chronicler Stow, their letters were delivered to Humphrey, the archbishops and the lords 'containing matter of rebuke and sharpe reprehension of the Duke of Gloucester, because he would not deliver his wife Jacqueline out of her grievous imprisonment, being then held prisoner by the Duke of Burgundy, suffering her to remaine so unkindly, contrary to the law of God and the honourable estate of matrimony'.[26] Humphrey paid little attention to the petition and married Eleanor some time between 1428 and 1431. It has been suggested that Eleanor was the mother of Humphrey's two illegitimate children, Arthur and

Antigone, although this seems unlikely. Eleanor would not have later needed to seek potions to help her conceive a child, if she already had two; also, Humphrey made no attempt to legitimise them following the marriage, as his grandfather, John of Gaunt, had done with his Beaufort children by Katherine Swynford. Eleanor was beautiful and intelligent; Aeneas Sylvius described her as 'a woman distinguished in her form', while Jean de Waurin said she was 'beautiful and marvellously pleasant'.[27] Eleanor and Humphrey had a small but lively court at their residence of La Plesaunce at Greenwich. Humphrey had a lifelong love of learning, which Eleanor most likely shared, and the couple attracted scholars, musicians and poets to their court.

On 25 June 1431, as Duchess of Gloucester, Eleanor was admitted to the fraternity of the monastery of St Albans – to which her husband already belonged – and in 1432 she was made a Lady of the Garter. Eleanor's status rose even higher in 1435, with the death of John, Duke of Bedford. While Henry VI was still childless, John had been heir presumptive. He died having had no children and so the position passed to Humphrey, Duke of Gloucester. With her heightened status, Eleanor received sumptuous Christmas gifts from the king; and her father was given custody of the French hostage, Charles, Duke of Orleans, who had been a prisoner since the battle of Agincourt in 1415. But Eleanor's dramatic downfall came in 1441.

Master Thomas Southwell, a canon of St Stephen's Chapel at Westminster, and Master Roger Bolyngbroke, a scholar, astronomer and cleric – and alleged necromancer – were arrested for casting the king's horoscope and predicting his death. Southwell and Bolyngbroke, with Margery Jourdemayne, known as the Witch of Eye and renowned for selling potions and spells, were accused of making a wax image of the king, '... the which image they dealt so with, that by their devilish incantations and sorcery they intended to bring out of life, little and little, the king's person, as they little and little consumed that image.'[28] Bolyngbroke implicated Eleanor during questioning, saying she had asked him to cast her horoscope and predict her future; for the wife of the heir to the throne, this was a dangerous practice. It suggested she might have her eye on the throne itself.

On hearing of the arrest of her associates Eleanor fled to sanctuary at Westminster. Of the twenty-eight charges against her, she admitted to five. Eleanor denied the treason charges, but confessed to obtaining potions from Jourdemayne in order to help her conceive a child. Awaiting further proceedings, as Eleanor remained in sanctuary, pleading sickness, she tried to escape by river. Thwarted, she was escorted to Leeds Castle on 11 August and held there for two months. On being brought to Westminster, Eleanor was examined by an ecclesiastical tribunal on 19 October and on 23 October, she faced Bolyngbroke, Southwell and Jourdemayne, who accused her of being the 'causer and doer of all these deeds'.[29] Eleanor was found guilty of sorcery and witchcraft; she was condemned to do public penance and to perpetual imprisonment. Her co-accused suffered even more terrible fates: Bolyngbroke was hanged, drawn and quartered, Southwell died in the Tower of London and Margery Jourdemayne was burned at the stake at Smithfield. Eleanor's own chaplain, Master John Hume, had also been arrested, although he was accused only of knowing of the others' actions and was later pardoned.

On three occasions Eleanor was made to do public penance at various churches in London; on the first of such, on 13 November 1441, bareheaded and dressed in black carrying a wax taper, she walked from Temple Bar to St Paul's Cathedral, where she offered the wax taper at the high altar. Following two further penances, at Christ Church and St Michael's in Cornhill, Eleanor was sent first to Chester Castle and then to Kenilworth. Her circumstances much reduced, Eleanor was allowed a household of only twelve persons. Her conviction for witchcraft discredited her husband; Humphrey was marginalised and on 6 November 1441 his marriage was annulled. Humphrey's enemies, Margaret of Anjou (Henry VI's queen) and the Earl of Suffolk, convinced the king that his uncle was plotting against him. In February 1447, Humphrey was arrested and confined in Bury St Edmunds. He died a week later; some claimed it was murder, but the most likely cause of death is a stroke. Eleanor was moved to Peel Castle on the Isle of Man, in 1446, and finally, in 1449, she was transferred to Beaumaris Castle on Anglesey. Still a prisoner, she died there on 7 July 1452; she was buried at Beaumaris, at the expense of Sir William Beauchamp, the castle's constable.

Eleanor's downfall was very public and dramatic. Witchcraft was a convenient charge to use against a woman; this wasn't the first time such a charge was laid against a high-profile lady. Indeed,

Humphrey's step-mother, Joanna of Navarre, wife of Henry IV, had also faced similar accusations, made by her stepson, Henry V. Perhaps the most surprising part of the scandal is that there is a smattering of truth among the accusations, which is probably what made them more credible and damaging in the minds of her judges. Eleanor Cobham, as with most of the other women whose lives were mired in scandal, paid the price with her freedom, she was imprisoned for eleven years.

As we have seen, however, scandal, no matter how dramatic and public, did not always signal the end of a woman's life and freedom. Joan of Kent, Princess of Wales and Joan, Lady of Wales, both managed to ride out the storms that threatened to engulf them, and ended their lives in relative peace, heroines for many women who had tried to forge their own paths, despite the restrictions placed on medieval women.

5

The Disinherited Heroines

Women throughout the medieval period faced the danger of losing their inheritance, either through an inability to physically fight for their rights or through the unscrupulous actions of their male relatives, or a combination of the two. For one such heroine, it meant the loss of one crown, but the recovery of another; while for others it meant truly miserable marriages. Remarkably, few of these women took their treatment lying down; they fought for their rights as best they could, although with varying degrees of success.

Isabella of Gloucester is a shadow in the pages of history. There are no pictures of her, not even a description of her personality or appearance. No one even seems certain of her name; she has been called Isabel, Isabella, Hawise, Avice – but Isabella is how she appears in the Close Rolls. Isabella was the youngest daughter and co-heiress of William, 2nd Earl of Gloucester, and his wife, Hawise, daughter of Robert de Beaumont, 3rd Earl of Leicester. Isabella's only brother Robert had died in 1166, making her and her two sisters co-heiresses to the earldom of Gloucester. Although her date of birth has been lost to history, it seems likely she was born in the early 1160s. She was betrothed, in 1176, to Prince John, the youngest son of Henry II and Eleanor of Aquitaine. John was nine years old at the time of the betrothal, with Isabella probably a few years older. The marriage was to be a way for Henry II to provide for his youngest son. After the Earl of Gloucester's death in 1183, his entire estate had passed to Isabella; her married older sisters, Mabel and Amicia, had been explicitly excluded from the estate to prevent the division of the comital inheritance and they received annuities of £100 each in compensation.[1] Henry II therefore seized all the Gloucester lands, took Isabella into wardship and made the income available for John's use, as her future husband.

Henry II, however, kept his options open and had not finalised John's marriage to Isabella by the time of his death, in case a more suitable alliance had come along. Richard I, on the other hand, thought it expedient to get his brother safely married, on his own accession to the throne in 1189. The wedding took place at Marlborough Castle in Wiltshire on 29 August 1189; John was twenty-one and Isabel was probably approaching thirty.[2] Baldwin, the Archbishop of Canterbury at the time, opposed the marriage as the couple were related within the prohibited degrees; they were second cousins, being great-grandchildren of Henry I. The archbishop placed an interdict on John's lands but this was removed after the intervention of the papal legate, Giovanni di Anagni, and John promised to seek a papal dispensation to overcome Baldwin's objections, although it appears this was never obtained.

Although Isabella and John were married for ten years, it is possible they never, or rarely, lived together. They never had any children and it is during this time in his life that John's illegitimate children were born, a further suggestion the couple were not close. In 1193, as part of his plotting with Philip II Augustus, King of France, John promised to marry the French king's half-sister, Alice, who had previously been betrothed to John's own brother, Richard. Nothing eventually came of the marriage proposal, but it was an implicit rejection of Isabella as his wife. John succeeded to the throne on the death of his older brother Richard the Lionheart, on 6 April 1199. He was crowned on 27 May 1199; the fact that Isabella was not crowned with him suggests that John was already looking for a way out of the marriage. Isabella would never be styled 'queen' and it was possibly as early as August 1199, but certainly by 1200, that John obtained a divorce on the grounds of consanguinity, the very difficulty for which he was supposed to have obtained a dispensation. The Bishops of Lisieu, Bayeux and Avranches, sitting in Normandy, provided the required judgement. One chronicler said of John that 'seized by hope of a more elevated marriage, he acted on wicked counsel and rejected his wife.'[3]

Keen to keep his hold on the substantial Gloucester lands, John took Isabella into wardship, again, holding her in 'honourable confinement' for the next fourteen years. The title of earl and a small portion of the estates were conferred on Amaury, Count of Évreux, Isabella's nephew by her sister, Mabel, in compensation for John's surrender of Évreux to France in the treaty of Le Goulet in 1200.[4] In 1213, however, Amaury died childless and Isabella was once again heir to the earldom of Gloucester. In anticipation of her death, possibly after succumbing to an illness, Isabella made a will in that same year, disposing of all her movable goods. However, she was still among the living in 1214, when this second wardship ended and she was given another chance at marital bliss.

This new marriage, arranged for her by John, was to a man who was more than sixteen years her junior. In 1214 she was married to Geoffrey de Mandeville, Earl of Essex, who had paid the considerable sum of 20,000 marks to become her second husband and Earl of Gloucester *jure uxoris* (by right of his wife); the new earl was granted all the Gloucester estates, save for the valuable manor of Bristol, which was retained by the crown. The marriage was politically motivated, and driven by John as a means of raising cash. Indeed, given the age difference, it is possible that Mandeville was a most reluctant groom, but it didn't pay to upset one's monarch, especially when it was King John.

Mandeville was to pay the 20,000 marks in instalments throughout 1214 and his failure to keep to the payment schedule meant the confiscation of the Gloucester estates. Although John restored them and offered to renegotiate Mandeville's debt, the Earl and Countess of Gloucester nevertheless joined the growing baronial rebellion. However, just two years later, on 23 February 1216, Geoffrey de Mandeville died from wounds he had received in a tournament. As one of the Magna Carta sureties, de Mandeville was in a state of rebellion against the crown when he died; as a result, all his lands and titles, including the earldom of Gloucester, were forfeit to the crown, leaving Isabella with little but liberty – she was almost joyfully styling herself 'Countess of Gloucester and Essex in my free widowhood'.[5]

It was not until the year after King John's death that Isabella's lands were finally returned to her, on 17 September 1217. At about the same time, or shortly after, Isabella was married for a third and final time, to Hubert de Burgh, Earl of Kent. De Burgh had become Chief Justiciar of England in 1215 and rose to be one of the regents during the minority of Henry III. This final marriage was, sadly, very short-lived and Isabella was dead within a month, possibly only a few weeks, of her wedding day and almost exactly a year after the death of her first husband, King John. Isabella died on 14 October 1217, probably at Keynsham Abbey near Bristol, and was buried at the Cathedral of Christ Church, Canterbury. Despite her three marriages, Isabella never had children and the earldom of Gloucester went to her nephew, Gilbert de Clare.

We can't know, of course, whether Isabella would have ever become a mother, nor whether it was through infertility, miscarriages or John's indifference that she did not have a family during their ten years of marriage. Isabella appears to have had very little control over her own life, even less than many women of her time; to the extent that one hopes beyond reason that the year of freedom she experienced following the death of Geoffrey de Mandeville was at least a happy one. Isabella endured the whims of John, first as her husband and then as king, through many years, even decades. Her life and future, and her inheritance, were constantly subject to John's desires and political machinations. Her lands and income were taken from her on at least three occasions; making it even more remarkable that she managed to pass her earldom of Gloucester, in its entirety, on to her nephew.

Isabella was far from being the only medieval heroine to suffer from the ruthless ambitions of her husband. The story of Alice de Lacey is something straight from a novel, with rebellion, kidnappings and love all featuring in the life of this countess. Alice was born at Denbigh Castle on or about 25 December 1281; she was the daughter of Henry de Lacey, 5th Earl of Lincoln. Through her mother Margaret she was the granddaughter of William (II) Longspée, Earl of Salisbury, and a descendant of Nicholaa de la Haye, the formidable lady who defended Lincoln Castle against the French invaders in 1217. Alice was one of three children and with two brothers, Edmund and John, she was, of course, not expected to inherit her father's earldom. However, two family tragedies made Alice one of the richest, and most desirable, heiresses in England. Young Edmund, it appears, drowned in a well at Denbigh Castle and John fell to his death from the parapet at Pontefract Castle, leaving Alice as her parents' sole heir. In 1294 Alice's marriage was arranged by no less a person than the king, Edward I, who saw her as a suitable bride for his nephew Thomas, Earl of Lancaster and son of the king's brother Edmund Crouchback. Alice and Thomas were married on or before 28 October 1294; he was about sixteen years old and Alice was not yet thirteen. It seems to have been one of the most disastrous marriages of the age, with Alice apparently playing no part in her husband's life.

Edward I had shown his unscrupulous nature in the marriage settlement in that Thomas was given part of the Lacey inheritance on the marriage, with the rest to pass to Thomas, not Alice, on her father's death. The settlement further stipulated with one stroke of the pen that the de Lacey lands would pass to Lancaster in the event of Alice's dying without issue; excluding all collateral heirs to the earldoms of Salisbury and Lincoln. Alice's mother Margaret, Countess of Salisbury in her own right, died in 1309 and by June 1310, Alice's father had remarried; probably in the hope of securing an heir for his earldom. In the event, it was not to be and the Earl of Lincoln died in 1311, with his estates passing, through his daughter, to Thomas, Earl of Lancaster and Leicester.

With five earldoms to his name, Thomas now became one of the richest and most powerful men in the kingdom. Although he was initially a supporter of the new king, his cousin Edward II, he would soon turn against him and his favourites, making enemies along the way. Poor Alice got caught in the middle of one of Thomas's feuds. According to the chronicler Walsingham:

> The Countess of Lancaster ... was seized at Canford, in Dorset, by a certain knight of the house and family of John, Earl Warenne, with many English retainers called together for the detestable deed, as it is said, with the royal assent. ... With them was a certain man of a miserable stature, lame and hunchbacked, called Richard de St Martin, exhibiting and declaring constantly his evil intentions towards the lady, so miserably led away.[6]

Alice was kidnapped in 1317 from her manor in Canford, Dorset, by John de Warenne's man, Sir Richard de St Martin, supposedly with the king's knowledge. Several reasons for the abduction have been put forward; one is, of course, that Alice and St Martin were having an affair, while another is that the affair was between Alice and John de Warenne, Earl of Surrey, himself. Given the king's involvement, a more likely explanation is that the kidnapping was organised by de Warenne in retaliation for the Earl of Lancaster's objections to de Warenne's attempts to divorce his wife, Joan of Bar, in 1315/16. Joan was a cousin of Thomas of Lancaster and a niece of King Edward II, but her marriage to John de Warenne was a disaster and John lived openly with his mistress, Maud Nerford. When he attempted to divorce Joan, Lancaster was one of his most vocal opponents; the divorce was eventually refused and de Warenne was even excommunicated for a time.

Following her abduction, Alice was held at Reigate Castle, Surrey. The kidnapping set off a private war between the two magnates, with Lancaster in retaliation targeting Warenne's Yorkshire estates and successfully besieging the earl's castle at Conisbrough. The Earl of Lancaster, however, seems to have made little or no effort to actually rescue his wife and there is no record of how and when she was eventually released. Alice and Thomas's marriage does not appear to have been a happy one and there is some evidence that they were actually divorced in 1318, with Thomas retaining Alice's earldoms after enforcing the marriage contract. The divorce was supposedly on account of her adultery with the Earl of Surrey's squire, Sir Eubolo Lestrange (although this may be a confusion of facts from her abduction and her later marriage). It has also been claimed that Alice and her abductor, Richard de St Martin, were pre-contracted before her marriage to Thomas of Lancaster. However, although this is not impossible, it does seem unlikely, given Alice's tender age on her wedding day.[7]

Whether or not Alice and Thomas did divorce is open to debate. If the divorce occurred, it did not protect her from the reprisals meted out after her husband's failed rebellion and defeat at the Battle of Boroughbridge, in March 1322. Following the execution of Thomas, the now-widowed Alice, with her step-mother Joan, was imprisoned in York Castle. It must have been a truly terrifying time for the two women; with no protectors, they were at the mercy of the king's favourite, Hugh le Despenser the Younger, and his father, also called Hugh le Despenser. Threatened with execution by burning, they were forced to surrender most of their estates.

Alice was allowed to keep her titles of Countess of Salisbury and Lincoln, and a life interest in lands to the value of 500 marks.[8] Although she would eventually recover Lincoln Castle, many of her estates were given to her erstwhile abductor, John de Warenne, and only returned to her by Edward III, many years later; all except the lordship of Denbigh, which was never returned to her.

By November 1324 Alice had married again, this time to a minor baron from the Welsh Marches, Sir Ebule, or Eubolo, Lestrange of Shropshire. The marriage demonstrated that Alice had managed to come out of the disaster of her first husband's downfall with enough income and property to make her an attractive proposition as a wife – although, it does seem possible that this marriage was a love-match, as it appears to have been a happier one. The facts that Sir Eubolo moved to Lincolnshire to look after his wife's interests and that it was with Sir Eubolo that Alice chose to be buried, when the time came, also attest to Alice's contentment. Alice and Sir Eubolo were married for more than ten years although during the latter part of the marriage Lestrange was away campaigning in Scotland, where he died in September 1335. In a demonstration of his trust in her, Alice was named as one of the executors of his will and he was buried in Barlings Abbey, Lincolnshire.

Following his death, Alice took a vow of chastity and looked determined to settle into a life of quiet retirement. However, her adventures were not quite at an end and in 1335, or early 1336, poor Alice was kidnapped for a second time; she was abducted from her castle at Bolingbroke, and allegedly raped, by Sir Hugh de Freyne. Freyne was a Herefordshire knight and royal keeper of the town and castle of Cardigan.

There appears to be some suggestion that Alice was in collusion with Sir Hugh, the abduction being a way for her to evade her vow of chastity. However, Edward III was furious and ordered their imprisonment. The imprisonment was of short duration, as the couple were reconciled with the king in 1336 and were allowed to marry. The marriage did much to improve Freyne's status and brought him a summons to Parliament in November 1336. Unfortunately, such success was short-lived and Freyne died at Perth in December 1336 or January 1337.

Shortly after the death of her third husband, the Bishop of Lincoln issued a demand that Alice keep to her prior vow of chastity. As there were no further marriages – or abductions – we can probably assume that she did so. Alice died on 2 October 1348 at what in those days would have been seen as the grand age of sixty-six. She was buried with her second husband at the Premonstratensian House of Barlings, in Lincolnshire. Having had no children from any of her three marriages, Alice's lands and titles, as according to the original marriage settlement fifty-four years earlier, passed to the house of Lancaster and her husband's nephew, Henry of Grosmont, 1st Duke of Lancaster and father of Blanche of Lancaster, John of Gaunt's first wife. It is remarkable that it was only after losing most of her inheritance that Alice appears to have found contentment in her life and marriages. The fact she was no longer a prize on the marriage market seems to have given her a freedom that escaped poor Isabella of Gloucester.

However, while Alice's inheritance was taken from her on her marriage, there was one little girl, in France, whose inheritance was taken out of her hands due to the scandalous actions of her mother. In 1312 a daughter was born into the French royal family. Although some sources say she was born as early as 1309 or 1311, most seem to settle on January 1312. However, the news was delivered to Edward II and Queen Isabella by Jeannot de Samoys, usher to Margaret of Burgundy, in March 1312, suggesting the baby had been born on 28 January of that year.[9] Jeanne de France was to be the only surviving child of her parents, Louis of France and Margaret of Burgundy. Louis had become King of Navarre on the death of his mother in 1305 and was married to Margaret later in the same year, when Louis was sixteen years old and Margaret was about fifteen. Louis was dauphin of France, the eldest of the three surviving sons of Philip IV *le Bel*, King of France and Navarre, and Jeanne I, Queen of France and *de jure* Queen of Navarre. Louis' sister, Isabella, was married to Edward II of England. It was a tight-knit family, with Louis' brothers, Philip and Charles, married to two sisters, Blanche and Joan of Artois, who were also cousins to Margaret, being the daughters of her uncle Otto IV, Count of Burgundy.

As described earlier, in 1314 a scandal rocked the French monarchy to its very core, leaving a question mark over Jeanne's legitimacy that is still there today. The Tour de Neslé Affair saw two-year-old Jeanne's mother, Margaret, convicted of adultery, and imprisoned in the Chateau-Gaillard for the rest of her life. Margaret's cousin and sister-in-law, Blanche, was convicted with her. Although Blanche's sister, Joan, with the support of her husband Philip, was cleared of the charges, she was held under house arrest for a short time as it was believed she knew of the adulterous liaisons of her sisters-in-law. The two knights in question were brothers, Gautier and Philip d'Aunay; who were tortured and castrated before being brutally executed by being 'broken on the wheel' and decapitated. How much Jeanne would have known of these events is uncertain. At just two years old, she would have been in the royal nursery and shielded from events, but it is not inconceivable that she was treated differently following the discovery of her mother's adultery.[10]

Although Jeanne was already two, no one could say how long Margaret's betrayal of her husband had been going on, or even if she had had other lovers, which meant that Jeanne's legitimacy was now in question. Within months, the situation became more acute. In November 1314, Jeanne's grandfather Philip IV died and her father succeeded to the French throne as Louis X. King Louis was now desperate to produce a male heir and with the papacy dragging its heels over his divorce from Jeanne's mother, it is possible he took matters into his own hands. Whether it was from natural causes after her rough treatment – or, more likely, strangulation on Louis' orders – Margaret died shortly after Louis' accession.

Louis then married Clementia of Hungary and the couple were jointly crowned at Reims in August 1315. Nothing is recorded of the relationship between Jeanne and her stepmother, or of how Jeanne's status changed as the daughter of the king. However, doubts over Jeanne's legitimacy must still have been at the forefront of people's minds as on his deathbed in June 1316, Louis X made a point of stating that Jeanne was his legitimate daughter. Clementia was pregnant at the time of Louis' death, which had happened after he played a particularly strenuous game of tennis; their son John the Posthumous was born five months later but died just five days after birth, causing a succession crisis.

In most countries, Jeanne would automatically have become queen regnant on the death of her baby brother. However, her tender years – she was only four years old, after all – and the questions over her legitimacy, meant she was practically overlooked as a candidate for the crown. Jeanne's uncle, Philip, the younger brother of Louis X, had acted as regent during Clementia's pregnancy and he now acted to take the crown, his experience and forceful personality gaining him support among the leading nobles. He was crowned King Philip V at Reims and solemnly recognised as king by the leading men of the kingdom of France, from nobles, to churchmen, to the rich bourgeois. One faction had supported Jeanne's succession, however, and although Salic law was not actually raised as a reason to bar Jeanne from the throne, the argument that a woman could not succeed to the throne of France was approved at a meeting of the Estates General, called by Philip V after his accession.[11]

It fell to Jeanne's maternal grandmother, Agnes of France, Duchess of Burgundy, and maternal uncle, Odo IV, Count of Burgundy, to press Jeanne's claims to the crown of Navarre, but they were unsuccessful. In 1318 Odo came to an agreement with Philip that should he have no male heirs, the counties of Champagne and Brie would go to Jeanne, while Jeanne would relinquish her claims to the thrones of France and Navarre – and would swear to this once she reached her majority, probably at the age of twelve.

In the same agreement, Odo was to marry Philip V's daughter Joan, and Jeanne would marry her cousin, Philip d'Evreux. Philip was the grandson of Philip III of France and his second wife, Marie of Brabant; he was the son of Louis d'Evreux, half-brother of Jeanne's grandfather, Philip IV. At just six years old Jeanne was married to twelve-year-old Philip on 18 June 1318. She was then given into the care of Philip's grandmother, the Dowager Queen Marie of Brabant, to continue her education.

There is no evidence that Jeanne relinquished her claims to the thrones of France and Navarre on her 12th birthday – and the situation changed, again, when Philip V died in 1322 and was succeeded by his brother, Charles IV. Charles IV reigned for only four years and a succession crisis arose yet again when he died on 1 February 1328, leaving no children, although his wife, Jeanne d'Evreux was pregnant. France was again left in limbo, with a regency under Philip of Valois until the baby prince or princess was born. Jeanne d'Evreux was delivered of a daughter, Blanche, on 1 April 1328, leaving Jeanne, the daughter of the oldest son of Philip IV, as the senior direct claimant to the French and Navarrese thrones. However, with the declaration by the Estates General that women were not eligible to accede to the throne of France, the crown was offered to Philip of Valois. Philip was the grandson of Philip III, through his father, Charles of Valois, and acceded to the throne as Philip VI. Philip, however, had no claim to the crown of Navarre as it had come to the French crown through the marriage of Philip IV with Queen Jeanne I of Navarre.

With a tradition of female rulers in its history, and having no laws barring women from the throne, therefore, the crown of Navarre finally came to Jeanne, after the extinction of the male line. Her inheritance was publicly acknowledged by the new King of France and the General Assembly of Navarre proclaimed Jeanne as Queen in May 1328, with a stipulation that her husband, Philip, would reign jointly with her, but only until their eldest son attained his majority.

After years in the shadows and aged just seventeen, Jeanne and her husband were jointly crowned as King Philip III and Queen Jeanne II of Navarre, at Pamplona on 5 March 1329. Several property agreements with the French crown meant Jeanne and Philip had extensive lands in Normandy, Champagne and Philip's County of Evreux, as well as their kingdom of Navarre. Their marriage also appears to have been successful, with at least seven children being born between 1326 and 1341, three of which were boys. Their eldest child, Maria, became the first wife of Peter IV of Aragon; while the next eldest, Blanche, born in 1330, was betrothed to John of France before marrying his father, Philip VI – who was forty years her senior – in 1349, just months after her mother's death.

One of their other daughters, Agnes, born in the mid-1330s, married Gaston, Count of Foix. According to Froissart, Gaston accidentally killed their only son, another Gaston, during a quarrel.[11] Jeanne's youngest daughter, Joan, was born in 1339 and would marry John II Viscount Rohan. Some sources mention another daughter, Joan, born around 1324, who would become a nun at Longchamp. However, it seems highly likely that Joan was an illegitimate daughter of Philip d'Evreux, rather than the eldest daughter of the Philip and Jeanne.

Jeanne and Philip's eldest son and heir, Charles II the Bad, was born in 1330 and later married Joan, daughter of John II of France. Charles was implicated in the assassination of the Constable of France, Charles de la Cerda, and intrigued with the English, against the French, during the Hundred Years War. He even escaped from imprisonment in Chateau-Gaillard, but was ultimately defeated by the French, who, nevertheless, allowed him to remain as King of Navarre. Another son, Philip, Count of Longueville was born in 1336 and married Yolande of Flanders; while their youngest son, Louis, was born in 1341 and would become Duke of Durazzo in Albania by right of his wife, Joanna.[12]

Jeanne and Philip shared their time between all their lands, with French governors installed to rule Navarre during their absences. As rulers of Navarre, Jeanne and Philip followed active legislation and building programmes and tried to maintain peaceful relations with neighbouring states. As a couple, they appear to have worked closely together; more than forty-one decrees were issued jointly in their names. Philip died in 1343, aged thirty-seven, while on Crusade against the Muslim kingdom of Granada in Spain. He was mortally wounded by an arrow during the Siege of Algeciras and died shortly after. His body was returned to Pamplona for burial, while his heart was taken to Paris and interred at the Couvent des Jacobins. After her husband's death, Jeanne ruled alone, dying of the plague on 6 October 1349 at the Chateau de Conflans. She was just months short of her thirty-eighth birthday, having ruled Navarre for twenty-one of her thirty-eight years. Jeanne was buried in the royal Basilica of St Denis but her heart was laid to rest beside her husband's in the Couvent des Jacobins, the taint of bastardy no longer an issue.

Jeanne of Navarre was not the only heroine to be refused her rightful place in the line of succession to a crown. Although Jeanne was set aside by others who were claiming the crown for themselves, there was a young princess in England who was specifically excluded by her own grandfather, Edward III. Princess Philippa of Clarence was born at Eltham Palace in Kent on the 16 August 1355. She was named after her grandmother, Philippa of Hainault, Edward III's queen, who was one of her godparents. The first grandchild of Edward III, young Philippa was the only child of Lionel of Antwerp, Duke of Clarence, and his first wife, Elizabeth de Burgh. Lionel was the first of King Edward and Queen Philippa's children to marry; he was their third son but the second to survive childhood. Born in 1338, he was married to Elizabeth de Burgh in the Tower of London on 9 September 1342. Lionel was almost four years old and his bride was six years older, born in 1332. Elizabeth was the daughter and heiress of William de Burgh, 3rd Earl of Ulster, who had died the year after her birth. It seems that from 1352, when Lionel was fourteen and Elizabeth twenty, the couple lived together as husband and wife. Lionel became Earl of Ulster by right of his wife and took possession of vast estates in Ireland and the Honour of Clare, in Suffolk; from which he was created Duke of Clarence by Parliament on 13 November 1362.

Philippa lost her mother when she was just eight years old. Elizabeth died in Dublin in December 1363 and was buried at Clare Priory in Suffolk. Lionel married again five years later, in May 1368, in Milan, to Violante Visconti, daughter of the Lord of Milan. He died at Alba just five months after the wedding, in October 1368, and was buried at Pavia; his body was later reinterred to lie beside Elizabeth at Clare Priory in Suffolk. The dukedom of Clarence became extinct on Lionel's death, but the earldom of Ulster and Honour of Clare passed to Philippa, his only daughter and heiress. Although an orphan at the tender age of thirteen, Philippa's future had been settled many years before.

When only in her fourth year, in February 1359, Philippa was betrothed, at the Queen's Chapel in Reading, to seven-year-old Edmund Mortimer. The children would probably not have seen much of each other before their wedding; Edmund was given in wardship to William of Wykeham, following his father's death. They were finally married in 1368, shortly before Lionel departed for Milan, although Edmund would not come of age until about 1372.[13] Edmund was the great-grandson of Roger Mortimer, 1st Earl of March and lover of Edward II's queen, and Edward III's mother, Isabella of France. Roger Mortimer had been executed on Edward III's orders in 1330 and the marriage, of Edmund and Philippa, was viewed as a reconciliation with the Mortimer family, powerful lords on the troublesome Welsh Marches. The children's wedding was also the first in a string of royal marriages. Philippa was married before any of her aunts and uncles; but weddings for her uncle, John of Gaunt, to Blanche of Lancaster, and her aunt Margaret to John Hastings, 2nd Earl of Pembroke, followed in May that year. The marriage alliances were all part of Edward III's policy to provide for his large brood of children and tie the great baronial families of the kingdom to the crown, by bringing them into the Royal family.[14]

Edmund Mortimer succeeded to his father's earldom as the 3rd Earl of March in 1372 and the couple spent their time between properties in England, Wales and Ireland. Their first child was born when Philippa was fifteen; she gave birth to a daughter, Elizabeth, at Usk in Monmouthshire, in February 1371. Three more children followed; Roger born at Usk in September 1373, Philippa, who was probably born at Ludlow in Shropshire around 1375, and finally Edmund, who was born at Ludlow in November 1377. Marriage to Philippa had brought her husband Edmund power and influence. Through his steward, Peter de la Mare, he was instrumental in the Good Parliament of 1376, which argued against the influence of Edward III's lover, Alice Perrers, and her friends, on the government of the kingdom. He spoke up for royal legitimacy and, using similar language to that used against his grandfather, Roger Mortimer, decried the influence an adulterous affair was having on the dignity of the crown. The Good Parliament led to serious division and long-term repercussions in the relationship between Edmund and John of Gaunt. Edmund resigned his position as Constable of England, for fear of assassination, and was sent to Ireland, ostensibly to put some distance between him and Gaunt.[15]

Following Edward III's death in 1377, until her own death six months later, Philippa was, technically, heiress presumptive to the crown of her cousin, Richard II. However, in a supplementary document to his will, in late 1376, Edward III had essentially disinherited his eldest granddaughter. He settled the inheritance to the throne on his grandson, Richard, son of his eldest son, Edward, the Black Prince and then, in turn, starting with John of Gaunt, on his surviving sons and their sons, excluding the descendants of his second son, Lionel of Antwerp. Edward had thus attempted to destroy any claim Philippa might have had to the throne, while simultaneously revoking the royal status of the Mortimer Earls of March.[16]

Although there appear to be several death dates for Philippa, the spring of 1377 or 1378 seem the most likely. She had made a will in November 1376, just before Edmund's birth, but this was quite common practice for a young woman about to be brought to childbed, in case of complications with the birth. She was buried at Wigmore, Herefordshire, the traditional burial-place of the Mortimers. Her epitaph reads:

A noble Countess here entombed doth lie,
In deeds of charity she strove;
Though sprung from kings,
the friend of poverty;
Forever may she live in heaven above![17]

Her husband Edmund's star, however, continued to rise and he was appointed Lieutenant of Ireland by Richard II on 22 October 1380. He died at Cork on 26 or 27 December 1381, and his body was brought back to Wigmore for burial. He was succeeded as 4th Earl of March by his eldest son, Roger, who had succeeded Philippa as Earl of Ulster on her death. Roger spent many years in wardship following his father's death. He was courageous, but had a reputation for religious and moral laxity. He was killed in Ireland in 1398, while acting as the King's Lieutenant. Roger was almost certainly named as Richard II's heir, at some point, although, whether Richard seriously considered Roger his successor, or merely used him as a tool to discomfort the Lancastrians, John of Gaunt and his son, Henry, is open to considerable debate.

Of Philippa and Edmund's other children, Elizabeth married Sir Henry 'Hotspur' Percy sometime before May 1380. They had two children, but he was killed at the Battle of Shrewsbury in 1403, fighting against King Henry IV. Elizabeth then married Thomas, 1st Baron Camoys, with whom she had a son who died young.

She died on 20 April 1417 and was buried at Trotton in Sussex, with her second husband. Philippa's daughter and namesake, Philippa, is first mentioned in her father's will in 1380, she married John Hastings, 3rd Earl of Pembroke. As a child, Hastings had been married to John of Gaunt's daughter, Elizabeth of Lancaster, although the marriage was never consummated, and was eventually annulled. Following Hastings' death in 1389, Philippa married Richard FitzAlan, 11th Earl of Arundel, who was executed in 1397 for his opposition to Richard II. Her third marriage was to Thomas Poynings, 5th Baron St John of Basing, around November 1399. She died in 1400 or 1401 and was buried at Boxgrove Priory in Lewes, Sussex.

Philippa and Edmund's youngest son, Edmund, his father's namesake, was married on 30 November 1402 to Catrin, the daughter of Owain Glyn Dwr. They had several children, but all died young. Edmund himself died sometime before February 1409, when his wife and children were taken prisoner, following the fall of Harlech Castle.[18] Philippa's grandson, Roger's son, Edmund, succeeded his father as Earl of March and Ulster; he became the king's ward following his father's death and, after Richard II's fall, he was kept close-at-hand, in Henry IV's family circle.

Edmund seems to have displayed a lack of ambition and when some barons tried to place him on the throne in 1415, it was Edmund himself who revealed the Southampton Plot to Henry V. Edmund died of plague in Ireland in January 1425, but it is through his sister, Anne Mortimer, who had been married to Richard of Conisbrough, that Philippa's claim to the throne was passed to Anne and Richard's son, Richard, Duke of York. This laid the foundations for the Wars of the Roses and the accession of Edward IV and, later, his brother, Richard III. Edward III's attempt to disinherit Philippa was thus lost or forgotten over the intervening years.

Philippa of Clarence was, in many ways, an exception. Her grandfather's attempt to deny her claim to the throne had little to no effect on her personally, and no long-term implications. Philippa lived her life as a princess, married a powerful baron, and did not have to fight for the privilege. The fight for her inheritance would come in the succeeding generations, particularly the House of York.

Jacqueline of Hainault, also known as Jacoba of Bavaria, was not so lucky in her inheritance. She is one of those medieval ladies who seems to have slipped under the radar of history and yet her life is one of the most colourful I have ever come across. Born in July 1401, either at The Hague or Le Quesnoy in Hainault, Jacqueline was the daughter of William VI, Count of Hainault, Holland and Zeeland, and Marguerite of Burgundy. Through her mother, Jacqueline's grandfather was Philip the Bold, Duke of Burgundy. Although she had at least nine illegitimate siblings, Jacqueline was her father's sole heir. And to strengthen her position, William arranged a marriage for Jacqueline while she was still an infant. In 1406 she was betrothed to John of Valois, Duke of Touraine, the fourth son of King Charles VI of France, and only three years older than Jacqueline. With little chance of inheriting the French throne, and with a view to him eventually ruling Hainault, the responsibility for John's education was handed over to Count William; he was sent to Holland, to be raised alongside his future wife.[19]

The young couple married on 6 August 1415 at The Hague. Only four months after the wedding John's older brother Louis, dauphin of France, died, and John became dauphin and heir to the French throne. Within two years John himself was dead, on 4 April 1417, with rumours circulating that he was poisoned, although this is far from certain and a natural death is just as likely. His younger brother, Charles, became dauphin and Jacqueline was a widow at only sixteen.

In the meantime, although Holland was not subject to Salic law (meaning a woman could not inherit), Jacqueline's father had been having a hard time persuading his people and Sigismund, the Holy Roman Emperor, to accept Jacqueline as his heir. His territories were large and strategically significant, too significant to be trusted to a female ruler. The various counties were divided in their views, but Jacqueline's succession was finally refused outright in 1416. When Count William died on 31 May 1417, only two months after her husband, Jacqueline was accepted as Countess of Hainault; however, Holland and Zeeland recognised her uncle, John of Bavaria, backed by Sigismund, as their count.

At this point, Jacqueline's mother and uncle stepped in. Margaret of Burgundy and her brother, John the Fearless, Duke of Burgundy, started looking around for a suitable husband for Jacqueline. Unfortunately, for Jacqueline, they decided on her cousin John IV, Duke of Brabant. The Duke of Burgundy saw the marriage as an opportunity to expand his influence over Jacqueline's lands, and applied for a papal dispensation. The dispensation was initially granted, but withdrawn just over two weeks later, following intense pressure from Sigismund. The couple married anyway, in March 1418, but the marriage was a disaster, politically and personally. John managed to antagonise both his wife and her subjects. Initially Jacqueline's husband helped in the fight against her avaricious uncle, her father's brother, John of Bavaria, Bishop-elect of Liège. He was intent on pursuing his claim to Holland and Zeeland, so much so that by November 1417, he had resigned his see, as bishop, and was installed in Dordrecht, as count, thus initiating civil war. In February 1419 John of Brabant agreed to a humiliating truce at Woudrichem. Jacqueline refused to accept it, only for her husband to then mortgage Holland and Zeeland to John of Bavaria for a period of twelve years. Jacqueline ran away; first to her mother in Hainault and then on to England, where she was welcomed by Henry V. The king granted Jacqueline a pension of £100 a month from the dower estates of his stepmother, Joan of Navarre, and invited her to be godmother to his only son, the future Henry VI.[20]

In 1421 Jacqueline repudiated her marriage to John of Brabant, with the support of Antipope Benedict XIII in Avignon; and in 1422, with a view to strengthening England's position against France, she married the King of England's younger brother Humphrey, Duke of Gloucester in a ceremony so secret that the date remains unknown, although a dispensation had been obtained from the antipope. The public were behind the marriage and even supported Humphrey's attempts to recover Jacqueline's lands. As Duchess of Gloucester, Jacqueline was made a Lady of the Garter in 1423, and, at some point, accepted Eleanor Cobham into her household as a lady-in-waiting; Eleanor would later go on to supplant Jacqueline and become Humphrey's second wife.

In 1424 Jacqueline gave birth to her only recorded child, who was stillborn. In the same year, Humphrey and Jacqueline led an army to the Low Countries; an expedition intended to recover Jacqueline's inheritance. Although Humphrey managed to recover much of Hainault, he came up against opposition from the new Duke of Burgundy, Philip III the Good, destroying the Anglo-Burgundian alliance. Many of Jacqueline's subjects, moreover, considered Humphrey an invader and, refusing to recognise him as count, gave their support to Burgundy. As a result, in 1425, Humphrey returned to England, alone; Jacqueline's mother had objected to her returning with him, so she moved on to Mons.

The officials of Mons had promised to protect Jacqueline but, once Gloucester was gone, she was handed over to the Duke of Burgundy and imprisoned in Ghent. In the same year, her uncle, John of Bavaria, died and her lands were handed over to Burgundy, as regent, by John of Brabant. Jacqueline escaped her imprisonment, dressed as a man, and fled, escorted by two knights, to Gouda. From Gouda, she led the Dutch resistance to the Burgundian takeover. However, when Burgundy besieged Gouda, she was forced to surrender. In the meantime, Pope Martin V had authorised an investigation into the state of Jacqueline's marriages. In 1428 he declared her marriage to Humphrey of Gloucester null and void, as her marriage to John of Brabant was legally valid. John of Brabant had died in 1426, so a remarriage between Humphrey and Jacqueline would have been acceptable – had Humphrey's attentions not already turned to Eleanor Cobham.

Jacqueline still had sympathisers in England, however, and the ladies of London petitioned Humphrey, according to the chronicler Stow their letters contained 'matter of rebuke and sharpe reprehension of the Duke of Gloucester, because he would not deliver his wife Jacqueline out of her grievous imprisonment, being then held prisoner by the Duke of Burgundy, suffering her to remain so unkindly, contrary to the law of God and the honourable estate of matrimony'.[21] Humphrey had managed to obtain a grant of 9,000 marks from the king's council, in 1427, to help Jacqueline recover her lands; however, John, Duke of Bedford, put a stop to plans for the expedition by opening up negotiations with the Duke of Burgundy. Therefore, in 1428, Jacqueline of Hainault found herself a prisoner of the Duke of Burgundy, with no prospect of help from England. With few options left to her, she came to an agreement with Philip the Good. In the Treaty of Delft, of 3 July 1428, Jacqueline retained her title of countess, but administration for her three counties passed to Philip. Philip the Good was confirmed as her heir, should she die childless; and she was not to marry without the consent of Philip, her mother and the three counties.

Philip, however, broke the treaty by mortgaging the revenues of Holland and Zeeland to members of the Borselen family from Zeeland. In 1432 Jacqueline secretly married a member of the family, Francis Borselen, governor of Holland and Zeeland since 1430. Whether or not this was a plot to overthrow Burgundian rule in Holland, Philip the Good certainly saw it that way and acted accordingly. Francis was imprisoned in October 1432 and Jacqueline was forced to abdicate as countess in 1433, relinquishing her titles in return for an income from several estates. After years of civil war, Jacqueline's financial position, prior to the settlement, had been desperate. Jacqueline and Francis's relationship appears to have been a love-match and, in July 1434 they had a second, public, marriage ceremony at Maartensdijk Castle. After such an adventurous life, and having fought so hard for her inheritance, Jacqueline settled down to married life. She retired to her castle at Teilingen, where she indulged a passion for hunting and, according to Dutch tradition, pottery. Her happiness was short-lived, however, as Jacqueline died at Teilingen on 8 October 1436, probably of tuberculosis. She had asked to be buried in her lordship of Sint-Maartensdijk, in Zeeland, but, at her mother's insistence was buried in the court chapel in The Hague.

Jacqueline led an incredible fight to retain her inheritance. She had one major attribute in common with all the women in this chapter, an absolute refusal to accept their lot and a determination to be more than a dynastic pawn. Their options were limited by their sex, but each woman found her own way to fight her corner, even if it resulted in only limited degrees of success. That they tried and didn't give up, despite the odds against them, makes them all heroines.

6

The Pawns

Many medieval women had little or no say in the direction of their lives. Not in the big decisions, anyway. However, this does not mean that they were not, in many ways, heroines. Even though they could not choose their own husbands, or decide where their future lay, they could still find ways to take control of their lives, or to make a difference in their home countries or, indeed, their adopted ones. The way these women conducted themselves, in the lives which they were given, is remarkable. They showed strength of character, a willingness to adapt, and an ability to strengthen diplomatic ties that few in modern times are forced to experience.

One such princess who was sent abroad to strengthen these diplomatic links was Matilda of England, the eldest daughter and third child of, arguably, medieval Europe's most glamorous couple. Born in London in June 1156, Matilda was the daughter of Eleanor of Aquitaine and Henry II and was baptised by Theobald, Archbishop of Canterbury, in the Priory Church of the Holy Trinity, Aldgate.[1] As her parents ruled an empire that stretched from the Scottish borders to the Pyrenees, travel was to be a constant part of Matilda's childhood. She experienced her first sea voyage, across the English Channel, at just two months old, travelling with her mother and older brother, Henry, to join her father in Anjou; before moving on to Aquitaine in October. Throughout her childhood, Matilda is often seen accompanying her mother throughout the vast Angevin domains. Although the eldest brother, William, died the same year she was born, Matilda and Henry would, eventually, be joined in the nursery by three younger brothers, Richard, Geoffrey and John, and two younger sisters, Eleanor and Joan, who survived into adulthood.

Despite the fact that she was only eight years old, negotiations began for Matilda's marriage in February 1165; the marriage would form part of an alliance with the German Emperor, Frederick Barbarossa, in opposition to Louis VII of France and the pope, Alexander III. It was one of a series of dynastic marriages, which included her younger sisters, aimed at strengthening their father's position among the European rulers. Matilda was the first of her parents' daughters to be married, her dowry and the celebrations for her departure cost around £4,500, about a quarter of England's annual revenue. The money was raised by taxes specifically levied for the occasion. The twelve-year-old princess was given a trousseau worth £63, including saddles with gilt fittings, 'two large silken cloths, and two tapestries and one cloth of samite and twelve sable skins'. Thirty-four packhorses were needed to transport all her belongings.[2] In July 1166, the emperor's envoys arrived in England to escort Matilda to Germany. Her mother accompanied her to Dover, where she embarked on a German ship, and the wedding to Henry V 'the Lion', Duke of Saxony and Bavaria, finally took place in Minden Cathedral, Germany, on 1 February 1168. Henry the Lion was twenty-seven years Matilda's senior; his first marriage, to Klementia of Zahringen, had been annulled in 1162.

The marriage appears to have been successful and produced ten children, although the fates of some seem to be in question, and several did not survive childhood. Their eldest daughter, Richenza, whose name was later changed to Matilda, was born around 1172 and was married, firstly, to Geoffrey III, Count of Perche, and secondly to Enguerrand III, Lord of Coucy. Henry, born in 1173, would succeed to the Duchies of Saxony and Bavaria on his father's death in 1195. Their second son, Otto, Earl of York and Count of Ponthieu, born around 1175, would become Holy Roman Emperor as Otto IV in 1209. Otto was briefly considered as heir to the English throne by his uncle Richard I, although Richard's brother, John, eventually claimed the crown. A third son, William, Duke of Luneberg and Brunswick, was born in England in 1184 and would be the ancestor, in the direct male line, of the House of Hanover, kings of Great Britain in the 18th century.[3]

In 1180 Henry V quarrelled bitterly with the Holy Roman Emperor, Frederick Barbarossa, who held him responsible for the failure of a campaign in Italy. Henry, it seems, had grown very powerful in his own domains and Barbarossa, following the dispute, deprived him of his fiefs and sent the Duke of Saxony and Bavaria into exile for seven years. Henry, Matilda and their children left Germany and sought refuge at the Angevin court of Matilda's father, in autumn 1181. Henry II welcomed his daughter to his court in Normandy and, while energetically lobbying the German emperor on his son-in-law's behalf, gave his daughter the palace of Argentin as a family residence. Matilda was heavily pregnant and remained with her father while her husband left on pilgrimage to Compostela, in Spain. The family was together again by Christmas 1182, spending the festive period with Matilda's siblings at Henry II's court in Caen.

Matilda and her family spent 1183 in the Angevin lands on the Continent; although she was pregnant again, Matilda accompanied her father to England in 1184, and it was at Winchester that she gave birth to her son, William, in June. While at the Angevin court Matilda was instrumental in getting the restrictions eased on her mother's imprisonment; Eleanor of Aquitaine had been held, probably at Old Sarum, following her complicity in a failed rebellion by her sons in 1173–4. Although she was still in the custody of guards, Eleanor was allowed to reside with Matilda at various locations in England, including Windsor and Berkhamsted. When Eleanor was allowed to cross the Channel to take possession of the Vexin Castles, Matilda accompanied her.

In early 1185, having asked the pope to intervene with the emperor, Henry II finally secured agreement for his son-in-law to return to his German domains; although Henry would not be fully restored to Imperial favour until 1190, when he made peace with the new Holy Roman Emperor, Heinrich VI. Matilda and Henry arrived back in Germany in October 1185, although their children, Otto, William and Matilda had remained at Henry's court, to be raised by their grandparents. Henry the Lion would be exiled from Germany again, when Frederick Barbarossa left on Crusade; however, this time Matilda stayed in Germany to oversee their family domains. Matilda died at Brunswick on 28 June 1189, aged only thirty-four; she was buried in the city's Cathedral of St Blasius, of which she was co-foundress. Henry II died just eight days later, probably before the news of his daughter's death could reach him. Matilda's husband would be buried next to her, following his death on 6 August 1195.[4]

There seems to be no surviving description of Matilda; however, Bertran de Born, troubadour to Matilda's brother Richard (the Lionheart) composed a song about her and compared Matilda's beauty to that of Helen of Troy. Her marriage had been a political arrangement by her father, but proved highly successful. Despite their difficulties with Frederick Barbarossa, they were obviously a hardy, supportive couple; proof, perhaps, that not all arranged marriages were disastrous. Matilda's younger sister, however, would have a very different experience; of the three daughters of Henry II, it would be the youngest who had the hardest time in her marriages.

Matilda's baby sister, Joanna of England, was born in October 1165 at Angers Castle in Anjou, the seventh child and youngest daughter of Henry II of England and Eleanor of Aquitaine. Ten years younger than her eldest brother, Henry the Young King, Joanna was born at a time when their parents' relationship was breaking down; her mother would eventually go to war against her husband, before being imprisoned by him for the last sixteen years of Henry's reign. Joanna's first Christmas in 1165 was the first one her parents had spent apart, with Henry still in England, dealing with a Welsh revolt. He spent that Christmas at Oxford, possibly in the company of his new mistress, Rosamund Clifford, and he would not meet his new daughter for several months.[5] Joanna spent much of her childhood at her mother's court in Poitiers, although she and her younger brother, John, spent some time at the magnificent Abbey of Fontevrault. It was during her stay at Fontevrault that Joanna was educated in the skills needed to run a large, aristocratic household; she was also given schooling in several languages – English, Norman French and rudimentary Latin.

When Eleanor and her sons rebelled in 1173, Henry II went to war against his wife. When she was captured by knights loyal to Henry in 1174 while she was riding to seek asylum with Louis of France and wearing men's clothes, Henry sent her to England for imprisonment. Joanna joined her father's entourage and frequently appeared at Henry's Easter and Christmas courts. Three years later, Eleanor was allowed to travel to Winchester to say goodbye to her youngest daughter, who had been betrothed to King William II of

Sicily. Joanna was provided with a trousseau, probably similar to her sister Matilda's on her marriage to Henry the Lion. Joanna was not yet eleven years old when she set out from Winchester at the end of August 1176. She was escorted by Bishop John of Norwich and her half-uncle, Henry II's illegitimate brother, Hamelin de Warenne, Earl of Surrey. Her escorts were ordered not to return to England until they had seen 'the King of Sicily and Joanna crowned in wedlock'.[6]

Joanna's entourage must have been a sight to see. Once on the Continent, she was escorted from Barfleur by her brother Henry, the Young King. Her large escort was intended to dissuade bandit attacks on her impressive dowry, which included fine horses, gems and precious metals. At Poitiers, Joanna was met by another brother, Richard, who escorted his little sister to Toulouse in a leisurely and elegant progress. Having finally reached Sicily, eleven-year-old Joanna was married to twenty-four-year-old William, in Palermo Cathedral, on 13 February 1177. The marriage was solemnised by Walter, Archbishop of Palermo, in front of a host of bishops, counts, barons, clergy and the people; the ceremony was followed by her coronation as Queen of Sicily. Joanna must have looked magnificent, her bejewelled dress cost £114 – an enormous sum at the time.[7]

Sicily was an ethnically diverse country; William's court was composed of a mixture of Christian, Muslim and Greek advisers. William himself spoke, read and wrote Arabic and, in fact, kept a harem of both Christian and Muslim young women within the palace. Although she was kept secluded, it must have been a strange life for a young girl, partly raised in a convent. Joanna and William only had one child, Bohemond, Duke of Apulia, who was born – and died – in 1181. When William died without an heir in November 1189, Joanna became a pawn in the race for the succession. William's sister Constance was the rightful heir, but she was married to Heinrich VI, Holy Roman Emperor, and many feared being absorbed into his empire should Constance be allowed to inherit. William II's illegitimate nephew, Tancred of Lecce, seized the initiative. He claimed the throne and, in need of money, imprisoned Joanna and stole her dowry and the treasures left to her by her husband.

Who knows how long Joanna would have remained imprisoned if it had not been for her brother's eagerness to go on Crusade?

Having gained the English throne in 1189, Richard I, the Lionheart, had wasted no time in organising the Third Crusade and arrived at Messina in Sicily in September 1190. Richard demanded Joanna's release; and fearing the Crusader king's anger Tancred capitulated and freed Joanna, paying 40,000 ounces of gold towards the Crusade in fulfilment of William II's promise of aid.[8] Described as beautiful and spirited, Joanna had been Queen of Sicily for thirteen years and it seems that while at her brother's court, she caught the eye of Richard's fellow Crusader and recently-widowed Philip II, the king of France. Richard and Philip did not have the best of relationships so England's king was having none of it. He moved Joanna to the Priory of Bagnara on the mainland, out of sight and hopefully out of mind. Richard stayed in Sicily for some time, negotiating a treaty with Tancred that would recognise Tancred as rightful king of Sicily in return for the remainder of Joanna's dowry and nineteen ships to support the Crusade. He was also waiting for his bride, Berengaria of Navarre, to catch up with him.

During Lent of 1191 Joanna had a brief reunion with her mother, Eleanor of Aquitaine, when she arrived in Sicily, having escorted Richard's bride. Joanna became Berengaria's chaperone and they were lodged together at Bagnara. Unable to marry in the Lenten season, Richard sent Joanna and Berengaria on ahead of the main army, and departed Sicily for the Holy Land. Unfortunately, the royal ladies' ship was driven by a storm to Limassol on Cyprus. After several ships were crippled and then plundered by the islanders, the ruler of Cyprus, Isaac Comnenus, tried to lure Joanna and Berengaria ashore. Richard came to the rescue, overcame Cyprus in three weeks and clamped Comnenus in chains; silver ones, apparently, as Richard had promised not to put him in irons. Once Lent was over, Richard and Berengaria were married with great pomp and celebration, before the whole party continued their journey to the Holy Land, arriving at Acre in June 1191.

Joanna's time in the Holy Land was spent in Acre and Jaffa, accompanying her sister-in-law and following, at a safe distance, behind the crusading army. She spent Christmas 1191 with Richard and Berengaria at Beit-Nuba, just 12 miles from Jerusalem. However, although he re-took Acre and Jaffa, Richard fell out with his allies and was left without a force strong enough to take Jerusalem. Joanna became a pawn on the marriage market again when Richard, in attempts to reach a political settlement with the Muslim leader, Saladin, offered her as a bride for Saladin's brother, Saphadin, also known as Malik al-Adil. His plans were scuppered, however, when a furious Joanna refused outright to even consider marrying a Muslim, despite the fact Richard's plan would have seen Saphadin converting to Christianity and Joanna installed as Queen of Jerusalem. We'll never know how serious Richard was in making his offer; the proposal came to nought as Saladin insisted the wedding take place within six weeks, and Richard insisted it would take at least six months to obtain the papal dispensation required for the second marriage of a king's widow.

When a three-year truce was eventually agreed with Saladin, Joanna and Berengaria were sent ahead of the army, leaving Acre on 29 September 1192, to Sicily and on to Rome where they were to await Richard's arrival. But Richard never made it. Although he left Acre on 9 October, he fell into the hands of Duke Leopold of Austria and was handed over to his enemy, the Holy Roman Emperor. With Richard imprisoned, Berengaria and Joanna continued their journey and arrived back in Poitiers. Berengaria herself set out to help raise the ransom money of 100,000 marks for Richard's release, which finally came about in February 1194.[9]

Joanna spent the next few years at her mother's and brother's courts, her wealth having been squandered by Richard's Crusade. But at the age of thirty-one she was proposed as a bride for Raymond VI, Count of Toulouse. Her title of Queen of Sicily would give him greater prestige while bringing the county of Toulouse into the Plantagenet fold, a long-time aim of Eleanor's. Three-times-married Raymond does not seem to have been ideal husband material, however – he had been excommunicated for repudiating his first wife and was placed under further papal sanction for marrying his third wife, even though he was still married to his second. He now repudiated wife number three, confining her to a convent, in order to marry Joanna. Despite this colourful marital history, the wedding went ahead and Joanna and Raymond were married at Rouen in October 1196, with Queen Berengaria in attendance. Although it was not a happy marriage, Joanna gave birth to a son, Raymond, around 1197 and a daughter, possibly called Mary, in 1198. Little is known of Mary, and it is possible that she died in infancy. Raymond succeeded his father as Raymond VII, Count of Toulouse, and married twice. Raymond VI was not a popular Count of Toulouse and while he was away in the Languedoc, in 1199, dealing with rebel barons, Joanna herself tried to face down her husband's enemies. She even laid siege to a rebel stronghold. Mid-siege, however, her troops turned traitor and set fire to the army's camp, including setting Joanna's tent alight; Joanna managed to escape, but may have been injured.[10]

A pregnant Joanna was then trying to make her way to her brother Richard when she heard of his death. She changed course and finally reached her mother at Niort. On seeing her daughter was hurt, distressed, pregnant, and in need of care, Eleanor sent Joanna to Fontevrault to be looked after by the nuns. With no allowance from her husband, Joanna returned to her mother and brother – King John – in Rouen in June 1199, pleading poverty. Eleanor managed to persuade John to give his sister an annual pension of 100 marks. Joanna's last few months must have been a desperate time. Too ill to travel and heavily pregnant, she remained at Rouen. In September, King John gave her a lump sum of 3,000 marks, to dispose of in her will; she specifically mentioned a legacy towards the cost of a new kitchen at Fontevrault and asked Eleanor to dispose of the remainder in charitable works for the religious and the poor.[11]

Knowing that she was dying, Joanna became desperate to be veiled as a nun at Fontevrault; a request normally denied to married women, especially when they were in the late stages of pregnancy. However, seeing how desperate her daughter was, Eleanor sent for Matilda, Abbess of Fontevrault but, fearing the abbess would arrive too late, she also asked Hubert Walter, the Archbishop of Canterbury, to intervene. The archbishop tried to dissuade Joanna, but was impressed by her fervour and convened a committee of nuns and clergy, who agreed that Joanna must be inspired by heaven. In Eleanor's presence, the archbishop admitted Joanna to the Order of Fontevrault. Joanna was too weak to stand and died shortly after the ceremony; her son, Richard, was born a few minutes later and lived only long enough to be baptised. Joanna of England, Queen of Sicily and Countess of Toulouse, died a month short of her thirty-fourth birthday. Joanna and her baby son were interred together at Fontevrault, the funeral cortège having been escorted there by

Eleanor of Aquitaine and King John. The Winchester annalist described Joanna as 'a woman whose masculine spirit overcame the weakness of her sex'.[12]

Joanna enjoyed a more adventurous life than most English princesses. We cannot know if she was content in her first marriage, although we can hope there was some happiness in those twelve years. Her second marriage was, probably, always doomed to failure in the light of Raymond's chequered marital history, so Joanna was unlikely to have expected a 'happily ever after' marriage. However, it did give her the opportunity to have the children denied her with William; and at least she was closer to her family, close enough to visit them. Although she had little say in her marriages, she did manage to stand by her refusal to marry Saladin's brother. As a princess, she knew her life was not her own, but she nevertheless managed to make an adventure out of it.

Joanna was far from being the only royal bride to experience misfortune on the marriage market. Her niece and namesake, Joan of England, had an experience that would not look out of place in the pages of the wildest romance. Joan was the oldest daughter of King John and his second wife, Isabella of Angouleme. Born 22 July 1210, she was the third of five children; she had two older brothers, and two younger sisters would join the family by 1215. Even before her birth, she was mooted as a possible bride for Alexander of Scotland, son of William I, King of Scotland. A verbal agreement between the two kings, in 1209, provided for John to arrange the marriages of William's two daughters, with a view to one of these daughters marrying a son of John's, and Alexander marrying one of John's as-yet unborn daughters. Following the death of William I, a further treaty in 1212 agreed to the marriage of the new King of Scotland, fourteen-year-old Alexander II, to two-year-old Joan. However, the agreement seems to have been made as a way of preventing Alexander from looking to the Continent – in particular, France – for a potential bride, and by extension, allies.

Nevertheless, this did not stop John from looking further afield for a more favourable marriage alliance for Joan. Nor did it stop Alexander II from siding with the barons against King John; Alexander was, in fact, one of the signatories of Magna Carta. John refused a proposal from his old ally, King Philip II of France, for Joan to marry Philip's son John, and settled instead, in 1214, for a marriage with his old enemies the de Lusignans. In 1214 Joan was betrothed to Hugh X de Lusignan. Hugh was the son of John's rival for the hand of Isabella in 1200; Isabella's engagement to Hugh IX was broken off in order for her to marry John. Following the betrothal Hugh, Lord of Lusignan and Count of La Marche, was given custody of Joan and of the towns of Saintes, Saintonge and the Isle of Oleron as pledges for her dowry. Joan was just four years old when she travelled to the south of France to live with her future husband's family. She was away from England at the height of the Baron's War, and her father's death in October 1216. It is possible that she was reunited with her mother in 1217 when Isabella of Angoulême left England, abandoning her four other children, in order to govern her own lands in Angoulême.

In 1220, in a scandalous volte-face, Hugh repudiated Joan and married her mother, his father's former betrothed – so poor nine-year-old Joan's erstwhile future husband was now her step-father. Isabella of Angouleme wrote to her twelve-year-old son, King Henry III, excusing her actions and saying Sir Hugh de Lusignan could not yet marry Joan, on account of her tender years, but was in desperate need of an heir. Isabella claimed she married him herself to prevent him looking to France for a suitable bride, and to safeguard the Plantagenet lands of Poitou and Gascony.[13] However, instead of being sent back to England, as you might expect, Joan, now only ten years old, went from being Hugh's betrothed to being his prisoner. She was held hostage to ensure Hugh's continued control of her dower lands, and to ensure the transfer of his new wife's dower. At the same time, England was withholding Queen Isabella's dower against the return of Joan's dower lands. Negotiations to resolve the situation were ongoing.

In the meantime, despite her captivity, Joan's older brother, Henry III, and his advisers were already looking to arrange a new marriage for her. On 15 June 1220, in York, a conference between Alexander II and Henry III saw the Scots king agree to marry Joan, with a provision that he would marry Joan's younger sister, Isabella, instead if Joan was not returned to England in time. Negotiations for Joan's return were long and difficult and not helped by the fact Hugh was threatening war in Poitou. Eventually, after papal intervention, agreement was reached in October 1220 and Joan was surrendered to the English. Joan and Alexander II were married on 19 June 1221, at York Minster. Joan was just weeks from her eleventh birthday, while Alexander was twenty-two. The Archbishop of York performed the ceremony, which was witnessed by Henry III and the great magnates of both realms. Henry III's Pipe Rolls suggest the wedding was followed by three days of celebrations, costing £100.[14] According to the *Chronicle of Melrose* 'having celebrated the nuptials most splendidly, as was befitting, with all the natives of either realm rejoicing, [Alexander] conducted [Joan] to Scotland.'[15]

The day before the wedding Alexander had assigned dower estates to Joan, worth an annual income of £1,000, including Jedburgh, Crail and Kinghorn. However, part of the dower was still held by Alexander's mother, the Dowager Queen Ermengarde, and Joan was not entitled to the income until after her mother-in-law's death in 1233. This left Joan financially dependent on Alexander from the beginning. There is a suggestion that Joan was not enamoured with Scotland and its society. She was hampered by her youth, her domineering mother-in-law and, eventually, by the fact she failed to produce the desired heir. Joan's position was further hindered from time to time by tensions between her husband and brother. In this, though, she seems to have found her purpose. Joan regularly acted as intermediary between the two kings. Alexander often used Joan's personal letters to her brother as a way of communicating with Henry, bypassing the formality of official correspondence between kings. One such letter is a warning, possibly on behalf of Alexander's constable, Alan of Galloway, of intelligence that Haakon IV of Norway was intending to aid Hugh de Lacy in Ireland. In the same letter, she assured Henry that no one from Scotland would be going to Ireland to fight against Henry's interests.[16] Another letter, this time from Henry, was of a more personal nature; written in February 1235, it informed Joan of the marriage of their 'beloved sister' Isabella to the Holy Roman Emperor Frederick II, news at which he knew Joan 'would greatly rejoice'.[17]

In December 1235 Alexander and Joan were summoned to London, possibly for the coronation of Henry's new queen, Eleanor of Provence. This would have been a long and arduous journey for the Scots monarchs, especially in the deepest part of winter. Henry's use of Joan as an intermediary suggests she did have some influence over her husband; this theory is supported by the fact that

Joan accompanied Alexander to negotiations with the English king at Newcastle in September 1236 and again at York in September 1237. In 1234, Henry had granted Joan the manor of Fenstanton in Huntingdonshire, and during the 1236 negotiations she was granted that of Driffield in Yorkshire, giving Joan an income independent of Scotland. Many have seen this as an indication that Joan was intending to spend more time in England, especially seeing as the chronicler Matthew Paris hints at an estrangement, although we cannot be certain.[18]

The 1236 and 1237 councils were attempts at resolving the ongoing claims by Alexander that King John had agreed to gift Northumberland to Alexander, as part of the marriage contract between Alexander and Joan. Henry, of course, denied this. With the mediation of a papal legate, agreement was eventually reached in York at the 1237 council, with both queens, Joan and Eleanor of Provence, present. Alexander gave up the claim to Northumberland in return for lands in the northern counties with an annual income of £200.[19]

Following the 1237 council, Joan and her sister-in-law Eleanor of Provence departed on pilgrimage to the shrine of Thomas Becket at Canterbury. Given that Joan was now twenty-seven and Eleanor already married for two years, it is possible both women were praying for children, and an heir to their respective husbands' thrones. Joan stayed in England for the rest of the year; much of the stay seems to have been informal and pleasurable. She spent Christmas at Henry's court and was given new robes for herself, her clerks and servants, in addition to gifts of deer and wine. Her sister Eleanor, Countess of Pembroke, widow of William II Marshal and future wife of Simon de Montfort, was present, with the Countess of Chester and Joan's cousin, the captive Eleanor of Brittany. In late January arrangements were being made for Joan's return to Scotland, but she fell ill before she could travel north. Only twenty-seven years of age, Joan died on 4 March 1238 at Havering-atte-Bower in Essex. Her brothers, King Henry III and Richard, Earl of Cornwall, were at her side. According to Matthew Paris 'her death was grievous, however she merited less mourning, because she refused to return [to Scotland] although often summoned back by her husband.'[20]

Even in death Joan chose to stay in England. Her will requested that she be buried at the Cistercian nunnery of Tarrant in Dorset.

The convent benefited greatly from Henry III's almsgiving for the soul of his sister; in 1252, more than thirteen years after her death, the king ordered a marble effigy to be made for her tomb (which unfortunately has not survived). Talking of her wedding day, the *Chronicle of Lanercost* had described Joan as 'a girl still of a young age, but when she was an adult of comely beauty'.[21] Alexander II married again just over a year after Joan's death, to Marie de Coucy, and their son and longed-for heir, Alexander III, was born in 1241. Alexander II died of a fever in 1249.

The debacle of Joan's betrothal and imprisonment by Hugh de Lusignan, and her unhappy marriage to Alexander II, are prime examples of the lot of a Plantagenet princess. However, Joan rose above her marriages and found a purpose in her pursuit of peace between England and Scotland. She was a conduit to maintain communications, even when relations were tense. Joan was also lucky to enjoy a happy, close relationship with her siblings, especially her brothers, Henry III and Richard, Earl of Cornwall, despite having spent her formative childhood years hundreds of miles away, in France.

Whereas Joan became a building block between England and Scotland, her niece, Eleanor de Montfort, was more of a stumbling block to peace between England and Wales. Born on 29 September 1252, at Kenilworth Castle, Eleanor de Montfort was the only daughter and sixth child of Eleanor of England. Her mother was the fifth and youngest child of King John and Isabella of Angoulême, and sister of Henry III. Her father was Simon de Montfort, Earl of Leicester, leader of the rebels in the Second Barons' War (1264–1267). Eleanor had five older brothers: Henry, Simon, Amaury, Guy and Richard. Her father is remembered as one of the founders of representative government. He and his eldest son, Henry, were killed at the Battle of Evesham on 4 August 1265. On her father's death, Eleanor fled into exile in France with her mother and brothers. Eleanor's brothers continued to Italy, where Guy and Simon went to seek knightly employment, while Amaury studied medicine and theology at the university in Padua. Eleanor and her mother settled at the abbey at Montargis, until the elder Eleanor's death there in 1275.

In 1265, in return for Welsh support, Simon de Montfort had agreed to the marriage of his daughter, Eleanor, to Llewelyn ap Gruffydd, Prince of Wales. De Montfort's downfall had postponed the marriage but, in 1275, in a move guaranteed to rile Edward I, King of England, Llewelyn reprised his marriage plans and the couple were married by proxy while Eleanor was still in France. Shortly afterwards, Eleanor set sail for Wales, accompanied by her brother, Amaury, a papal chaplain and Canon of York. Believing the marriage would 'scatter the seeds which had grown from the malice her father had sown', Edward arranged for Eleanor to be captured at sea.[22] When Eleanor's ship was intercepted in the Bristol Channel, the de Montfort arms and banner were found beneath the ship's boards. Eleanor was escorted to Windsor Castle, where she was held, while her brother Amaury was imprisoned at Corfe Castle for six years. In 1276, with his bride in Edward I's custody, Llewelyn refused to pay homage to Edward I, and was declared a rebel. Faced with Edward's overwhelming forces, and support slipping away, within a year Llewelyn was forced to submit. The Treaty of Aberconwy reduced his lands to Gwynedd, but paved the way for his marriage to Eleanor, at last; it is possible that the marriage was one of the conditions of Llewelyn's submission.[23]

The marriage of Eleanor de Montfort and Llewelyn ap Gruffydd was an extravagant affair, celebrated at Worcester Cathedral on the Feast of St Edward, 13 October 1278. The illustrious guests included both the English king, Edward I, and Alexander III, King of Scots. Edward's brother, Edmund of Lancaster, gave Eleanor away at the church door, and Edward paid for the lavish wedding feast. While the marriage did not prevent further struggles between the Welsh and the English king, there was relative peace for a short time and Eleanor may have encouraged her husband to seek political solutions. She is known to have visited the English court as the Princess of Wales, and was at Windsor on such a visit in January 1281. However, on 22 March 1282, Llewelyn's younger brother, Dafydd, attacked the Clifford stronghold of Hawarden Castle and Llewelyn found himself in rebellion against Edward I yet again. At the same time, Eleanor was in the final few months of her pregnancy and Llewelyn held off taking the field until the birth of his much hoped for heir.[24]

Eleanor and Llewelyn's only child, a daughter, Gwenllian, was born on or around 19 June 1282; Eleanor died two days later. Llewelyn himself was killed in an ambush on 11 December of the same year, at Builth, earning himself the name of Llewelyn the

Last – the last native Prince of Wales. Little Gwenllian was just a year old when she was taken into Edward I's custody, and sent to be raised at the convent at Sempringham, where she eventually became a nun. She died there on 7 June 1337, the last of her father's line. Eleanor de Montfort was the first woman known to have used the title Princess of Wales. She was buried alongside her aunt Joan, illegitimate daughter of King John and wife of Llywelyn the Great, at Llanfaes on the Isle of Anglesey.

While many princesses were used as pawns through their marriages, it was Eleanor's fate that Edward I used her as a pawn initially to prevent her marriage. When he did finally allow it, on his terms, he hoped to use Eleanor to control her husband – an eventually futile attempt, given that Welsh and English aims were so diametrically opposed at the time. Eleanor, however, had tried to ease relations and had succeeded, if only for a short time. And, although ultimately tragic, her story is still less so than that of Margaret, the Maid of Norway.

The story of Margaret, the first ever Queen Regnant of Scotland, is short and sad, and a tragedy not only for the little girl, but for Scotland itself. Little Margaret died before her eighth birthday, and before she had ever set foot in the country of which she was queen. Her death set in a motion a chain of events that would see Scotland torn apart by war for years to come. Margaret's claim to the Scottish throne came from her grandfather, Alexander III. Alexander had come to the throne at the age of eight and, over the years, had proved to be a very capable and strong monarch. On 26 December 1251, he had married Margaret, the daughter of Henry III of England and Eleanor of Provence and a sister of Edward I. Margaret and Alexander had three children. Their eldest child, their daughter Margaret, was born in February 1261, at Windsor Castle, and their two sons were Alexander, born in 1264 at Jedburgh, and a younger son, David, was born in March 1273. Queen Margaret died in February 1275 at Cupar Castle, when, as a joke, she had tried to push a courtier into the river, but she herself fell in and drowned when the strong current washed her away.[24] Further tragedy struck the king in June 1281, when his younger son, David, died at Stirling Castle, at just eight years old.

One happy event in the midst of the family's grief was the marriage of twenty-year-old Margaret of Scotland to thirteen-year-old Erik Magnusson around 31 August 1281. Erik had become

King Erik II of Norway the year before, with a royal council ruling for the under-age king. The marriage was intended to engender peace between the two nations, and to put a stop the continuing Scandinavian incursions into Scottish territory.[25] Eric came of age in 1282 and the following year, on 9 April 1283, Margaret gave birth to a daughter, also named Margaret, at Tonsberg, Norway. Sadly, the queen died giving birth to her daughter, and was buried in Christ's Kirk at Bergen. For Alexander III, even more tragedy was to follow in January 1284 when his son and heir, Alexander, died aged just twenty. The young heir's death sparked a succession crisis for Scotland's king. He had no brothers or uncles to succeed him and his only heir was his eight-month-old granddaughter, Margaret, across the sea in Norway. In the same year, Alexander managed to obtain recognition of Margaret's right to succeed to the throne, from his nobles, should he fail to produce any further heirs.

With the death of his last surviving child and his entire dynasty resting on the life of his toddler granddaughter, Alexander started the search for a new wife. In February 1285 he sent a Scottish embassy to France for this sole purpose. Their successful search resulted in Yolande de Dreux arriving in Scotland that summer, accompanied by her brother John. Yolande was born into a cadet branch of the French royal family, probably sometime in the mid-1260s. Her father was Robert IV, Count of Dreux, who died in 1282, and her mother was Beatrice de Montfort, who died in 1311. One of six children, little is known of Yolande's childhood but we can imagine that as a junior member of the Capetian dynasty, she grew up amid some privilege and splendour.

Alexander and Yolande were married at Jedburgh Abbey, Roxburghshire, on 14 October 1285, the feast of St Calixtus, in front of a large congregation made up of Scottish and French nobles. Yolande was probably no more than twenty-two years of age, while Alexander was in his forty-fourth year. The marriage was one of the shortest in British royal history – and the shortest of any English or Scottish king, lasting less than five months. Tragedy struck in March of 1286. Alexander had spent the day attending a council meeting in Edinburgh. When the meeting broke up he set off on horseback to join his wife at Kinghorn Castle in Fife. It was said he wanted to be there to celebrate her birthday and he may also have recently discovered that she was pregnant with the much-desired heir. For whatever the reason, he was eager to get to his bride, and took only a small escort of three men and two local guides. It seems that, with bad weather closing in and daylight fading, several people counselled against continuing the journey, including the ferryman at the River Forth and the bailie at Inverkeithing, who argued that Alexander should stay the night and continue his journey in the morning as a heavy storm was brewing. Only 8 miles from his destination, Alexander would hear none of it and insisted on continuing his journey. He somehow lost his escort in the dark and the worsening weather, but continued alone. The next morning his body was found on the foreshore of Pettycur, just a mile from his destination. The most likely explanation was that his horse had stumbled, throwing the king whose neck was broken in the fall, although at least one historical fiction writer has suggested foul play, while others have suggested the king was drunk.

Months of uncertainty followed in Scotland. The country had lost one of her most energetic and successful kings, and the succession was in turmoil. Little Margaret, the Maid of Norway, had been recognised by the council as Alexander's heir, but his queen was pregnant and, if she gave birth to a boy, he would be king from his first breath. A regency council was established to rule until the queen gave birth. In the event, however, Yolande either suffered a miscarriage, or the child was stillborn. Within weeks of Alexander's death Robert Bruce and John Balliol had both made attempts on the crown and the south-west was raised in rebellion. Nevertheless, the majority of Scots, represented by the six Guardians, gave their backing to Margaret, the Maid of Norway, and Bruce and Balliol were forcibly held in check.

As early as 1284 Alexander III had, following the death of his last son, floated the idea that England and Scotland might unite through marriage. In response to a letter of condolence from his brother-in-law, Edward I, Alexander had suggested that, through his tiny granddaughter, 'much may yet come to pass'.[26] The prospect at the time had not been without risk, however – should Alexander have a son to inherit, England would have been committed to a disadvantageous marriage with a Norwegian princess, rather than a Scottish queen. Nonetheless, with Alexander's death, and the queen's child dead, Margaret's accession seemed certain. With the Guardians maintaining an uneasy peace between the competing claims of Margaret, Robert Bruce and John Balliol, Erik II of

Norway sought the help of Edward I of England. Messengers were sent between the English and Norwegian courts and in spring 1289, serious negotiations began.

On 6 November 1289, an international summit was held at Salisbury. The Norwegian ambassadors met with Edward and his advisers. It's possible the Scottish Guardians had also sent representatives, but some sources say the Scots were excluded from these initial talks. The summit proved successful and it was agreed Margaret would marry Edward of Caernarfon, Edward I's son and heir, within the next twelve months. For the Scottish, the marriage alliance promised an end to the years of uncertainty and to the latent threats they had been facing since 1286. For Margaret, a marriage alliance with England gave the Maid a powerful protector. In March 1290, the community of Scotland, comprising more than 100 Scotsmen of substance, met to ratify the marriage agreement. They wrote to Edward expressing their will to proceed with the wedding.

The Guardians of Scotland, however, had sworn an oath to preserve Alexander III's kingdom intact and undiminished for his eventual heirs, and their overriding concern now was to safeguard Scotland's future independence. It was agreed at Brigham that although Edward and Margaret were not yet of marriageable age, they would be regarded as married on Margaret's arrival from Norway – and Edward of Caernarfon would be King of Scotland from that moment. The business of Scottish government and its legal system were to remain in Scotland and be run by a resident viceroy or lieutenant. There was no common ground, however, on the issue of royal fortresses: Edward I wanted to appoint all custodians as a guarantee of security but the Scots saw this as a demand for the surrender of sovereignty. In the final agreement, ratified at Northampton, the point is glossed over with an agreement that keepers would be appointed by the 'common advice of the Scots and the English king'.[27]

The reason Edward acquiesced on – or, rather, failed to push – the castles issue was the news that Margaret had already left Norway. Edward wanted the deal signed and sealed before the Scots' hand was strengthened by the physical possession of their queen. In the final agreement, the Scots were given a clear statement safeguarding their independence. Edward promised that Scotland should remain 'free in itself, and without subjection from the Kingdom of England'.[28] Margaret set sail in September 1290, accompanied by Bishop Narve of Bergen; she was bound for Leith. In preparation for the Maid's arrival, Edward I sent the Bishop of Durham, and gifts of jewellery, north to welcome his future daughter-in-law. The great magnates of Scotland began to assemble at Scone Abbey, Perth, in anticipation of the enthronement of their new queen. However, storms drove the Maid's ship off course and she landed at St Margaret's Hope, South Ronaldsay, on Orkney. Scottish and English representatives rode north to Orkney to meet her. Sadly, Margaret died at Orkney, in the arms of Bishop Narve, supposedly from the effects of a severe bout of seasickness. She was seven years old.

As the Scottish and English messengers returned south with news of the Maid's death, Margaret's body was returned to Norway. She was buried beside her mother, in the north aisle of Christ's Kirk, in Bergen. Her father confirmed the identity of the body before her burial, an act that proved significant in 1300, a year after Erik's death, when a woman turned up in Bergen, claiming to be Margaret. Reports say the woman appeared to be forty years old, when Margaret would have only been seventeen, yet the woman gained popular support, despite the king's identification of Margaret's body. She was eventually convicted as 'the False Margareth' and was burned at the stake in 1301.

Although Scotland's first Queen Regnant, she never actually bore the title of 'queen'. That could only have been conferred at her coronation at Scone; before and after her death she was known to the Scots as 'Lady of Scotland'.[29] The tragedy of Margaret's death brought an end to the rule of the House of Dunkeld, begun with Malcolm III Canmore in 1058. Scotland was plunged into a crisis that would last for decades. Edward I's intervention with his judgement of the Thirteen Competitors for the Crown, and his backing of John Balliol as the next king, saw the beginning of Scotland's Wars of Independence. Marred not only by English invasion but also the in-fighting among the Scottish nobles, it was not until King Robert the Bruce emerged victorious, after the battle of Bannockburn in 1314, that Scotland began to find her feet again.

Margaret's story is, by far, one of the saddest stories of the Middle Ages. Her life was cut unbelievably short because of how valuable she was as a marriage prize and the need to get her to Scotland as quickly as possible, for the safety and security of the nation. At only seven years old, she had no control or say over the journey, over the choosing of her husband, or over leaving her father and everything she knew in Norway, to rule a country she had never set foot in. Her life was tragically short and her death had far-reaching consequences for Anglo-Scottish relations. However, she was a heroine because the fact she lived had such an impact on history itself. Indeed, all the princesses in this chapter, despite the lack of control over their own lives, made contributions to the stories of their individual families and their nations, the ones into which they were born, and the ones into which they were married.

7

Captive Heroines

Many women, throughout history, have suffered imprisonment – and worse – for their beliefs or actions, or simply because of who they were, and their ancestry and aristocratic claims were little protection against unscrupulous lords and kings. They are heroines because they spoke out, because they stood by their beliefs or, simply, because they endured and refused to give up.

The story of Ingeborg of Denmark is a strange one. She was the daughter of Valdemar I the Great, King of Denmark, and Sofia of Minsk, and was the youngest of their eight surviving children. Ingeborg was born around 1176 and it was only six years later, in 1182, that her father died. Valdemar was succeeded by Ingeborg's older brother, Knut (or Canute) VI; and it fell to Knut to arrange Ingeborg's future. I could not find any details of Ingeborg's childhood, although she was probably educated to the standard expected of princesses of the time to make her attractive in the international royal marriage market. A princess was expected to be able to manage a household, to sew, play music, sing, dance and much more. In 1193 Knut arranged a spectacular marriage for Ingeborg, to the King of France.

Philip II Augustus had acceded to the throne of France in 1180, at the tender age of fifteen. His bitter rivalry with the English Plantagenet kings, especially Richard I, the Lionheart, led him to search for alliances that would help him against his enemies. Philip's first wife, Isabella of Hainault, died in 1190. She was the mother of the French king's son and heir, the future Louis VIII, who was born in 1187. On 14 March 1190 Isabella gave birth to twin boys, Robert and Philip, and died of complications the next day, aged just nineteen; the babies died three days after their mother. With only one living son, Philip II was soon looking around for a new wife. Ingeborg held many political attractions, her brother not only had a claim to the English throne, stretching back to the time of Cnut the Great, who ruled England in the 11th century, but he also possessed an impressive navy, one Philip would rather have with him, than against him. Such an alliance also helped France and Denmark to stand up to the expansionism of the Holy Roman Empire, under Emperor Heinrich VI.[1]

On the conclusion of negotiations with Knut's representatives, Philip sent an embassy to Denmark to escort his bride back to France. The envoys were given a lavish reception at the Danish court, where the formal arrangements for the marriage were finalised. Ingeborg was provided with a dowry of 10,000 marks in gold and set out for a new life in France, accompanied by the French envoys and many Danish dignitaries, probably not expecting to ever see her homeland again.[2] Ten years older than Ingeborg, Philip met his bride for the first time on their wedding day, 14 August 1193, in the cathedral church at Amiens. Ingeborg was crowned Queen of France the next day, by the Archbishop of Reims; her name changed to Isambour, to make it more acceptable for use in the French language. At seventeen years of age, contemporary sources praised her excellent qualities; in addition to the obligatory courtly praise of her appearance, comparing her beauty with that of Helen of Troy, she was a model of virtue. Ingeborg was described as 'very kind, young of age but old of wisdom' by Étienne de Tournai, who knew her well and said that the beauty of her soul overshadowed that of her face.[3] Remarkably, given subsequent events, even those chroniclers devoted to her husband Philip II, such as Guillaume le Breton, spoke of the new queen with respect.

Unfortunately, no one knows what happened on the wedding night but poor Ingeborg had one of the shortest honeymoons in history; and by the end of the coronation ceremony the king had such an aversion to Ingeborg that he tried to get the Danish envoys to take her home with them. Ingeborg, however, refused to go, saying that she had been crowned Queen of France and her place was now in France. Queen Ingeborg sought sanctuary in a convent in Soissons, from where she wrote an appeal to the pope, Celestine III. Three months later, Philip established a friendly ecclesiastical council in Compiègne in an attempt to have the marriage annulled. Ingeborg was present but speaking no French, she had little understanding of the proceedings until they were interpreted for her. The French king protested that the marriage was not consummated, a claim that Ingeborg vehemently denied. Philip then went on to claim that Ingeborg was related to his first wife, therefore the marriage was within the prohibited degrees of consanguinity, going so far as to falsify his family tree to bolster his claim. As a result, the sympathetic churchmen determined that the marriage was void. When Ingeborg was informed of the decision, she appealed to Rome, protesting loudly *'Mala Francia! Roma! Roma!'*[4] Her homeland finally took notice of Ingeborg's plight and following a meeting with a Danish delegation, who produced their own genealogy showing that Ingeborg and Philip had very little blood in common, the pope declared the decision by Philip's ecclesiastical council to be invalid; he further ordered that Philip should take back his wife, and was not to remarry.

Philip II's sudden repudiation of Ingeborg is one of the greatest mysteries of the medieval period. It has been suggested that the Danish alliance was not as beneficial as he had hoped, but he would have known that when the details of the marriage were finalised, before the actual wedding day. Another suggestion comes from Philip's claim that he was bewitched by Ingeborg, leading to him being unable to consummate the marriage; however, Ingeborg never wavered from her assertion that the marriage had been consummated. Philip was a capricious being when it came to his wives, indeed, he had attempted to repudiate his first wife, Isabella, citing her failure to produce an heir, despite the fact she was only fourteen at the time. Unfortunately for Philip, Isabella was a popular queen and the support of the people forced the king to take her back; she gave birth to the desired son and heir three years later. Although physical attraction was not the primary requirement for a royal marriage, Philip may well have decided that Ingeborg was not the one for him, expecting her to acquiesce without any trouble. Thwarted by Ingeborg's stubbornness, Philip decided to force the issue by making Ingeborg's life as uncomfortable as possible. She was placed under house arrest; first at an abbey near Lille, then at the monastery of Saint Maur des Fossés and at various other convents afterwards, her treatment becoming gradually harsher the longer she refused to give in. For seven years, the French court saw nothing of her; Étienne de Tournai reported to the Archbishop of Reims, that 'she spent all her days in prayer, reading, work; solemn practices fill her every moment'.[5] Ingeborg would spend twenty years incarcerated in various castles and abbeys, contesting any annulment. The longer her imprisonment, the more desperate her situation became; Ingeborg was forced to sell or pawn most of her possessions, even down to her clothing, to sustain herself.[6] She later described herself, in a letter to the pope, Celestine III, as '... discarded like a dried and diseased branch; here I am, deprived of all help and consolation'.[7]

As the consanguinity argument was not working for Philip in his pursuit of a divorce, and with his counsellors already having an eye on a new bride for the king, another argument was advanced; that of non-consummation. Ingeborg, however, remained steadfast, insisting that she and Philip had slept together on their wedding night. The pope again took Ingeborg's side, admonishing the French clergy for acceding to Philip's demands for a divorce, and ordering Philip to return to his wife, though not as forcefully as he could have. Philip, therefore, disregarded the pope's decree – he took a new wife, Agnes of Merania, a German princess, in 1196. They had two children, Philip and Marie, illegitimate due to their father's bigamous marriage to their mother. However, in 1198, the new pope, Innocent III, younger and more confrontational than Celestine, asserted his authority and declared the marriage invalid, that Philip was still married to Ingeborg and ordering the king to return to his true wife. Philip responded by making Ingeborg's imprisonment even harsher. Not to be thwarted, following vigorous correspondence between Paris and the papacy, and Philip's tacit refusal to put Agnes aside, Innocent responded with his most powerful weapon – excommunication. On 15 January 1200, the whole of France was put under interdict, all churches were closed. There were to be no church services or offices; no sacraments were to be performed, save for the baptism of newborns and the last rites of the dying, until Philip acquiesced to the pope's demands and, at least, renounced Agnes, even if he didn't return to Ingeborg. This last was a concession on the pope's part, largely because he needed Philip's help in his disputes with the Holy Roman Empire.

Towards the end of the year Philip finally gave in. Agnes was sent away and stripped of her status as Philip's wife; she died in July 1201, heartbroken. Her two children by Philip were legitimised by the pope shortly after. For Ingeborg, however, nothing changed. Philip refused to take her back and appealed again for an annulment, this time claiming that she had bewitched him on their wedding night. The appeal, again, was refused but Philip responded by moving Ingeborg to a harsher confinement in the castle at Étampes, allowing her little or no human contact. After Ingeborg complained to the pope about her treatment, her conditions were finally eased in 1207; but she wasn't released until 1213. Philip's change of heart was not out of any sense of guilt, affection or justice, but more for practicality's sake. The situation in England was ripe to be exploited after King John's barons had risen against him, and Philip needed peace with Denmark in order to concentrate his attentions on the greater prize, the English throne.[8]

Ingeborg had been a prisoner in France for twenty years. Now, because of political expediency, she was not only free, but reinstated as queen, accorded the respect and dignity she had had a right to since her wedding day in 1193. Following decades of isolation, deprivation and maltreatment, she feasted and dressed as Queen of France; the sudden change in her situation must have been simultaneously welcome but bewildering. Her husband never returned to her bed, their marriage was for appearances only; Ingeborg was Philip's queen-consort, but only in public. Philip's son Louis now had his own son and heir, so there was no need for Philip to be with Ingeborg to secure the succession. Ingeborg was queen-consort of France for the next decade, until Philip's death in 1223. On his deathbed, Philip II Augustus asked his son to treat Ingeborg well; while in his will, he left her 10,000 livres.[9] The new king, Louis VIII, and his son, Louis IX, would both treat Ingeborg well and accord her all the respect due to her rank as Dowager Queen of France, even after her retirement from court. Such action was politically useful to Louis; by recognising Ingeborg as the legitimate Queen of France he emphasised that Agnes had not been and that, therefore, her children, especially Louis's half-brother, Philip, had no right to the throne (despite his legitimisation by the pope).

After Philip's death Ingeborg paid for Masses to be said for his soul, whether out of duty or as a sign of forgiveness we'll never know. A dignified and pious widow, she then retired to the priory of St Jean de l'Île, Corbeil. She died in 1238, surviving her husband by more than fourteen years and was buried in a church in Corbeil, having spent twenty of her forty-five years as queen, as a prisoner of her husband. Her steadfast refusal to accept the annulment of her marriage, her perseverance in her rights as wife and queen were rewarded in the end, making her a true heroine for women and their right to be heard.

On the other side of the English Channel, King John of England was just as harsh in his treatment of women who crossed him, if not harsher, than Philip had been. Matilda (or Maud) de Braose was probably born in the early 1150s in Saint-Valery-en-Caux, France, to Bernard IV, Seigneur de Saint-Valery and his wife, Matilda. Contemporary records describe her as tall and beautiful, wise and vigorous.[10] Made famous by her husband de Braose's spectacular falling out with King John – and the manner of her death – very little is known of Matilda's early years, though she probably spent time at her family's manor of Hinton Waldrist in Berkshire. Sometime around 1166, she married William de Braose, 4th Lord of Bramber, a Norman lord with land on the Welsh Marches. William was highly favoured by both Richard I and, later, his brother King John. While William was away campaigning in Normandy, Matilda would have been left to manage their estates in Wales. In 1198, Matilda defended Painscastle in Elfael against a massive Welsh attack by Gwenwynyn, Prince of Powys. She held out for three weeks until English reinforcements arrived, earning the castle its nickname of Matilda's Castle.

One of Matilda's titles was the Lady of Hay and Welsh folklore has her building the Castle of Hay in one night, single-handed, carrying the stones in her skirts. The couple had around sixteen children, who married into some of the most powerful families of the time. Their eldest son, William, married Maud de Clare, daughter of the Earl of Hertford. Another son, Giles, became Bishop of Hereford. Of their daughters, Loretta, married Robert de Beaumont, 4th Earl of Leicester and another, Margaret, married Walter de Lacy, Lord of Meath. A third son, Reginald, married, as his second wife, Gwladus Ddu, daughter of Llewelyn the Great, Prince of Wales. Reginald's son, William, by his first wife, married Eva Marshal, daughter of the great knight, William Marshal. It was this William de Braose who was ignominiously hanged by Llewelyn the Great, after being 'caught in Llywelyn's chamber with the King of England's daughter, Llywelyn's wife'.[11] William had been at the Welsh court to arrange the marriage of his daughter, Isabel, to Llewelyn and Joan's son, David. Interestingly, the marriage still went ahead, although it was to be childless.

William de Braose was greatly favoured by King John in the early part of his reign. He was given Limerick in Ireland for 5,000 marks and also received the castle at Glamorgan and the lordship of Gower.[12] William de Braose was the knight who captured the rival to John's throne, Arthur of Brittany, at the Siege of Mirebeau in 1202 and it is highly likely that he witnessed Arthur's brutal murder in Rouen at Easter 1203. It was following Arthur's murder that things started to go wrong for the Lord and Lady of Bramber. John became increasingly suspicious of de Braose's loyalty and turned against him. This could have been for several reasons, not least being de Braose's knowledge of Arthur's fate. Elsewhere, de Braose had fallen behind in his payments to the Exchequer for the honour of Limerick, but he had also sided with his friend William Marshal in his disagreements with the king. In addition, de Braose's son, Giles, had been one of the bishops to approve a papal interdict against John. Whatever the reason or reasons, in 1207 King John moved to make a public example of one of his most powerful barons, and punish him for his debts to the Exchequer. John demanded William and Matilda give up their sons as hostages.

Matilda refused and Roger of Wendover recorded her response to the soldiers sent to collect the boys, as; 'I will not deliver my sons to your lord, King John, for he foully murdered his nephew Arthur, whom he should have cared for honourably.'[13] There is some suggestion that William and Matilda realised she had gone too far, William told his wife, 'You have spoken like a foolish woman against our lord the King' and promised the king's men that he would make amends to the king for any offence caused.[14] But it was too late. John took possession of de Braose's castles and moved to arrest William. Forewarned, the couple fled with two of their sons to Ireland, where they took refuge with Walter de Lucy, their son-in-law and Lord of Meath. John was not to be thwarted and launched an invasion of Ireland to capture the fugitives, bringing other recalcitrant barons to heel along the way. While William de Braose tried to come to terms with the king, Matilda and their eldest son William escaped by taking a ship to Scotland.

Nevertheless, Matilda, her daughter Annora and her son William, with his wife and children, were captured in Galloway by Duncan of Carrick, who was richly rewarded by his distant cousin, King John. John sent two ships, crossbowmen and sergeants as an escort to bring his prisoners to him in Carrickfergus. When John returned to England, he took Matilda and her family with him; they were imprisoned, initially in Bristol Castle. King John made an agreement with both William and Matilda; freedom for her and a pardon for William in return for 50,000 marks, with Matilda remaining imprisoned until the sum had been paid in full. William was allowed to leave court to raise the money, but managed to evade his escort and escaped to France. Informed of her husband's escape, Matilda proved defiant, refusing to pay the fine, saying she had only fifty coins and 15 ounces of gold left to her.[15] Matilda and her son were moved from Bristol to imprisonment at either Windsor or Corfe Castle, the sources can't seem to agree. William was outlawed and after he escaped into exile in France, disguised as a beggar, he remained there until he died in 1211. Matilda's fate was more gruesome; she and her son were left to starve to death in John's dungeons (whether this was at Corfe or Windsor is unclear). Tradition has it, that when their bodies were found, William's cheeks bore his mother's bite marks, where she had tried to stay alive following his death. Anonymous of Bethune described the scene;

> On the eleveneth day the mother was found dead between her son's legs, still upright but leaning back against her son's chest as a dead woman. The son, who was also dead, sat upright, leaning against the wall as a dead man. So desperate was the mother that she had eaten her son's cheeks. When William de Braose, who was in Paris, heard this news, he died soon afterwards, many asserting that it was through grief.'[16]

John's treatment of the de Braose family did not lead to the submission of his barons, as John had intended, and the remainder of his reign was marred by civil war. However, it has gone down in history in that when Magna Carta was written in 1215, Clause 39 may well have been included with Matilda and her family in mind: '

> No man shall be taken, imprisoned, outlawed, banished or in any way destroyed, nor will we proceed against or prosecute him, except by the lawful judgement of his peers or by the law of the land.[17]

Not many women prisoners could claim to have made an impact on the laws of so many nations. Magna Carta and the right to judgement by peers can be seen in the United States' 1791 Bill of Rights, the 1948 Universal Declaration of Human Rights and the 1950 European Convention on Human Rights.

Some female prisoners have very little as a claim to fame; in fact, their perpetual imprisonment was more in the hope that they would be forgotten, erased from history. John's own niece, Eleanor of Brittany, was one such. Born around 1184, Eleanor was the daughter of Geoffrey Plantagenet, Duke of Brittany by right of his wife, and Constance of Brittany. Described as beautiful, she has been called the Pearl, the Fair Maid and the Beauty of Brittany. A granddaughter of Henry II and Eleanor of Aquitaine, she was the eldest of her parents' three children; Matilda, born the following year, died young and Arthur was killed by, or at least on the orders of, King John in 1203.

Initially, Eleanor's life seemed destined to follow the same path as many royal princesses – marriage. Richard I, her legal guardian after the death of her father in 1186, following his sister Joanna's adamant refusal, offered Eleanor as a bride to Saladin's brother, Al-Adil, in a failed attempt at a political settlement to the Third Crusade. After that, at the age of nine, Eleanor was betrothed to Friedrich, the son of Duke Leopold VI of Austria, who had made the betrothal a part of the ransom for Richard I's release from imprisonment by the Duke. She travelled to Germany with her grandmother, Eleanor of Aquitaine, and the rest of the ransom and hostages. Young Eleanor was allowed to return to England when Duke Leopold died suddenly, and his son had 'no great inclination' for the proposed marriage.[18] Further marriage plans were mooted in 1195 and 1198, to Philip II of France's son Louis, the dauphin, and Odo, Duke of Burgundy, respectively; although neither came to fruition and

Eleanor was returned to her mother's custody. Eleanor's fortunes changed drastically when her brother Arthur rebelled against Richard's successor, King John, in the early 1200s. He was captured while laying siege to his grandmother, the formidable Eleanor of Aquitaine, at Mirebeau on 1 August 1202. Eleanor was captured at the same time, or shortly after. And while her brother was imprisoned first at Falaise, and then Rouen where he died under mysterious circumstances, she was sent into perpetual imprisonment in England.

If the laws of primogeniture had been strictly followed, Eleanor would have been sovereign of England after her brother's death. John and his successor, Henry III, could never forget this. Although her confinement has been described as 'honourable' and 'comfortable', Eleanor's greater right to the throne meant she would never be freed, or allowed to marry and have children. King John gave her the title of Countess of Richmond on 27 May 1208, but Henry III would take it from her in 1219 and bestow the title elsewhere. From 1219 onwards she was styled the 'king's kinswoman' and 'our cousin'. Eleanor's movements were restricted, and she was closely guarded. Her guards were changed regularly to enhance security, but her captivity was not onerous. She was provided with 'robes', two ladies-in-waiting in 1230, and given money for alms and linen for her 'work'.[19] She was granted the manor of Swaffham and a supply of venison from the royal forests. The royal family sent her gifts, but throughout her captivity she is said to have remained 'defiant'.[20] It seems Eleanor did spend some time with the king and court, particularly in 1214 when she accompanied John to La Rochelle to pursue his war with the French. John planned to use Eleanor to gain Breton support and maybe set her up as his puppet Duchess of Brittany, replacing her younger half-sister Alice; but his plans came to nought. It is difficult to pinpoint exactly where Eleanor was imprisoned at any one time. Corfe Castle is mentioned at times, and it seems she was moved away from the coast in 1221 after a possible rescue plot was uncovered. She was also held at Marlborough for a time, and she was definitely at Gloucester Castle in 1236. However, by 1241 she was confined in Bristol castle where she died at the age of about fifty-seven, after thirty-nine years of imprisonment, achieving in death, the freedom that had eluded her in life. She was initially buried at St James's Priory Church in Bristol but her remains were later removed to the Abbey at Amesbury, a convent with a long association with the crown.

Eleanor of Brittany was not the only princess of royal blood to be imprisoned for her lifetime. Although Eleanor was always treated according to her royal status, imprisoned in a gilded cage, the last Princess of Wales was never accorded such privilege. Gwenllian was the only child of Llywelyn ab Gruffuddd, also known as Llywelyn the Last, Prince of Wales. Her mother was Eleanor de Montfort, who was the daughter of Eleanor of England, sister of Henry III, and Simon de Montfort, Earl of Leicester. Llywelyn and Eleanor had married in Worcester Cathedral in October 1278, in a lavish ceremony attended by Edward I, King of England, and Alexander III, King of Scots. Gwenllian, a descendant of both Welsh and English royalty, was born in June 1282 at the palace of Garth Celyn, Abergwyngregyn, near Bangor; her mother died giving birth to her. Shortly after her birth, Edward I concluded his conquest of Wales. Gwenllian's father, Llywelyn, was killed in an ambush on 11 December 1282 – just six months after her birth, Gwenllian was an orphan. Her uncle Dafydd, Llywelyn's younger brother, became the little princess's legal guardian. After his brother's death, Dafydd continued the fight for Welsh independence but was betrayed to the English, in June 1283. Dafydd, his wife, children and little Gwenllian were captured at Bera Mountain in Snowdonia, where they had been in hiding.

At just one year old, Gwenllian was taken, by sea, probably to thwart any attempt at rescue, from the land of her birth, Wales. She would never see her homeland again. The baby girl was placed behind the high walls of the Gilbertine priory of Sempringham, in Lincolnshire, just south of the great city of Lincoln. Her female cousins, the seven daughters of Dafydd, were also placed in various nunneries, so it is possible some of her cousins were with her. Dafydd's legitimate daughter, Gwladus, who was a similar age to Gwenllian, was placed in Sixhills, another Gilbertine priory, in the Lincolnshire Wolds. Dafydd's two sons, Llywelyn and Owain, were imprisoned in Bristol Castle; Llywelyn died there in 1287, just four years after his capture, Owain was still living in 1325, every night securely incarcerated in a specially constructed timber cage within Bristol Castle. Dafydd himself suffered the horrendous 'traitor's death'; he was hung, drawn and quartered at Shrewsbury.

The Gilbertines were the only wholly-English monastic community. Their founder, St Gilbert, had some form of physical deformity, which prevented him from pursuing a career as a knight. He trained as a clerk in France, studying under Master Anselm at Laon. He eventually entered the household of the Bishop of Lincoln and, in 1129, was appointed Vicar of Sempringham and West Torrington. He established the first priory there in 1131, with seven local women vowing to live a life of chastity, poverty and obedience. Sempringham Priory was a double-house, housing both men and women in segregated quarters. At its height, the priory housed 200 nuns and forty canons. The order followed strict rules, based on those of the Augustinian and Premonstratensian monasteries. By the time of Gilbert's death in 1189 there were thirteen priories in England; this number had risen to twenty-five at the time of the Reformation.[21]

Gwenllian was a prisoner at the Gilbertine Priory of St Mary, at Sempringham, for the rest of her life. A prisoner of three English kings, Edward I, Edward II and Edward III, she was a rallying figure for the subjugated Welsh and too valuable to ever be freed. Edward I wrote to the Prior and Prioress of Sempringham of his decision to place Gwenllian in their custody, on 11 November 1283: '… Having the Lord before our eyes, pitying also her sex and her age, that the innocent may not seem to atone for the iniquity and ill-doing of the wicked and contemplating especially the life in your Order'.[22] Although Edward wanted Gwenllian to be forgotten, he could not afford to forget her, and four years after she was placed in the convent, Edward ordered Thomas Normanvill to 'go to the places where the daughters of Llewellyn and of David his brother, who have taken the veil in the Order of Sempringham, are dwelling, and to report upon their state and custody by next Parliament'.[23] How much Gwenllian knew about her history and homeland is far from certain. Indeed, she is said not to have spoken a word of Welsh and may not have even known how to spell her name; she is referred to as 'Wencillian', in a document sent to Edward III at the time of her death.

Gwenllian was probably well-cared for, Edward III endowed her with a pension of £20 a year, which was paid to the priory for her food and clothing. Whether Gwenllian was treated according to her rank at the priory is unknown; however, it is highly likely that she was aware of some of her history and her family connections, especially when she was older. She is said to have received gifts from her cousin the king, and may have spent time in Edward III's company, when he visited the priory at Easter-time in 1328; the young king issued a charter from Sempringham on 2 April of that year.[24] Gwenllian may also have spent time in the company of Joan Mortimer, the daughter of Roger Mortimer, supposed lover of Isabelle of France, Edward III's mother, and ruler of England after the deposition of Edward II. Joan was held at Sempringham following her father's downfall in 1330. Joan was only eighteen at the time, however, so would have had little in common with Gwenllian, a woman now in her late forties who had spent her entire life in conventual seclusion.

The profound difference between Joan and Gwenllian, of course, is that Joan was released after a short time. Gwenllian only found release in death, hers occurred on 7 June 1337, the same month as her fifty-fifth birthday. She was buried at the priory where she had spent all but eighteen months of her life. Her grave was lost at the time of the dissolution of the monasteries, in the 16th century. However, a memorial plaque was placed near St Andrew's Church in Sempringham in 1993, stating:

> In memory of Gwenllian, daughter of the last Prince of Wales.
> Born at Abergwyngregyn 12.06.1282.
> Died at Sempringham 7.6.1337.
> Having been held prisoner for 54 years.[25]

Also, in 2009 a mountain in Snowdonia in Wales, formerly known as Carnedd Uchaf, was renamed Carnedd Gwenllian in the lost princess's honour. Although she left very few physical marks on the world, a child whose very future was stolen by Edward I, Gwenllian's remarkable story merits her inclusion as a heroine.

Gwenllian was not, however, the only victim of Edward I whose story is remarkable and harrowing. One of the most famous collections of female prisoners in medieval history were the women of Robert the Bruce's family – his wife, sisters, daughter and Isabel Buchan, the woman who risked everything to assert her family's right to crown Bruce as Scotland's king. Their collective and individual stories are remarkable. This is one of those periods in history that holds a particular fascination for me. Robert the Bruce, the grandfather of the Stewart dynasty and hero of Scotland, started his career with some very divided loyalties. Initially a supporter of the English king, Edward I, it was only the arrival of William Wallace that started Bruce on his journey to become the champion of Scottish independence. Through the murder of his greatest rival and the Battle of Bannockburn, Bruce proved himself determined and resourceful, overcoming defeat to emerge victorious and master of his realm. Bruce suffered greatly for the crown, but his family and friends suffered equally.

Christian Bruce was one of the children of Sir Robert le Brus, Lord of Annandale, and his wife Marjorie, Countess of Carrick in her own right. Christian was one of 11 children, with five boys and five girls surviving infancy. Unfortunately, we don't know when Christian was born, nor whether or not she was an older or younger sibling of Robert the Bruce. She was probably born at her father's castle of Turnberry sometime in the 1270s or early 1280s. Christian's grandfather was another Robert le Brus, one of the Thirteen Competitors for the throne of Scotland following the death of Margaret, the Maid of Norway; when the vacancy of the Scottish throne was resolved by Edward I of England in favour of John Balliol. And when Balliol's kingship proved disastrous it was Christian's brother, Robert the Bruce, who became one of the leading candidates for the Scottish throne.

There are some question marks over Christian's marital history. Some sources claim she married Gartnait, Earl of Mar in the 1290s, and was the mother of Donald of Mar. However, this has recently been disputed. Christian never seems to have been addressed, or described, as the Countess of Mar, and there seems to have been little communication between Christian and her supposed son, Donald, even though they were both held prisoner in England at the same time. The main argument against the marriage appears to be that Abbot Walter Bower had stated that Gartnait had been married to the 'eldest Bruce daughter', a description never applied to Christian. However, if the elder daughters were already married, Christian may well have been the eldest 'unmarried' Bruce daughter, so we really don't know. By 1305, however, Gartnait was dead and Christian had married Sir Christopher Seton (*c.* 1278–1306); Sir Christopher was a knight with lands in Annandale and northern England. He was a stalwart supporter of Robert the Bruce, his family having had a long tradition of serving the Bruce family.

We know little to nothing about Christian's short marriage to Sir Christopher; their relationship took a back seat to the national events of the time. Sir Christopher was with Christian's brother on the fateful day in the Greyfriars Church in Dumfries when Robert the Bruce fatally stabbed John Comyn, his rival to the Scottish throne. Whether Comyn's death was accidental or murder, we'll probably never know. Robert then made the dash for Scone, hoping to achieve his coronation before the Christian world erupted in uproar over his sacrilege. An excommunicate could not be crowned. His sisters Christian and Mary accompanied him to Scone Abbey, as did his wife Elizabeth and his daughter Marjorie. The Stone of Scone was the traditional coronation seat of the kings of Scotland and, although the stone had been stolen by the English and spirited away to London, holding the coronation at the Abbey sent a message of defiance to the English king, Edward I.

On 25 March 1306 Christian and her husband were present when her brother was crowned King Robert I by William Lamberton, Bishop of St Andrews, just six weeks after Comyn's murder. The ceremony was repeated on 27 March, following the late arrival of Isabella MacDuff, Countess of Buchan, who claimed her family's hereditary right to crown Scotland's kings (despite her being married to a Comyn). Robert's coronation was the start of the most desperate period of his life – and that of his supporters. Edward I of England was never one to acquiesce when his will was flouted; he sent his army into Scotland to hunt down the new king and his adherents. After Robert's defeat by the English at Methven in 1306, he went into hiding in the Highlands. Robert sent his wife and daughter north to what he hoped would be safety. Christian, her sister Mary and the Countess of Buchan accompanied them, escorted by the Earl of Atholl and Christian's brother, Sir Neil Bruce. It is thought that the Bruce women were heading north to Orkney to take a boat to Norway, where Robert's sister, Isabel, widow of King Erik II, was still living. Unfortunately, they would never make it. The English caught up with them at Kildrummy Castle and laid siege to it. The defenders were betrayed by someone in their garrison, a blacksmith who set fire to the barns, making the castle indefensible. The women managed to escape with the Earl of Atholl, but Neil Bruce remained with the garrison to mount a desperate defence, to give the queen, his niece and sisters enough time to escape. Following their capitulation, the entire garrison was executed. Sir Neil Bruce was subjected to a traitor's death; he was hung, drawn and quartered at Berwick in September 1306. Christian and her companions did not escape for long; they made for Tain, in Easter Ross, probably in the hope of finding a boat to take them onwards. They were hiding in the sanctuary of St Duthac when they were captured by the Earl of Ross (a former adherent of the deposed king John Balliol), who handed them over to the English. They were sent south, to Edward I at Lanercost Priory in Cumbria.

Christian had been separated from her husband shortly after the coronation. Sir Christopher Seton had been sent to hold Loch Doon Castle against the English. Following a desperate siege, the castle was surrendered by its governor, Sir Gilbert de Carrick, and its defenders were taken into English custody. Seton was executed on the orders of Edward I; the poor man was hanged. Edward I's admirer, Sir Maurice Powicke, said Edward treated his captives with a 'peculiar ferocity'.[26] Christian's sister Mary was treated particularly harshly by Edward I. The English king had a special cage built for her, although within the castle and not, as previously believed, hung from the walls of the keep at Roxburgh Castle, exposed to the elements and the derision of the English garrison and populace. In contrast, Christian was sent into captivity to a Gilbertine convent at Sixhills, an isolated location, deep in the Lincolnshire Wolds; she was probably told of her husband's death – and the manner of it – during the journey south. Christian languished at Sixhills for eight years, until shortly after her brother's remarkable victory over the English at Bannockburn, in 1314. Despite Edward II escaping the carnage, King Robert the Bruce had managed to capture several notable English prisoners, including Humphrey de Bohun, 4th Earl of Hereford and Essex. Suddenly in a strong bargaining position, the Scots king was able to exchange his English captives for his family, held prisoners in England for the last eight years.

Once home in Scotland, Christian joined her brother's court. In no hurry to remarry, she accompanied the king and his family on a short progress around Tyndale, an area of Northumberland that was officially in Scottish hands. Sometime after her return to Scotland, Christian had also been granted the Bruce lands of Garioch in Aberdeenshire. The Scottish Wars of Independence took a heavy toll on Christian's family. Having lost her brother and husband in 1306, she had lost her two younger brothers on the same day in 1307. Thomas and Alexander Bruce had been leading a force into Galloway when they were overwhelmed by the forces of Dungal MacDougall, a supporter of the Comyn faction. The brothers, both in their early twenties, were handed over to the English and were beheaded at Carlisle on 9 February 1307. Robert and Christian's surviving brother, Edward, was killed in battle in Ireland in 1318. The sad losses must have seemed endless to Christian. In 1323 Christian's sister Mary died; Mary had survived four years imprisoned in a cage at Roxburgh Castle before being transferred to a more comfortable imprisonment in 1310. It wouldn't be surprising if her inhumane incarceration had contributed to Mary's death in her early forties.

Christian remained unmarried for many years. Although their marriage had been a short one, Christian kept her husband's memory alive for many years; in 1324 she founded a chapel in Dumfries in his honour. There is a possibility she was the Bruce sister mooted as a bride for Sir Andrew Harclay, Earl of Carlisle, as part of a peace treaty with England in 1323. However, negotiations broke down and the marriage never took place. Christian eventually married in 1326, to a man who was probably about twenty years her junior.

Her second husband was Sir Andrew Murray of Bothwell, posthumous son of the Sir Andrew Murray who had fought beside Sir William Wallace in the victory at Stirling Bridge. Christian and Andrew were to have two children, both sons. Their eldest, John, married Margaret Graham, Countess of Mentieth, sometime after 21 November 1348. John died in 1352 and Margaret would go on to marry Robert, Duke of Albany, brother of Robert III and a great-grandson of King Robert the Bruce. A second son, Thomas, would marry Joan, a daughter of Maurice Moray, Earl of Strathearn, and died in 1361.

On the death of Christian's surviving brother, Robert the Bruce, in 1329, Scotland was once again thrown into turmoil. His five-year-old son, David, was proclaimed king, with regents to rule for him. As a member of the royal family, Christian took part in David's coronation in 1331; she shared a room in Scone Palace with her nieces, the new king's sisters. The English, however, saw the Bruce's death as an opportunity and backed Edward Balliol's invasion of Scotland. Edward was crowned king in 1332, but could not consolidate his position. In the same year, Murray was chosen as Guardian of Scotland and spent the next five years fighting the English and repulsing their attempts to return Balliol to the throne. Again Christian found herself in the thick of the fighting when Sir Andrew installed her as keeper of Kildrummy Castle. In 1335 she was besieged by one of Balliol's commanders, David Strathbogie, Earl of Atholl. Her husband marched to her aid with a force of more than 1,000 men; he was able to surprise Atholl and defeated him at Culblean.[27]

Christian remained in possession of Kildrummy Castle even after Sir Andrew's death; her husband had died at Avoch Castle in Ross in 1338, having retired from national politics the year before. Christian is known to have entertained her nephew's wife, Queen Joan, at Kildrummy Castle in 1342 and David II was generous to his aunt, providing her with an income from a number of sources, including the customs of Aberdeen. It is believed Christian died sometime in 1356, the last time she was mentioned in the exchequer rolls.[28] She must have been well into her seventies, a great age for the time. I couldn't find any source to confirm where she was buried; however, her husband was initially buried in the chapel at Rossmarkie, but later reinterred in Dunfermline Abbey, suggesting that this is also Christian's resting place. It would be appropriate if it was, as so many of her ancestors and family are buried there; including her husband, brother Robert, and niece Marjorie.

Edward I's treatment of the women associated with Robert the Bruce varied depending on the person. Robert the Bruce's wife suffered a no less punishing life in support of her husband but her treatment in English custody was probably the least harsh of all his women relatives, thanks to her father's relationship with the English king. The daughter of Richard de Burgh, Earl of Ulster and Connaught, and his wife, Margaret, Elizabeth de Burgh was born around 1289 and was a goddaughter of Edward I. In 1302, at thirteen, Elizabeth was married to Robert the Bruce, Earl of Carrick, probably at his manor of Writtle, near Chelmsford in Essex. It is possible the marriage was arranged by Edward; he certainly encouraged it, as a way of keeping the young Scottish noble loyal to his cause. However, events in Scotland would soon push the Bruce away from his English alliances; the killing of his greatest rival for the throne, John Comyn, in the Chapel of the Greyfriars in Dumfries meant that Robert could claim the Scottish throne. Aware that he would be excommunicated for his actions, Bruce raced to Scone to be crowned before a papal bull could be issued. Elizabeth was at Robert's side when he was crowned at Scone on that spring day in March 1306.

Unfortunately, as we have already seen, the coronation was not the end of trouble for the Bruces. If anything, things were about to get much worse. After the fall of Kildrummy Castle, and the desperate race north to Tain, Queen Elizabeth and her companions were captured by the Earl of Ross, a former adherent of the deposed king, John Balliol, who took them from sanctuary at St Duthac and handed them over to the English. As we have seen, they were sent south, to Edward I at Lanercost Priory.

Elizabeth's capture would have been a hard blow for Robert the Bruce. The new king of Scotland still lacked a male heir, and had no chance of having one while his wife was in English hands. This made his hold on the throne even more precarious than it already was. However, although she was imprisoned, Elizabeth was treated more kindly than her step-daughter and the other adherents to Robert the Bruce. Her father was a close ally of Edward I and the king did not want to alienate him. The Queen of Scots was, therefore, sent to Burstwick Manor in Holderness, Yorkshire, under house arrest. It was from there that she wrote to Edward I, in an undated letter, complaining that she only had three changes of clothes, and no bed linen.[29] She then spent four years at Bisham Manor in Berkshire, before she was moved again in 1312. With her husband gaining strength and raiding into Yorkshire, she was moved to a more secure location, probably the Tower of London (although some sources say Windsor Castle). By this time, she was allowed six attendants and was given a regular allowance. Elizabeth was later moved to Shaftesbury Abbey in Dorset, just as the political situation was about to change in her husband's favour.

After Robert the Bruce's not inconsiderable victory at the Battle of Bannockburn, over Edward II and his English forces, negotiations led to a prisoner exchange and Elizabeth and the rest of the Bruce ladies, finally returned to Scotland after eight years of imprisonment. Reunited at last, Robert set about consolidating his kingdom, with his queen at his side. Between 1315 and

1323 Elizabeth and Robert had two daughters, Margaret, who married William, 5th Earl of Sutherland, and died in childbirth in 1346 or 1347, and Matilda, who married Thomas Isaac and had two daughters; she died in 1353.The much longed-for son and heir, David, was born in 1324 and would succeed his father at the age of five, as King David II. A second son, John, was born in 1327 but died young. Elizabeth herself died on 27 October 1327, possibly due to complications following John's birth, although sources are silent on the reasons for her death. She was buried in Dunfermline Abbey; Robert the Bruce was buried beside her when he died eighteen months later.

The youngest of Edward I's Scottish prisoners was Marjorie Bruce. Dead before her twentieth birthday, her short life was filled with tragedy and adversity from the moment of her birth. I could find no pictures of her – just ones of her tomb, which just about sums it up for poor Marjorie. Marjorie was born at a time of great upheaval in Scotland; Edward I was claiming overlordship of the country, and the right to choose its next king. John Balliol was chosen as king, only for Edward to humiliate and dethrone him a short time later, publicly removing the royal blazon from his surcoat, earning him the nickname Toom Tabard, meaning 'empty surcoat'. Marjorie's father, Robert the Bruce, was one of the chief claimants of the Scottish crown. Marjorie was the only daughter of Robert the Bruce, Lord of Annandale and Earl of Carrick, and Isabella of Mar. Isabella was the daughter of Donald, 6th Earl of Mar, and Helen, possibly an illegitimate daughter of Llewelyn the Great, Prince of Wales (although this seems to be far from certain). Isabella and Robert had married in 1295 and Marjorie arrived about two years later. Heartbreakingly, at the age of only nineteen, Isabella died shortly after giving birth and Marjorie was left motherless, with a father who was away fighting, alternately for and against the English. Named after her paternal grandmother, Marjorie, Countess of Carrick in her own right, it seems highly likely that given her motherless status and with her father embroiled in the problems of the kingdom, Marjorie's care was handed to one of her father's sisters, either Mary or Christian.

At six years old, Marjorie acquired a new step-mother when Robert married Elizabeth de Burgh. Although Edward I appears to have arranged the marriage in order to keep the Bruce's loyalty, it was only a short while after the marriage that Robert the Bruce finally decided to join William Wallace and fight for Scotland. In 1306, following his coronation as King of Scots at Scone Abbey, little eight-year-old Marjorie was suddenly a Princess of Scotland as the daughter of King Robert I. She was not her father's heir, however. Her uncle, Edward Bruce, Robert's brother, was afforded that status; probably due to the fear that a girl would not be up to the task of defending the kingdom against the English. Within months of the coronation Marjorie was in the hands of Edward I. When they reached London, her escort during the failed escape north, the Earl of Atholl, suffered the same fate as her uncle Sir Neil had at Berwick; Atholl was the first earl to ever suffer the traitor's death of hanging, drawing and quartering.

Although Edward did not order the executions of the women folk, it cannot be said he treated them kindly. They were used to set an example; a demonstration of the price of rebellion against Edward. For Marjorie Bruce, these events must have been terrifying. Edward ordered her confined in an iron cage in the Tower of London, where no one was to speak to her. Whether Edward relented of his own free will, or was advised against such treatment of a child of not yet ten years old, the order was rescinded and she was confined to a convent at Watton in Yorkshire.[30] Although loyal to their king, we can only hope that the nuns took pity on the poor child, and treated her kindly. She was held at Watton for eight years and it was only her father's victory at Bannockburn in 1314 that eventually secured her freedom.

On Marjorie's return to Scotland, King Robert almost immediately set about arranging her marriage. With the queen yet to produce a child, the now-seventeen-year-old Marjorie was needed to produce an heir for the Bruce dynasty. Walter Stewart, the wealthy and powerful 6th High Steward of Scotland was just five years older than Marjorie and the ideal candidate as a husband. Loyal to Scotland's king, Walter had distinguished himself as a commander at the Battle of Bannockburn, and was the man entrusted by Bruce to bring his family home from their English captivity. Walter and Marjorie were married shortly afterwards, with Marjorie's dowry including the Barony of Bathgate in West Lothian. Whatever happiness – if any – Marjorie derived from the marriage, however, was short-lived.

In 1316, while heavily pregnant, she fell from her horse while out riding near Paisley Abbey. Going into premature labour,

Marjorie was taken to the Abbey, where she was delivered of a son, Robert, on 2 March 1316. It is possible that Robert was delivered by caesarean section as his mother was close to death; in the medieval period, a caesarean was a death sentence for the mother, but was performed when it offered the only chance of survival for the child. This mother survived the birth by just a few hours and died the same day. Marjorie Bruce was dead at the tender age of nineteen – the same age as her mother before her – having lived through some of the most turbulent years of Scottish history. However, she had secured Scotland's future, had she lived she would have seen her son succeed her brother David II, as Robert II, founder of the Stewart dynasty in 1371. Marjorie had spent eight of her nineteen years imprisoned in a convent in England, harsh treatment for a young girl, kept away from her family and her homeland.

However, as with Mary Bruce, it was also Isabel MacDuff, Countess of Buchan, who suffered the horrendous force of Edward I's not inconsiderable wrath. Isabel was probably born around 1270; she was the daughter of Colban, Earl of Fife, and his wife, Anna. Isabel was married to John Comyn, Earl of Buchan, and was first mentioned in 1297, when she was in England, managing her husband's estates while he was in Scotland. Captured after the Scottish defeat at Dunbar in 1296, the Earl of Buchan had been sent north by Edward I, ordered to take action against Andrew Murray; however, he only took cursory action against the loyal Scot and soon changed sides, possibly fighting for the Scots at Falkirk in 1298. The Comyn family were cousins of Scotland's former king, John Balliol, and constantly fought for his return to the throne, putting them in direct opposition to Robert the Bruce.

Isabel's story remained unremarkable throughout Scotland's struggles in the early years of the 1300s; until Robert the Bruce made his move for the throne in 1306. By birth, Isabel was a MacDuff, her father had been Earl of Fife and, in 1306, the current earl was her nephew, Duncan, a teenager who was a loyal devotee of Edward I. The Earls of Fife had, for centuries, claimed the hereditary right to crown Scotland's kings. Although Duncan had no interest in being involved in the coronation of Robert the Bruce, Isabel was determined to fulfil her family's role. It cannot have been an easy decision for her. Isabel's participation was an act of bravery and defiance. She went against not only Edward I but her own husband, the Earl of Buchan. Isabel's husband and the murdered John Comyn, Lord of Badenoch, were not only cousins but had a close relationship. It seems likely that Isabel's husband was in England at the time of Bruce's coronation, and she did not have to face him personally; but she would have known that her actions would mean there was no going back. Supporting Robert the Bruce, the man who stood accused of John Comyn's murder, meant she turned against her husband and his entire family, people she had lived among for her entire married life.

Robert the Bruce had raced directly to Scone following the death of John Comyn, Lord of Badenoch, in Greyfriars Church, Dumfries, on 10 February 1306. Bruce was crowned at Scone on 25 March, by William Lamberton, Bishop of St Andrews. Two days later Isabel reached Scone and insisted on her family's hereditary right to crown the new king. There are some rumours of a more intimate relationship between Isabel and Bruce, but these seem to be without foundation and are only to be expected, given that Isabel acted so decisively – and publicly – against her husband.[31]

There was no going back for Isabel – crowning Robert the Bruce meant she was on her own; she couldn't go back to her family, so she stayed with the royal party, travelling with Elizabeth de Burgh, the new queen, when Bruce sent her, his daughter and sisters, north for their safety. Isabel was with them when they escaped Kildrummy Castle by the skin of their teeth, and when they reached the shrine of St Duthac at Tain and were captured by William, Earl of Ross, in September 1306. As the party were sent south, Isabel must have faced the future with trepidation. Her placing the crown on Robert the Bruce's head was the clearest challenge to Edward I and guaranteed that she would receive no sympathy from England's king.

Even knowing that she would receive harsh treatment, it is doubtful that she, or indeed anyone, could have foreseen the punishment that Edward I would mete out. He ordered the construction of wooden cages, for Isabel and Bruce's sister Mary; the two women were to be imprisoned in these cages close to the Scottish border, Isabel at Berwick Castle and Mary at Roxburgh Castle. Tradition has these cages were suspended from the walls of the castles' keeps, open to the elements and the harsh Borders weather, the only shelter and privacy being afforded by a small privy. According to the *Flores Historiarum*, written at the Abbey of St Albans, Edward I said of Isabel's punishment:

[o]ne who doesn't strike with the sword shall not perish by the sword. But because of that illicit coronation which she made, in a little enclosure made of iron and stone in the form of a crown, solidly constructed, let her be suspended at Berwick under the open heavens, so as to provide, in life and after death, a spectacle for passers-by and eternal shame.[32]

It is doubtful, however, that the St Albans annalist was present when the order was given. The original royal writ still survives, written in French and reads a little differently;

It is decreed and ordered by letters under the privy seal sent to the Chamberlain of Scotland, or his Lieutenant at Berwick-upon-Tweed, that, in one of the turrets within the castle at the same place, in the position which he sees to be most suitable for the purpose, he cause to be made a cage of stout lattice work of timber, barred and strengthened with iron, in which he is to put the Countess of Buchan.[33]

This type of cage, within a room in the keep, was also used by Edward I to hold Owain, the son of Daffydd ab Gruffuddd; he had been held at Bristol Castle since 1283 and had been secured in a cage, overnight, since 1305. The construction of the cages was intended to humiliate their occupants and, at the same time, Scotland's new king. They were also a taunt; placing Isabel and Mary in these cages, on the borders of Scotland, it is possible they were intended as a challenge to Robert the Bruce, showing him that he was not powerful enough to protect his women, but also teasing him, hoping he would be drawn into a rescue attempt that would, almost certainly, lead to the destruction of his limited forces.

Despite Edward's death in 1307, Isabel, Countess of Buchan was held in her little cage in Berwick Castle for four years in total. Attempts to secure her release were made by Sir Robert Keith and Sir John Mowbray, by appealing to Duncan, Earl of Fife, but the appeals came to nought. It was only in 1310 that Mary and Isabel were released from their cages; Isabel was moved to the more comfortable surroundings of the Carmelite friary at Berwick. In 1313 she was put into the custody of Sir Henry de Beaumont, who was married to Alice, niece and co-heir of Isabel's husband, John Comyn, Earl of Buchan. This is the last we hear of Isabel, Countess of Buchan, as she slips from the pages of history. It seems likely that Isabel died within the next year, probably due to her health being destroyed by the years of deprivation; she was not among the hostages who were returned to Scotland following the Scots' victory at Bannockburn.

These women were imprisoned because they threatened the State and the status quo in some way. It cannot have been easy for Eleanor of Brittany and Princess Gwenllian, to have been imprisoned merely for their royal blood, and the threat that blood posed to the incumbent rulers. However, the fact they endured, even if they were never freed, makes them heroines in the eyes of many. Gwenllian even has her own society. Many women were imprisoned at the whim of a king, such as poor Ingeborg, who provides a forewarning of things to come; who cannot compare her fate to the fates of Henry VIII's wives, particularly Catherine of Aragon? That most of these women survived their imprisonment makes them heroines; they faced adversity and their sheer perseverance saw them through. And poor Maud de Braose, starved to death for having spoken out of turn – but who wouldn't do the same to protect their family? Knowing what John had done to Arthur, would you willingly place your children in his custody?

8

Warrior Heroines

My research into medieval women uncovered several who broke the mould of that time almost beyond recognition, those who strayed far away from the sphere of domestic influence to which most women were consigned. Of course, everyone has heard of Joan of Arc, and a book on medieval heroines would not be complete without the French teenager who orchestrated the defeat of the English in the Hundred Years War; however, she was not alone in fighting for her country and her people.

Not as well-known as Joan, the Maid of Orléans, even to British people, is the daughter of Alfred the Great, King of Wessex, one of England's greatest kings. Æthelflæd was born about 870, the eldest child of King Alfred and his wife, Ealhswith. Alfred's biographer, Asser, says Ealhswith was a member of the Mercian royal house through her mother, Eadburh.[1] Around 886 Æthelflæd was married to Æthelred, ealdorman of Mercia and a trusted lieutenant of her father. Æthelred ruled over the English half of the Mercian kingdom, which had been dissected by the Vikings but submitted to King Alfred's overlordship. The marriage was a political alliance, intended to strengthen Saxon resistance to the Danes, who were now occupying Northumbria, Yorkshire and East Anglia. The resulting close relationship of Mercia and Wessex was only further strengthened by the renewed Viking attacks of the 890s.

During the early years of their marriage the young couple appear to have settled in London, the city that had been entrusted to Æthelred's care by Alfred. Æthelflæd seems to have taken after her father – she was a strong, brave woman and is often regarded more as a partner to Æthelred than a meek, obedient wife. The couple jointly presided over provincial courts. The 'Mercian Register', a fragment of a Mercian chronicle, included in some versions of the *Anglo-Saxon Chronicle*, records that Æthelflæd was exercising regal powers in the region even before her husband's death. In his final years Æthelred increasingly suffered from illness, during which time Æthelflæd assumed greater authority. The couple had only one child, a daughter, Ælfwynn. According to William of Malmesbury (writing in the 12th century) the lack of more children was due to Æthelflæd's avoidance of marital relations, possibly due to a fear of dying in childbirth. Malmesbury quotes her as saying it was 'unbecoming a daughter of a king to give way to a delight, which after a time produced such painful consequences'.[2] Æthelred died in 911, though whether this was from wounds received in battle or from illness remains unclear. He was buried at Gloucester.

Wessex had already adjusted to a change in ruler when Æthelflæd's father had died in 899 and had been succeeded by her younger brother, Edward 'the Elder'. When Æthelred died, Edward was happy to support his sister as sole ruler of Mercia, but he took personal control of the cities of London and Oxford, cities that could be used as bases from which Edward could launch campaigns against the Danes of the Midlands. The siblings seem to have had a trusting relationship for many years; Edward had entrusted his son Æthelstan, often viewed as the first king of England, to Æthelflæd and her husband, to be educated at the Mercian court. The first woman to rule an Anglo-Saxon kingdom – albeit as a client of her brother's more powerful kingdom of Wessex, Æthelflæd was accorded the title the Lady of the Mercians. She proved to be a vital ally to her brother and the siblings worked together to combat the threats of the Danes. In 909, according to the *Anglo-Saxon Chronicle*, Edward sent an army, made up of West Saxons and Mercians, into Danish territory in the north. It was probably this army that brought back to Mercia the relics of St Oswald, the 7th century Northumbrian Dane. They had been taken from Bardney in Lincolnshire and Æthelflæd had them translated to the new minster at Gloucester, which was renamed St Oswald in his honour.

Æthelflæd continued the policy, started by her father, of building *burhs* and established a ring of fortified centres around western Mercia. The *burhs* not only provided protection against the Danes, but served as bases from which to launch attacks on Danish-occupied regions. Each *burh* could provide a refuge for all villagers within a 20-mile radius; it would have a large garrison, depot and its own water supply. During Æthelred's lifetime, *burhs* had been established at 'Bremesburh', Worcester (between 887 and 899) and Chester (907). Later, on Æthelflæd's orders, in 913, fortresses were built at several further sites, including Bridgnorth, Tamworth and Stafford, in response to Viking raids into Edward's territories. Edward built two further *burhs* at Buckingham in 914, plugging a defensive gap between Tamworth and Hertford. At the same time, Æthelflæd built one at Warwick and another at Eddisbury; this latter, with a new *burh* at Runcorn in 915, helped to strengthen her northern defences. While the Danes appeared to be the greatest risk, Æthelflæd did not neglect her defences along the Welsh border, building a *burh* at Chirbury and one at the now-lost location of 'Wearburh'. In the same year, Edward fortified Bedford and in 916 he built a *burh* at Maldon to fortify Essex against seaborne raiding. While this building programme was going on, it also seems highly likely that Æthelflæd rebuilt and strengthened the defences of Gloucester and Hereford.[3]

Æthelflæd was no silent partner in Edward's reconquest of England. Most remarkably, she personally led successful military campaigns against the Welsh, the Norse and the Danes of York. The *Anglo-Saxon Chronicle* relates that on the feast of St Cyriac the Martyr, 16 June 916, the abbot Egbert and his retainers, were murdered for no known reason.[4] The Mercian abbot had been travelling in the Welsh mountain kingdom of Brycheiniog when he was attacked. Æthelflæd seems to have taken the murder as a personal affront; the abbot was, after all, under her protection. Three days later she invaded Wales; her army ravaged Brycheiniog, burning the little kingdom. Although King Tewdr escaped, Æthelflæd took his wife, Queen Angharad, as a hostage, with 33 others. Many of them were relatives of the Welsh king. Eventually, the king submitted to Æthelflæd, promising to serve her faithfully and to pay compensation. The incident not only demonstrates Æthelflæd's commitment to her people, but also shows her strength and determination, attributes she was to put to good use against the Danes.

In 917 Danish forces had taken the offensive, raiding English territories. By the end of the year Edward had subdued East

Anglia, with all the Scandinavian armies of the region submitting to him. While her brother was raiding in East Anglia and the East Midlands, Æthelflæd led her forces across the West Midlands. She marched on the Viking stronghold of Derby, personally leading the army on campaign. It would be the first of the Danes' 'Five Boroughs', which made up the Danelaw, to fall.

Although she managed to successfully storm the fort, her army suffered heavy casualties, including four of her most trusted and senior thegns. Thegns were the army's commanders and officers. The *Anglo-Saxon Chronicle* reported; 'With God's help Ethelfleda, lady of Mercia, captured the fortress known as Derby with all its assets. Four of her favoured ministers were slain inside the gates'.[5]

The Saxon victory was a great shock to the Danes. Their Viking myths told of an invincible woman who would appear at *Ragnarok*, the Norse apocalypse, and make brave warriors cower before her. Æthelflæd was relentless – in early 918 she and her army moved on to Leicester, while Edward headed for Stamford. Leicester was the centre of a heavily settled Danish colony, and Æthelflæd ravaged the countryside around the settlement. The Danes had no choice but to surrender in the face of her indefatigable forces. However, she was magnanimous in victory, displaying mercy and charity by distributing alms as she progressed into town.

The inexorable advance of Æthelflæd's army combined with her compassion for the defeated was to prove to be a clever strategy, demonstrating to those regions still controlled by the Danes that she was prepared to offer compromise if they would only submit to her. The Danes of York, the Viking capital, in particular, began to look at submitting to Æthelflæd as a serious option to avoid continued conflict. Their new king was Ragnall, a Viking pirate from Dublin, who had taken the throne by force; but the Danes knew that Edward and Æthelflæd would never make peace with him. In the summer of 918 the noblemen and magnates of York sent emissaries to Æthelflæd, promising that they would surrender to her.

In May, King Edward had marched his army to Stamford, building a new fort south of the river and accepting the surrender of the local Danes, who submitted to him as their new ruler. It was while he was still at Stamford that Edward received word of his sister, The *Anglo-Saxon Chronicle* made a cold, clinical report:

918 While he was there his sister Æthelflæd died at Tamworth two weeks before midsummer. The king took possession of Tamworth and the whole province of Mercia which she had governed.[6]

Æthelflæd died suddenly at Tamworth on 12 June 918. She was buried beside her husband, in the east chapel of the cathedral she had founded, St Peter's Church, Gloucester. Although she did not live long enough to see the successful conclusion to the work she and her brother had carried out, her achievements cannot be lightly brushed off. Between 910 and 920 all Danish territories south of Yorkshire had been conquered. Her nephew Athelstan consolidated the kingdom that had been created by the efforts of Edward and Æthelflæd. If Æthelflæd did not live to see the extent of her success, neither did she live to see her daughter, Ælfwynn, nearly thirty and still unmarried, briefly become the nominal ruler of Mercia; only to be 'deprived of all authority' six months later and taken to Wessex, from where nothing more is heard of her.[7]

The story of Æthelflæd mainly comes from the Mercian Register, embedded largely in the B, C and D texts of the *Anglo-Saxon Chronicle*. She appears only rarely in the primary text, text A, which focuses on Edward and Wessex. Text A tries to minimise Æthelflæd's significance, but could not wholly obscure her achievements. She was, after all, the daughter of Alfred the Great, the wife of the ealdorman of Mercia and a prominent woman in her own right, in an era when this was an incredible rarity. It is thought that it was Æthelflæd, the Lady of the Mercians, who inspired the 10th-century poem, 'Judith', who is 'white and shining', 'noble and courageous'. In the poem, Æthelflæd is depicted as the 'valorous virgin' who struck off the head of the hostile foe with her gleaming sword and 'ascribed the glory of all that to the Lord of Hosts'.[8] Recognising her vital role in the creation of England, the 12th-century Henry of Huntingdon declared Æthelflæd 'to have been so powerful that in praise and exaltation of her wonderful gifts, some call her not only lady, but even king'. In a poem he described her as 'worthy of a man's name' and 'more illustrious than Caesar', apparently high praise indeed – for a woman.[9]

What is surprising is that Æthelflæd is by no means unique in leading an army or fighting against her country's enemies.

However, each 'warrior' woman I have come across has had her own, very different wars to fight, and from varying social statuses. My personal favourite – and the original inspiration for this book – was a lady by the name of Nicholaa de la Haye (also written as de la Haie in some sources), a woman of formidable reputation, even in her own lifetime. Nicholaa was the daughter and co-heiress of Richard de la Haie and Matilda de Vernon. Richard was the hereditary constable of Lincoln Castle and Sheriff of Lincolnshire. Nicholaa was probably born in the 1150s, although nothing of her childhood is known. She married, firstly, William Fitz Erneis but he died in 1178 and there don't appear to have been any children from the marriage. Nicholaa was an attractive marriage prospect. As her father had died in 1169, the position of constable of Lincoln Castle was passed through Nicholaa to her husband, as well as her lands in England and Normandy. Although the de la Haie lands were a relatively small barony, holding only sixteen knights' fees in 1172, their hold of Lincoln Castle meant that Nicholaa wouldn't stay a widow for long and by 1185 she was married again, to Gerard de Canville. Gerard was the son of Richard de Canville, who had served both King Stephen and Henry II before his death in 1176. Gerard himself had been in royal favour during the reign of Henry II. In 1189 Gerard and Nicholaa travelled to Barfleur in Normandy to obtain a charter from the new king, Richard I, which confirmed Gerard de Canville in his lands in England and Normandy and in his position as castellan and, most likely, Sheriff of Lincolnshire, for a fee of 700 marks.[10]

However, Richard's reign was not smooth sailing for Gerard and Nicholaa; in 1191 Gerard quarrelled with William de Longchamp, chancellor and justiciar, while the king was away on Crusade. Longchamp had demanded that Canville relinquish the castle and swear allegiance to him as regent. Canville refused and, instead, swore his allegiance to the king's brother, John. Longchamp ordered Canville be stripped of his position, giving the post of sheriff to William de Stuteville, and besieged Nicholaa at Lincoln Castle, as Gerard joined John at Nottingham. The castle was under siege for forty days, but the tenacious Nicholaa held out. Richard of Devizes said that her defence was done 'without thinking of anything womanly'.[11] After taking the royal castles at Nottingham and Tickhill with apparent ease, John sent a message to Longchamp demanding that he lift the siege and reinstate

Canville as castellan. News of Longchamp's heavy-handedness and unpopularity had reached the king, at that time in Sicily, who sent Walter of Countances, Archbishop of Rouen, to mediate between the factions. The siege of Lincoln was lifted and Longchamp returned to London. A peace agreement, weighing heavily in John's favour, was eventually reached and Gerard de Canville was reinstated as Castellan of Lincoln.[12]

Nicholaa and Gerard would have three children. Their eldest son, Richard, married a widow named Eustachia and their daughter Idonea married William II Longspée, Earl of Salisbury, and inherited the de la Haie and de Canville estates. Of another son, named Thomas, no information beyond his name has survived. There was also a daughter, Matilda, of whom there is little information, save that her mother was fined 300 marks by King Richard, in 1194, for an agreement that she could marry her daughter to whomever she wished, except, of course, an enemy of the king's. Nicholaa was still accounting for this debt until 1212, and had renegotiated the amount with King John in 1200; in 1201 she still owed £20, 40 marks and one palfrey (horse).[13]

It was on Richard's return in 1194 that Gerard de Canville was stripped of both his positions as Sheriff of Lincolnshire and Castellan of Lincoln Castle. They probably retired to Nicholaa's Lincolnshire estate at Swaton, south of Lincoln, but were reinstated on the accession of King John in 1199. Nicholaa de la Haye and her husband are among the few barons who stayed faithful to John throughout his reign. Gerard de Canville died in 1215, but Nicholaa was able to retain Lincoln Castle. King John had managed to upset practically every baron in England, with his despotic and heavy-handed ways. In 1215 open rebellion was thwarted when John signed Magna Carta, a long, detailed document dealing with the barons' particular grievances, but touching the whole system of government and including arbitrary fines and the exploitation of wardship. John 'had broken the spirit of kingship'.[14] John was soon writing to the pope to have Magna Carta annulled and England was plunged into rebellion. The barons even invited the French dauphin, Louis, to join them and make a play for the throne. Louis was the son of John's erstwhile friend Philip II Augustus, King of France, and the husband of his niece Blanche, who was the daughter of his sister Eleanor, Queen of Castile. Louis and his men had landed on the Isle of Thanet on 14 May 1216. Louis advanced through Kent and took Canterbury before moving onto Winchester. John seems to have been undecided as to how to act; he sent his oldest son Henry to safety at Devizes Castle in Wiltshire. Dover Castle, under the command of Hubert de Burgh, held out against the French and rebel forces, as did Windsor and Lincoln. The northern barons 'were defeated in their attempts to take Lincoln. A certain lady called Nicola, who was the custodian's wife, freed herself from this siege with a money payment.'[15]

Even John's loyal barons were now beginning to turn on him, including his cousin the Earl of Warenne. John moved north, devastating the Isle of Axeholme 'with fire and sword'[16] before arriving at Lincoln in September 1216, just days after the besieging army had departed with their payment. Nicholaa met the king at the eastern postern gate of the castle. She offered the keys of the castle to the king, claiming she was unable to continue with the office of castellan due to her great age. John is said to have replied, 'My beloved Nichola, I will that you keep the castle as hitherto until I shall order otherwise.'[17] When Nicholaa spoke of her 'great age' she wasn't exaggerating. She was probably around sixty years old at the time, a great age in those days, but John still had great confidence in her and just a few days before his death, John granted Nicholaa the position of Sheriff of Lincoln in her own right, despite the fact her son Richard was now a grown man and able to inherit the position. As King John moved on from Lincoln, he contracted a violent fever and died of dysentery at Newark on 19 October 1216. The new king was now John's nine-year-old son, Henry III, with the famous and redoubtable William Marshal, Earl of Pembroke, acting as reluctant regent.

Support began to fall away from Louis, who returned to France to recoup his strength. In early 1217 he returned to continue the fight. An armed force under the Comte de Perche moved on Lincoln. He took the town, which was unprepared for attack, and laid siege to the castle, still in Nicholaa's charge. Louis himself travelled to Lincoln to request the surrender of the castle, promising Nicholaa there would be no reprisals, no one would be hurt. Nicholaa refused and settled in for another long siege. Despite the French army outside her walls, she may have been quietly confident; this was, after all, her third siege and no one had ever managed to breach the walls. Lincoln Castle is a rather large fortress, sitting opposite the impressive cathedral and perched on the top of a bluff – the hill going down to the town is not named Steep Hill for nothing. However, this siege was going to last longer than the others. From March through to May, Louis' forces battered the walls of Lincoln Castle. The French prince had brought impressive siege engines, leaving them at Perche's disposal when he returned to London, fully expecting to hear of Lincoln's capitulation within weeks, if not days.

However, he did not count on the tenacity of Nicholaa and her deputy, Sir Geoffrey de Serland, who rallied their troops and resisted the combined Anglo-French forces of the Comte de Perche, and awaited reinforcements. William Marshal was determined to relieve Lincoln – after all, it would have been 'dishonourable not to help so brave a lady'.[18] The *Histoire de Guillaume le Maréchal* tells how Peter des Roches, Bishop of Winchester, managed to sneak into Lincoln Castle by a secret entrance; he had been sent by William Marshal to reassure Nicholaa that relief was on its way.[19] Nicholaa was delighted to hear that, it must have bolstered the morale of the men under her command; all they had to do was sit tight and wait. Marshal mustered his forces at Newark on 17 May; the Royalist army was made up of 406 knights, 307 crossbowmen and a large number of followers, including non-combatants. The regent led the relief of Lincoln himself, but was accompanied by the great and the good, including the warrior-bishop, Peter des Roches, Ranulf of Chester, William Longsword, Faulkes de Bréauté, John Marshal and William Marshal, the regent's son. Marshal was eager to relieve Lincoln before the besiegers could receive reinforcements, which would increase the force to a complement of 600 knights.[20]

Marshal split his forces, with Ranulf of Chester approaching from the north, joining with Marshal, who came to the castle at the city's western gate and skirted the northern wall of the castle to the east gate. A large force of crossbowmen, led by Faulkes de Bréauté, gained entry to the castle through the west gate; they were positioned on the castle walls, looking into the town, and rained a deadly barrage of crossbow bolts into the Anglo-French army. It must have been a fine sight for Nicholaa and her garrison to watch their relief march straight through the castle and engage the enemy in battle. The siege engines were destroyed and fierce hand-to-hand fighting ensued. The leader of the Anglo-French forces, Thomas, Comte de Perche, was killed in a melee in front of Lincoln Cathedral. Marshal's army advanced down the hill into the town itself and the Anglo-French encampment. The Battle of Lincoln, on 20 May 1217, raged through the streets, the fierce fighting followed by looting and sacrilege in the medieval city. Sacking the city and attacking citizens who had collaborated with the French was considered a just punishment by the Royalist forces. Now known as the Lincoln Fair, it was one of two decisive battles that ended French hopes of winning the English throne. Support for Henry III grew and the young king's forces were soon marching on London to blockade Louis within the capital city. A sea battle near the Isle of Thanet prevented Louis from receiving much-needed reinforcements and on 12 September, the two sides came to terms, with Louis being paid 10,000 marks to go home.[21] In one of the most remarkable examples of ingratitude ever, and surely worthy of King John himself, Nicholaa was relieved of her duties as Sheriff of Lincolnshire just four days after the Battle of Lincoln. The position was handed to the king's uncle, William Longspée, Earl of Salisbury. Nicholaa's son, Richard, died in 1217 and his daughter, Idonea, was now the aged widow's heir. Idonea was married to Salisbury's son, William II Longspée; the couple inherited the de la Haie and Camville lands on Nicholaa's death. The settlement was not ideal, however, and some wrangling seems to have continued until Salisbury's death in 1226.

A staunchly independent woman, Nicholaa issued charters in her name, of which some 25 have survived. She made grants to various religious houses, including Lincoln Cathedral, and even secured a royal grant for a weekly market on one of her properties. A most able adversary for some of the greatest military minds of the time, and a loyal supporter of King John, she was unique among her peers. Although praised by the chroniclers, they seemed to find difficulty in describing a woman who acted in such a fashion; the *Dunstable Annals* refer to her as a 'noble woman', saying she acted 'manfully'.[22] It is impossible not to feel admiration for a woman who managed to hold her own in a man's world, who fought for her castle and her home at a time when women had so little say over their own lives – and at such an advanced age. Her bravery and tenacity saved Henry III's throne. Not surprisingly, Henry III referred to her as 'our beloved and faithful Nichola de la Haye'.[23] By late 1226 she had retired to her manor at Swaton. Having lived well into her seventies, Nicholaa died there on 20 November 1230.

She was buried in St Michael's Church, Swaton, in Lincolnshire. Her granddaughter Idonea succeeded to Nicholaa's lands in Lincolnshire, although her manor of Duddington in Northamptonshire reverted to the king.[24]

Nicholaa's steadfast hold on Lincoln Castle against an Anglo-French force saved England and turned the tide in favour of the regents of Henry III. Nicholaa's actions are remarkable, not only because she was a woman but also in view of her advancing years. At an age when even men would expect to be allowed to sit by the fire and reminisce about their past exploits, Nicholaa was standing firm, holding a key stronghold against an invading army.

And yet, she was not the only woman in medieval times to hold tenaciously to a castle under siege. It was more common than one might think. Maud de Braose (or Briouze), the Lady of Hay, was another such, who held her castle against the besieging Welsh; as was Agnes of Dunbar, known to history as Black Agnes and a woman who was a blight on English forces in Scotland. Agnes was a bold lady whose acts of defiance against the English would surely have impressed Nicholaa, nationalities aside, of course.

Agnes was the eldest daughter of Thomas Randolph, 1st Earl of Moray, and his wife Isabel, a daughter of Sir John Stewart of Bunkle. Thomas Randolph was a favoured nephew of Robert the Bruce, King of Scots, and one of his most stalwart supporters. Randolph was rewarded with the earldom of Moray and the appointment as guardian during the minority of King Robert's son and successor, David II, in 1329. There is very little known of the early life of Agnes, until about 1320, when she married Patrick, Earl of Dunbar. We can imagine that Agnes envisioned a life as a typical laird's lady, looking after the land and tenants while her husband was away fighting. Unfortunately, Agnes and Patrick would remain childless, so the countess was not preoccupied with raising children. Agnes's younger sister, Isabel, was married to Sir Patrick Dunbar, Earl Patrick's cousin, and it would be their son, George, who would be made heir to Earl Patrick and Agnes.

From the timing of the marriage, we can surmise that Agnes was probably born just after the turn of the century, into a country struggling to gain independence from its aggressive neighbour, England. It would, therefore, not be unreasonable to assume that she saw little of her father during her early years as he was frequently away fighting; even after the Scottish victory at

Bannockburn in 1314, Randolph continued in active service for the Scottish crown, fighting with Robert the Bruce in Ireland in 1317, and in the borders with England in 1318 and 1319.[25] Scotland's troubles continued long into the reign of David II, with the English backing David's rival, Edward Balliol, son of Scotland's former king, John Balliol. The throne would pass back and forth between the two claimants for several years. When Agnes's father died in 1332, he was succeeded by her brother Thomas, who was killed just weeks later, at the Battle of Dupplin Moor, fighting those who had been disinherited during the Wars of Independence. Thomas, in turn, was succeeded by another brother, John, who was killed fighting the English at the Battle of Neville's Cross in 1346.

On John's death, the earldom of Moray would pass to Agnes's husband in right of his wife. Agnes and Patrick were cousins within the prohibited degree of consanguinity and a dispensation had been needed for them to marry. According to the chronicler, Pitscottie, she gained her name of Black Agnes 'be ressone she was blak skynnit', suggesting Agnes had a dark complexion; her black hair, dark eyes and olive skin more common among Mediterranean countries than the northern fastness of Scotland.[26] The English attributed a different reason to her name, to them, Black Agnes was the most evil Scotswoman who ever lived.[27] Pitscottie went on to say of Agnes that she was 'of greater spirit than it became a woman to be', which, given her actions in the face of the enemy, is a fair appraisal of an incredible woman.[28] Agnes was not the only woman to become heavily involved in the Scottish Wars of Independence, which had been a different kind of war from the very beginning. Robert the Bruce's wife, daughter and sisters had been imprisoned for eight years by Edward I; his sister Christian would herself become involved in the fighting during her nephew David's reign, defending the castle of Kildrummy against the supporters of Edward Balliol, in 1335.

Most of Agnes Randolph's life is shrouded in mystery; there is very little mention of her existence until the English army appeared before her castle of Dunbar in January 1338. With the resumption of hostilities between England and Scotland in the 1330s, the castle of Dunbar became strategically important for both sides. The castle had been rebuilt, at the expense of Edward III, in 1333, but by 1337 it was standing against England's king. English affairs in the north lay in the hands of Richard (II) FitzAlan, Earl of Arundel, and William Montague, Earl of Salisbury, and it was these two experienced military leaders who decided to launch an English offensive by attacking Dunbar. An impressive stronghold, the castle was all but impregnable; it was built at the mouth of the Dunbar harbour, on separate rocks, with interlinking bridges and corridors. Strategically, the castle's position made it impossible for the English to march past it and leave it behind them, intact, able to harry the invaders and cut their lines of communication with England. Earl Patrick was away from home at the time, however, Scottish writer Nigel Tranter suggests that Agnes deliberately allowed herself to be besieged to give the Scottish forces time to rally and organise a resistance to the English invasion.[29] Even so, it must have been a terrifying sight for the countess to look out from the battlements and see an army approaching; and the English earls must surely have been confident that they could beat the countess and her reduced garrison. In January 1338, the English laid siege to Dunbar, surrounding it as best they could. The army had brought a legion of engineers with it, thus ensuring that a vast number of siege engines could be constructed and the castle's inhabitants would face an almost constant barrage from missiles. When Salisbury demanded that Agnes surrender, she is said to have responded,

> Of Scotland's King I haud my House,
> He pays me meat and fee,
> And I will keep my gude and house,
> While my house will keep me.[30]

The siege didn't go exactly as the English planned. Agnes mocked them at every opportunity, appearing on the battlements even during bombardments. She is said to have had her maids dusting the battlements where they had been struck by missiles. When a siege engine known as a sow (a battering ram) was brought to face the castle, Agnes is said to have taunted the English by shouting 'Beware, Montagow, for fallow shall they sow.' The Scots would use the displaced rocks, caused by the barrages, and the missiles that had been fired at them, and rain them back down on their enemies. As the sow was destroyed and the English took cover, Agnes is said to have shouted 'Behold the litter of English pigs.'[31] Attack after attack was repulsed by Agnes and her men; a ballad, said to have been written by Salisbury himself, demonstrates Agnes' steadfast attitude:

> She makes a stir in tower and trench,
> That brawling, boisterous, Scottish wench;
> Came I early, came I late,
> I found Agnes at the gate![32]

The English even tried subterfuge to win the castle, bribing one of the castle's guards to raise the gate and allow entry to the English attackers. However, the guard, having taken the money, went straight to Agnes:

> Believing that they were going to be entering the castle, the Earl and his soldiers arrived at the gate. The guards, thinking Salisbury would be first to enter, dropped the gate after the first soldier stepped into the castle. Fortunately for Salisbury, one of his men had passed him on the approach. The thwarted earl retreated back to his camp with Agnes yelling at him from the castle walls: 'Fare thee well Montague, I meant that you should have supped with us and support us in upholding the castle from the English!'[33]

The problem for the English lay in the fact that they could not entirely surround the castle. Although they could besiege it from the land, the castle was still accessible by sea. An English fleet was guarding the harbour, but Sir Alexander Ramsay of Dalhousie managed to replenish the castle's dwindling supplies by using a fleet of fishing boats, approaching in the early dawn from the cover of the Bass Rock. He managed to sneak through the enemy lines, making a dash for the harbour before the larger English vessels could get underway.[34] Ramsay managed to land vital supplies and reinforcements for the garrison through a partially submerged entrance. Agnes even sent the Earl of Salisbury some fresh-baked food when she knew the English supplies were running low, taunting the poor earl. Eventually, Agnes's resistance proved too much for the English army, and, after nineteen weeks, on 10 June 1338, they lifted the siege, claiming their men and resources were needed for the king's campaigns overseas. It had cost over £6,000, prompting one English chronicler to record that the siege had been 'wasteful, and neither honourable nor secure, but useful and advantageous to the Scots'.[35]

The struggle against the English continued for several more years, but David II and his queen, Joan of the Tower, the daughter of Edward II and sister of Edward III, returned to Scotland amid great rejoicing in 1341; only for David to become a captive of Edward III following the Battle of Neville's Cross in 1346. Scotland's king spent eleven years in English captivity, while Scotland was ruled by his nephew and heir, Robert the Steward. David returned in 1357, the same year that Patrick, Earl of Dunbar, participated in the raid that saw Berwick returned to Scottish sovereignty, for a short time at least. Earl Patrick continued to witness royal charters until July 1368 and remained active in Scottish affairs until his death in 1369. When Agnes also died in 1369, her father's earldom and that of her husband passed to her nephew, George Dunbar. With her death, Black Agnes passed into legend, her tenacity and stalwart defence of Dunbar Castle a shining example of what a mere woman can be capable of achieving.

In the following century, however, the actions of a young girl in France would far outshine the achievements of Nicholaa de la Haye and Black Agnes of Dunbar. The triumphs of Joan of Arc were remarkable due not only to the fact she was a simple country girl, but also because she was a teenager. The daughter of a tenant farmer, Joan came from a relatively wealthy peasant family. She grew up in a two-storey stone house, located close to the village church, suggesting the family enjoyed a high social status within their community.[36] She would have been illiterate; education of girls in any class in that era in France was a very low priority. Joan was born around 1412 in Domrémy on the border of Bar and Champagne, making her a subject of the King of France, rather than the Duke of Burgundy. At the time of her birth, France had endured years of intermittent warfare with successive English kings since Edward III attempting to assert their claims to its crown. Civil war between the Armagnac and Burgundian factions at the French court had practically paralysed the country at the turn of the century, making her susceptible to renewed English aggression. Far from being a united country, a great part of France was made up of semi-independent duchies, such as Burgundy and Brittany, whose rulers often sided with the English against their French overlord. In the early 1400s France was ruled by Charles VI, a king with such mental problems that, at times, he thought that he was made of glass. English 'diplomacy' following their great victory at Agincourt in October 1415 had persuaded Charles VI to disinherit his own son, the Dauphin Charles, and name Henry V of England as his heir. In England, Henry V had died in August 1422, leaving his nine-month-old son, Henry VI, as King of England and France (following Charles VI's death in October of the same year).

During Henry VI's minority, France was ruled by John, Duke of Bedford, brother of Henry V, as regent, while French resistance formed around Dauphin Charles, Charles VI's son and heir. In 1419 John the Fearless, Duke of Burgundy, had been assassinated by partisans of the dauphin, ensuring the Burgundians' alliance with England. The Anglo-Burgundian armies occupied much of northern France, including Reims, the traditional place for the coronation of France's kings, thus ensuring that Charles was still not consecrated King of France in 1427, five years after his father's death. Charles, however, was not the most pro-active of military leaders and it took the arrival of Joan of Arc to spur him into some sort of action. Joan's village of Domrémy was on the border of the two opposing factions; its residents had been forced to flee, more than once, when faced with Burgundian aggression. In her early teens, Joan began to experience visions and heard the voices of St Michael the Archangel, St Catherine of Alexander and St Margaret of Antioch.

While we are largely dismissive of such claims in the 21st century, in the early 15th century it was not unknown for maids to claim to be guided by saints and be believed. In a less scientific world, such events were received with far less cynicism. In May 1428, guided by her voices, Joan travelled to Vaucouleurs, the nearest garrison loyal to France and the dauphin, and asked the garrison commander, Robert de Baudricourt, for permission to join the dauphin. Baudricourt did not take her seriously and told Joan to return home. However, she returned to Vaucouleurs just months later, in January 1429. She had gained the respect of the people through her quiet firmness and piety and she finally managed to persuade Baudricourt that she was neither a witch nor feeble-minded. He gave her permission to travel to the dauphin at Chinon, with an escort of six men-at-arms. Joan left Vaucouleurs around 13 February. She had to travel across enemy territory, dressed in men's clothing, and reached Chinon after eleven days.[37]

Once at Chinon Joan immediately went to the castle, hoping for an audience with the dauphin. Charles seems to have been undecided as to whether he should meet Joan; his counsellors gave conflicting advice and it was two days before he granted an audience to the Maid. When he did agree to meet Joan, Charles was not above testing her from the first moment. He hid among his courtiers, hoping to trick the young girl, but she is said to have found him easily amid the crowd. It was at this meeting that Joan told Charles she wanted to go into battle against the English, and that she would see him crowned at Reims. Not surprisingly, Charles was still dubious and, with the fear of heresy never far from people's minds, he insisted she be interrogated by the ecclesiastical authorities. Escorted by Jean, duc d'Alençon, a cousin of Charles who would later prove a strong supporter of Joan, she was examined at the University of Poitiers for three weeks by eminent theologians allied to the dauphin's cause. The written record of the examinations is now lost, however, it seems Joan told her interrogators that proof of her mission would not be given at Poitiers, but at Orléans. The churchmen reported back to Charles with their approval, suggesting that given the desperate situation of Orléans, a city which had been under siege by the English for months, they might as well make use of Joan. In all honesty, they had little to lose. Joan returned to Chinon. By April, she was at Tours. The dauphin provided her with a military household; she was given a number of men, including Jean d'Aulon as her squire, and her own brothers, Jean and Pierre, were in her retinue. Her standard was painted with an image of Christ in Judgement and banner bearing the name of Jesus. When it came to a sword, Joan is said to have declared that it would be found in the Church of Sainte-Catherine-de-Fierbois and, apparently, it was.[38]

Throughout her time at the centre of the French campaign, Joan dictated letters to the English commanders in France. In one such, written in March 1429, at the time of the English siege of Orléans, Joan is confident in her address and demands. Here's an excerpt:

King of England and you, Duke of Bedford, who call yourself Regent of the Kingdom of France; you, William de la Pole, Earl of Suffolk, John, Lord of Talbot [he was, in fact, Earl of Shrewsbury]; and you Thomas, Lord Scales, who call yourselves

Bedford's lieutenants, do right by the King of Heaven. Hand over to the Maiden, who is sent by God the King of Heaven, the keys to all the towns which you have taken and violated in France. She has come here in the name of God to support the Royal Family [of France]. She is quite prepared to make peace, if you are willing to do right so long as you give up France and make amends for occupying it.

And you archers, soldiers both noble and otherwise, who are around the town of Orléans, in God's name go back to your own lands. And if you will not do so, await word of the Maiden, who will go to see you soon to your very great misfortune. King of England, if you do not do so, I am a commander, and wherever I come across your troops in France, I shall make them go, whether willingly or unwillingly, and if they will not obey, I will have them wiped out...

Duke of Bedford, the Maiden asks and requests that you will not cause your own downfall. If you will do right, you could yet come in her company to where the French will do the noblest deed which has ever been done for Christianity. And reply if you wish to make peace in the city of Orléans; and if you do not do so, you will shortly contemplate your great misfortunes.[39]

It is worth taking a moment to remember that Joan was still no older than seventeen when she dictated the letter and had been at the French court for less than two months. Her confidence in addressing the Duke of Bedford in such a way is impressive. On 27 April 1429, the several hundred French troops mustered at Blois set out for Orléans. The city was almost completely surrounded by the English, who had erected a ring of strongholds; it had been under siege since 12 October 1428, and its inhabitants must have been in a desperate situation. Although Joan and one of the French commanders, La Hire, managed to get supplies into the city, she was told that any assault must be postponed until further reinforcements arrived. However, on the evening of 4 May, probably inspired by her saints' voices, Joan announced that she must attack the English. Quickly arming herself, she made her way to an English fort east of the city, only to discover that fighting was already under way. Her presence renewed the vigour of the French attackers and the fort was taken. On the morning of 6 May, Joan and La Hire advanced toward another fort, which the English abandoned for a stronger position close by. Joan and La Hire stormed the English and took their position. Continuing the impetus of their assaults, the French attacked the fort of Les Tourelles early on the morning of 7 May. Joan was taken from the field, wounded, but soon returned to the fighting, an example that encouraged the French commanders to keep up the fight until the English were defeated. The next day, 8 May, the English began their retreat. Joan refused to allow any pursuit as it was Sunday. A city that had been besieged for six months was freed in four days.

On 9 May Joan left Orléans to meet Charles at Tours. She urged him to make haste to Reims for his coronation. Charles was reluctant as the more cautious of his counsellors were advising against such a move. However, although it was decided that they should first clear the English from other towns along the valley of the Loire, Joan's persistence eventually won the dauphin around. Joan and the Duc d'Alençon, now Lieutenant General of the French armies, advanced towards Beaugency, where the English retreated into the castle but eventually surrendered. On 18 June 1429, Joan's army came face to face with the English at Patay. Joan was confident of her troops' success, promising that Charles would win a greater victory than he had so far won. The English were routed; their reputation for invincibility was destroyed with the French achieving an impressive victory. The road was open for Joan's troops to advance on Paris; however, Joan and her commanders withdrew to rejoin the dauphin, staying with his adviser, Georges de Trémoille, at Sully-sur-Loire. Joan impressed upon Charles the need to act quickly, to advance on Reims and stage his coronation. Having listened to his advisers, who counselled delay, the dauphin again prevaricated. He made a slow progress, meandering through the towns of the Loire valley as Joan tried to impress upon him the need to act decisively. Finally, she managed to convince him to overcome the dangers and difficulties involved. The army began to assemble at Gien and it was from there that Charles sent out the traditional letters of summons to the coronation. Joan herself sent two letters at this time; one to the loyal people of Tournai and the other a challenge to the Duke of Burgundy.

The army finally set out on the march to Reims on 29 June 1429. Joan sent messages ahead, to the town of Troyes, promising pardon if it submitted to the dauphin. The town sent a popular preacher,

Brother Richard, to meet and assess her. Despite the good brother's enthusiasm for the Maid of Orléans, the townspeople chose to stay loyal to the Anglo-Burgundian regime. However, when Joan's forces assaulted Troyes the next morning, their resistance was short-lived and the town soon capitulated. When the army then marched on the previously defiant town of Châlons, the town offered no resistance and its Count-Bishop handed the keys of the town to Charles. The royal army finally reached the gates of Reims on 16 July; the city opened its gates to the dauphin, who was finally crowned on the following day. Joan attended the coronation, standing close to the altar, her banner alongside her, her mission accomplished. Following the ceremony, Joan knelt before Charles VII, addressing him as her king for the first time.

Still acting in her military role, on the same day as the coronation, Joan wrote to Philip the Good, Duke of Burgundy, encouraging him to make peace and requesting that he withdraw his garrisons from the royal fortresses. Paris was still in the hands of France's enemies and it was to this city that Joan now directed her focus. For weeks after the coronation, the French army marched through Champagne and the Île France as Joan made plans to attack Paris. On 2 August, however, Charles made the decision to retreat from Provins to the Loire, a move that would have meant abandoning a march on Paris and several loyal towns would have been left to the mercy of the enemy. Three days later Joan wrote to Reims, reassuring them of a two-week truce that had been made with the Duke of Burgundy, and a hope that Burgundy would hand Paris to the French at the end of the truce. English troops prevented the French army from crossing the Seine at Bray on 6 August, but no decisive action seemed imminent. A despatch was sent from the English camp on 7 August:

Letter from John, Duke of Bedford, Regent of France, to Charles de Valois, formerly called *dauphin de Viennois*, and now wrongfully called king, in opposition to the writer's sovereign lord Henry, the true, natural, and legitimate king of France and of England, complaining of his having occupied with his forces towns and castles rightly belonging to the said Henry, and of his deceiving superstitious people by the aid of a dissolute woman disguised as a man, and also of an apostate mendicant friar. He bids Charles to make peace with him, or meet him in battle,

as becomes a Prince. Dated at 'Mortereau ou soure Dyonne,'
7 Aug., A.D. 1429.'[40]

The French army then campaigned throughout the land surrounding
Paris. An engagement on 14 August, between the French and English,
was merely a skirmish. Despite Joan openly challenging the English,
carrying her standard as far as the enemy's earthworks, neither army
was eager to start a battle. The French army, nonetheless, managed
to take many of the surrounding towns, with Compiègne, Beauvais
and Senlis surrendering to the king. On 28 August a four-month
truce, covering all territory north of the River Seine, was agreed
with the Burgundians, meaning Joan could concentrate her efforts
on Paris. On 26 August she and Alençon had reached St Denis, on
the northern outskirts of Paris, as the defenders set about organising
their defences.[41] Charles joined the French army on 7 September
and an attack was finally launched on Paris the following day. The
main assault was concentrated between the gates of Saint-Honoré
and Saint-Denis, with Joan standing forward of the earthworks,
calling for the surrender of the defenders. Although wounded, Joan
continued to encourage her soldiers, but eventually the attack had
to be abandoned and when Joan and Alençon sought to renew
the assault the next day, they were ordered to retreat by Charles'
council. The army withdrew to Gien, where it was disbanded on
22 September, the king retired to the Loire, Joan with him, while
the remainder of his captains went home. While Alençon planned
a campaign in Normandy, Joan travelled with the king. In October,
she and her small army were sent to take the town of Saint-Pierre-
le-Moutier, which they took after a courageous assault. They then
besieged La Chanté-sur-Loire but ran woefully short of munitions.
Appeals to neighbouring towns for supplies were answered too late
and Joan had to abandon the siege after only a month.

With winter drawing in and the campaigning season coming to
a close, Joan rejoined the king, who issued letters patent ennobling
Joan, her parents and her brothers in the last days of December
1429. She was a peasant no longer, and her whole family was given
recognition for the contribution Joan had made to getting Charles
crowned, and to France's extraordinary recovery. However, the
fight was not yet over and in early 1430 the Duke of Burgundy was
once again threatening Brie and Compiègne. Joan sent a letter to
Reims, assuring the worried populace that she would march to their

aid. As the Duke of Burgundy marched towards Compiègne, Joan, her brother Pierre, her squire and a small company of soldiers, set off to intercept him. On arriving at Melun in the middle of April, the town declared for Charles VII, probably encouraged by Joan's presence. By the middle of May she was at Compiègne, where she joined with Renaud de Chartres, Archbishop of Reims, and Charles' cousin Louis I de Bourbon, Count of Vendôme. The combined forces marched to Soissons, but were refused entry. Renaud and Louis decided to withdraw to the south of the rivers Marne and Seine, while Joan decided to stay in the field and return to Compiègne.

During the march, she heard that the city was now under siege from a Burgundian force under John of Luxembourg. Joan entered Compiègne under the cover of darkness on 22 May and the next day led two attacks against the besieging force but was forced to withdraw when she was outflanked by the arrival of English troops, sent to reinforce the Burgundians. Joan stayed with the rearguard as her own forces retreated across the River Oise, but was unhorsed in the action. She had little choice but to surrender, her brother and her squire Jean d'Aulon stayed with her. Joan was taken to Margny where she came face to face with the Duke of Burgundy. Joan and her squire were sent to John of Luxembourg's castle in Vermandois, as her erstwhile allies abandoned her. When Renaud de Chartres informed Reims of her capture, he said she had 'rejected all good counsel and acted wilfully'.[42] Charles VII was trying to negotiate a treaty with the Duke of Burgundy. Keen to do nothing to put the truce in jeopardy, he did nothing to help the girl who had won him his crown.

Following Joan's attempts to escape the castle at Vermandois, desperate to return to Compiègne and aid its citizens, she was moved to a more distant fortress. Another escape attempt saw her jump into the moat from the top of a tower; she was unconscious as she hit the water – but she had suffered no serious injuries and was then moved to Arras, a town loyal to the Duke of Burgundy. When word of Joan's capture reached Paris, the theologians of the University, always on the side of the English, wrote to the Duke of Burgundy and to John of Luxembourg, requesting that she be given into the custody of the Church for judgement, either to the Chief Inquisitor or to the Bishop of Beauvais, in whose diocese she had been captured. On 14 July 1430, the Bishop of Beauvais went before the Duke of Burgundy asking, on behalf of himself and the English king, that Joan be handed over to him and offering a payment of 10,000 francs. This request was passed to John of Luxembourg and by 3 January 1431, Joan was in the Bishop's custody. Joan's active military career had lasted less than eighteen months. From the age of seventeen, this teenage girl had led armies and worked with the greatest men in France at the time. She had successfully relieved Orléans, recovered several towns and cities from English control and managed to get her king crowned in Reims. However, it was only now, still only eighteen, that she was to face her greatest trial – the trial for her life.

As the trial was to take place in Rouen, Joan was held in a tower in the castle of Bouvreuil; the castle was held by the English commander at Rouen, Richard Beauchamp, Earl of Warwick. But Joan was not to be tried for taking up arms against the English; she was to be tried in an ecclesiastical court on heresy charges. Joan's claims that she could communicate directly with saints threatened the established Church. A conviction for heresy, moreover, could discredit Charles VII and severely weaken his hold on the French throne. Joan's two judges were to be Pierre Cauchon, Bishop of Beauvais, and Jean Lemaître, vice-inquisitor of France. The trial began on 13 January 1431 with various statements from Lorraine and elsewhere read before the judges, which would be the outline for Joan's interrogation. Joan herself was brought before her judges on 21 February. She asked to be allowed to attend Mass beforehand, but this was refused due to the gravity of the charges against her – one of which was attempted suicide, referring to the escape attempt when she jumped into the moat. Joan faced her highly educated interrogators with a great deal of courage for one so young and with no formal education. She swore to tell the truth, but always refused to reveal the details of her conversations with Charles VII. When her judges informed her that she was forbidden to leave her prison, Joan insisted that she was morally free to attempt escape. However, such defiance resulted in Joan being chained to a wooden block, sometimes even put in irons, and she was under constant guard, even inside her cell.

Between 21 February and 24 March, Joan was questioned on many occasions; each time she was required to swear to tell the truth and each time she refused to speak of her conversations with her king, saying that although her judges were Frenchmen, they worked for the English and were, therefore, enemies of King Charles VII. When the report of the interrogations was read back to her on 24 March she admitted to its accuracy, save for two points. The full trial began just a few days later, with Joan facing seventy charges; it took two days for her to answer them all. Most of the charges were based on the blasphemy laws, particularly that she claimed her pronouncements had the authority of divine revelation, that she prophesied the future, that she professed to be assured of salvation and, lastly, that she wore men's clothes. One of the most serious charges against her was that she preferred to listen to what she believed were the direct commands from God over those of the Church. As the trial continued Joan was questioned again on 31 March, with the judges concentrating on her obedience to the court as being a test of her submission to the Church. However, she managed to avoid most of their traps, insisting that she knew the Church could not err, but that it was to God and her saints – St Michael the Archangel, Saint Catherine of Alexandria and St Margaret of Antioch – that she was answerable for her words and deeds. Her judges were hoping that she would admit to actions that might discredit and dishonour herself and her king.[43] The seventy charges were eventually reduced to twelve, which were sent to theologians in Rouen and Paris for deliberation.

Not surprisingly, given the stress and the restraints she was under, Joan fell sick in prison and was attended by two doctors. Still no more than nineteen years old, she was desperately ill and thought herself to be dying. When she was visited again by Cauchon and his assistants, on 18 April 1431, they exhorted her to submit to the Church even as she pleaded to be allowed to go to confession and receive Holy Communion and asked to be buried in consecrated ground. As they pressured her to acquiesce, ill as she was, her response remained constant; 'I am relying on our Lord, I hold to what I have already said.'[44] The pressure on Joan to submit was relentless; on 9 May she was threatened with torture if she would not clarify certain points. Her response was that no matter the extent of the torture, her answers would remain the same and that should she answer differently under torture, she would afterwards maintain that it had been extorted by force. Her interrogators thus concluded that torture would prove fruitless.

Joan's story was now drawing to its inevitable, dramatic climax. On 23 May 1431, she was informed of the decision of the learned theologians of the University of Paris – that should she persist in her errors, she would be surrendered to the secular authorities for punishment. The Church could not carry out the death sentence of a condemned heretic, only the secular authorities could do that. The following day, 14 May 1431, Joan was taken to the cemetery at Saint-Ouen, where her sentence was to be passed; it was the first time she had left her prison in four months. She was forced to listen to a sermon by one of the theologians, vehemently criticising Charles VII. Joan interrupted him, saying he had no right to attack the king but should direct his censures at her alone. Once the sermon was ended, Joan asked that all the evidence be sent to the pope in Rome but her judges ignored her appeal and read out the sentence, abandoning her to the secular authorities. The nineteen-year-old girl was sentenced to perpetual imprisonment and ordered to be returned to her cell. On hearing the dreaded pronouncement, Joan declared that she would do everything the Church required of her. She was presented with an instrument of abjuration, which she signed after some hesitation, declaring that she signed on condition that it was 'pleasing to our Lord'.[45] She obeyed an order, by the vice-inquisitor, to dress in women's clothes; however, just two or three days later, when she was visited by the judges, she was dressed in male clothing and insisted that she had done so on her own desire, preferring men's clothes. The declaration encouraged the judges to question Joan further. Upon hearing her declaration that her saints, St Catherine of Alexandria and St Margaret of Antioch, had reproached her 'treason' in signing the abjuration, the judges and thirty-nine assessors unanimously agreed that this was a sign of relapse into heresy and decided on 29 May that she should be handed over to the secular authorities for punishment. Events moved very quickly after that, giving Joan little chance to dwell upon what was to come.

The next morning, Joan was allowed to make confession and receive communion, a concession that was unprecedented for a relapsed heretic. She was then escorted to the *Place du Vieux Marché*, in Rouen, accompanied by two Dominican friars, where she was subjected to another sermon before the sentence, handing her over to punishment by the secular authorities (her enemies, the English) was proclaimed in front of her judges and a vast crowd.

Joan maintained to the last that her voices were sent from God. She was then taken by the executioner, tied to the stake and the pyre lit. One of the Dominican friars did his best to console Joan, she asked him to hold a crucifix high over his head, so that she could see it above the flames, and to shout out assurance of her salvation, loudly so that she could hear above the roar of the fire.

An inquiry into the trial of Joan of Arc, in 1456, heard from those present at her execution, who said that they didn't doubt her salvation and that she died a faithful Christian. The inquiry had been ordered by Pope Calixtus III following appeals from Joan's family. Charles VII had conducted an initial inquiry in 1450, but the pope's hearings went further, revoking and annulling the 1431 sentence; Joan was innocent. However, she would not be canonised until the 20th century – on 16 May 1920 Pope Benedict XV declared her a saint with her feast day on 30 May, the date of her death.[46]

Joan of Arc is the epitome of the medieval heroine. It is incredible to think what she achieved at such a young age, in so short a time period; her story takes up less than three years of French history, and yet it resonates through the ages. Her military career lasted just eighteen months but in that time she took numerous towns and cities, her greatest achievement being the relief of Orléans, which secured the loyalty of much of northern France to the French crown. She revitalised the French army and people, saw her king crowned, almost took Paris and put France on the road that would eventually see it victorious in the Hundred Years War. At a time when boys were trained in warfare from an early age, Joan, with no formal military training, led armies into battle at seventeen; the fact she was wounded on a number of occasions testifies to her presence in the thick of the fighting. With no education, she advised her king on policy and military tactics, and managed to hold her own against the greatest theologians her enemies could bring against her. And yet, she was still a pawn for powerful men in the greater conflict; the English saw her destruction as essential to victory over the French and Charles VII would not lift a finger to help her, for fear it would jeopardise the brokering of peace with the Duke of Burgundy.

Æthelflæd of Mercia, Nicholaa de la Haye and Agnes of Dunbar had been women of status, raised to command households, if not men, who stepped up to the mark when the occasion demanded it. Although they were not educated in military techniques and tactics, they had lived within a world that was constantly on a war footing and when faced with a fight, they rose to the challenge. Joan, on the other hand, was a peasant girl educated in little beyond the life of her village. War didn't seek her out, she sought it. Her saintly voices showed her a way to help France and it was her own tenacity that saw her through, to fight for her king. It is remarkable how much she achieved, and the loyalty she evinced from common soldier and noble alike, in such a short time. Her legend has spanned the centuries and she is still seen as a heroine today – on both sides of the English Channel.

9

Women who Ruled

Very few women in the medieval era were able to take the reins of government. Their role was primarily confined to the domestic sphere, with men taking on the job of governance – whether of lands, as a count or duke, or of a country, as king – because that was seen as their domain. Some women, however, did manage to rule, and to rule efficiently, although not without opposition. Most examples of women who took the reins of power follow the early deaths of their husbands, when they were called upon to rule as regents until their sons were old enough to rule alone.

One such woman was Anne of Kiev, sometimes called Agnes. Born some time between 1024 and 1036, Anne was the daughter of Yaroslav the Wise, Grand-Duke of Kiev, and Ingegerd of Sweden. Yaroslav and Ingegerd had nine children, several of whom had made royal marriages. Of their daughters, Anastasia had married Andrew I of Hungary, and Elizabeth was the wife of Harold of Norway. One son, Isiaslav, was married to the sister of the king of Poland, while another son, Vsevolod, married a daughter of the Byzantine emperor.

In 1051, Anne was to make the most prestigious marriage of all, when she became the second wife of Henry I, King of France. Following the death of his first wife, Matilda of Frisia, during childbirth, and in an attempt to find a wife who was not related to him within the Church's prohibited degrees of kinship, Henry had sent an ambassador to Kiev, laden with gifts, in search of a bride. Anne is said to have been renowned throughout Europe for her 'exquisite beauty, literacy and wisdom'.[1] Anne and Henry were married at the Cathedral of Reims on 19 May 1051; Anne was probably around twenty years old, while Henry was around forty-three. As a demonstration of her superior level of education, Anne signed the marriage contract in her own hand, using her full name, whereas Henry could only manage a cross. At her coronation at Reims, Anne used a Slavic gospel to say her vows, which she had brought with her from Kiev, rather than the traditional Latin Bible. Anne brought no land with her marriage dowry, but she did bring connections and wealth. The jewels she brought with her probably included a jacinth, which Abbot Suger later mounted in a reliquary of St Denis.[2] Although it lasted only nine years, Anne and Henry's marriage appears to have been a great success. The couple had three sons, of whom the oldest, Philip, born in 1052, succeeded his father as Philip I. He was known as Philip 'the Amorous' and reigned for forty-eight years, marrying twice; firstly to Bertha of Holland and secondly to Bertrade de Montfort, having three children – two sons and a daughter – with each wife. Anne and Henry's second son, Robert, born in 1054/5, died young and the youngest, Hugh, born in 1057, became Count of Vermandois on his marriage to Adelaide, Countess of Vermandois. Hugh was vilified for failing to fulfil his Crusader vows by returning home early from the First Crusade, he died, in 1101, of wounds received in battle with the Turks after returning to the Holy Land.

Anne appears to have thought of France as provincial compared to her homeland of Kiev; she wrote to her father in 1050 saying, 'What a barbarous country you sent me to – the dwellings are sombre, the churches horrendous and the morals – terrible'.[3] Anne, however, appears to have made an effort to settle into her adopted country, she learned the language and participated, to some extent, in government; she and Henry worked in partnership as king and queen. Several decrees include the phrase 'With the consent of my wife Anna' or 'In the presence of Queen Anna'.[4] Towards the end of Henry's reign, Anne was counter-signatory to at least four charters, including a 1058 charter of concession to the monastery of St Maur-les-Fosses, signed 'including my wife Anna and sons Philip, Robert and Hugh' and a donation to the monastery at Hasnon, which was signed by King Henry, Prince Philip and Queen Anne.[5]

The situation changed in 1060 when King Henry died. With Anne's son Philip then only seven years old, a regency was set up with Baldwin V of Flanders, husband of King Henry's sister Adele, given the post of regent. However, at the time, the Bishop of Chartres described Philip and his mother Anne as his sovereigns; moreover, Philip himself declared that, as a child, he ruled the kingdom jointly with his mother. The young king valued his mother's advice and Anne signed numerous royal acts during her son's reign; her signature was always either the first signature on the document or the second after that of King Philip. The acts included donations to monasteries, the renunciation of customs grants of exemptions and a charter to the Abbot of Marmoutier to build a church. In all, there are at least twenty-three acts that mentioned Anne, or carried her signature, between 1060 and 1075.[6]

Anne was held in high regard by many. Among her admirers was Pope Nicholas II himself, who wrote to her with high praise;

> Nicholas, Bishop, servant of the servants of God, to the glorious queen, greeting and apostolic benediction. We give proper thanks to almighty God, the author of good will, because we have heard that the virile strength of virtues lives in a womanly breast. Indeed it has come to our ears, most distinguished daughter, that your serenity overflows with the munificence of pious generosity for the poor, sweats forth with the zeal of most devoted prayer, administers the force of punishment on behalf of those who are violently oppressed, and fulfills with other good works, insofar as it belongs to you, the office of royal dignity...[7]

In 1061 Anne was involved in a scandal in France when she married Raoul, Count of Crepy and Valois, in what appears to have been a love-match. Raoul was an ally of the young king, but was already married to Eleanor of Champagne. The count had repudiated Eleanor, on the grounds of adultery, in order to marry Queen Anne. However, Eleanor appealed to the pope, Alexander II, who ordered the Archbishop of Reims to investigate the matter. Raoul was ordered to take Eleanor back, and was excommunicated when he refused; he and Anne left court as a result of the furore. However, Raoul and Anne were both important allies of the king, and continued advising Philip and acting as signatories to his royal acts, despite being exiled from the court. The king eventually forgave his mother and she was welcomed back to court following Raoul's death in 1074. Her return to her family was probably

Conisbrough Castle, South Yorkshire, built by Hamelin and Isabel de Warenne in the late twelfth century. (Author's collection)

Sandal Castle, Wakefield, also owned by Hamelin and Isabel de Warenne. Conisbrough and Sandal also feature in the life of Joan of Bar and came under attack from Thomas, Earl of Lancaster, following John de Warenne's abduction of Thomas's wife, Alice de Lacey. (Author's collection)

The remains of Bolingbroke Castle, Lincolnshire, birthplace of Blanche of Lancaster's only surviving son, Henry IV. (Author's collection)

Pontefract Castle. The staircase leading up to the keep. Part of the inheritance of Alice de Lacey. It was at Pontefract that Alice's husband, Thomas, earl of Lancaster, was executed following his defeat at the Battle of Boroughbridge. (Author's collection)

Kettlethorpe, Lincolnshire, home to Katherine Swynford and her first husband, Sir Hugh Swynford. (Author's collection)

Church of St Peter & St Paul, Kettlethorpe, Lincolnshire. (Author's collection)

Re-erected fourteenth century Gate House, the only surviving piece of Katherine Swynford's home, Kettlethorpe Manor. (Author's collection)

All that remains of Barlings Abbey, Lincolnshire, final resting place of Alice de Lacey and her second husband, Eubolo LeStrange. (Author's collection)

Jedburgh Abbey Scotland, scene of the wedding of Yolande de Dreux and Alexander III of Scotland. The death of Alexander, four months later, and Yolande's failure to produce a living child, led to the accession of Margaret, the Maid of Norway. (Author's collection)

Jacqueline d'Hainault, also known as Jacoba of Bavaria, countess of Holland and Zeeland, duchess of Gloucester. Painted by Pieter Willem Sebes, 1879. (Courtesy of the Rijksmuseum)

The wedding of Jacoba of Bavaria (Jacqueline d'Hainault), Countess of Holland, and Jan IV, Duke of Brabant, 10 March 1418. Painted by Jacob Joseph Eeckhout, 1839. (Courtesy of the Rijksmuseum)

The Tower of London, where Joan, the Fair Maid of Kent, sought refuge during the Peasants Revolt, and Joan of Bar was given apartments during the breakdown of her marriage with John de Warenne, earl of Surrey. (Courtesy of Karen Mercer, Bexlin Photography)

The gatehouse to Canterbury Cathedral, where Isabella of Gloucester, first wife of King John, was buried in 1217. (Author's collection)

Windsor Castle, royal residence and prison. It was at Windsor that Eleanor de Montfort was confined before she was allowed to marry Llywelyn, prince of Wales. Windsor is also a possible location for the dungeon in which Maud de Braose and her son were starved to death. And it was where James I of Scotland first fell in love with Joana Beaufort. (Author's collection)

York Minster, where King John's daughter, Joan, married Alexander II, king of Scots. (Author's collection)

Memorial to Gwenllian, princess of Wales, at Sempringham, Lincolnshire. (Author's collection)

St Andrew's Church, Sempringham, probably stands on or near the site of the Gilbertine Priory. (Author's collection)

Church of All Saints, Sixhills. It was at the Gilbertine monastery at Sixhills that Christian Bruce was held during her imprisonment by Edward I. (Author's collection)

The walls of Berwick. It was in the castle at Berwick that Isabel MacDuff, countess of Buchan, was imprisoned in a purpose-built cage. (Author's collection)

Melrose Abbey, where Robert the Bruce's heart is buried. (Author's collection)

Lincoln Cathedral. Katherine Swynford is buried in the south side of the Angel Choir. The French commander, the Count of Perche was killed in front of the Cathedral doors, during the Battle of Lincoln, known as the Lincoln Fair, in 1217. (Author's collection)

The West, or postern gate, of Lincoln Castle. Lincoln Castle was in the possession of the formidable Nicholaa de la Haye at the time of the 1217 Battle of Lincoln. (Author's collection)

St Michael's Church, Swaton, final resting place of Nicholaa de la Haye. (Author's collection)

The gatehouse of Cawood Castle, where Margery Kempe was questioned by the Archbishop of York. (Author's collection)

Beaumaris Castle, final prison of Eleanor Cobham, Duchess of Gloucester. (Courtesy of Tina Walker)

Joan of Arc by Arnoud Schaepkens, after Theodor Scaepkens, 1831-1904. (Courtesy of the Rijksmuseum)

La Tour Jeanne d'Arc, Rouen, France, supposedly the tower in which Joan was questioned by her interrogators, before her execution. (Courtesy of Kristie Dean)

Hildegard of Bingen, Romeyn de Hooghe, 1701. (Courtesy of the Rijksmuseum)

Fair Rosamund and Queen Eleanor, by Edward Burne-Jones, 1833-1898, (Courtesy of the Paul Mellon Fund, Yale Centre for British Art)

Skipton Castle, family home of Maud Clifford, Countess of Cambridge. (Author's collection)

Roche Abbey, final resting place of Maud Clifford, Countess of Cambridge. (Author's collection)

Church of St Mary the Virgin, Ewelme, final resting place of Alice Chaucer, duchess of Suffolk. (Courtesy of Kristie Dean)

One of the most famous and formidable women of the medieval era was Eleanor of Aquitaine. Pictured is her tomb at Fontevrault Abbey. (Courtesy of g0ng00zlr)

short-lived, however, as it seems likely that Anne died in 1075, although the exact date of her death, and her final resting place, are lost to the thousand years that have passed since then.

However, Anne left a mark on history in the remarkably high regard in which both her husband, Henry I, and her son Philip held her. She was a well-educated, pious woman whose advice and opinions were respected, not only within her family, but by such exalted persons as the pope and French bishops. She proved that a woman could act wisely, at least in politics, if not in her second marriage, at a time when women were not expected, or allowed, to rule. The nature of her rule appears to have been a gentle hand on the shoulder of her son, whereas other women were more forceful as rulers – such as Adela, the daughter of William the Conqueror, King of England, and Matilda of Flanders.

Although most sources give Adela's date of birth around 1061 or 1062, recent research argues that she was born after the Norman Conquest, as a contemporary poet, Godfrey of Reims, suggests she was born as the daughter of a king, with the lines; 'The royal virgin obtained by fate that her father would be king. In order for Adela to be the daughter of a king, the Fates allowed the father to establish himself as king'.[8] Adela was one of nine or ten children born to William and Matilda, with at least four sisters and four brothers. Given her high level of literacy, and her patronage of poets in adulthood, it is likely that Adela was very well-educated as a child – either through tutors or possibly through residence in a convent, as were many daughters of the nobility at that time. As a child, it seems, a marriage was arranged for Adela and Simon Crispin, Count of Amiens; however, when Crispin chose to take monastic vows rather than marry, another groom had to be found. As part of an alliance directed against the aggressive counts of Anjou, Adela was then betrothed to Stephen of Blois, son of Theobald III, Count of Blois and Champagne. Stephen was about twenty years her senior. The formal betrothal took place at Bourgueil and was later followed by a lavish wedding ceremony in Chartres Cathedral in 1081 or 1082, although it may have been a few years later, as the first charter in which Adela appears is 1085.[9] Poetry from the time of her wedding describes Adela as valorous, learned and generous. The Archbishop of Dol praised her 'beauty, dignity and grace', saying she had 'the brilliance of a goddess'.[10]

Adela and Stephen would have about eleven children in all, with at least two sons born before Stephen succeeded his father as Count of Blois and Champagne in 1090. Adela paid particular attention to their education, ensuring all her children were well versed in their studies. Adela and Stephen's eldest son, Humbert, Count of Virtus, died young and their second son, William, survived into adulthood but appears to have been disinherited at an early age. William, described as an 'idiot' by some, was married to Agnes, the daughter of Giles, Lord of Sulli, and was given the titles Count of Chartres and Lord of Sulli, but he was not allowed to inherit the richer County of Blois, which went to his younger brother, Theobald. Theobald, who was knighted in 1107, became Count of Blois and Champagne, and married Matilda, the daughter of Ingelbert II, Duke of Carinthia. Stephen, named after his father, was born around 1096/7 and was created Count of Mortain sometime before 1115; he became Count of Boulogne in right of his wife, Matilda of Boulogne, before 1125.

On the death of Henry I of England, Stephen claimed the throne ahead of his cousin, Matilda. He was crowned at Westminster Abbey on 26 December 1135; his actions plunging England into a civil war that last almost twenty years, known as The Anarchy. Stephen and Adela's youngest son, Henry, was born around 1099 in Winchester, England. He was given to the priory at Cluny, in France, as a child and had a highly successful career in the Church. He later transferred to Bermondsey Abbey, just outside London, where he eventually became abbot, before being elected abbot of the prestigious abbey at Glastonbury, Somerset, in 1126. He was consecrated Bishop of Winchester on 17 November 1129; he died in August 1171, and was buried in Winchester Cathedral. He was a great support to his older brother, Stephen, when he claimed the throne of England on his uncle Henry's death in 1135.

Of Adela and Stephen's five daughters, Matilda married Richard d'Avranches, 2nd Earl of Chester. The couple drowned in the disaster of the White Ship, in 1120; a tragedy that also deprived Henry I of England of his only son and heir, William the Ætheling. Another daughter, Eleanor, married Raoul, Count of Vermandois and died in 1147. Of three other daughters Agnes married Hugh III de Puisset, Alice married Reginald III, Count of Joigni, and Adela (or Lithuise) married Miles de Brai, Viscount of Troyes and Lord of Montlheri, but the marriage was later annulled.

Adela was a lot like her mother, not only in character and appearance, but also in her political acumen. She seems to have been a great asset to her husband, who included her in charitable donations and even in his early judicial rulings. She developed a cordial relationship with Bishop Ivo of Chartres, which worked well to maintain the peace between the laity and the clergy in the county. Malmesbury said she was 'a powerful woman with a reputation for her worldly influence'.[11] In 1095, when Stephen of Blois took the cross and became one of the leaders of the First Crusade, Adela was left as head of the family and regent of his domains. Letters the count sent home to his wife indicate a great degree of affection and trust; Adela was given charge of the family's finances as well as their lands. However, Stephen's return from Crusade appears of have been less than happy. Stephen arrived home while the Siege of Antioch was still in progress, and before he had fulfilled his vow to reach Jerusalem. Adela was highly critical that he had not satisfied his Crusader's vow and her reproach may have been a contributing factor in his return to the Holy Land in 1101 – she certainly encouraged him to return. Stephen was killed in combat in the Holy Land, during the Siege of Ramallah, in May 1102. He was succeeded as Count of Blois by his second surviving son, Theobald. Theobald was knighted in 1107, by which time his older brother, William, had already been removed from the succession to the county. William inherited the lesser title of Count of Chartres. Following Stephen's death, Adela continued to act as regent until Theobald attained his majority. Even after Theobald came of age, mother and son ruled jointly until Adela retired from public life in 1120. Adela was particularly close to her younger brother, Henry, who became King Henry I of England in 1100. She even supported him against their oldest brother, Robert, when Henry claimed the English crown.

An able administrator and negotiator, Adela settled many disputes among monasteries, and even between monasteries and laymen, in her own domains and beyond. Anselm, Archbishop of Canterbury during the reign of William II and Henry I, praised her skills as negotiator and peacemaker following her success at achieving a temporary truce between Anselm and her brother in 1105. Anselm described her as an ardent supporter of papal reform, and enjoyed her hospitality during his exile from England.[12] Adela hosted many other Church dignitaries, including Archbishop Thurstan of York and Pope Paschal II. Her family's prestige and power was bolstered by her friendships with the leading ecclesiastic figures, both in France and England. An avid patroness of the arts, Adela corresponded with such dignitaries as Hildebert, Bishop of Le Mans and Abbot Baudri of Bourgeuil – later Bishop of Dol – who both wrote poems dedicated to the countess. The book *Ecclesiastical History Together with the Deeds of the Romans and the Franks*, written by Hugh of Fleury, was dedicated to Adela.[13]

An active ruler, Adela regularly toured the family's domains – both as regent and mother of the reigning count. She also maintained links with the Anglo-Norman and Capetian kings. In 1101 Adela sent knights to help Philip I of France's son, Louis, battling against rebels north of Paris. However, by 1107 her son Theobald had joined the revolt and relations with France were to deteriorate further in 1113 when the allied forces of Theobald, Henry I and Adela defeated a Capetian-Angevin army. After further conflict in 1118, Adela used her wealth and diplomatic skills to benefit her family. Theobald's two sons, Henry and Theobald, would later marry Marie and Alice, the two daughters of Louis VII of France by his first wife, Eleanor of Aquitaine; while Theobald's daughter, Adela, as Louis VII's third wife, would be the mother of Louis' long-desired son and heir, Philip II Augustus.

In 1120 Adela stopped using the title of countess and retired to the Cluniac Priory of Marcigny; the same year that her daughter Matilda died in the White Ship disaster off Barfleur in Normandy. Adela continued to be active in political affairs and lived to see her son, Stephen, claim the throne of England, in 1135, although she did not witness the twenty years of conflict that ensued. Aged almost seventy, and having been a widow for half her life, this most remarkable woman, Adela of Normandy, former Countess of Blois and Chartres, died in 1137, possibly on 8 March. Although later tradition has her buried with her mother at Holy Trinity in Caen, contemporary sources say she was buried at Marcigny.

Adela had proved herself to be an able ruler of her husband's lands, both before and after his death. Her diligence and hard-working nature saw the county through conflict with France and the minority of her son, Theobald. She was a shining example of what a woman could achieve if she was allowed to rule. However, as with Anne of Kiev, she had only been allowed to rule as regent. Women in medieval Europe were rarely rulers in their own right. One of the few examples can be found in Poland, where Jadwiga ruled as a female king, because they had no word for a ruling queen.

King Jadwiga, or Hedwig in Hungarian and German, was born in 1073 or 1074, in Krakow, Poland. She was the daughter of Louis I, King of Hungary and Poland, and his wife, Elizabeth of Bosnia. Jadwiga spent a lot her childhood in Hungary but when her father died in 1382 her older sister, Maria, inherited the crowns. However, Maria was married to Sigismund, Duke of Brandenburg and brother of Wenceslas, the Holy Roman Emperor. Sigismund was entirely too German for Polish tastes and they decided to end the hated union of the two crowns, by electing nine-year-old Jadwiga as their new ruler. She was crowned *Rex Poloniae*, King of Poland – rather than queen, to make it clear that she was monarch in her own right – at Krakow's Wawel Cathedral on 15 October 1384.

At the time of her coronation, Jadwiga was intended to marry her own German prince, Wilhelm Habsburg, however, the Polish nobles and clergy managed to persuade Jadwiga that this marriage wasn't in the best interests of her people, nor of the pagans in Lithuania whom she could bring into the comfort of the Church if she married the groom suggested by her lords. Although she seemed quite fond of Wilhelm, Jadwiga gave him up and married the husband chosen for her; Jogaila, or Władysław II Jagiełło in Polish, the Grand Duke of Lithuania. It was hoped that such a union would counteract the threat posed to both Poland and Lithuania by the Teutonic Knights, who were based in Prussia. Lithuania then comprised most of Ukraine and Belarus so the marriage would therefore increase the prestige and territory of the little kingdom of Poland after its recent split from Hungary. As for Lithuania, the marriage also promised the prospect of the conversion of its people, most of whom were pagans, to Christianity. The fact the union would open vast areas in the east, for both trade and settlement, was also an attractive proposition.

The Union of Krewo finalised the details of the marriage in 1385, with Jagiełło accepting Roman Catholicism for himself and his people. The pope, Urban IV, encouraged the union and the proposed Christianisation of Lithuania. Jagiełło was, in fact, baptised at Wawel Cathedral in Krakow on 15 February, 1386, with most of his brothers and his cousin, Vytautas, who was also his main rival for power back home in Lithuania.

The Archbishop of Gniezno presided over the baptisms and also officiated at the wedding, of Jadwiga and Jagiełło, which took place just days later, on 18 February 1386. Jagiełło was then crowned in a ceremony on 4 March of that year. Although Jadwiga and Jagiełło ruled jointly, Jadwiga remained the leading personality in the realm.

Jagiełło was an adept politician, capable of great cunning and diplomatic duplicity when needed. He was quiet and introspective, drank no alcohol and ate sparingly. By no means a king of great sophistication, he had no enthusiasm for music or the arts. He did, however, have a passion for hunting. Soon after the marriage, he led a force into Lithuania, accompanied by priests, to start his country's conversion to Christianity. A Polish Franciscan was named as Bishop of Vilnius and ordered the construction of a new cathedral in the city. Franciscans were the preferred order for handling pagans because they were experienced and renowned for their tolerance of non-Christians. By the end of 1387, Jagiełło had also extended Polish control over Moldavia and Wallachia, taking advantage of Sigismund of Hungary's attention being elsewhere; the pope eventually intervened to prevent war between the two countries.

Young Jadwiga was quite the opposite. She was happy to let her husband spend as many days hunting as he wished; she was a pious, devout Christian whose greatest pleasures were church services and good works. She appears to have shied away from court entertainments, and only fulfilled her duties as a wife when necessary.[14] Jadwiga could speak German, Hungarian, Latin, Polish and Serbian; although she could not speak Lithuanian, and her husband's Polish was rudimentary in the early years of their marriage. A patron of the arts, religion and scholarship, Jadwiga founded a college for Lithuanians in Prague, funded a restoration project at the university at Krakow, remodelling the university on that of Paris and making it a centre of Polish civilisation. It was later named the Jagiellonian University in her honour.

Jadwiga played an active role in politics and although her husband led most of the military expeditions, dealing with conflict in Lithuania, Jadwiga herself led two military forays in 1387 when she succeeded in reclaiming Red Ruthenia from Hungary. She was also a good friend of the Grand Master of the Teutonic Knights and acted as mediator between the Prussian Crusaders and her husband over the Knights' occupation of parts of Samogitia, a Lithuanian province. By 1400, however, the Crusade was over and considered a success, with most Lithuanians now converted to Christianity and peace established between Jagiełło and the Teutonic order, allowing them to turn their attentions to the Tatar threat coming out of the Russian steppes.[16]

Three miracles are associated with Jadwiga. The first was that Christ was said to have spoken to her from a crucifix in Wawel Cathedral; the crucifix remains within the cathedral to this day. The second miracle was that of 'Jadwiga's footprint'; while visiting the construction site of the Church of the Visitation of the Blessed Virgin Mary, Jadwiga gave a piece of jewellery to one of the poor workers. After her departure, the stonemason noticed her footprint embedded in plaster that had long-since dried. The third miracle was the most remarkable; she is said to have resurrected a child who had drowned in the River Wisła, in Krakow; he was revived after she covered his body with her own cloak.[15]

Jadwiga's reign lasted almost fifteen years. She died in childbirth on 17 July 1399 when she was no more than twenty-six years old; her baby Elizabeth Bonifacia died a few days earlier. Jadwiga was buried in Wawel cathedral in Krakow, where her relics are buried beneath the crucifix from which Christ spoke to her. She was canonised as a saint by Pope John Paul II on 8 June 1997. Jagiełło continued to rule alone, as king, marrying a further three times, with four children surviving to adulthood. On his death on 1 June 1434, he was succeeded by his son by his fourth and last wife, Sophia of Halshany, who reigned as Władysław III.

Jadwiga of Poland had been every inch a king. She had played an active role in the politics and culture of Poland and is one of their most celebrated monarchs. Poland has to be admired for allowing a woman to truly govern in her own right. The rest of Europe was not so forward-thinking and the best chance for a woman to rule remained as regent for her son, although even this was rarely without difficulty. Catherine of Lancaster, as Queen of Castile, was one such regent.

Catherine had illustrious parentage. She was the daughter of John of Gaunt, Duke of Lancaster and the third surviving son of Edward III of England, and his second wife, Constance of Castile. Constance's father, Pedro the Cruel, King of Castile, had been at war with his illegitimate half-brother, Henry of Trastámara, who eventually gained the advantage and murdered Pedro with his own hands in 1369. Catherine's parents had married in 1371, after John had brought Constance and her younger sister, Isabella, to England to escape the civil war; Isabella would later marry John's brother, Edmund of Langley. The marriage of Constance and John of Gaunt was not a love-match, but one that John hoped would gain him a crown. With her father's death, Constance had inherited his claim to the throne of Castile, a throne which was now in the hands of her uncle, Henry of Trastámara, and John hoped to claim this crown in his wife's name.

Catherine, or Catalina in Castilian, was probably born in 1372, at Hertford Castle, the year after her parents' wedding, and certainly no later than the spring of 1373. As Catherine was to be Constance's only living child – it is possible that she later gave birth to a boy, John, who did not survive long – she would eventually inherit her mother's claim to Castile. She had two older half-sisters, Philippa was twelve and Elizabeth was eight years old, and a half-brother, Henry – the future Henry IV – who was only about five years older than Catherine, from her father's first marriage to Blanche of Lancaster. She would also have younger half-siblings from her father's long-running affair with Katherine Swynford. Although their birth dates are uncertain, it seems likely that the eldest, John Beaufort, was born a year after Catherine. He was followed by two more brothers, Henry and Thomas, and a sister, Joan.

With her sisters almost grown up, little Catherine was not raised in their household, but given her own. Between 1380 and 1382 she was in the custody of the widowed Joan Burghersh, Lady Mohun, a kinswoman of her father. By 1381, she was being referred to as *Katerine d'Espaigne*, perhaps to suggest that her future lay in Spain, or to emphasise her father's aims in the Iberian Peninsula.[17] Given the careful education that her older sisters received, it is safe to assume that Catherine was also educated to a high standard – with languages, poetry, dancing and deportment, included in her syllabus.

The affair between Katherine Swynford and John of Gaunt came to an end, at least for a time, in 1381. The vehemence of the populace's hatred for John of Gaunt during the Peasants' Revolt caused him to repudiate Katherine and she retired to Lincoln, living in a house close to the cathedral. John asked his wife for her forgiveness and relations between the couple were more cordial after that. John needed Constance's forgiveness because he needed her co-operation in his forthcoming expedition to Spain.

After years of planning and false starts, by 1385 John of Gaunt was now ready to claim his wife's patrimony. He had been using the title King of Castile and Leon since his marriage, but it was more an honorific than a reality. Henry II, of Trastámara, the man who had killed Constance's father, had died in 1379 and his son, John I, was now King of Castile and Leon. In August 1385, Portugal had beaten Spain at the battle of Aljubarrota and another John, or João, was confirmed as John I, King of Portugal. John of Gaunt had been recognised as the legitimate ruler of Castile and Leon by Pope Urban VI and now John of Portugal offered the English prince an alliance to launch a military expedition against Castile.

On 9 July 1386, the English force of ninety ships and thousands of men left Plymouth harbour and set sail for Spain. They were led by John of Gaunt, who was accompanied not only by his wife Constance, but also his daughters Philippa and Elizabeth, and Catherine, now thirteen years old. The force arrived at Corunna on 25 July and remained there a month before heading south to Santiago de Compostela, where Gaunt was immediately recognised as king. He and his family settled in Ourense, where they established a court for the winter of 1386/7 and Gaunt received the homage of the local, friendly Galician nobles. Gaunt then met with John I of Portugal to finalise the details of the invasion of Spain. The plans also included a more permanent union with Portugal, by way of a marriage. Although Catherine was initially suggested as the bride for King John, it was decided that Philippa would be more suitable, given the hostility, within Portugal, to all things Castilian, as Catherine had Castilian blood.[18]

Philippa married John of Portugal on 2 February 1387, but there was no honeymoon; her husband left on campaign almost immediately. In March 1387 the combined English and Portuguese forces crossed the River Douro to engage with the forces of John I of Castile. Catherine, her mother and her sister Elizabeth accompanied the army. The campaign was a disaster; according to Froissart, 'they found the country all laid waste and the English suffered much from the climate'.[19] The troops soon succumbed to sickness, which crippled the army, and John of Gaunt and John of Portugal were quarrelling. In the end the only option was to come to terms with Castile.

The Treaty of Bayonne was concluded in 1388, John of Gaunt and Constance renounced their claims to Castile and agreed to return their Galician conquests in return for an initial payment of 600,000 gold francs plus an annual payment of 40,000 francs. It was also agreed that Catherine, now fifteen, would marry John I of Castile's nine-year-old son, Henry. The treaty meant that although Castile was lost to Gaunt and Constance, Catherine would eventually become Queen Consort of her mother's homeland. It also gave legitimacy to the usurping House of Trastámara, uniting the legitimate and illegitimate descendants of Alfonso XI of Castile and reuniting the royal lines.

Catherine and young Henry were married on 17 September 1388, in Palencia Cathedral; they were the first to receive the title Prince and Princess of Asturias, the title now borne by the heir to the throne of Spain. The towns of Ateinza, Deza, Molina, Soria and Almazàn were provided for Catherine's dower. Henry succeeded to the throne just two years later, in 1390, as King Henry III after his father was killed in a riding accident. Catherine was visited by her mother in October of that year, when Constance took the opportunity to have her own father's remains reburied among his ancestors. It was probably the last time Catherine saw her mother, who died at Leicester Castle in March 1394. Her father spent 1395 in France, looking after his interests as Duke of Aquitaine, so it is possible that Gaunt visited Catherine; however, it would have been one of the last times as when he returned to England, as a widower, he married his mistress, Katherine Swynford, in January 1396, and died in February 1399.

Henry's early reign proved to be an unsettled period; with the young king still a minor and in need of a regency, the encircling nobles caused chaos in their attempts to increase their own areas of influence. His personal rule, however, began in 1393 when, still only fourteen years old, he was declared of age. He immediately set about pacifying the nobles and restoring royal power. During his reign, he also reorganised the kingdom's economy, started the colonisation of the Canary Islands, and prevented another invasion by the Portuguese – a truce was signed in 1402.

Henry and Catherine seem to have had a harmonious marriage and they had three children. A daughter, Maria, was born in 1401; she married Alfonso V 'the Magnanimous', King of Aragon and Naples, and died childless in 1458. A second daughter, Catherine, was born sometime between 1403 and 1406. She married Henry of Aragon, Count of Albuquerque and Ampurias, and died in 1439. Their son and heir, John, was born in 1405. Catherine and Henry were married for eighteen years, with Catherine devoting herself to religious patronage and good works while her husband ruled. However, all this changed in 1406 when Henry died at the age of twenty-seven, while campaigning in Granada.

Catherine was left widowed at the age of thirty-three, with three young children to raise. Her youngest, John, was not yet two years old and was now King John II of Castile and Leon. Henry obviously trusted Catherine as the terms of his will made her joint regent for her son, with Henry's brother, the Infante Ferdinand. It must have been a blow for Catherine, however, when custody of the young king was to be entrusted to two nobles, Diego López de Stúniga and Juan Fernández de Velasco. Unwilling to relinquish her baby son into anyone else's custody, Catherine retreated to the Castle of the Alcázar of Segovia and prepared to defend herself and her family. Ferdinand, however, brokered a deal which allowed the little king to remain with his mother.

Despite this initial entente between the two regents, they agreed on very little. Distrust built up, especially over Ferdinand's plans to lead the campaign into Granada that had been started by Henry II. Their constant differences of opinion led to a division of rule. The royal council divided the territories, with Catherine getting control of the northern kingdoms of Castile and Leon. However, further bickering between the two regents was caused by Catherine's favouritism of Velasco and Stúniga, and in 1409 Ferdinand succeeded in obtaining their expulsion from court. Catherine then co-operated more with Ferdinand and agreed to help fund his campaign in Granada. Her favouritism of particular people was a recurring problem, and as a result, she was twice forced to banish ladies from her household.

Through her family connections, Catherine was able to foster friendlier relationships with both England and Portugal. She was on good terms with her cousin, Richard II, and with his successor, her half-brother, Henry IV, in England, and with her sister, Philippa, who was Queen Consort of Portugal. Although there was no formal peace treaty with England, trade between the two countries prospered. Indeed, Catherine's international policies boosted the prosperity of many Castilian communities, despite the drain caused by Ferdinand's warring. She also helped to end the Western Schism, when the papacy was split between two popes, one in Rome and one in Avignon, by recognising Martin V as pope. Ferdinand gained the throne of Aragon in 1412, but died in 1416. The death of her co-regent meant that Catherine's authority and influence diminished, as those who had supported her because they were enemies of Ferdinand, no longer saw the necessity to do so.

The country's rule was coming increasingly under the control of a regency council, especially after Catherine suffered a stroke. She surrendered the custody of her son, who was now approaching twelve years of age. Catherine's final years appear to have been greatly restricted by ill health. In addition to the stroke, she had also gained a lot of weight and developed gout. Fernán Pérez de Guzmán gave us a description of the queen, her appearance and character, towards the end of her life:

> The Queen was tall of body and very fat. She was pink and white in her complexion and fair. In her figure and her movements she seemed as much like a man as a woman. She was very virtuous and reserved in her person and in her reputation; generous and magnificent in her ways but very much devoted to favourites and greatly ruled by them – a thing, which, in general, is a vice common to royal personages. She was not very well ordered in her body and had a serious affliction of the palsy which did not leave her tongue properly loose or her bodily movements free.[20]

Although Catherine did have flaws in her adherence to her favourites, she was a successful regent. Her constant desire to pass on a stable country to her son, and to see her son safely attain his majority, helped to shape domestic and foreign policy – with great success. John II started his personal rule in 1418 and married his first wife, Maria of Aragon, in the same year. Of their four children, only John's eventual successor, Henry, survived infancy. Following Maria's death, John married Isabella of Portugal, granddaughter of his mother's half-sister, Philippa. John and Isabella were, in turn, the parents of Isabella of Castile, the mother of Henry VIII's first wife, Catherine of Aragon.

Catherine of Lancaster, Queen and Regent of Castile, died after another stroke, at Valladolid, on 2 June 1418. She was forty-five years old and was buried with her husband in the Capilla de los

Reyes Nuevos in the Cathedral at Toledo. Her effigy can still be seen there. Catherine had steered Castile through difficult times; when war between the various Spanish nations was almost constant, she had used her family connections to foster trade and friendship. She was a woman who had held considerable power and, for the most part, used it wisely. She was not the only woman who had shown great political intelligence and aptitude when it came to ruling, however; Anne de France, also known as Anne de Beaujeu, was regent of France during the minority of her younger brother, Charles VIII.

Anne was the third child born to her father, Louis XI of France, and his second wife, Charlotte of Savoy, but she was the first to survive infancy. She was born at Genappe, near Brussels, in April 1461. At the time of her birth her father was still dauphin of France. However, just a few months later, Anne's grandfather, Charles VII, the man who had attained the crown thanks to the efforts of Joan of Arc, died. The unfortunate king had had a fractious relationship with his son and heir, Louis; they did not see each other for the last fifteen years of Charles VII's life. Louis plotted intrigue with his neighbours and had even raised an army against his father in 1455, following arguments over Louis' marriage to Charlotte. He eventually fled to Burgundy with his wife after his father threatened to invade his lands in the dauphiné. He refused to return to France, despite being told that his father was dying; Louis waited at the French border for news that he was king. Charles VII died of starvation on 22 July 1461, after a tumour in his jaw prevented him from eating, and Louis immediately returned to France for his coronation.

Louis XI was thirty-eight years old when he became king; he was not a likable man but possessed a keen intelligence and few scruples. His main political aim was to expand his kingdom, using whatever methods would achieve this. He was pious and cultivated, in contrast to the ostentation and debauchery of his predecessors. His web of political intrigues often got him into international hot water, such as the adventure of Péronnne in 1468, when Louis incited the people of Liège to revolt against the Duke of Burgundy. Under the pretext of negotiation, Louis was arrested by the Duke and forced to offer him financial aid.[22] However, these initial setbacks did not last. Louis was a wily diplomat, at home and abroad. He managed to extend French territory by acquiring the French duchy of Burgundy, Picardy, Anjou, Maine and Provence. Louis relied on men of modest means to run his administration, rightfully anticipating that they would be more dependent on him and his goodwill than wealthy nobles. He encouraged the bourgeoisie and initiated the beginnings of the Grand Conseil. He also increased the number of military companies who came directly under the command of the king, rather than his nobles.

On his accession to the throne, Louis' daughter, Anne, was installed in the Chateau at Amboise, away from the court, with her mother, Charlotte of Savoy, and grandmother, Louis' mother, Marie of Anjou. Anne was given her own attendants, including chambermaids, nurses and a cradle-rocker. Her mother, Charlotte of Savoy, was in charge of Anne's education. The queen had an extensive library, including classics, such as Cicero, romances, psalters, histories and books on government. Anne inherited the books on her mother's death; they were still in her library at Moulins when she herself died.[23] While still in the cradle, in fact as soon as her father was on the throne, Anne was the most eligible princess in Europe. She was considered as a bride for Edward IV in England, Duke Francis II of Brittany and even her uncle Charles, Duke of Berry. Any age difference did not matter to her father, who offered the four-year-old princess to the thirty-two-year-old Count of Charolais – Charles the bold, the future Duke of Burgundy. A betrothal to Nicholas, Duke of Lorraine, came to nothing when the duke broke it off to pursue Mary, Duchess of Burgundy. When she was twelve, almost thirteen, Anne's future was decided, when she married Pierre de Bourbon on 3 November 1473; at thirty-four, Pierre was twenty-one years her senior.

Pierre's brother, the Duke of Bourbon, allowed him to use the courtesy title of Lord of Beaujeu and gave him rule of the Beaujolais. However, the newly married couple resided in the king's court at Plessis-lès-Tours. For Anne, the next ten years were spent at the court and, particularly, with her father – during which time Louis XI said Anne was 'the least foolish woman in France but a wise one there was not'.[24] Anne, who would be called '*Madame La Grande*' had a sharp political intelligence, combined ith great energy; many thought her the mirror image of her her in her keen political mind, although not in other ways.

She had a handsome face but was not considered beautiful. She fell pregnant in 1476, but little is known of the outcome of the pregnancy, it is possible that she had a short-lived son, Charles, Count of Clermont, but the details are sketchy. In 1481 Anne was given the County of Gien by her father, to allow her to finance her own household. And in April 1483 she was despatched to Hesdin, to bring her little brother's bride, three-year-old Margaret of Austria, to France. The little princess was to be brought up at the French court until she was old enough to marry the thirteen-year-old dauphin, Charles.

Anne was twenty-two years old when Louis XI died on 30 August 1483, at Plessis-lès-Tours in the Loire Valley; he was sixty years old. He was succeeded by his son, Charles VIII, who was thirteen years old. Louis had not provided for a regency – young Charles was ten months short of his majority – although he had intended to set up a regency council, which would include the young king's mother, Charlotte of Savoy, and Louis, Duke of Orléans. Louis was a great grandson of Charles V and brother-in-law to the king and his sister, Anne de Beaujeu, being married to Jeanne de France; he was also Charles VIII's heir until he produced a son of his own. Anne's husband Pierre, Lord of Beaujeu, was to be appointed the council's president. However, Anne and her husband had also been appointed Charles's guardians and it seemed a natural progression for them to take over the government of the realm. Charles was crowned on 30 May 1484 and, in the same year, to appease the populace, an Estates General was called. The body which brought together representatives from the Three Estates (nobility, clergy and commons) had last met in 1439. Their grievances, such as requests for reductions in the *tailles* and no taxation without the consent of the Estates, were heard and promises made; and the representatives went home content they had been listened to, even though their demands were not entirely met. The nobility, who had control of the army, and Louis d'Orléans, in particular, were not happy with the arrangements. Encouraged by Archduke Maximillian of Austria and Duke Francis of Brittany, Louis and his supporters took up arms in what became known as 'the mad war' or 'the silly war'. They were soundly defeated, their army crushed at Saint-Aubin-du-Cormier in July 1488, and the Duke of Orléans taken prisoner.

Anne's greatest success, however, was in Brittany, a semi-autonomous duchy within France. The Duke of Brittany, Francis, died in 1488 leaving a thirteen-year-old daughter, Anne, as his sole heir. Before his death, in an attempt to keep Brittany from being swallowed up by the French crown, the Duke offered his daughter's hand in marriage to Maximillian of Austria. However, Maximillian was too far away to protect the duchy when the French army invaded. Anne of Brittany was forced to agree to marry Charles VIII; although Brittany would remain in Anne's hands. This move eventually led to the annexation of Brittany by the crown. No longer needed as a bride, little Margaret of Austria was sent home and Charles VIII married Anne of Brittany on 6 December 1491. The marriage treaty had one unusual clause in that should Charles die before they had children, Anne was to marry Charles' heir, the next king of France.

This diplomatic coup was one of the last of the Beaujeu regency as Charles VIII was now twenty and of an age and desire to rule. In 1488, Anne de Beaujeu had become Duchess of Bourbon following the death of Pierre's older brother, John; the title had initially passed to another older brother, Charles, an Archbishop, who was persuaded to relinquish the title after holding it for just two weeks, following Pierre's invasion of the duchy. Anne and Pierre, now the Duke and Duchess of Bourbon, had become the richest, most powerful nobles in the realm. Although she still acted as an advisor to her young brother, Anne de Beaujeu now turned her attention to her new duchy, familiarising herself with her lands and its administration. She started a building programme, which included the rebuilding of the ducal castle at Gien, and the palace at Moulins; she also reorganised the duchy's administration, codified its laws and raised taxes. Their court was the epitome of the flowering Renaissance, with the couple patrons of the arts and literature; Anne particularly loved paintings, tapestries and books.

Anne finally gave birth to a surviving child, a daughter, on 10 May 1491, who was named Suzanne. Suzanne was carefully educated by her mother, who wrote a book, *Les Enseignements d'Anne de France, Duchesse de Bourbonnais et d'Auvergne, à sa fille Suzanne de Bourbon*, giving advice to her daughter on the proper behaviour expected of a noblewoman.[26]

Anne de Beaujeu was made regent again in 1494, when her brother Charles VIII led his army into Italy. She financially supported the king's campaign by loaning him 10,000 livres; she made him pay it back in instalments and had recovered the full amount within a year. Charles died in 1498, after striking his head on a door lintel, leaving no direct heir. His distant cousin Louis, Duke of Orléans, succeeded him as King Louis XII. He immediately applied to the papacy for an annulment of his marriage to Anne de Beaujeu's sister, Jeanne, in order to marry the dowager queen, Anne of Brittany, as the terms of her original marriage contract dictated. In return for Anne de Beaujeu's support of his accession, and repudiation of her sister, Louis agreed to waive royal rights to the duchy of Bourbon and the Auvergne, and to allow these rights to pass to Suzanne, should Anne produce no male heir.

In 1503, Pierre de Beaujeu, Duke of Bourbon, fell ill while returning home to Moulins, from the French court. He succumbed to a fever, which attacked his body for two months, before he died on 10 October. Pierre arranged for Suzanne to marry a prince of royal blood, Charles d'Alençon, and called him to Moulins so the wedding could take place before his death. However, Charles arrived too late and could only act as chief mourner at Pierre's funeral, rather than as bridegroom to Suzanne. Suzanne's mother then broke the marriage contract and Suzanne would marry her cousin, Charles III of Bourbon-Montpensier, Constable of France, but died in 1521, childless.

Anne de Beaujeu, Duchess of Bourbon, died on 14 November 1522 at the Château of Chandelle, Coulandon. She was buried alongside her husband and daughter in the abbey at Sauvigny. Her lands and personal title, at her own request, passed to her son-in-law, Charles of Bourbon-Montpensier. Anne de Beaujeu was regent of France at a time when the country was transitioning from the medieval to the early modern era. She successfully steered the country through civil unrest, and initiated the merging of Brittany into the French crown, which would be definitively sealed in 1532.

Anne, as with most of the heroines in this chapter, was called upon to steady the ship of state until the legitimate ruler was old enough to govern. She, like Anne of Kiev, Adela of Normandy and Catherine of Lancaster before her, did not shirk the responsibility – and each proved themselves the equal of men. It is telling that only Jadwiga of Poland ruled by right, although not without a husband by her side, and with the title of King as Poland had no provision for a ruling queen. There were other women who ruled, either as regents or in their own right, and I am only sorry I could not include them all. However, they were few in number in comparison to the number of men and they only had the opportunity when no suitable man was around to accept the responsibility. Each woman distinguished herself in that she was ready, willing and able to not only take on the responsibility, but to also face down the natural hostility that came from the lords and priests, when a woman took up the reins of government.

10

True Love

Time and time again in the medieval era, we see young girls married off for land or money, given little to no say in who their prospective husbands would be. However, there were rare instances when a woman managed to marry the man of her choice. Some of these marriages were often a heroine's second or third marriage, when she had a little more say over her destiny than a young girl. The relationships were not always successful, but at least the poor woman had succeeded in gaining some control over her own future. And there were other women who found love and contentment in the marriage their parents arranged for them.

Given the loving relationship between Edward I and Eleanor of Castile, it should probably not come as too big a surprise that two of their daughters managed to find true love. Although with Joan of Acre, her love-match definitely did not please her father! Joan had an exotic start in life; she was born in Palestine in the spring of 1272, while her parents were participating in the Ninth Crusade. Joan's parents, Prince Edward of England and Eleanor of Castile, had arrived in Palestine in May 1271. The Crusade had very little success and the nominal King of Jerusalem, Hugh III of Cyprus, brought it to an end by signing a ten-year truce with Baibars, the Mamluk leader, in May 1272. The couple could not return home immediately after the truce was signed as Eleanor had just recently been delivered of her daughter Joan, and an assassin's attack had nearly cost Edward his life so they were forced to stay in the Holy Land a little while longer.

Edward and Eleanor finally set sail for Europe in September, taking their baby daughter home. They stopped in Sicily on their way, before spending Christmas on the Italian mainland. It was during their stay in Italy that English messengers arrived with the news of Henry III's death a few months before, in November 1272. As Henry III's eldest son and heir, Edward was now King of England. The news did not hasten Edward's return to England, however, and he and Eleanor continued their progress through Europe, visiting Eleanor's mother Joan, Countess of Ponthieu, in France. They left their two-year-old daughter, little Joan of Acre, with her grandmother at Ponthieu and she remained there for the next few years.[1]

The couple now travelled on to England, arriving in Dover on 2 August 1274, and to Edward's coronation on 19 August. By the time Joan finally arrived in England, in 1278, her father was in the process of arranging a marriage for her to Hartman, son of the King of the Romans. Joan had been brought back to England, escorted by Stephen of Pencestre and his wife Margaret, in 1278 so that she would be home in time for her wedding to Hartman, which was expected to take place in 1279. Unfortunately, the wedding was not to be as Hartman was drowned in a boating accident in December 1278, when his boat hit a rock midstream.

Once back in England Joan, with her elder sister Eleanor and her younger brother Alfonso, were allowed to accompany the royal court – for parts of the year at least. They would have been permitted to take part in the Christmas and Easter celebrations with their parents, as part of their education, while their younger siblings remained in the royal nursery. Little is known of Joan's every-day life. She joined the court on an almost permanent basis once she was old enough to deal with the gruelling travel itinerary. Joan was supervised by a governess until her marriage in 1290; Edeline was the wife of Philippe Popiot, a knight in Queen Eleanor's household who had previously served the queen's mother, Jeanne of Ponthieu. Margerie, the wife of another of Queen Eleanor's knights, John de Hengham, also served in Joan's household.[2] Joan may have been close to her baby brother, Edward – the future Edward II – as she lent him the use her own seal when he was at odds with his father. It is said that she was distant from her parents; however, this idea stems from their leaving Joan with her grandmother during her early years and doesn't necessarily mean the same relationship continued when she finally arrived in England.

Edward and Eleanor travelled relentlessly, and not always with their children. Nevertheless they did make time for their family, with weeks at Leeds Castle and Windsor built into their itinerary; such a holiday took place in 1285 when Edward combined a pilgrimage to the tomb of Thomas Becket with a family week at Leeds Castle, before a week of hunting and then the journey to Amesbury, where Joan's little sister, six-year-old Mary, was veiled as a nun.[3] In 1286, however, Edward and Eleanor left England for their domains in France and the children would not see their parents again until 13 August 1289, when Joan, her four sisters and five-year-old Prince Edward greeted them when their ship docked in Dover.

What is certain is that Edward planned for the future of the children through their marriages. Following the death of Joan's first intended husband, Hartman, Edward started looking for an alternative. He finally settled on Gilbert de Clare, 8th Earl of Gloucester and 7th Earl of Hertford, also known as Gilbert the Red. Gilbert had been married to Alice de Lusignan, half-sister of Henry III, in 1253 when Gilbert was ten years old. The marriage was finally annulled in 1285. By offering Joan in marriage to one of the most powerful barons in England, Edward intended to bind Gilbert to the royal cause, thus weakening baronial opposition. With the promise of a position at the centre of royal politics, Gilbert relinquished his titles to the Crown; they were returned to him on his marriage to Joan as a new grant that gave the lands and titles to the couple, jointly, as opposed to just Gilbert. Joan and Gilbert were married in a private ceremony in the royal chapel at Westminster on 30 April, 1290. Joan was eighteen years old and Gilbert forty-six. Although Joan's dress was second-hand, she was presented with gifts from her parents of a headdress from France and a matching 'magnificent zone [belt], of all gold with emeralds and rubies'.[4]

Joan's temperament was said to be as fiery as her mother's. She refused to marry until she had the same number of attendants as her sisters. The king resolved the situation by hiring temporary servants, just until her wedding day. The princess is also said to have run up considerable debts after refusing to accept money from her own wardrobe keeper, following a heated argument. Instead of chastising the princess, her father simply paid the debt on her behalf. Joan's tetchiness was again in evidence during preparations for the wedding of her sister Margaret, just a few months after her own. Joan initially refused to attend, preferring to retire to Gilbert's estates. Edward and Eleanor retaliated by taking back seven dresses they were intending to give her, and making them part of Margaret's trousseau.[5]

It was at the celebrations of the wedding of Margaret to John II, Duke of Brabant, that Gilbert and Joan, with many members of the court, took the cross, swearing to go on Crusade to the Holy Land. Events in Scotland changed Edward's priorities and the Crusade never happened; the death of Alexander III's granddaughter, Margaret, the Maid of Norway, in September 1290, left the Scottish throne vacant, and gave Edward the opportunity to extend his influence north of the English border.

Joan lost her mother, Eleanor of Castile, in the same year as her marriage. She saw her mother one last time before her death, having been summoned north to Lincolnshire when it became apparent that the ailing queen would not survive the journey south. Eleanor died in November 1290, before any of her daughter's children were born. Joan and Gilbert had one son and three daughters. Their son, also called Gilbert, succeeded his father as Earl of Gloucester and Hertford, but was killed at the Battle of Bannockburn in 1314; he was married to Matilda, daughter of Richard de Burgh, Earl of Ulster, and sister of Elizabeth de Burgh, Robert the Bruce's queen. Of Joan's daughters by Gilbert, Eleanor would firstly be married to Hugh le Despenser, the Younger, the favourite of her uncle Edward II, who was executed in 1326. She then married William la Zouche de Mortimer, and died in 1337. Margaret was married to the first favourite of her uncle Edward II, Piers Gaveston, Earl of Cornwall, who was executed in 1312; she went on to marry Hugh Audley, and died in 1347. Their sister, Elizabeth, an influential patron of the arts, married three times; John de Burgh, Theobald de Verdon and Roger Baron d'Amory.

Joan and Gilbert were married for five years; then Joan was widowed when Gilbert died at Monmouth Castle on 7 December 1295. As the land and titles were held jointly by Gilbert, Joan remained in charge of the estates after Gilbert's death. The estates, spread across England, Wales and Ireland, produced an annual income of £6,000 and the widowed Joan paid homage for them to

Edward I, on 20 January 1296. Edward wasted no time in trying to find her a suitable new husband; his choice was Amadeus V, Count of Savoy. The betrothal document was dated 16 March 1297. However, it seems Joan had had other ideas.

In late 1296 she sent one of her late husband's squires, Ralph de Monthermer, to her father, the king, asking that he be knighted. Shortly after, in a secret ceremony in January 1297, Joan married the erstwhile squire, thus thwarting Edward's plans for her marriage with the Count of Savoy. Edward was so furious that he is said to have thrown the crown he was wearing into the fire. He ordered Ralph's arrest and had him imprisoned in Bristol Castle; he refused to receive Joan and confiscated all the lands and castles she had inherited from her late husband. Joan is said to have sent her three daughters by Gilbert to their grandfather to try to appease him, and the Bishop of Durham also attempted to mediate. Edward soon mellowed, however, possibly when he discovered that Joan was pregnant with Ralph's child. Monthermer was released and the de Clare estates were restored to the couple; although Tonbridge and Portland remained in the king's hands until 1301. Ralph performed homage for his lands on 2 August 1297, when he was summoned to the August parliament as Earl of Gloucester and Hertford, by right of his wife. Joan and Ralph had two sons and two daughters. Their eldest son, Thomas, was killed at the Battle of Sluys in 1340 and their second son, Edward, died in the same year. Of their daughters, Mary married Duncan, the 10th Earl of Fife, while Joan became a nun at Amesbury Abbey in Wiltshire, the same abbey where her mother's sister, Mary, was a nun and where Eleanor of Provence had spent her last days.

After ten years of marriage, Joan of Acre died at Clare in Suffolk, on 23 April 1307, from an unknown ailment, aged just thirty-five. She was buried in the Augustinian Priory there, of which she was a benefactress, and where she had founded the Chapel of St Vincent. The earldoms of Gloucester and Hertford passed to her son by Gilbert, also called Gilbert, and Ralph was given the title 1st Baron Monthermer in recompense.

Joan was not the only daughter of Edward I to have found love and contentment in her marriage. Although Elizabeth of Rhuddlan was not able to choose her own husband, her father's choice of husband proved to be suitable, the second time around, at least. King Edward I was in the middle of subduing Wales as his wife,

Eleanor of Castile, was reaching her final month of pregnancy, in July 1282. Unlike most royal wives, who would have stayed at home in one of their sumptuous palaces, Eleanor was in Wales with her husband. After all, Eleanor had been on Crusade with Edward and had even given birth to Joan in the Holy Land. Wales could hardly be more of a difficulty.

Rhuddlan Castle had been 'civilised' for the queen's use with the addition of gardens, decorative seating and a fish pond to aid Eleanor's comfort. However, it was still Edward's headquarters, where troops were mustering and messengers were coming and going at all hours – hardly the most comfortable and peaceful place for a queen to give birth. Elizabeth of Rhuddlan was born around 7 August 1282. She was the youngest surviving daughter of the king and queen's fifteen children – a sixteenth and final child, Edward (the future Edward II), would be born in 1284. Although the castle must have been bustling during Elizabeth's birth, one can imagine the rooms surrounding the birthing chamber were kept as serene as possible. Indeed, it seems Eleanor was allowed the 'laying-in' of a whole month following Elizabeth's birth with her churching at the end of it – a luxury that did not arise all that often for Edward's queen.

Eleanor's wardrobe accounts show the queen purchased several small items for her baby daughter's use; a basin, some tankards, a storage chest and a bucket.[6] And, unlike her siblings, Elizabeth remained with her mother during the first few years of her life. It's possible she was with her fulltime until the age of two, or was at least visited regularly by Eleanor. Elizabeth was still with her mother when her baby brother and the king's heir, Edward, was born at Caernarfon in 1284. When Edward was established in his own household, Elizabeth went with him. She spent most of her childhood in her brother's company; her education was supervised by her mother, often from a distance. Elizabeth is known to have had a fondness for books; books are recorded as forming part of her marriage goods on her first marriage, and the Alphonso Psalter was known to be in her possession at some time.[7] In 1285, Elizabeth and Edward spent the summer with their parents and older sisters. They visited Thomas a Becket's shrine at Canterbury and spent a week at Leeds Castle in Kent before travelling to Amesbury in Wiltshire. Amesbury Priory was the retirement home of the dowager queen, Eleanor of Provence;

and it was during this visit that Elizabeth's six-year-old sister, Mary, was veiled as a nun.

Edward I and Eleanor of Castile are famous for having had a close, loving relationship. They appear to have travelled everywhere together. Their children, however, were often left behind, usually in the care of their grandmother, Eleanor of Provence, Henry III's queen and Edward I's mother. In 1286, when Elizabeth was still only three, the king and queen left England for the Continent to broker peace between France and Aragon and in the hope of launching a new Crusade. Although the Crusade never materialised, Edward and Eleanor were absorbed in their Continental possessions until 1289. However, the children were not forgotten. While in Paris, Eleanor bought little items of jewellery for her daughters and sent them other pieces that had been given to her as gifts. She was also known to make offerings for her children's health at the major shrines she visited. When they finally returned home, arriving at Dover after a three-year absence, Edward and Eleanor were greeted by their children, although the youngest, six-year-old Elizabeth and four-year-old Edward, probably had little or no memory of their parents. Following celebrations of their return in Canterbury, the royal family would spend the next two weeks at Leeds Castle, getting to know each other again.

Elizabeth and Eleanor were not especially close. Eleanor had spent half of her daughter's life away on the Continent and Eleanor's health began to fail shortly after her return. Elizabeth spent the summer of 1290 touring the countryside with her brother, only attending the court for the weddings of their sisters; Joan, in April, and Margaret, in July. In October 1290, Elizabeth was summoned to her ailing mother's bedside at the royal hunting lodge of Clipstone in Nottinghamshire. She and her little brother, Edward, were just in time to say goodbye, as Eleanor died at Harby in Lincolnshire on the 28 November 1290. The king accompanied his queen's body on her final journey to London, for burial at Westminster Abbey, ordering stone crosses to be erected at the places they stopped along the route. We have no record of how Elizabeth reacted to her mother's death, she was just eight years old and had rarely seen her mother over the last four years. We can assume that she was saddened, but that otherwise life carried on pretty much as normal, with her day-to-day life remaining constant. In 1297 she and her sister Mary paid to have a special

Mass held in honour of their mother, demonstrating their affection, and that she hadn't been forgotten.[8]

In 1297 Elizabeth's marriage was celebrated, to John, Count of Holland after his father's death the year before. John had been educated at Edward's court following his betrothal to Elizabeth in 1285. He had been one of the competitors for the Scots throne, though with only an outside chance as his claim was through Ada of Huntingdon, sister of William I, the Lion, King of Scotland – whereas the claims of Robert the Bruce and John Balliol came through William's brother, David. Elizabeth is said to have thrown a tantrum before the wedding when not all her jewels were ready in time. However, the royal wedding went ahead, at Ipswich Priory on 8 January 1297. Elizabeth was just fourteen years old and John was about thirteen. It seems Elizabeth was very fond of her father – there is some suggestion, too, that she was his favourite – and she was loath to leave him, and England. The king himself threw Elizabeth's coronet into the fire during an argument over Elizabeth's refusal to leave England with her husband. It took several letters from Count John, and much cajoling from the king, to persuade Elizabeth to accompany her husband to her new country. In the event, however, the arguing proved unnecessary as Count John died at Haarlem on 10 November 1299. Elizabeth, a childless widow at seventeen, returned home to her father's court.

Almost exactly three years after the death of her first husband, on 14 November 1302, Elizabeth married again. This time there would be no arguments about leaving England as her husband was Humphrey de Bohun, 4th Earl of Hereford and Essex. Before the wedding, as had Gilbert de Clare prior to his marriage to Joan of Acre, Humphrey had relinquished all his lands and titles to the crown, including that of Constable of England. They were re-granted, jointly, to Humphrey and his new wife after the wedding. Elizabeth's second marriage appears to have been highly successful. The couple were incredibly fond of each other and Humphrey and Elizabeth weathered the storms of change together. Humphrey had been a stalwart of Edward I's Scottish campaigns and in 1306 had been rewarded with the forfeited estates of Robert the Bruce. When Elizabeth's father died in 1307, Humphrey was initially a supporter of the new king, Elizabeth's brother and childhood companion, Edward II. He is witness to the document that created Piers Gaveston, Edward's controversial favourite, Earl of Cornwall. However, in 1310, he was named one of the Lords Ordainers, set up to reform the king's household and government. He was stripped of his position as Constable of England for refusing to accompany the king on his Scottish campaign of 1310–11, but was reinstated the following year. In 1314 Humphrey was one of the commanders of the English forces facing Robert the Bruce at Bannockburn. It is believed his arguments with Gilbert de Clare, Earl of Gloucester, over who should have precedence, was a major factor contributing to England's defeat. Gloucester was killed in the fighting and Humphrey was captured by the Scots, the highest-profile English prisoner. His freedom came when he was exchanged for Robert the Bruce's queen, Elizabeth de Burgh, who had been held captive by the English since 1306.[9]

Between 1303 and 1316, the couple were to have eleven children, including twin boys. Eight of the siblings survived childhood, six boys and two girls. Their eldest daughter, Eleanor, married James Butler, 1st Earl of Ormonde and, following his death, Sir Thomas Dagworth, who was murdered in 1350. Their youngest surviving daughter, Margaret, married Hugh de Courtenay, Earl of Devon, and lived until 1391. Two of their sons John and Humphrey would succeed, consecutively, to the earldoms of Hereford and Essex. William de Bohun, twin brother of Edward (who drowned in 1334) would be granted the title of Earl of Northampton by his cousin and close friend Edward III. The twin brothers had both been involved in Edward III's escape from Nottingham Castle and from the control of his mother's lover, Roger Mortimer. Of the two remaining sons, Eneas died before 1343 and Edmund married Matilda, the daughter of Nicholas de Segrave, Baron Stowe.

Sadly, Elizabeth died in childbirth on 5 May 1316 and her last daughter, Isabella, died with her. They were buried together at Walden Priory (Waltham Abbey) on 23 May. Humphrey survived his wife by six years; he was killed at the Battle of Boroughbridge in March 1322, fighting with the forces of Thomas of Lancaster against the king. Despite his will requesting he be buried beside his wife at Walden Priory, he was laid to rest at the Church of the Friars Preachers in York. Elizabeth and Humphrey were the ancestors of the Lancastrian kings through their great-granddaughter, Mary de Bohun, who married Henry Bolingbroke (the future Henry IV) and was the mother of five children, including the victor of the 1415 battle of Agincourt, Henry V.

Princesses of England are often shadowy figures, hidden in the background. Many of these ladies were married off to foreign courts or dedicated to convents, their lives and futures decided by the king, their father. Isabella of Woodstock is, to some extent, an exception. She appears to have been very close to her parents, and spent most of her life at the English court. The eldest daughter and second child of Edward III and his queen, Philippa of Hainault, Isabella was born in June 1332 at the Royal Palace of Woodstock. Edward and Philippa had a large family, with at least twelve children (possibly more), of whom nine survived infancy. They maintained a close relationship with their children and often travelled with them. When Edward left England in July 1338, Philippa and their daughters accompanied him. Isabella was six years old and was given a pair of decorated silver basins by her father, in the days before they set sail.[10] The older children, including Isabella, were with Philippa in Antwerp when their baby brother, Lionel, was born in November 1338.

From Isabella's infancy, Edward was making plans for her marriage. In 1335 negotiations were opened for her to marry the heir to the Castilian throne; in 1344 it was a son of the Duke of Brabant and, in 1349, it was Emperor Charles. But all these plans eventually came to nought. In 1351, aged nineteen, Isabella was to marry Bernard, the heir to Lord Albret. Her trousseau included a mantle of Indian silk, furred with ermine; circlets of silk and pearls, decorated with a gold *agnus dei* set on green velvet, in addition to jewellery and dresses. Her departure was set for a few short weeks before Christmas, but one week before she was due to leave, Isabella pointedly refused to board the boat waiting to take her to Gascony.[11] Edward III does not seem to have been too put out by this. He continued to support Isabella and described her as 'our very dear eldest daughter, whom we have loved with special affection'.[12] Edward indulged Isabella, she was with him almost constantly – far more than any of his other children. In 1348, during a tournament in Lichfield, she was one of the ladies given blue and white robes – to match those of the knights – by the king. In 1354 Edward paid for a new balcony to be built outside Isabella's suite of rooms at Woodstock so that she would have a better view of the park. By late 1361, Isabella was her parents' last surviving daughter. Her sister, Joan, eighteen months her junior, had died in France in 1348, of plague while on her way to her marriage in Castile. And her younger sisters, Mary and Margaret, just teenagers, died within a short time of each other in 1361.

Isabella finally married in 1365, at the comparatively late age of thirty-three, in what appears to have been a love-match. Her husband, Enguerrand VII Lord of Coucy, was seven years her junior, and a hostage for the fulfilment of the Treaty of Bretigny. Edward III is said to have approved of the match as he enjoyed family entertainments and Enguerrand had a fine singing voice.[13] On marrying Isabella, he was released without ransom. Hoping that Enguerrand and Isabella would remain in England, Edward gave Enguerrand the earldom of Bedford in 1366 and, later, made him Count of Soissons. Two daughters quickly followed, in 1366 and 1367. Mary was born at the Château of Coucy, in France, and would later marry Henry of Bar. Their second daughter, Philippa, was born at Eltham, and would later marry Robert de Vere, Earl of Oxford and Duke of Ireland. The marriage was not without its difficulties, however, and in later years the shine appears to have worn off. In 1368, Enguerrand left England for the continent, going on to fight in Italy. He renounced all his English titles following Edward III's death, choosing to give his allegiance to France.

Isabella remained at her father's court, with her daughters, using the title of Countess of Bedford, even after her husband had resigned the earldom. She received robes as a Lady of the Garter in 1376. She remained at court even during the dark times, when Alice Perrers' influence over Edward III chased many others away. Edward's will gave to his 'very dear daughter' Isabella, an income of 300 marks per year, until her daughters were married.[14] She died, probably in 1379, aged forty-seven – although 1382 also has been suggested – and was laid to rest at the Greyfriars Church in Newgate, London. Although it had turned sour, she had broken convention by marrying for love; in her stubbornness and outright refusal to marry her father's choice of husband, Isabella had been given greater control over her own life than most English princesses, before and after her. The marriage's later problems were a sad epilogue.

The story of King James I of Scotland and his queen, Joan Beaufort, is probably the greatest love story of the medieval era. He was a king in captivity and she a beautiful young lady of the court of the Lancastrians. The son of Robert III of Scotland, James had been on his way to France, sent there for safety and to continue his education, when his ship was captured by pirates in April 1406. Aged only eleven, he was handed over to the English king, Henry IV, and imprisoned in the Tower of London. Within a couple of months of his capture, James's father died and he was proclaimed King of Scots, but the English would not release their valuable prisoner. James was closely guarded and regularly moved around, but he was also well-educated while in the custody of the English king and became an accomplished musician and poet. He was held at various castles including the Tower of London, at Nottingham Castle, where he was allowed to go hunting, and Windsor.

His future bride, Joan Beaufort, was probably born in the early 1400s. Lady Joan was the daughter of John Beaufort, 1st Earl of Somerset and the legitimated son of John of Gaunt (himself the third son of Edward III) by his mistress and, later, wife Katherine Swynford. Joan's mother was Margaret Holland, granddaughter of Joan of Kent, (later the wife of Edward the Black Prince) from her first marriage to Thomas Holland, 1st Earl of Kent. Joan was very well-connected; she was a niece of Henry IV, cousin to Henry V, great-niece of Richard II and great-granddaughter of Edward III. Her uncle, Henry Beaufort, was a cardinal and the Chancellor of England. Little seems to be known of her early life but she was at court by the early 1420s, when James first set eyes on her. James wrote of his love for Joan in his famous poem, *The Kingis Quair*. According to Nigel Tranter, James was with the court at Windsor, when he saw Joan for the first time; she was walking her little lapdog in the garden, below his window.[15] The narrow window afforded him only a limited view but the Lady Joan walked the same route every morning and James wrote of her;

> *Beauty, fair enough to make the world to dote,*
> *Are ye a worldy creature?*
> *Or heavenly thing in likeness of nature?*
> *Or are ye Cupid's own priestess, come here,*
> *To loose me out of bonds*[16]

One morning James managed to drop a plucked rose down to Lady Joan, which he saw her wearing the following evening at dinner. Nigel Tranter suggests Lady Joan grieved over James's imprisonment and even pleaded for him to be released. Their romance grew apace but was interrupted when James had to accompany Henry V on his French campaign. Henry was hoping that James's presence would make the Scots, who were fighting with the French, think twice about engaging with him. However, the strategy had little effect. James's imprisonment lasted for eighteen years. His uncle Robert Stewart, Duke of Albany and Guardian of Scotland in James's absence, refused to ransom him, in the hope of gaining the throne himself. He never quite garnered enough support, but managed to keep the Scottish nobles in check. However, when he died in 1420, control passed to his son Murdoch, who had also been imprisoned by the English for twelve years, but was ransomed – instead of James – in 1414, and Scotland fell into a state of virtual anarchy.

Henry V had finally decided that it was time for James to return to Scotland. However, his untimely death left the details to Henry's brother, John, Duke of Bedford. As regent for the infant Henry VI, it was Bedford who set the terms of James's freedom. James was charged 60,000 marks in ransom – to cover the costs for his upkeep and education for eighteen years, it was claimed. The agreement included a promise for the Scots to keep out of England's wars with France, and for James to marry an English noble woman – not an onerous clause, given his love for Lady Joan Beaufort. Written in the winter of 1423/24, the autobiographical poem, *The Kingis Quair*, gives expression to James' feelings for Joan;

> I declare the kind of my loving
> Truly and good, without variance
> I love that flower above all other things[17]

James and Joan were married at the Church of St Mary Overie in Southwark (now Southwark Cathedral) on 2 February 1424. The wedding feast took place in the adjoining hall, the official residence of Joan's uncle Henry Beaufort, Bishop of Winchester. James and Joan made their way north shortly afterwards and the couple were in Scotland by the end of March. They were crowned together at Scone in a ceremony officiated over by Henry de Warlaw, Bishop of St Andrews, on 21 May 1424.

James and Joan had eight children, seven of whom survived childhood. Their six daughters helped to strengthen alliances across Europe. The oldest, Margaret, was born in the royal apartments at the Dominican Friary in Perth, on Christmas Day in 1424. At the age of eleven she was sent to France to marry the dauphin, Louis – the future Louis XI – narrowly escaping her father's fate when the English fleet tried to capture her *en route*. Sadly, Margaret never became Queen of France as she died in 1445, leaving no children. Five more daughters were born in the next nine years; Isabella, Eleanor, Joan, Mary and Anabella. The royal couple finally had twin sons in 1430. Born on 16 October, Alexander died within a year of his birth, leaving the younger twin, James, as Duke of Rothesay and heir to the throne. He would eventually succeed his father as James II and married Mary of Gueldres. He died during the siege of Roxburgh Castle, when a cannon known as 'The Lion' exploded next to him. He was thirty years old and was succeeded by his nine-year-old son, James III.

On his return to Scotland, James immediately set about getting his revenge on the Duke of Albany's family and adherents; executing some, including Murdoch, Albany's son and heir. Two other claimants to James's throne were sent to England, as hostages for the payment of his ransom. James and Joan ruled Scotland for thirteen years; James even allowed Joan to take some part in the business of government. Although the Scots were wary of her being English, Queen Joan became a figurehead for patronage and pageantry; she granted her chaplain the hospital at Linlithgow in 1426. In recognition of her piety, Pope Eugene IV corresponded with her, requesting that she aid the king in his reforms of the Scottish Church.[18] The English hope that Joan's marriage to James would also steer the Scots away from their Auld Alliance with France, was short-lived, as the 1436 marriage of Margaret to the French dauphin formed part of the renewal of the alliance.

James' political reforms, combined with his desire for a firm but just government, made enemies of some nobles, including his own chamberlain Sir Robert Stewart, grandson of Walter, Earl of Atholl, who had been James's heir until the birth of his son. Sir Robert and his grandfather hatched a plot to kill the king and queen. In February 1437, the royal couple was staying at the Blackfriars in Perth when the king's chamberlain dismissed the guard and the assassins were let into the priory. The locking bar to the king's quarters had been removed; the king was relaxing with the queen and her ladies when they heard the men approaching. On seeing the locking bar missing, Joan's lady, Kate Douglas, used her own arm to bar the door, earning he the name 'Kate Bar-lass'. The queen hid the king in an underground vault as Kate's arm broke and the plotters gained entry. There is a legend that the vault had originally been an underground passage, however, the king had ordered the far end to be sealed, when his tennis balls kept getting lost down there. Unfortunately, that also meant James had blocked off his own escape route. The assassins dragged James from his hiding place and stabbed him to death; Joan herself was wounded in the scuffle.

The plotters, led by Walter, Earl of Atholl, had expected to seize power, but were arrested and executed as the nobles rallied around the new king, six-year-old James II. James I was buried in Perth and Joan took her young family to the security of Dunbar Castle. Little James was crowned on 25 March at Holyrood Palace, the new king's great-uncle Walter, Earl of Atholl, was executed as a traitor the following day. In his late seventies, the ageing prince had endured three days of torture before his execution. There was limited support for Joan as regent; the usual objections to a woman ruling over men were raised and, eventually, Joan had to be satisfied with retaining the guardianship of her son, while the ruling of the kingdom went to Archibald Douglas. When Douglas died two years later, a power struggle erupted, between the rival factions of Douglas, Livingstone and Crichton. Alexander Livingstone came out on top and took possession of the child-king. To shore up her own position, and possibly with some affection on both sides, Joan married a loyal supporter of the late Archibald Douglas, forty-year-old Sir James Stewart, the Black Knight of Lorne and son of the Scottish ambassador to England. However, the newlyweds had little time to enjoy their marital bliss and were arrested on 3 August, just days or weeks after their July wedding. Joan was held under house arrest in the castle apartments at Linlithgow, while her husband was sequestered in the castle dungeons.

They were only freed once Joan agreed to Livingstone being allowed to keep custody of the king, and transferred her dowry to Livingstone to pay for his maintenance. Joan retreated to Dunbar Castle, with her daughters. Over the next five years, Joan gave birth to three sons; John, James and Andrew. Queen Joan also arranged the marriages of her five younger daughters. Isabella married Francis I, Duke of Brittany; she had two daughters and died in 1494. Eleanor married Sigismund, Archduke of Austria, and died in 1480. Joan was born mute and, after several false starts on the marriage market, she married James Douglas, Earl of Morton, and had four children – her eldest son, Sir John Douglas, 2nd Earl of Morton, was probably killed at Flodden in 1513. Joan herself died in 1486. Another daughter, Mary, was created Countess of Buchan in 1444; she married Wolfert, Count of Grandpre, of the Netherlands, and gave birth to two sons who died young before she died in 1465. A last daughter, Anabella, initially married Louis of Savoy but following their divorce in 1458, she married George Gordon, 2nd Earl of Huntly. They had two children before divorcing on the grounds of consanguinity in 1471.

Although James II turned fourteen in 1444, the age when he could assume personal rule, Livingstone was still in control of the country. In 1445 he ordered Sir James Stewart's arrest and had him arraigned for speaking out against Livingstone, who still held the king in his custody at Edinburgh Castle. Queen Joan retreated to her stronghold of Dunbar Castle, where she was besieged by Livingstone's forces. Whether it was as a result of falling masonry, murder or a missile, Joan was killed during the fighting on 15 July 1445, and castellan Adam Hepburn was forced to surrender. Joan was laid to rest beside her first love, King James I, in the Carthusian Priory at Perth. Their magnificent tomb was destroyed in 1559, during the Scottish Reformation. Their story of true love was cut short by an assassin's dagger in 1437, but the literary story lives on in James' own work, *The Kingis Quair*, written in Middle Scots when the royal lover was still imprisoned by the English.

It is comforting to think that Joan found some happiness with her second husband; the birth of three sons in four years suggests they were close. Even if her second marriage was not as passionate and poetic as her first, and although it was a rare occurrence, she would not have been the only woman in medieval history to have found love twice in one lifetime. Elizabeth of Lancaster could also lay claim to such a special experience.

Elizabeth of Lancaster was the youngest surviving daughter of one of the 14th century's golden couples, John of Gaunt, third surviving son of Edward III, and Blanche of Lancaster, daughter of Henry Grosmont, Duke of Lancaster. Elizabeth was born before 21 February 1364; her older sister, Philippa, had been born in 1360 and baby brother, Henry – the future Henry IV – was born in 1367. Although her early education would have been overseen by her mother, Elizabeth was only four years old when Blanche, only about twenty-three years old herself, died in childbirth at

Tutbury in September 1368. Elizabeth and her sister were raised together in one household, with Blanche Swynford, the daughter of their mother's lady-in-waiting, Katherine Swynford. John of Gaunt provided his daughters with an annual allowance of £200 and in 1369 Blanche, Lady Wake, a cousin of their father, was appointed as governess of the Lancaster children.[19] It seems likely that Katherine Swynford also remained with the girls, her long-running love affair with their father probably started in 1371, following the death of Katherine's husband in that year.

Elizabeth had a further loss when her grandmother, Queen Philippa, died at Windsor Castle in August 1369. Black mourning cloth was ordered for both Elizabeth and Philippa, and it must have been a very subdued Christmas they celebrated that year at Kings Langley with their father, John of Gaunt, and grieving grandfather, King Edward III. The queen was finally laid to rest in Westminster Abbey in January 1370. The Lancaster children would have seen their father only infrequently, with John of Gaunt often acting as his father's lieutenant in the family's French possessions. However, her father's absence would not have unduly affected Elizabeth's day-to-day life, with the girls having their own household and servants and guardians to cater to their every need.

In September 1371 Elizabeth and her siblings got a new stepmother, their father's new bride Constance of Castile. Constance was the daughter of Pedro the Cruel, the deceased King of Castile who had been murdered by his half-brother, Henry of Trastámara, in March 1369, leaving Constance as *de jure* Queen of Castile, although Henry of Trastámara was in physical possession of the country and ruling as King Henry II. Elizabeth gained another sister, Catherine of Lancaster, when Constance gave birth to a daughter in 1372–3.

Elizabeth was made a Lady of the Garter in 1378 and, in 1380, when she was seventeen years old, her future appeared to be decided when she married John Hastings, Earl of Pembroke, at Kenilworth Castle. However, the young Earl was only about seven years old at the time, being Elizabeth's junior by ten years, and the princess soon tired of waiting for her bridegroom to grow up. The unconsummated marriage was eventually dissolved around the same time that it was discovered that Elizabeth was pregnant by Sir John Holland, half-brother of Elizabeth's cousin, King Richard II. John was the third son of Richard's mother, Joan, the Fair Maid of Kent, by her first husband, Sir Thomas Holland.

John was already rumoured to have been having an affair with Elizabeth's aunt, Isabella of Castile, wife of Edmund, Duke of York, and was rumoured to be the father of Edmund's youngest son, Richard of Conisbrough.

Whether Elizabeth was seduced by John Holland, or whether they fell in love, we cannot be certain. However, once the affair was discovered, Elizabeth and Holland were hurriedly married, near Plymouth, on 24 June 1386. Within two weeks, the couple were aboard ship with John of Gaunt, his wife Constance, and daughters, Philippa and Catherine; ninety ships and thousands of men were in an expedition aimed at winning the throne of Castile for Constance and John. The invasion force landed at La Coruña on 25 July, moved on to Santiago de Compostela and spent the winter of 1386–7 at Ourense, building support and recognition for John as King of Castile. It was probably during their time at Ourense that Elizabeth gave birth to her daughter Constance, in early 1387. She would have been nursing the infant throughout the disastrous campaign in Castile, which saw the army decimated by a combination of sickness, the unfriendly climate and dwindling supplies. By May 1387, John of Gaunt and his ally, John I of Portugal, the husband of Elizabeth's older sister Philippa since February, had agreed peace terms with Castile. At the end of May 1387, Elizabeth, her husband and their baby girl left the army and returned to English soil, after receiving a safe-conduct from the enemy to travel through Castile.

On 2 June 1388 John was created Earl of Huntingdon by his half-brother, the king; he would be elevated to Duke of Exeter on 29 September 1397. The marriage produced at least four children, three sons and a daughter. Constance, the oldest, married Thomas Mowbray, 4th Earl of Norfolk. Of the sons John, Richard and Edward, John eventually succeeded to his father's title of Duke of Exeter. The late 1390s proved turbulent times for Elizabeth. Her brother Henry Bolingbroke was banished from England by their cousin, Richard II, in 1398; the sentence was extended to life following the death of their father, John of Gaunt, on 3 February 1399. When Henry retaliated by invading England and taking the king prisoner, it must have been a difficult time for Elizabeth. Her brother was now King Henry IV, but she was married to the former king's brother.

Her youngest son, Edward was not yet a year old when John Holland joined the conspiracy to restore his brother to the throne. Holland and his fellow conspirators, Salisbury, Kent, Rutland and others, planned to kill the usurping king at the New Year jousts. However, Henry IV learned in advance about the Epiphany Rising so he did not appear at the jousts and the conspirators were arrested. John Holland was executed at Pleshey Castle on 9 January 1400, his head placed on London Bridge and his body buried in the Collegiate Church at Pleshey. He was attainted by parliament, his honours and lands forfeit to the crown. However, Elizabeth, as sister of the king, would not suffer for her husband's treason, and was granted 1,000 marks a year for her maintenance.[20] John and Elizabeth's eldest surviving son, John, would eventually become Duke of Exeter, in a new creation, in 1444.

Within months of John Holland's execution, it seems that Elizabeth, now in her late thirties, had an experience that few medieval women were ever privileged to. She fell head over heels in love with Sir John Cornwall, after watching him defeat a French knight in a joust at York, in June or July, 1400. Cornwall was a career soldier who had fought in Scotland and Brittany, and would soon be fighting to defeat Owain Glyn Dwr's revolt in Wales.[21] Although considerably younger than Elizabeth, he also fell for the Lancastrian princess and within months, and without obtaining the king's permission, the couple were married in a secret ceremony. When he discovered the marriage, the king had Cornwall arrested and thrown into the Tower of London. Cornwall's considerable charm, and most likely the pleas from his sister, soon saw the knight released and restored to favour, becoming 'an indispensable royal servant in the process'.[22] A widely respected soldier and one of the great chivalric heroes of his day, Cornwall was accepted into the Order of the Garter in 1409 and was one of Henry V's most formidable captains during the Agincourt campaign of 1415.

The couple were to have two children – a daughter, Constance and a son, John, who was born before 15 February 1405, when King Henry IV stood as his godfather.[23] Constance would marry John FitzAlan, 14th Earl of Arundel, and died around 1427. Young John would come to a tragic end in 1421, when the teenager was killed at the Siege of Meaux, his father a devastated witness to the tragedy. Elizabeth died at her husband's estate of Burford, in

Shropshire, on 24 November 1425. She was buried in Burford Parish Church, where her magnificent effigy, showing a tall, slender princess in colourful robes, can still be seen today. Sir John Cornwall was created Baron Fanhope in 1432 and Baron Milbroke around 1441; he died at his great estate of Ampthill in Bedfordshire on 11 December 1443 and was buried in a chapel he had founded, in the cemetery of the Friars Preacher near Ludgate in London. His two children having died before him, Cornwall bequeathed 800 marks to be divided between two illegitimate sons, and his estate at Ampthill was sold to his friend Ralph, Lord Cromwell.[24]

Elizabeth of Lancaster had led an eventful life, following her father to war, with an infant daughter on her hip and married for love, not once, but twice. She and Joan Beaufort were the exceptions amongst medieval women everywhere; they had chosen the men they would marry, and enjoyed and experienced love in their married lives, even if their marriages were tragically cut short by violence. They proved that women could create their own destinies and have happiness and affection, as well as a dynastic marriage. One can only assume that each woman in this chapter knew how lucky she was, from watching the arranged marriages of those around them, to find contentment and love with their spouses.

Literary Heroines

It is impossible to write a book about medieval heroines without writing about the writers. The literate world of the chroniclers was largely reserved for the men – and monks in particular – but there were women who made just as great an impact, if not greater. They give the lie to the argument that women were uneducated and illiterate. Not all women were educated, of course and, as with men, education depended on a woman's social position; many young girls of the nobility were given tutors, or sent to convents to be taught to read and write. We have already seen now Julian of Norwich wrote the first spiritual autobiography of a woman, and how Margery Kempe dictated her own mystical experiences. However, the medieval world was also the realm of Heloise, a prolific writer of letters to her one-time lover, Peter Abelard, and Christine de Pisan, arguably the first feminist and the first woman to earn a living from her writing.

There was also the rather brilliant Hildegard of Bingen. Hildegard was born in 1098 in Bremersheim in the Rhineland. Born into a noble family, she was the tenth child of Hildebert and Mechtild and was destined for life in a convent from an early age. She was around eight years old when she was placed with Jutta of Sponheim, a reclusive (possibly an anchorite), religious noblewoman who supervised the education of young girls from noble families. In 1112, at the age of fourteen, Hildegard, along with other girls in Jutta's charge, took her vows at the monastery at Disibodenberg. Under Jutta, who became prioress at Disibodenberg, Hildegard was taught to read, and Latin, although she was not proficient in the latter, and in later life she relied on her secretaries to correct her Latin grammar.

Hildegard was a woman of many talents, she was a visionary, a musician, philosopher, theologian and an expert in medicine. She lived at the monastery of Disibodenberg for more than thirty years. It was in her early years there that she first experienced visions, which would make her famous even in her own lifetime. Initially, she only revealed her prophetic visions to her mentor, Jutta, and it was only when God commanded to her record them, that she revealed them to her friend and secretary, Volmar. With the permission of the Abbot of Disibodenberg, Kuno, and with the encouragement of Volmar and a fellow nun, Richardis of Stade, Hildegard started writing down her visions when she was in her forties. It was only after much encouragement from her Archbishop, Henry of Mainz, that her first work, *Scivias*, was published. The beautifully illustrated work was given approval from a commission set up by Pope Eugene III and was also supported by the saintly Bernard of Clairvaux.

Abbot Bernard of Clairvaux was one of a number of theologians with whom Hildegard maintained a correspondence. She regularly asked the venerable abbot for advice and guidance, and help in interpreting her visions. In one letter, she would tell him,

> I have from earliest childhood seen great marvels which my tongue has no power to express but which the Spirit of God has taught me that I may believe ... Indeed, I have no formal training at all, for I know how to read only on the most elementary level, certainly with no deep analysis. But please give me your opinion in this matter, because I am untaught and untrained in exterior material, but am only taught inwardly, in my spirit.[1]

Hildegard corresponded with the great personalities of her time, with emperors, popes and even queens. Sometime between 1154 and 1171, she responded to a letter from Eleanor of Aquitaine, asking for advice, with the words 'Your mind is like a wall which is covered with clouds, and you look everywhere but have no rest. Flee this and attain stability with God and men, and God will help you in all your tribulations. May God give you his blessing and help in all your works'.[2]

In 1148 Hildegard had a vision in which God commanded her to take her nuns and establish her own nunnery. Although Abbot Kuno was reluctant to see Hildegard leave Disibodenberg – her reputation had brought the monastery pilgrims and prestige – she eventually prevailed and established a new convent at Rupertsberg. Hildegard's convent admitted only noblewomen, she did not believe in mixing the classes within a convent, writing that different 'classes of people should not be mixed, or they will fall out through deceit or arrogance, and the shame occasioned by their differences. The greatest danger of all is a breakdown in peaceful manners through mutual backbiting and hatred when the upper class pounce on the lower or when the lower is promoted above the higher.'[3]

It was at Rupertsberg that Hildegard wrote two medical works, *Causes and Cures* and *Physica*, after studying the illnesses of the sick who she cared for. Her writings suggested remedies for different ailments, using a wide variety of plants; for example, Hildegard explains how cloves could be used to remedy against gout, swollen intestines and hiccups.[4] She also extolled the virtues of the rose as a cure for many ills, saying:

Rose is cold, and this coldness contains moderation which is useful. In the morning, or at daybreak, pluck a rose petal and place it on your eyes. It draws out the humour and makes them clear. One with small ulcers on his body should place rose petals over them. This pulls the mucus from them. One who is inclined to wrath should take rose and less sage and pulverise them. The sage lessens the wrath, and the rose makes him happy. Rose, and half as much sage, may be cooked with fresh, melted lard, in water, and an ointment made from this. The place where a person is troubled by a cramp or paralysis should be rubbed with it, and he will be better. Rose is also good to add to potions, unguents, and all medications. If even a little rose is added, they are so much better, because of the good virtues of the rose.[5]

Hildegard's prolific writing career continued in her new surroundings. She produced religious poems, music and even a play, *Ordo Virtutum*. She also wrote two further books of her visions, *Liber vitae meritorum* (*Book of Life's Merits*) and *Liber divinonim operum* (*Book of Divine Works*), and a life of the abbey's patron saint, St Rupert. Ricardis of Stade and her friend and secretary,

Volmar, had accompanied Hildegard from Disibodenberg to Rupertsberg and continued to help her as secretaries and assistants. A succession of secretaries came after Volmar and Richardis, including Hildegard's nephew, Wesclein, her brother, Hugo of Tholey, and her last secretary, Guibert of Gembloux. Guibert and an earlier secretary, Godfrey of Disibodenbrg, both wrote biographies of Hildegard. The main purpose of the secretaries was to edit Hildegard's works as her Latin grammar was far from proficient; however, they were under strict instructions not to change any of her words as they came from God, exhorting 'Let no man be so audacious as to add anything to this writing lest he be blotted out from the book of life'.[6]

Hildegard was a prolific letter writer and, more than 800 years after her death, there are around 400 of her letters still extant today. Many wrote to her asking for advice and prophecies. Indeed, John of Salisbury said Pope Eugene III had consulted Hildegard for predictions about his reign, which had been accurate.[7] In her letters, Hildegard acts as a mediator within the monastic world, soothing arguments within convents, between abbesses and their nuns, and abbots and their monks. She was respected by men and women alike, noble and poor. Hildegard gave advice and support and remonstrated against injustice and corruption. She travelled widely and undertook four preaching tours, between 1158 and 1170, a practice ordinarily forbidden to women, who were expected not to teach or speak in church.

Hildegard of Bingen died in her eighty-fourth year, at Rupertsberg, on 17 September 1179, and was canonised as Saint Hildegard on 10 May 2012 by Pope Benedict XVI, who declared her a doctor of the Church, in the same year. She was a woman of extraordinary talents, a prolific writer, a poet and composer, a visionary, a mystic and a scientist. She was trusted and respected by the great men of her age and is considered to be the most influential woman in medieval Church history, a well-deserved accolade.

A contemporary of Hildegard's, and one who is just as famous, although for very different reasons, is Heloïse d'Argenteuil. Born around 1100, Heloïse was involved in one of the most famous and tragic love affairs of the medieval era. We know nothing of her parentage, except that her mother was named Hersende, a fact mentioned in Heloïse's obituary at the convent of Paraclete.[8] Her father is not named, which may suggest that Heloïse was illegitimate, but at this distance in time, we cannot be certain. Considered to be the most learned woman in Europe, Heloïse's education was supervised by her uncle, Fulbert, who was a canon at the Church of Notre-Dame on the Île-de-France in Paris. When Heloïse was around thirteen or fourteen, Fulbert employed his fellow canon, Peter Abelard, as her tutor in return for him lodging with them. Already an accomplished student, Abelard schooled her further in rhetoric, Latin, Hebrew, Greek and philosophy. Born in 1079, Peter was more than twenty years her senior and was an accomplished theologian; he was considered one of the most brilliant philosophers of the age, although his arrogance made him many enemies among the intellectual elite.

Abelard and Heloïse soon fell in love, with Abelard confessing 'My hands strayed oftener to her bosom than to the pages'.[9] Although her uncle, Fulbert, remained ignorant of the affair for a long time, once Heloïse fell pregnant, the secret could be kept no longer. Abelard wrote about Heloise's pregnancy, saying,

A little after, the young woman discovered she was pregnant and wrote me as soon as she could, asking me what she should do. One night, when her uncle was away, I took her and once we were reunited I took her immediately to Brittany, where she stayed with my sister until the day she gave birth to a son who she named Astrolabe.[10]

Abelard's sister would raise little Astrolabe, whose name means 'one who reaches the stars'.

Even before the birth, Abelard wanted to marry Heloïse but she was reluctant, fearing that marriage would ruin his career, writing to him that: 'The condition of philosophers is not like that of rich people and those who seek a great fortune or whose lives are given up to the things of this world rarely devote themselves to the study of Scripture and philosophy'.[10] Heloïse insisted 'It would be dearer and more honourable to me to be called your whore', rather than ruin his career as a theologian.[12] Abelard continued the story in his *Historia Calimatatum*, 'We left our young child with my sister and returned to Paris in secret. Several days later we spent the night in vigil in a church, at dawn the next morning, in the presence of Heloïse's uncle and several of our friends and his, we were united in marriage'.[13] Fulbert, however, was not easily pacified and Abelard took Heloïse to the convent at Argenteuil to escape his wrath. Unfortunately, it seems this further incensed Fulbert, who believed Abelard had abandoned his niece. His revenge was terrible indeed, Fulbert sent his servants to Abelard's room, they broke in during the night and castrated him.

Mutilated, humiliated and filled with horror, Peter Abelard abandoned Heloïse and joined the abbey of Saint-Denis as a monk. He sent instructions to Heloïse that she should join the convent community at Argenteuil and, aged only nineteen, the poor girl took the veil. She eventually rose to be prioress at Argenteuil. Then Abelard arranged for Heloïse to be made abbess of a new foundation of nuns at the Paraclete, a religious hermitage that Abelard had helped to found. It would eventually have at least five daughter houses set up by Heloïse herself. Their love affair over and in the past, Heloïse now pursued a highly successful career as abbess; her learning, compassion and administrative skills earning her much admiration and respect. The letters between Heloïse and Abelard develop and change, transforming from love letters to those of a more professional relationship. Abelard exhorted her to turn her love for him into love for God. Although they continued to correspond, their letters were now of a more theological nature, with Heloïse asking for advice on the scriptures, or for material that could be used for study by her convent community.

Despite their new relationship, Heloïse's letters to Peter Abelard are still suffused with a desperate passion, now unfulfilled; one such starts 'To him who is especially hers, from her who is uniquely his. I do not wish to give you the slightest reason for accusing me of disobedience in anything. Following your command, I have put a rein on the expression of my boundless grief, so that I may restrain myself, at least in my letters, from writing words against which it is not merely difficult but impossible to guard oneself in speech'.[14] However, having embraced the monastic life, she then goes on to request '...that you draw up in writing and send to us a rule that is suitable for women, setting forth in its entirety the condition and character of our monastic life'.[15] Highlighting their new relationship, Abelard replied to one of Heloise's letters with the address '... my sister Heloise, once dear to me in the world, now dearest in Christ'.[16]

Peter Abelard was not Heloïse's only correspondent, however. She exchanged letters with many ecclesiastics, including Hugh Metel, an Augustinian canon, and with Peter the Venerable, Abbot of Cluny. Her correspondents also included the popes Alexander III, Eugene III and Innocent II, with a series of official letters relating to the administration of the Paraclete.

Peter Abelard had left the monastery in the 1130s and resumed teaching. He attracted the opposition of powerful clergymen, such as Bernard of Clairvaux, by insisting that the Cistercian teachings should be subjected to rational inquiry. He was condemned as a heretic in 1140 for insisting that intention was intrinsic in deciding whether a sin had been committed. Peter Abelard died two years later and was buried at the Paraclete, where Heloïse was still abbess. An extant letter that Heloïse wrote to Peter the Venerable thanks him for his visit to the Paraclete, sometime following the death of Peter Abelard, whom she refers to as 'our master', asking for absolution for Abelard, and a Church position for her son. She writes 'May it please you too to send me also under seal an open document containing the absolution of our master, to be hung on his tomb. Remember also, for the love of God, our Astralabe and yours, so that you may obtain for him some prebend either from the Bishop of Paris or in some other diocese'.[17]

When Heloïse herself died in 1164, she was buried beside Peter Abelard, in the cemetery at the Paraclete. Their bodies were later moved, in the 19th century, to the famous cemetery of Père Lachaise, the fame of their love undiminished by the passage of centuries.

Heloïse's writing fame came from her letters, rather than books, as was the case of Hildegard of Bingen. The passion and maturity in her letters led scholars to question that a woman could have written such intelligent prose, but write it she did. We know about Heloïse from her own letters, and from Peter Abelard's own account of his life, *Historia Calamitatum* (*The History of his Calamities*). However, there were women writers of the time about whom we know very little, such as Marie de France.

Marie de France was a poet in the late 12th century, who wrote three major works that can be definitively attributed to her, even though we don't know who she was. All that is left of Marie is her work, and the vague notion that she comes from France, because she wrote in her *Fables* 'Marie ai num, si sui de France'.[18] The traditional view is that Marie was a Frenchwoman writing at the court of Henry II of England based on the fact that if she was writing in France, she wouldn't have to say that she was from that country. However, France in the 12th century was far from one unified, indivisible country. In fact, it was a series of counties and duchies with their own rulers, who paid homage to the King of France; the French king's own domains at the time were the Île-de-France, which incorporated Paris and its environs.

Another argument for Marie writing in England, is that her *lais*, her poetic verses, were dedicated to a *'noble reis'*, or 'noble king', and this is thought to be Henry II of England. However, it could just as easily been intended for Louis VII of France, or his son Philip II Augustus. In turn the *Fables*, an adaptation of *Aesop's Fables*, were dedicated to a nobleman she identifies as 'Count William'. There were several earls in England at the time who were named William, including William Marshal, Earl of Pembroke; William Longspée, Earl of Salisbury; and William Mandeville, Earl of Essex; or even the son of King Stephen, William of Blois, Earl of Warenne and Surrey. However, William was a common name at the time, even on the Continent, where you could find many a *Guillame*.

Everything we think we know about who Marie was is pure conjecture. It has even been suggested that she was the illegitimate daughter of Geoffrey of Anjou, father of Henry II, and therefore a half-sister of Henry. She has also been variously identified as a nun at Reading Abbey, the abbess of Shaftesbury between 1181 and 1216, and Marie de Meulan, wife of Hugh Talbot of Cleuville.[19] We do know that Marie had a knowledge of Latin and English, and a familiarity with the works of Ovid and Wace's *Brut*, and wrote in an Anglo-Norman French.

Her works have been dated to the second half of the 12th century, with her poetry, the *lais*, dating between 1160 and 1199, the *Fables* between 1160 and 1190, and her last work, the *Espurgatoire,* has been dated to after 1189 and possibly as late as 1215.[20] *L'Espurgatoire Seint Patriz (The Purgatory of St Patrick)* is believed to have been written after 1189 as it appears to have been heavily reliant on the Latin text of Henry of Saltrey as her source, which was published around 1185. *L'Espurgatoire* is dedicated to 'H. abbot of Sartis', who may have been Hugh, Abbot of Wardon Abbey, in Bedfordshire, between 1173 and 1185 or 1186; the abbey was originally named St Mary de Sartis.[21] The only surviving manuscript of this treatise is now stored in the *Bibliothèque Nationale* in Paris.

The *lais* were a series of twelve poems, many of which were drawn from Celtic legends. Only one is based on Arthurian legends, specifically the story of the lovers, *Tristan and Iseult*. Many of the *lais* were translated into Old Norse in the 13th century, while two, *Lanval* and *Le Fresne* were translated and adapted into Middle English in the 14th century. The *lais* were narratives, written in verse and intended to be set to music. One such included the lines; 'when a good thing is well known, it flowers for the first time, and when it is praised by many, its flowers have blossomed.'[22] Her stories included fairy mistresses, twins separated at birth, and one relating the troubles of the wife of a werewolf. Her *lais* explored love and conflicting loyalties. They dealt with the issues of courtly behaviour and documented the struggles to fulfil the conflicting aims of individual needs and cultural expectations. The *lais* varied in length, with the shortest, *Chevrefoil*, having 118 lines and the longest, *Eliduc*, comprising 1,184 lines; this last was the story of a wife having to adapt when her husband brings home a second wife.

Marie's collection of *Fables*, known as *Ysopets* in French and written for the mysterious 'Count William', are based on the older *Aesop's Fables*, from antiquity, but she also adapted and added to the original stories. The *Fables*, a rhyming collection of works, demonstrate Marie's concern for the well-being of the lower classes and the poor, criticising the political and social conditions of the time. Her work was widely read and influential; the fable *Del cok e del gupil (The Cock and the Fox)* is one of the inspirations for Geoffrey Chaucer's *The Nun's Priest's Tale*, written in the 15th century. Marie ends The *Fables* with an epilogue, in which she includes a plea to be remembered,

> To end these tales I've here narrated
> And into Romance tongue translate,
> I'll give my name for memory:
> I am from France, my name's Marie.
> And it may hap that many a clerk
> Will claim as his what is my work.
> But such pronouncements I want not!
> It's folly to become forgot![23]

Wherever she came from, geographically and socially, Marie de France was a keen observer of the social undercurrents of the time, incorporating them into her *Lais* and *Fables*. We cannot say for certain that her work was produced in England, at the English court. With the Norman empire stretching from the borders of Scotland to the borders of Spain she may have travelled within Henry II's domains, but not necessarily with the court. Although we have few clues to her identity and origins, at least we have her works – her poetry through which she has lived on for more than eight centuries. That is more than we have for Margaret of Scotland, another female poet writing some 200 years after Marie de France.

Margaret of Scotland was the eldest daughter of King James I and his wife, Joan Beaufort. Her parents were that rare couple in medieval times – they married for love. James I had been held prisoner at the English court since 1406, the year he turned twelve. He had been King of Scotland since his father's death just two weeks after young James's ship was captured off the English coast. The ship had been taking him to safety in France. James fell in love with Joan Beaufort, the granddaughter of John of Gaunt and Katherine Swynford, while he was still a captive and they married at St Mary Overie in Southwark on 12 February 1424. James's release had been successfully negotiated in 1423 and the marriage was politically favourable to the English, who saw it as an opportunity to improve relations with Scotland while, at the same time, drawing Scotland away from France, their traditional ally.

After eighteen years of imprisonment, James I returned to Scotland in April 1424, with his new bride – and queen– at his side. Margaret, their eldest child, was born in December of the same year, possibly on Christmas Day. She was joined in the nursery by five sisters during the next ten years, Isabella, Eleanor, Joan, Mary and Annabella. Twin brothers were born in 1430, Alexander and James, but only James survived past the first few months.

Margaret's future was almost settled in 1428, when a French embassy arrived to renew the Franco-Scottish alliance. France's king, Charles VII had given his ambassadors the task of asking for Margaret's hand in marriage for his son, Louis, the dauphin. Born in July 1423, Louis was just eighteen months older than his future bride. However, James I hesitated, reluctant to give the French the army of 6,000 men that they wanted as part of the alliance. Charles VII was in a precarious position in France at the time. The Hundred Years War was raging and, despite the fact his father had died in 1422, he would not actually be crowned king until July 1429. In fact, Henry VI of England had also been crowned King of France and it was only due to the efforts of Joan of Arc that Charles VII's fortunes would change. James, therefore, held off from agreeing to the alliance, and used it to strengthen his position in negotiations with the English. As Charles VII's fortunes in France improved, he too was reluctant to commit to an alliance; until it appeared that an Anglo-Scottish treaty may become a reality, with Margaret or one of her sisters proposed as a bride for Henry VI.

In 1435, the marriage of Margaret and the dauphin was finally agreed and the young bride, still only eleven years old, set out for France the following year. She left by ship from Dumbarton in March 1436, with an entourage worthy of a princess; she was escorted by several of the leading lords of the realm, a household of 140 persons in royal livery and more than 1,000 troops. The French fleet in which she sailed landed on the Île de Ré, near La Rochelle, on 17 April and made a formal progress to Tours. On 24 June she met her future husband for the first time, in the great hall of the castle at Tours, and the young couple embraced formally. They were married the next day, in the castle's chapel.

Celebrated by the Archbishop of Reims, it was a rather subdued affair, for a royal wedding. The continuing state of warfare with England had stretched the French royal finances to the limit. The reception was not as lavish as the Scottish guests might have expected and was cut short to preserve funds, the scandalised Scots being quickly ushered out. Almost immediately after the wedding celebrations, most of Margaret's Scottish household was sent home, with just a handful of her native attendants allowed to stay with the Scottish Princess. Owing to the tender age of the young couple, they were not expected to consummate the marriage for another few years, so Margaret was given into the guardianship of Queen Marie and continued her education under the queen's supervision. Petite, pretty and delicate, Margaret soon became the darling of the French King and Queen. Louis, on the other hand, had a strained relationship with his father, one that would eventually be expressed in open rebellion; as a result, he was rarely at court.

When Louis asked the king for an allowance with which to set up a household for himself and his young wife, his father refused, despite being happy to give Margaret money to indulge herself. At one time, Charles VII gave Margaret 2,000 livres to buy herself furs and silks, and yet he refused to pay off Louis' debts. Relations between the dauphin and dauphine were not helped by Louis' strained relationship with his father and it seems that comparisons were made between Louis' unimpressive looks and Margaret's beauty – although malicious English chroniclers would insist that Louis was repelled by Margaret's 'evil soured breath'.[24] However, in 1437 their marriage was consummated and Margaret, now approaching her thirteenth birthday, was given her own household. In the same year, Margaret suffered a personal loss when her father was murdered back home in Scotland; her six-year-old brother was now King James II and, until her death, Margaret was his heir presumptive.

Although Louis' relationship with his father was deeply strained, Margaret remained on good terms with the king; she received grants directly from him, rather than her husband, as might have been expected. Margaret was allowed no part in court politics. The dauphine's role in France was limited to formal occasions and court ceremonials, such as the celebrations for the marriage of the king's niece, Margaret of Anjou, to Henry VI of England, which Margaret attended in 1445.

As with her father before her, Margaret had a passion and talent for writing poetry and, although she enjoyed court life, she became increasingly bored with it. She retreated more and more to her own chambers with her ladies and spent her days and evenings writing and reading poetry. Her evenings were so taken up in this style, that she often retired to bed long after Louis had fallen asleep. Margaret was also renowned as a patroness of literature. She had several poets in her household, including Jehanne Filleul, whose works have survived to this day, and the Viscount de Blosseville. De Blosseville wrote one of the three laments to the dauphine, written before her death. Another such lament was possibly written by her sister Isabella, it was certainly in her possession.

As the years passed and the marriage was still childless, Margaret's lifestyle caused further discontent within the marriage, and more unhappiness for the young princess as her husband expressed his displeasure. There is some suggestion that Margaret deliberately prevented falling pregnant by drinking vinegar, and by tightly lacing her bodices – although this may also have been for vanity, and to keep her svelte figure. There also followed accusations of impropriety within Margaret's rooms when, at Christmas 1444,

Jamet de Tillay, a member of the king's household, entered her chamber during one of her private poetry evenings and subsequently spread rumours about 'wanton princesses'. Margaret perceived it as a personal attack and became increasingly distressed, complaining that Jamet had turned the king and dauphin against her. This, coupled with strained relations with the queen over her household, caused the young princess increasing anguish. Although Jamet tried to apologise, Margaret would not hear of it. By the summer of 1445 the dauphine was very ill. Having accompanied the court on pilgrimage she fell ill on 7 August and by the next day she was feverish and suffering from fits of coughing. Her doctors diagnosed an inflammation of the lungs. In her delirium, she blamed Jamet de Tillay for her impending death, and swore she had never done Louis any wrong. As she approached death, Margaret calmed down and forgave Jamet, on her ladies' instigation. Having received the last rites, Margaret died shortly after 10pm on 16 August 1445, at Châlons-sur-Marne; she was just twenty years old. The dauphine was laid to rest in the Cathedral of St Étienne in Châlons; in 1479 her body was moved by her husband, now Louis XI, to the chapel of the Holy Sepulchre in the Abbey Church of Saint-Laon in Thouars, where Margaret had founded a chaplaincy.[25] Just over five years after Margaret's death, Louis married nine-year-old Charlotte of Savoy; he waited until Charlotte was fourteen to consummate the marriage and the couple went on to have three children, including the future Charles VIII and Anne de Beaujeu, Duchess of Bourbon and regent for her brother Charles.

Following her death, Louis destroyed every piece of poetry and writing that Margaret had ever produced. Whereas with Marie de France we have her writing but not her identity, with Margaret of Scotland we have the story of the young dauphine but none of her work survived her husband's purge. We can only speculate as to what she wrote about, and how much poetry she produced. However, her patronage of poets has at least ensured she had a worthy legacy. And it may be that the love of poetry that Margaret fostered at the French court encouraged more women to write, leading to the success of later writers, such as Christine de Pisan.

Christine de Pisan was born around 1364 in Venice, Italy; the family was from the village of Pizzano, just outside Bologna. Her father, Tommaso di Benvenuto da Pizzano, was a graduate of the University of Bologna and was a lecturer in astrology at the university, but moved to Venice in 1357. In the late 1360s Tommaso was invited to join both the Hungarian and the French royal courts. He chose France and moved his family, including Christine and her two brothers Paolo and Aghinolfo, to Paris, in December 1368, becoming royal physician and astrologer to Charles V. Christine's father paid particular attention to his daughter's education, allowing her to be taught to the same standards as a boy of her age, although her mother disapproved. She was tutored in history, literature, religion and the classical languages.[26]

In 1380, at the age of fifteen, Tommaso arranged a marriage for Christine with Etienne de Castel. Ten years older than Christine, Etienne was a graduate of the University of Paris and became a royal secretary in the year they married. The position of royal secretary was a lifetime appointment and only open to the intellectual elite, as they were often involved in diplomatic events. In the same year, on 16 September, Tommaso's patron Charles V died, leaving the family in a precarious financial position. Christine was further challenged by a series of tragedies toward the end of the decade. Her father, Tommaso, died in 1387, leaving Christine's mother and niece in his daughter's care. Around the same time, Christine lost a child, his name unknown; although two children, Marie and Jean, survived infancy. In 1390 her husband Etienne passed away at Beauvais and Christine was left with the responsibility of providing for herself and her young children, as well as her mother and niece.

Christine explained herself, in her book *Mutation of Fortune*, how she had to take on the mantle of the man of the house,

> Let me summarise this moment,
> Just who I am, what all this meant.
> How I, a woman, became a man by a flick of Fortune's hand
> How she changed my body's form
> To the perfect masculine norm.[27]

Etienne had taken care of all the family's financial dealings and it was a steep learning curve for Christine to learn to manage the accounts and pay off the family's debts. Shortly after Etienne's death, Christine found work as a copyist for a number of Parisian manuscript workshops. Eventually, around 1399, she began to compose her own prose and poetry as a means of supporting her family, and it was the grief of losing Etienne that informed

Christine's early works of poetry. Initially, she would send her works to members of the court, who sent her money in gratitude, with patrons eventually including Louis, Duke of Orléans, the Duke de Berry and France's queen, Isabella of Bavaria. And as Christine's fame spread beyond France, she could also count Philip II the Bold, Duke of Burgundy, and Thomas Montagu, 4th Earl of Salisbury, among her patrons. Writing in ballads and *lais* (poetry put to music), Christine could express her love and grief for Etienne and the sense of loss and loneliness she now felt,

> Like the mourning dove I'm now alone,
> And like a shepherdless sheep gone astray,
> For death has long ago taken away
> My loved one whom I constantly mourn...[28]

Christine de Pisan's poems, amounted to ten volumes of verses, including *L'Épistre au Dieu d'Amours* (*Letter to the God of Loves*) which was published in 1399. In the early 1400s she also published *Letters on the Debate of the Romance of the Rose*, a response to Jean de Meun's *Le Roman de la Rose* (*The Romance of the Rose*) attacking the traditional view of women causing the sins of men. Christine is, above all, remembered and revered for her work, *Le Livre de la Cité des Dames* (*The Book of the City of Ladies*), published in 1405. Well received in France, even in her own lifetime, it was later translated into Flemish and English. The book tells of the lives of past and present heroines, including pagan, Hebrew and Christian ladies who were renowned for being examples of exemplary womankind, famed for their chastity, loyalty and devotion. It included the lives of female saints who remained steadfast in their devotion to God in the face of martyrdom. *City of Ladies* was Christine's response to the misogynistic portrait of womankind that was present in many works of the era, in which women were blamed for the misery in which men found themselves. The book suggests that women were capable of being anything, from warriors to artists and teachers, but stops short of suggesting that her contemporaries should pursue such careers.[29]

In the same year, 1405, the sequel to *City of Ladies*, entitled *Le Livre des Trois Vertus* (*The Book of the Three Virtues*) was also published. This text was more of an instructional treatise, showing women how they should behave and how they could make a significant contribution to society from their various social spheres. In it Christine recommends that women should be modest and obedient as virgins, tolerant and humble as wives, and courageous and dignified as widows. It is possible that *Le Livre des Trois Vertus* was written as a book of instruction for eleven-year-old Marguerite de Nevers, the daughter of the Duke of Burgundy and bride of Louis of Guyenne, the heir to the throne of France. Although the book appears to be a contradiction of Christine's own life, when she was making a name for herself as a writer to support her family, it has to be remembered that Christine was living in a male-dominated era, rather than the 21st century. She has often been advanced as the first feminist, but while she wanted to correct the negative view of women and improve the conditions of women, advancing arguments for better education and a role beyond the home, she was not intending to be revolutionary.

Christine's writing proved so successful that she managed to pull herself out of debt and make a living at it; she was the first woman to ever become a professional writer. Her ability to write for varied audiences meant her work was often sought after. She eventually started receiving commissions to write specific items for her noble patrons, including political and moral works. A biography of Charles V, *Le Livre des Fais et des Bonnes Meurs du Sage Roy Charles V* (*The Book of the Deeds and Good Character of the Wise King Charles V*), which Christine wrote in 1404, was commissioned by the late king's brother Philip, Duke of Burgundy. Her other works included *The Book of the Body Politic* and *Feats of Arms and Chivalry*. The latter was published anonymously as Christine doubted it would be taking seriously if a woman was identified as the author.

As Charles VI increasingly slipped into bouts of madness in the early 15th century, and France found itself on the verge of civil war, Christine would write about peace and the necessity of stable government. However, as France was dragged back into the Hundred Years War against England, she became increasingly marginalised. She retired from public life and retreated to the convent at Poissy, where her daughter was a nun. Her last work, in 1429, *Le Ditié de Jehanne d'Arc* (*The Poem of Joan of Arc*), extolled the virtues of Joan, the Maid of Orléans, as valiant and brave, chaste and pure; it was the only work written about Joan during her own lifetime. Writing at the height of Joan's success. it portrayed the Maid, the leader of the revival of French fortunes in the war against the English, as the embodiment of the women Christine had written of in *City of Ladies*. However, Christine does not appear to have lived long enough to see the final chapters, and the tragedy, of Joan's life – her imprisonment and death at the hands of the English. Christine probably died in 1430, the year before Joan.

Christine de Pisan was one of the most remarkable women of her age. In her world, women were denied their own voice and independence. There were strictures placed on every aspect of their lives, by tradition and society. And yet she circumvented these strictures, not only by writing, but by writing to make a living, and by giving a voice and identity to women everywhere. She was not a feminist; the notion of feminism simply did not exist. However, she was a forerunner for the feminist movement, and a sign of the independence that women would eventually achieve.

Each of the women in this chapter was a heroine in her own right. They forged a path for all women writers who came after them, including me. Even if their work has not survived, as with Margaret of Scotland, or their identity, as in the case of Marie de France, their contribution is immeasurable. What is just as remarkable is the variety and extent of the writings of these women. Hildegard of Bingen was respected and admired by the great men of her time, consulted for her wisdom and knowledge, she wrote on medicine, God and her own visions and admonished injustice and corruption; whereas Heloïse, who wrote of love and loss at such a young age, was proof that women were capable of great literature. The poet and political and social observer Christine de Pisan was the culmination of these remarkable trailblazers, proving that women were just as capable as men of making successful careers as writers.

The Survivors

The last chapter of this book must be dedicated to those heroines who endured, who are heroines because they survived everything that medieval life threw against them. These women had to persevere through the hard times, through their father's, or husband's, execution for treason; through abandonment by their husbands; through war and loss of freedom. They endured and even found some satisfaction and contentment in life – eventually.

A book about medieval heroines would not be complete without the most famous woman of the middle ages. Eleanor of Aquitaine is the only woman to have ever worn the crowns of both England and France. Eleanor was the ultimate survivor and, despite many setbacks, lived to a great age, revered and respected to the very end. Her life story has filled many a volume over the years; she has even been promoted as the first feminist. However, Eleanor lived within the bounds of medieval society, even if she did break the mould in many ways. Eleanor was born in the early 1120s, probably around 1122–4. Her father was Guillaume, 8th Count of Poitou and 10th Duke of Aquitaine. Her mother was Alienor, or Aenor, daughter of Aimery I, Vicomte of Châtellerault. Eleanor was one of three children; she had a sister called Petronilla and a brother, Guillaume. Little Guillaume died during childhood, shortly before the death of the children's mother. After the death of her brother, Eleanor became her father's heir, at least until he remarried.

Duke William died unexpectedly during Easter week 1137, while on pilgrimage to Santiago de Compostela. Eleanor was somewhere in her mid-teens at the time of her father's death, and was not expected to be able to rule the valuable inheritance of Aquitaine alone. Just months after her father's death, in July 1137, she was married to Louis VII of France. It is entirely possible the marriage had been planned during her father's lifetime and brought forward due to the Duke's untimely death. At the time of the wedding, Louis was heir to the French throne. Although he had been crowned as junior king in 1131, during his father's lifetime, a tradition in the French royal house, a way of securing or at least signalling the succession. Shortly after the wedding on 1 August 1137, he succeeded as sole King of France, when his father, Louis VI, died of dysentery. During the years of the marriage the significance of Eleanor's lands was highlighted by the fact Louis went by the combined title of 'King of the French and Duke of Aquitaine'.[1]

There seems to have been some issue concerning Eleanor's fertility, with her first child not arriving until eight years into the marriage. There is a story that the revered abbot, Bernard of Clairvaux, had a meeting with Eleanor sometime around 1144, at St Denis, and promised to intercede with God for a son and heir to the French throne. Although Eleanor's first surviving child was born soon after, in 1145, it was a daughter, Marie, rather than the much-desired son. The year 1144, however, also saw the fall of Edessa, far away in the Holy Land, prompting the pope to call for a new Crusade. A Crusade appealed to Louis, who was seeking atonement for an atrocity committed in his name during the invasion of Champagne, in support of Eleanor's sister, Petronilla. Petronilla had caused scandal at the French court, by running away with Raoul of Vermandois and marrying him, despite the fact he already had a wife, the niece of the Count of Champagne. As a consequence, the two lovers were both excommunicated. However, conflict with Champagne soon followed. When Louis' men took the town of Vitry, some 1,300 men, women and children sought sanctuary in the town's church. Every single one of them perished when the church was burned to the ground by Louis' marauding soldiers.

It may well be that Eleanor joined the Second Crusade in the hope that God looked favourably on her, enough to give her a son. Maybe she wanted to help her uncle, Raymond of Toulouse, who was Prince of Antioch, who had sent presents accompanied by appeals for help, to his niece and her husband.[2] Or maybe it was Eleanor's own desire for adventure. Whatever her reason, it was both Eleanor and Louis who took the cross at Vézelay on Easter Day, 31 March 1346, following an inspiring call to arms by Bernard of Clairvaux.

The Second Crusade proved to be the defining point of Eleanor's marriage to Louis. Led jointly by Louis and the German emperor, Conrad III, it was an unmitigated disaster. Louis lost his personal bodyguard in the heavy defeat by the Seljuk Turks, at Laodicea, in January 1148, while still en route to Outremer. The French forces finally reached the Holy Land, arriving at Antioch, the home of Eleanor's uncle, Raymond, just a few months later. The warm welcome and lavish attention to his niece soon brought about rumours that Raymond and Eleanor were more than niece and uncle. The persistent rumours of Eleanor's infidelity, and incest with her uncle, led Louis to put her under close guard, despite a lack of any firm evidence of wrongdoing. She remained under such supervision – although discreetly, so as not to offend her vassals from Aquitaine, who made up a considerable part of Louis' army. Looking at the evidence today, it is impossible to know whether the rumours, which included not just infidelity but also the birth of a child, had any foundation in truth or were merely fanciful accusations.

Louis fulfilled his pilgrimage by entering Jerusalem in 1148, making the final leg of the journey to the Holy Sepulchre, on foot and fasting, just like countless pilgrims before him. In a council at Acre, Louis and his allies then decided that the best course of action was to take Damascus, with the original aim of the Crusade – to retake Edessa – being forgotten or sidelined. However, attempts to retake the city ended in failure and Louis returned, first to Antioch and then to Jerusalem. The Second Crusade was at an end and, owing to the rumours of infidelity, Louis and Eleanor's marriage had been dealt a fatal blow.

In 1149, Louis celebrated Easter in the Holy City of Jerusalem, before embarking at Acre for the return journey to France. Eleanor and her ladies travelled separately in another ship. They were reunited in September 1149 and were given a magnificent reception at Potenza, by King Roger of Sicily. From Sicily, they visited the pope, Eugenius III, at Tusculum. Eugenius attempted mediation in the royal marriage, going so far as to insist that they sleep together in a bed which he had personally blessed.[3] Some temporary reconciliation must have been achieved, as their second daughter,

Alix, was born within a year. However, with the failure to produce the desired male heir, a permanent reconciliation escaped them and a divorce, on the grounds of consanguinity, was finally proclaimed during Lent of 1152.

Louis attempted to retain control of Aquitaine by insisting that he approve of any prospective husband of Eleanor's; but the duchess rode away from the French court, and her daughters, returning to her own lands in Aquitaine in the spring of 1152. Eleanor's marriage – and Aquitaine – was a coveted prize and her journey home was not without its perils. She is said to have narrowly escaped ambushes by the Count of Blois and Geoffrey of Anjou, second son of Empress Matilda and Geoffrey, Count of Anjou. Nevertheless, it seems likely that Eleanor had already decided her future even before her divorce was proclaimed by the clerics at Beaugency. A year earlier, Henry of Anjou and his father, Count Geoffrey, husband of Empress Matilda, had been in attendance at the French court for Henry to swear fealty for the Duchy of Normandy, and to settle disputes over the northwestern county, the Vexin. Although the Vexin issue was far from settled, Henry rode away, confirmed as Duke of Normandy and, possibly, with a promise of marriage from the soon-to-be divorced queen.[4]

Although the marriage of Henry and Eleanor is often presented as a love-match, it was a marriage of hardheaded practicality with mutual benefits. Eleanor needed a husband who was strong enough to stand up to Louis. As Duke of Normandy and Count of Anjou, and with the possibility of the crown of England tantalisingly close, Henry was the ideal choice as Eleanor's new husband. They were married in Poitiers Cathedral in May 1152; Eleanor was around thirty years old and Henry was nineteen. Louis was furious and called Henry to court to explain himself for having married without the permission of his liege lord. When Henry failed to appear, Louis formed a coalition against him, persuading King Stephen to attack Normandy from England, while he attacked from the south. Stephen was keen to oblige, hoping to secure the English succession for his son, Eustace, and neutralise the threat posed by Henry. Louis' other allies included Thibault of Blois, recently betrothed to Alix, the two-year-old daughter of Louis and Eleanor; and Henry of Champagne, who was now married to seven-year-old Marie, Louis and Eleanor's eldest daughter, and Eleanor's heir to Aquitaine, at least until Eleanor and Henry had a son.

Louis had thought Henry was preoccupied with plans for invading England. Instead, he quickly reacted to the French king's aggression, conducting a lightning campaign, which caught Louis off guard. The French king was completely outmanoeuvred and was quick to acquiesce when the Church called for peace. Henry could then turn his attention to England, which he invaded in 1153. However, the death of Stephen's oldest son and heir, Eustace, in August of that year ultimately led to the Treaty of Winchester, with Stephen bypassing his youngest son, William, in order to settle the succession on Henry and bring to a close the twenty years of warfare, known as the Anarchy. When Stephen died the following year, Henry's accession followed peacefully. Henry and Eleanor were crowned, together, in a magnificent ceremony in Westminster Abbey, on 19 December 1154. They now ruled an empire that stretched from the borders of Scotland in the north, to the borders of Spain in the south.

By the time of her marriage to Henry, Eleanor had already survived the birthing chamber on at least two occasions, with the births of her daughters, Marie and Alix, by Louis VII. Although she had only produced two children in fifteen years of marriage to Louis, by the time of her coronation Eleanor had already provided Henry with a son and heir, William, born in August 1153. William died in England in 1156, aged just three, with his mother by his side, and his father away in the family's Continental domains. However, he had already been joined in the nursery by another son, Henry, born in February 1155, and a daughter, Matilda, who was two months old when little William died. Childbirth was a dangerous time for women, with no guarantee that having survived once, twice or three times, you would survive a fourth or fifth confinement. Nevertheless, after William's death, Eleanor safely delivered another five children into the world. Her favourite son, Richard, who was her choice as heir to Aquitaine, was born in September 1157 and another son, Geoffrey, who became Duke of Brittany when he married the duchy's heiress, Constance, arrived twelve months later. Eleanor, who would become Queen of Castile, was born in October 1162, and Joanna, who would initially marry the King of Sicily and then Raymond VI of Toulouse, arrived in October 1165. Eleanor's fifth son, and tenth and last child, John, was born at Christmas, 1167.[5] Having given birth to ten children over the course of twenty-two years, Eleanor had survived the most perilous aspect of any medieval woman's life. She would have been well aware of the risk she was taking every time she entered the birthing chamber, knowing that either she or the baby, or both, may not survive.

During their married life together Henry was constantly on the move, travelling between his vast domains, dealing with restless barons, dispensing justice and holding court. Eleanor joined him when she could, depending on her state of pregnancy or recent childbirths. In 1156, for example, still grieving for her three-year-old son William, Eleanor crossed the English Channel with her surviving son, eighteen-month-old Henry, and daughter Matilda, when Matilda was just two months old, journeying to join Henry in Anjou, before moving on to Aquitaine in October. Travel had its own dangers; the English Channel is not the calmest of sea roads and Henry's own uncle, William, son and heir of Henry I, had been killed in the *White Ship* tragedy in 1120, when his ship had foundered leaving harbour, killing all but one of the people on board.

Land journeys could be equally hazardous. Indeed, Eleanor was almost kidnapped or killed in April 1168, when travelling through the hills of Poitou, escorted by Patrick, Earl of Salisbury, and his men. The party were ambushed by Eleanor's rebellious vassals, Geoffrey and Guy de Lusignan. Salisbury and his men were travelling, unarmoured, when the de Lusignans fell upon them. The earl 'sent the Queen on to the castle' at Poitiers while he and the remainder of his men held off the attackers, giving the queen time to make it to safety.[6] The earl was killed by a lance during the vicious skirmish; his nephew, William Marshal, was wounded in the thigh and captured after having his horse killed under him. William spent several months in captivity, his wounds healing despite the harsh treatment meted out by the de Lusignans. William was a young, penniless knight and was finally released when Queen Eleanor agreed to pay his ransom.[7] William then joined the queen's household, before joining that of her son, Henry. William Marshal would faithfully serve five English kings – Henry II, Henry, the Young King, crowned during his father's lifetime, Richard I the Lionheart, King John and, finally, Henry III, for whom the aged Marshal was regent.

The years 1169 to 1173 were spent, almost exclusively for Eleanor, in her duchy of Aquitaine with her son, Richard, who she was training as her eventual successor. Richard was invested as Count of Poitou and, in 1169, paid homage to Eleanor's first husband, King Louis, for the Duchy of Aquitaine. In 1173, however, news reached Henry II that his sons were plotting against him. The boys – now men – were tired of frequently having the possibility of power and responsibility dangled before them, only for their father to withdraw it at the last minute. Henry's eldest son, Henry, the Young King, fled to the court of Louis VII, his father-in-law since his marriage to Louis' daughter, Marguerite, in 1160. For unknown reasons, Eleanor sided with her sons against their father. It was later suggested that Eleanor had been incensed at Henry's relationship with Rosamund Clifford – the Fair Rosamund – and that, wounded by this betrayal, had joined or incited her sons' rebellion.

Unfortunately, there is no contemporary evidence that the affair caused Eleanor's rebellion and her reasons remain obscure. She may have resented the restrictions of power placed on her, or the fact Henry would not allow their sons any exercise of power. Whatever the reason, Eleanor joined the rebellion, and lost. Her sons were outmanoeuvred and defeated by Henry. Far from humiliating them, however, Henry came to terms with his sons and an uneasy peace ensued. On the other hand, Henry was not so forgiving of Eleanor, who was captured while trying to escape Poitou; she had tried to reach the safety of the French court, dressed in men's clothing. In 1174, Henry sent his queen to imprisonment in England, possibly at Salisbury, under heavy guard.

Eleanor was kept securely at first, but her imprisonment was relaxed as the years passed, especially after the death of her son, Henry, the Young King, who had pleaded with his father from his deathbed in 1183, that his mother be treated less harshly. In subsequent years, Eleanor was allowed at court for some ceremonial occasions, and was allowed visits by her daughter, Matilda, who had been exiled with her husband, Henry of Saxony, from their German lands. Matilda was instrumental in getting the restrictions eased even further and, although she was still in the custody of guards, Eleanor was allowed to reside with Matilda at various locations in England, including Windsor and Berkhamsted. However, fifteen years of imprisonment in England, far away from her homeland and court in Aquitaine, cannot have been easy for a queen used to riding freely across the vast domains she and her husband possessed.

The queen was only released after Henry's death in 1189; indeed, ordering his mother's release was one of the first acts of her son, Richard I. And the queen was there to welcome him for his ceremonial entry into Winchester in August 1189. Now in her mid-sixties, Eleanor was given a new lease of life, and lived it with the same energy and vigour she had in the years before her imprisonment. Almost immediately, Eleanor was trusted with the oversight of the government of England. In 1190 she travelled to Navarre, to collect Richard's bride, Berengaria, and deliver the princess to her son, then en route to the Holy Land on the Third Crusade. After a winter journey over the Alps, the queen, now almost seventy, escorted Berenagria to a rendezvous with Richard at Messina in Sicily in March 1191. Having fulfilled her mission, Eleanor set off home, almost immediately; although not before what must have been an emotional reunion with her youngest daughter, Joanna, who was Queen of Sicily and had been widowed in November 1189, but held prisoner by her husband's successor, Tancred. Richard affected her release and his sister was now to be a companion for his bride; Joanna accompanied Richard and Berenagria to the Holy Land.

Eleanor was later instrumental in securing her son's release from captivity in Germany. Richard had been captured by Leopold V, Duke of Austria, on his return journey from the Holy Land, in December 1192. He was handed over to the Holy Roman Emperor, Heinrich VI, in March 1193. During Richard's captivity, Eleanor was inexhaustible in her attempts to raise the ransom, some 150,000 marks and to keep her son, John, in check. John took the opportunity created by Richard's absence to make a play for power; he and Philip II Augustus, King of France, went so far as to offer Heinrich 80,000 marks to keep Richard incarcerated. John was still in open opposition to his brother when Eleanor finally secured Richard's release, on 4 February 1194. Eleanor travelled to Germany to personally hand over the ransom payment and escort Richard home. As news of Richard's release reached England, John fled to France.

Richard's death in April 1199, must have come as a horrific blow for Eleanor; the loss of her favourite son, at just forty-one years of age, caused immense grief. Richard's death was soon followed by that of Joanna, Eleanor's youngest daughter, who, heavily pregnant and hurt, had sought refuge with her mother at Rouen. Eleanor was by her daughter's side as she gave birth to a son, Richard, who lived only long enough to be baptised. Joanna died within moments of her son, in September 1199, and mother and baby were buried together at the Abbey of Fontevrault.

Having lost two of her children in quick succession, and with her youngest son, John, now on the English throne, Eleanor undertook one final, diplomatic mission. Nearing her eightieth year, Queen Eleanor journeyed across the Pyrenees to Castile, in search of a bride for Louis, the dauphin of France and grandson of her first husband, Louis VII. England's Dowager Queen was received at the court of Alfonso VIII and her own daughter, Eleanor, Queen of Castile, with all the pomp and pageantry the Castilians could muster. She stayed there for more than two months, taking the opportunity to spend some time with her daughter and getting to know her granddaughters. Eleanor of Aquitaine seems to have decided that twelve-year-old Blanca would make a more suitable bride for Louis than her sister, Uracca. Eleanor then brought Blanca back to France and delivered her to her bridegroom, Louis; the couple were married in Normandy, as France was under papal interdict at the time, owing to the marital indiscretions of Louis' father, King Philip II Augustus.

Following her delivery of Blanca to her new husband, Eleanor retired to the Abbey at Fontevrault. She did not take the veil as a nun, but lived in her own house within the abbey's precincts. However, the eighty-year-old queen had one final adventure in 1202, when she was besieged by her fifteen-year-old grandson, Arthur, Duke of Brittany, at Mirebeau. Arthur had rebelled against his uncle, King John, and made an attempt on the English throne. In a remarkable forced march, John quickly came to his mother's rescue, capturing Arthur and his sister, Eleanor, and raising the siege.[8] Arthur disappeared into King John's dungeons at Rouen and probably died there during Easter, 1203. His sister, Eleanor, was sent to England, to a perpetual, if comfortable, imprisonment.

The event was Eleanor's last major adventure; increasingly frail, she retreated to Fontevrault, where she died on 31 March 1204, aged around eighty-two. She had outlived all but two of her children, with only Eleanor in Castile, and John in England, still living. She was buried in the abbey church alongside her second husband, Henry II, and her son, Richard, and daughter, Joanna.

Eleanor of Aquitaine had survived the Second Crusade, several kidnap attempts, fifteen years of imprisonment and giving birth to ten children. She was the most remarkable woman of the medieval age, the ultimate survivor and a heroine to the core.

She was not the only medieval woman who endured, and survived, rejection by a husband. It might be expected that a man who was given a king's granddaughter as a wife would relish the glamour and connections such a bride brought. However, this was not always the case, as the life and marriage of Joan of Bar proves. Joan was the granddaughter of the mighty Edward I, King of England, and his queen, Eleanor of Castile. Her mother was Eleanor, Edward and Eleanor's eldest surviving child. Eleanor of England had been born in June 1264 and was married to Alfonso III, King of Aragon, by proxy on 15 August 1290 at Westminster Abbey. Unfortunately, the groom died before the marriage could be consummated so Eleanor married again at Bristol on 20 September 1293, to Henry III, Count of Bar. Henry and Eleanor had at least two children. Their son, Edward, and daughter, Joan, were born in successive years, in 1294 and 1295,[9] although there seems to be some confusion about who was the eldest. A possible third child, Eleanor, is said to have married Llywelyn ap Owen of Deheubarth; but her existence seems to be in question.

As usual with medieval women – even royal ones – we know very little of Joan's childhood. Her mother died in Ghent in 1298; her body was brought back to England and buried in Westminster Abbey, London. Joan's father, the Count of Bar, died in 1302, possibly as a result of injuries received in battle while fighting in Sicily. The count was succeeded by his only son, Edward, who was then only six or seven years old. During little Count Edward's minority, the County of Bar was to be run by his grandfather, Edward I, with the child's uncle John of Puisaye and the Bishops of Liege and Metz acting as governors. It is likely the children came to live at the English court, or at least spent some time there. By 1310 Edward's majority was declared and he married Mary, daughter of Robert II, Duke of Burgundy, in that year.

By this time, young Joan had already been married for four years. It was during the parliament of 1306 that Edward I had settled Joan's future. On 15 March, Edward had offered Joan's hand in marriage to nineteen-year-old John de Warenne, 7th Earl of Surrey, who had recently been granted his grandfather's lands, despite the fact he hadn't yet reached the required age of twenty-one. Once the betrothal was finalised, Joan was sent for and arrived in England, landing at Dover on 13 April.[10]

John de Warenne was not without his own royal connections. His aunt Isabella had been married to Scots king John Balliol, and their son, John's cousin, was Edward Balliol, John's ward; Edward would be, briefly, King of Scots in the 1330s, but would eventually lose out to his rival, David II, son of Robert the Bruce. John de Warenne was the grandson of Edward I's good friend, also named John de Warenne, the 6th Earl of Surrey and former Warden of Scotland. Young John's father, William de Warenne, had died in a tournament in the same year John was born, 1286. As a consequence, John was raised by his grandfather, until the 6th Earl's death in 1304, when John's wardship passed to the king himself. In the week following the betrothal of John and Joan, and in anticipation of a new expedition against Scotland, Edward I held a magnificent ceremony for the knighting of his eldest son, Edward; the king knighted the prince, who then went on to knight the other candidates, in the glorious setting of Westminster Abbey. The ceremony was also to bestow knighthoods on almost 300 men, John de Warenne included:

> The yong Erle of Warenne with grete nobley was thare
> A wif thei him bikenne, the erles doubter of Bare.[11]

As the celebrations continued a number of weddings also took place, involving several barons and nobles. John de Warenne and Joan of Bar were married on 25 May, with John's sister, Alice, marrying Edmund FitzAlan, 9th Earl of Arundel, at about the same time. Edmund had been a ward of John's grandfather. The two young men were very close in age and were political allies and friends. Barely ten years old, Joan was escorted to the palace at Westminster with great pomp and she and John were married in the presence of the ageing king.

Following the wedding John and his child-bride lived on the Warenne's Yorkshire estates, sharing their time between their castles at Conisbrough and Sandal. In the wider world, Edward I died in the summer of 1307 and was succeeded by his son, Edward II. Initially, John de Warenne was a supporter of Edward; witnessing the charter which made Edward's favourite, Piers Gaveston, Earl of

Cornwall and accompanying the king to France to claim his bride, Isabella, daughter of Philip IV of France.[12] However, John was not immune to the turbulence and distrust of Edward's reign and changed sides several times in the arguments between the king and his barons. The uncertainty of Edward's reign cannot have helped the marriage of John and Joan, but neither, it seems, did John. The couple was soon estranged; Joan was half John's age when they married, and not yet old enough to consummate the marriage. This must have put an incredible strain on the relationship. There had been indications of problems as early as 1309, when the king had given John permission to name whoever he wished as his heir, as long as any children he may have by Joan were not disinherited. By 1313, although Joan was now eighteen and the marriage had most likely been consummated, there were still no children, and the couple were obviously unhappy.

In the spring of that year, Edward sent his yeoman, William Aune, to bring Joan to the king. She was taken from Warenne's castle at Conisbrough and lodged in the Tower of London, at the king's expense. John, on the other hand, was openly living with his mistress, Maud Nereford, for which he was threatened with excommunication in May; a sentence that was finally carried out by the Bishop of Chichester when Edward's attempts to prevent it failed. A long legal battle followed. Eager to marry Maud and legitimise his two sons by her, John attempted to dissolve his marriage to Joan on the grounds of consanguinity – they were related in the third and fourth degrees. He also claimed that he was pressured into marrying Joan against his will. Maud added her own suit to the legal proceeding by claiming that John had contracted to marry her before his marriage to Joan.

The Church council registered disapproval of John and Maud's relationship; as did a council of nobles, which included the king's cousin and most powerful nobleman in the land, Thomas, Earl of Lancaster. John had even been Thomas's retainer in the early years of the king's reign. However, relations had soured following the murder of Gaveston. John had captured Gaveston at the siege of Scarborough Castle and was taking him south when Lancaster had taken Gaveston from John's custody, held a mock trial and executed him on 19 June 1312.[13] Thomas of Lancaster's objection to John's divorce would spark a feud between the two men that only ended with Lancaster's death.

In May 1313, John was told by the Archbishop of Canterbury; 'Countess Joanna, that good lady, his consort, who so languished in expectation of his good pleasure and favour, was nevertheless his true and lawful wife, and that he could never be legally separated from her while she lived, for any reason that they had heard.'[14] The divorce case would drag on for two years, with John unable to find a friendly ecclesiastical court who would pronounce in his favour. Clearly unhappy with John's treatment of his cousin, Edward II also ordered the confiscation of High Peak, the castle, town and manor the king had given to John in gratitude for the earl's services in the Scottish campaign of 1310.[15] In the meantime, Joan had left England for France, accompanying the king and queen. Being of a similar age to the young queen, Joan and Isabella of France were close friends. For practical reasons, in view of his absence from England, Edward II ordered the Bishop of Norwich to defer excommunicating John de Warenne, so that he could act as keeper of the peace during Edward's absence.[16] In 1316 John agreed to pay Joan a sum of £200 annually while the suit was ongoing, and to provide Joan with lands worth 740 marks once the marriage was dissolved.[17] As the hopes of an annulment faded, John enlisted the help of Aymer de Valence, Earl of Pembroke, who was on an embassy to Avignon for Edward II, in presenting a petition to the pope, seeking a papal annulment; Pembroke was abducted while crossing the County of Bar, on his return journey.

It seems likely that Pembroke's capture and imprisonment was ordered by Joan's brother, Edward, Count of Bar, unhappy with John's mistreatment of his sister. Joan was among a number of high-profile nobles, including the kings of England and France, who successfully petitioned the Count of Bar to release Pembroke; he was freed in June 1317.[18] At about the same time, John rearranged his estates, surrendering them to the king to have them re-granted with specifications that some of the lands could pass to his sons by Maud Nereford on his death, first to the eldest, John, and then to his brother Thomas. John's support for Edward II remained steadfast, he even went so far as to abduct Alice de Lacey, wife of Thomas of Lancaster, possibly at the instigation of the king himself, in 1317. Lancaster retaliated by attacking John's Yorkshire strongholds, and even took Conisbrough Castle after a very short siege.[19] John was forced to come to terms with Lancaster, although it meant giving up most of his Yorkshire estates in exchange for land in Devon and Somerset. The rebellion of Thomas of Lancaster was crushed at the Battle of Boroughbridge in 1322, but war simmered on with France adding to the king's troubles by demanding he personally pay homage for his French lands.

While the troubles in England intensified, John's marriage troubles seem to have somewhat abated. In 1325, John de Warenne was appointed captain of an English expedition to Aquitaine and was away from home for the next year. John's Yorkshire lands, taken into the king's custody following Lancaster's downfall, were finally returned to him in 1326. Joan had been in France at the same time, having accompanied Edward II's queen, Isabella, on her diplomatic mission to her brother the King of France, to discuss peace; and stayed with her when the queen refused to return to England because of her husband's infatuation with Hugh le Despenser the Younger. Indeed, Joan was one of the people to whom Edward II wrote in the hope of persuading the queen to return home.[20] Some sources say that when Warenne returned to England in 1326, Joan accompanied him and they even received permission to go abroad in February 1327 – as a couple.

Following the downfall of Edward II, his son and the new king, Edward III, in gratitude for her service to his mother, Queen Isabella, settled lands on Joan for life, and granted her some of the goods forfeited by Edmund FitzAlan.[21] John's erstwhile brother-in-law had been caught up in the turbulence of Edward II's downfall and executed. John de Warenne proved a faithful servant to Edward III, acting as keeper of the realm, jointly with young prince Edward, during the king's absences in 1338 and 1340. Joan was in John's company and treated as his wife in the years between 1331 and 1337. In 1331 John gave grants to the priory at Lewes, a de Warenne foundation, for the souls of himself and Joan.[22] However, Joan went abroad with her entire household in 1337 shortly after her brother's death; Edward, Count of Bar, had died in a shipwreck on his way to the Crusades and it is possible that Joan was acting as regent for her nephew, Henry IV, Count of Bar.

By the 1340s Maud Nereford was now dead and her sons had both joined the Knights Hospitallers, but John had a new lover in Isabella Holland, daughter of Sir Robert Holland, a leading retainer of Thomas of Lancaster. And it seems he was again contemplating divorce. In a 1344 letter from the Bishop of Winchester charges him to hold Joan in marital affection and honour the dispensation that had been granted for his marriage. Joan was abroad again, possibly acting as regent for her great-nephew, Edward II Count of Bar. Amid fears that John de Warenne would try to take Joan's lands, Edward III acted to guarantee them in her absence. By 1345, in one final attempt to dissolve his marriage John was claiming that he had had an affair before marrying Joan, with his wife's maternal aunt Mary of Woodstock, when he was nineteen and Mary twenty-seven years of age.[23] This was indeed a drastic claim, as Mary had been a nun since she was about seven years old, and it was probably born out of desperation; John was getting increasingly infirm and still had no heir to succeed him. It was a last ditch attempt to marry Isabella and have legitimate children. It failed, however, and John died at Conisbrough Castle between 28 and 30 June 1347, aged sixty-one. His will, written just before his death and dated 24 June 1347, left various gifts to Isabella and his illegitimate children – but nothing to Joan, his wife.[24] Warenne left several illegitimate children, including at least three boys and three girls. John died on 30 June and was buried amongst his ancestors, in the Church of St Pancras at Lewes Priory. Joan de Bar was abroad when her husband died. She lived for another fourteen years, retaining the title of Countess of Surrey until her death; Richard FitzAlan, John's heir, took possession of the Warenne estates on John's death, but didn't use the title Earl of Surrey until after Joan died. The king granted her an annual income of £200 as her dower; in 1350 she was granted a safe-conduct by Edward III, to go on pilgrimage on the Continent, visiting several shrines. In the 1350s Joan is said to have often visited the French king, Jean II, who was a prisoner of Edward III in London; she was also a regular visitor at court, dining with the queen, on occasion, and with other members of the royal family. After a long and turbulent life, and at around sixty-six years of age, Joan died in London on 31 August 1361. She was not buried in England, however; her body was conducted to France by her valet, where she was buried at Sainte-Maxe Collegiate Church in Bar-le-Duc in October 1361.

Joan's marriage must have been one of the most miserable of the medieval era. At a time of great upheaval, Joan did not even have the comfort and security offered by a faithful husband. Nevertheless, she found a life and a purpose in her home County of Bar, and in supporting her nephew during his minority. She also had the trust and friendship of Queen Isabella and later, Edward III and Philippa of Hainault, who recognised and valued her loyalty and support.

Another granddaughter of a king who faced many trials and tribulations was Anne of Woodstock. Born sometime around 1382 Anne was the daughter of Thomas of Woodstock, 1st Duke of Gloucester, and Eleanor de Bohun. Anne's parentage was impeccable. Her father was the youngest son of the late king Edward III and his queen, Philippa of Hainault, making Anne first cousins with the two subsequent kings, Richard II and Henry IV. With Henry IV's first wife, Mary de Bohun, Anne's mother was co-heiress of the Earls of Hereford. Anne grew up in a time of turmoil for England, her childhood marred by the political conflicts of Richard II's reign.

Richard had succeeded his grandfather, Edward III, in 1377, aged just ten years old. By the time he reached his twenties, Richard was gaining a reputation as a tyrannical ruler, highly dependent on personal favourites, whom he promoted to positions of power and influence. In the late 1380s, Anne's father had set himself up in opposition to the king's tyrannical rule – as a leader of the Lords Appellant he was responsible for curbing the king's power and in 1386 they established a commission to rule England for a year, keeping Richard II as little more than a figurehead. Having defeated the king's favourite, Robert de Vere, Earl of Oxford, at Radcot Ridge, the Lords Appellant arrested and executed many of the king's supporters, although de Vere and another favourite, Michael de la Pole, Earl of Suffolk, fled abroad and were sentenced to death *in absentia*; they both died in exile, Michael de la Pole in France in 1389 and Robert de Vere in Belgium in 1392.[25]

Anne was probably born at Pleshey Castle, in Essex, which was also the scene for the celebrations of her first wedding. In June 1391, aged only eight or nine, Anne was married to Thomas Stafford, 3rd Earl of Stafford, who was about fifteen years her senior. Thomas died in the following year, before Anne was even old enough for the marriage to be consummated. However, even before Thomas Stafford's death, it seems, it had been agreed that, should he die, Anne would marry one of Thomas's younger brothers. These brothers, William and Edmund Stafford, were wards of Anne's father. The elder of the two, William, died in 1395, when he was about nineteen years old; Anne was married to the youngest, Edmund, now 5th Earl of Stafford, in 1396. In the year following her marriage, Anne was to suffer further tragedy when her father, recovering from illness at the family's home of Pleshey Castle, was personally arrested by the king. Thomas was transported to imprisonment in Calais to await trial, under the care of the Earl of Nottingham. His death was reported in September of that year. A later inquiry established that Thomas Duke of Gloucester had been murdered, most likely on the night of 8 September 1397, and probably smothered under a mattress.[26]

The Duke was declared a traitor and his lands and property were forfeited to the crown. Anne's only brother, Humphrey, was made a ward of King Richard II and was with the king in Ireland two years later, when Henry Bolingbroke invaded England and claimed the crown as Henry IV. Henry had been a political ally of Anne's father and so with his accession, Anne's family's fortunes were destined to improve. However, although the new king ordered Humphrey's return to England, the young man died on the voyage home in August 1399, aged just eighteen. Anne's life was hit by two further losses in close succession. Her mother, Eleanor de Bohun, died on 3 October 1399. The chronicler, Walsingham, said she died of a broken heart, following the deaths of her husband and only son so close together.[27] A year later, Anne's unmarried sister, Joan, died in August 1400. Anne's only surviving sibling, Isabel, then took the veil at the Minoresses in London, in April 1402, on her sixteenth birthday.

With her sister Isabel joining a convent, Anne became the sole heiress of her father, and one of the greatest heiresses in the kingdom. From 1399 she was recognised as Countess of Buckingham, Hereford and Northampton and was made a Lady of the Garter in 1405. In these years, Anne gave birth to two daughters and a son. Of her daughters, Philippa died young and Anne would marry consecutively her cousins Edmund Mortimer, Earl of March, and John Holland, 3rd Duke of Exeter. Anne's only son by Edmund Stafford, Humphrey, was born in 1402 and would go on to be created 1st Duke of Buckingham in 1444. Loyal to Henry VI at the outbreak of the Wars of the Roses, he would be killed at the Battle of Northampton in 1460. Humphrey's son, Henry, would be husband to Henry VII's mother, Margaret Beaufort.[28]

On 21 July 1403 Anne was widowed for the second time when Edmund was killed fighting for the king at the Battle of Shrewsbury. Still only in her early twenties, Anne was left with two young children and a dower income of £1,500 a year. However, with her dower properties stretched across the strategically important Welsh Marches, Anne's remarriage was of great interest to Henry IV. Of immediate concern was the security of those dower properties, given the king's ongoing conflict with Owain Glyn Dwr and the Welsh. Sir William Bourchier, Count of Eu, was dispatched to help protect Anne and her properties from any Welsh incursions. And it was with this same knight that Anne, taking her future into her own hands, contracted a secret marriage some time before 20 November 1405. The king was displeased with the clandestine marriage and the couple were fined 'great sums'. However, Bourchier, it seems, was highly charismatic, a capable soldier and valued administrator; all factors which, when added to his proven loyalty to the Lancastrian king, helped to ensure that the couple was soon forgiven. Sir William Bourchier would continue his impressive career under Henry V; fighting at Agincourt in 1415, after which he was appointed Constable of the Tower of London and took responsibility of the high-profile French prisoners captured in the battle. In letters Anne described with pride 'the valiant prowess, wisdom and good governance' of her husband.[29]

Anne and William seem to have been genuinely in love and soon had a nursery full of children, with four sons and a daughter all born before 1415. Anne promoted the careers of all her children and arranged marriages for them. William and Anne's eldest son, Henry, 1st Earl of Essex, was married to Isabel of Cambridge, daughter of Richard of Conisbrough and sister of Richard, Duke of York. A Yorkist supporter, Henry Bourchier fought at the Second Battle of St Albans and at Towton, dying in April 1483. Thomas Bourchier, most likely Anne and William's second son, went to Oxford and then joined the Church. He rose to become Archbishop of Canterbury in 1454 and was made a cardinal in 1467. Although he was Chancellor for a short time, in the reign of Henry VI, Thomas was a loyal supporter of the Yorkist cause and it was Edward IV himself who wrote to the pope urging for Thomas's promotion to cardinal. In his position as Archbishop of Canterbury, Thomas crowned both Richard III and Henry VII; he died in 1486 and was buried next to the high altar in Canterbury Cathedral. Of their other sons; William Bourchier became Baron FitzWarin in right of his wife, and Sir John Bourchier was created Baron Berners following his marriage to Margery Berners and was

Constable of Windsor Castle in the 1460s. Anne and William's only daughter, Eleanor Bourchier, married John de Mowbray, 3rd Duke of Norfolk, and was the mother of another John, the fourth Duke. Eleanor was the grandmother of little Anne de Mowbray, child bride of Edward IV's second son Richard, Duke of York. She died shortly before her ninth birthday.

Although they seem to have been on opposing sides of the political spectrum, with Humphrey Stafford being a loyal Lancastrian, Humphrey remained close to his mother and his Bourchier half-siblings.[30] Anne was widowed for a third and final time when William died at Troyes in 1420. His body was sent back to England for burial at Llanthony Priory in Gloucestershire. Anne had an enduring friendship with the Prior at Llanthony, John Wyche, and corresponded with him in both French and English. Although not yet forty, Anne never remarried. Throughout her marriages – and after – she was personally involved in estate management and her letters demonstrate a sound business acumen. Anne had loyal and talented administrators who helped her fight for her interests. As Earl of Buckingham, Anne's father had revenues of £1,000 a year from the lordships of Oakham, Rutland and Holderness, in Yorkshire. While Oakham was returned to Anne in 1414 she only recovered Holderness in 1437, the year before she died.[31]

While Anne was cousin to the king, Henry V, both he and his father had resented the unequal division of the Bohun inheritance in her favour. Henry V was to eventually force a new settlement on the recently widowed countess, in 1421, this time heavily weighted for the king's benefit, leaving Anne just £1200 a year from her mother's inheritance; and even this often fell into arrears. Anne had shared a love of the Church with her mother and was known for her piety and love of learning. She died in October 1438, aged around fifty-five. Her will, written 'in the Englyshe tonge for my most profit redyng and vnderstandyng', remembered her 'most trewe and diligent' retainers.[32] A granddaughter of Edward III, she was buried beside her second husband, William, at Llanthony Priory; in 1453, the Bourchier children set up a perpetual chantry for the welfare of the souls of their parents.

Anne of Gloucester was the mother of combatants on both sides of the Wars of the Roses. She had survived her father's murder and attainder to find happiness in her second marriage. She was an astute business woman, loyal wife and a devoted mother, and managed to keep the two branches of her family, politically diverse as they were, on friendly terms during one of the most famous conflicts of the medieval era, the Wars of the Roses.

A contemporary of Anne of Woodstock, Maud Clifford, was another woman who had to negotiate the marital and political pitfalls of the 15th century. Maud Clifford was born around 1389, at Brough Castle in Westmoreland. Maud (or Matilda) was the daughter of Thomas Clifford, 6th Baron Clifford, and his wife Elizabeth de Ros. Maud's brother, John, has also been given 1389 as his possible year of birth. It may be that John and Maud were twins, or that they were born within a year of each other. Their early childhood cannot have been very pleasant as it was marred with loss. Their paternal grandfather, Roger Clifford, died in July of 1389, probably of a stroke. And in October 1391, their father, Thomas, died. While in Königsberg Thomas had had a disagreement with Sir William Douglas, illegitimate son of the Earl of Douglas; Douglas was killed in the ensuing brawl and Clifford, overcome with guilt, went on pilgrimage to Jerusalem in penance. He died on an unidentified Mediterranean island while on the way to the Holy City. Thomas and his wife, Elizabeth, had a close, loving relationship; as a widow, Elizabeth de Ros referred to Thomas as 'my most dear lord and husband'.[33]

Some time before 1406, Maud was married to John Neville, Lord Latimer. For some unknown reason the marriage was never consummated and Maud successfully sued for an annulment. The marriage was dissolved with very favourable terms for Maud; some of the Neville lands had been put in trust for Maud and, even though the marriage had been declared invalid, she was allowed to keep them. Maud was, therefore, a very attractive bride for a landless earl. Richard of Conisbrough lived at Conisbrough Castle in Yorkshire, as the tenant of his older brother, Edward, 2nd Duke of York. Richard was a widower with two small children; his wife, Anne Mortimer, had died sometime after 1411, when she had given birth to their second child, Richard, the future Duke of York, probably at Conisbrough Castle. It is not known when Anne died, but it was before 1414, which is the probable date of Maud's marriage to the Earl of Cambridge. It was also in 1414 that Richard was created Earl of Cambridge by Henry V; with no land settlement accompanying the title, he was the poorest – and only landless – earl in England, and struggled financially to adequately maintain his position as earl.[34]

Unfortunately, the marriage between Richard and Maud, proved to be short-lived; it probably lasted less than a year. In 1415 Richard became involved in the Southampton Plot, a plan to overthrow king Henry V and replace him with his own brother-in-law, Edmund Mortimer, Earl of March. However, March revealed the plot to the king and Richard and his accomplices were arrested. With Henry V heading out on the campaign that would see the English victory at Agincourt in October of that year, the conspirators were swiftly dealt with and Richard of Conisbrough was beheaded for treason on 5 August 1415. Richard of Conisbrough was not attainted, so his lands, such as they were, were not forfeit to the crown. Maud was allowed to remain at Conisbrough Castle, and her stepson, Richard, would be allowed to inherit the Dukedom of York from his uncle, Edward, who was killed fighting at Agincourt, on 25 October 1415.

It is not clear how much contact Maud had with her step-children. The eldest child, Isabel, had been born around 1409; she had been betrothed in 1412 to Sir Thomas Grey and it is possible that she was raised in the household of the Grey family. Thomas Grey's father had been a co-conspirator in the Southampton Plot and was executed three days before Isabel's own father. Thomas Grey junior died before 1426, when Isabel married Henry Bourchier, 1st Earl of Essex and son of Anne of Woodstock. As Duke of York, Isabel's brother, Richard was a valuable pawn; his wardship and marriage was a great prize, and would eventually go to Ralph Neville, Earl of Westmoreland, with York marrying Neville's daughter, Cecily. The Yorks' eldest and youngest sons would become the Yorkist kings of England; Edward IV and Richard III, respectively.

Maud would continue to use Conisbrough Castle as her main residence throughout her life; she received an annuity of £100 from the Earl of March, perhaps to assuage his guilt in the part he played in her husband's downfall.[35] As Dowager Countess of Cambridge, Maud seems to have led a full and active life, and remained very close to her Clifford family; they stayed with her often and she was a regular visitor to the Clifford ancestral home of Skipton Castle. Her nephew Thomas and his family lived with her at Conisbrough for a year in 1437, while his castle at Skipton was undergoing extensive works. On 8 April 1435 Maud's great-nephew, John

Clifford – the future 9th Baron Clifford – was born at Conisbrough Castle. He was the grandson of Maud's brother, John, and son of her nephew, Thomas, and his wife, Joan Dacre. Baby John would have been born either in the solar of the keep itself, or in the family apartments above the great hall of the inner bailey. Either way it's most likely he was baptised in the small private chapel within the keep; with Maud as his godmother. The chapel is built into one of the keep's six buttresses and, despite the years and water damage, it is a wonder to behold, with exquisite designs carved into the stone columns, and the vaulted ceiling.

Maud's brother, John, was killed at the siege of Meaux in 1422 and her nephew, Thomas, would be killed at the First Battle of St Albans in 1455, supposedly by Richard, Duke of York, himself. And so it was, that on the 30 December 1460, at the Battle of Wakefield, John Clifford is said to have taken his revenge by killing York's son Edmund, the seventeen-year-old Earl of Rutland. Whether or not Clifford uttered the words 'Thy father slew my father; therefore, die,' as he killed young Edmund, is entirely debatable, but the event serves to highlight how closely the noble families of the Wars of the Roses were related.[36] There is some suggestion that Maud remarried in 1429. The supposed groom was John Wentworth of North Elmsall, Yorkshire. However, this seems to be more of a family legend among the Wentworth family and only arose over 100 years after Maud's death.

Maud's will demonstrates her closeness to her family, and serves as an insight into her comfortable life and the sumptuous furnishings of the castle,

> To Thomas, Lord Clifford, my relation: a 'hall' of arras [a fine woven wall hanging from Arras] bought from Sir Robert Babthorpe; my bed of Arras with three curtains; four cushions of red silk; two long cushions of cloth.
>
> To John Clifford, my godson: 12 silver dishes, 6 salt cellars signed with the 'trayfulles' [trefoils] and a shell.
>
> To Beatrice Waterton, my relation: a gold cross, which belonged to my mother; my green Primary [a book of readings from the Bible]; a diamond; my best furred robe with 'martes' [marten fur].
>
> To Katherine Fitzwilliam: the brooch that I wear everyday; a small black Primary; a jewel called Agnus Dei covered with silver

and written around with pearls; my best robe furred with miniver [white stoat fur].

To Maud Clifford, my goddaughter: my best gold belt.[37]

Having lived for more than thirty years as a widow, Maud died of an unknown illness, at Conisbrough Castle, on 26 August 1446. She was around fifty-six years of age. Maud was buried at Roche Abbey, just a few short miles away; a religious foundation that had benefited greatly from her generous patronage.

By dying in 1446, Maud just missed the upheaval that would see England plunged into the civil war that was to become known as the Wars of the Roses, fought between the Yorkists and Lancastrians, with her stepson Richard, Duke of York, fighting the Lancastrian king, Henry VI, for the ultimate prize, the throne. Maud's family would fight on both sides of the conflict, which would claim the lives of her stepson, her nephew and many others of her family and affinity.

A near contemporary of Maud, Alice Chaucer, would lose her own husband in this legendary power struggle. Alice was the granddaughter of the famous poet, Geoffrey Chaucer, author of *The Canterbury Tales*. She was the only child, and heir, of Geoffrey's son, Thomas Chaucer. Geoffrey Chaucer had married Philippa de Roelt (or Rouet), sister of Katherine Swynford, the third wife and Duchess of John of Gaunt, and the mother of Gaunt's legitimised children, the Beauforts, loyal supporters of their Lancastrian brother, King Henry IV. Alice's mother was Maud (or Matilda) Burghersh, co-heir of the Burghersh estates, which included the manor of Ewelme in Oxfordshire, where Alice was probably born, sometime around 1404.

Nothing is known of Alice's childhood, although, given her later success in estate management and preserving her son's inheritance, we can assume that she had some level of education. She is first mentioned in 1414, when she was around ten years old, when Alice became the wife of Sir John Phelip, who was some twenty-four years her senior. Poor Alice had little time to get used to married life, and was still not old enough to consummate the marriage when she was widowed, on 2 October 1415, when Phelip died at Harfleur. In his will, Alice was left a gold cup and all the furniture from one room of Phelip's house at Grovebury.[38] Still a minor, Alice probably returned home to her family after Phelip's death.

However, she was married again by 1421, this time to Thomas Montagu, Earl of Salisbury. Salisbury's daughter by his first wife, Eleanor Holland, was also called Alice, and was of a similar age to her new stepmother. Alice Montagu would marry Richard Neville, son of Joan Beaufort and Ralph Neville, Earl of Westmorland. Through his mother, Richard Neville was a grandson of John of Gaunt and first cousin, once removed, of Alice Chaucer.

Alice's new husband was a soldier, and fought in the Hundred Years War in France. It was during a visit to France in 1424, to her husband, that Alice was at a banquet in Paris, hosted by Philip the good, Duke of Burgundy. Renowned for her beauty, it appears that Duke Philip was far too attentive to the Earl of Salisbury's wife, infuriating the earl in his attempts to seduce poor Alice. Relations between the duke and the earl soured significantly, with Salisbury going against the interests of Burgundy in besieging Orléans. The siege was a disaster for Salisbury, the French were rallied by Joan of Arc and he was struck in the face by a splinter from a French cannon on 27 October 1428, and died a week later, on 3 November. During the same engagement, Salisbury's good friend, William de la Pole, Earl of Suffolk, was captured by the French. Suffolk, it seems, was also fond of Alice and it is thought Alice was the mystery woman to whom he wrote love poetry during his two years of captivity.

Salisbury's death left Alice a widow for a second time, but this time she was a very wealthy one. According to the terms of Salisbury's will Alice was left half of his net goods, 100 marks in gold and 3,000 marks in jewellery and plate, plus the revenues of his Norman lands. As a sign of his trust in Alice and her abilities, Salisbury had also named her as the supervisor of the will.[39] As a wealthy and beautiful widow, it is not surprising that by 1432, and possibly as early as 1430, Alice had made her third and final marriage. Her husband was the same William de la Pole, Earl of Suffolk, friend of her husband and, apparently, an admirer of Alice. It seems likely that they married shortly after his release from his French imprisonment.

William de la Pole's family had risen from being wealthy wool merchants to the nobility, to nobility themselves. His grandfather, Michael de la Pole, was a favourite of Richard II, who had been promoted to the peerage as Earl of Suffolk. However, when Richard II's personal rule was curbed by the Lords Appellant, Suffolk was one of those to take the brunt of the criticism. He fled into exile in 1388 and was sentenced to death *in absentia*; he died in Paris the following year. His son, another Michael and William's father, was allied with the Appellant Lords and saw his goods and titles forfeit when Richard II regained control. They were restored to him in 1398. Michael de la Pole, 2nd Earl of Suffolk, had five sons, of whom William was the second oldest. The de la Pole family gave everything fighting in the French wars, the second earl died of dysentery in 1415, during the siege of Harfleur, and his oldest son, another Michael, died in October of the same year, as one of the few noble casualties of the Battle of Agincourt; he was nineteen and had held the title Earl of Suffolk for just one month. William therefore succeeded to the earldom of Suffolk, but would lose his three remaining brothers to the French over the next twenty years: Alexander was killed in 1429, at the Battle of Jargeau, John died a prisoner in France and Thomas died while acting as hostage for his brother, William.

William himself spent decades fighting in France, as one of Henry VI's senior military commanders. This military service may well be the reason why, although William and Alice were married in the early 1430s, their only known child, John de la Pole, was not born until 27 September 1442. When still a child, John would be betrothed to his parents' ward, Margaret Beaufort, sole heiress of Alice's cousin, John Beaufort, Duke of Somerset.

William and Alice appear to have had a genuinely close, affectionate and trusting relationship. In his will of 1448, William appoints Alice as his sole executrix, giving her guardianship of their son, John, stating; 'And last of all, with the blessing of God and of me as heartily as I can give it, my dear and true son, I bequeath between him and his mother love and all good accord and give him to her wholly'.[40] Although William's family seat was a house at Wingfield, the couple spent most of their time at Alice's house at Ewelme, where they enlarged the manor house, even receiving a papal dispensation to have a font installed in the chapel. They also rebuilt the parish church of St Mary the Virgin and established a school to educate local boys, the master of which was to be selected from the University of Oxford. William and Alice also built a series of almshouses, known as God's House, to house thirteen almsmen and two priests, one of whom was to be the schoolmaster.[41]

William de la Pole was deeply involved in the politics of the time. One of Henry VI's most trusted advisers, it was William who led the embassy to arrange the king's marriage to Margaret of Anjou, a cousin of the King of France. In November 1444, Alice accompanied her husband to France, along with the Earls of Shrewsbury and Salisbury, to bring back the king's bride. Alice was to act as Margaret's senior lady-in-waiting for the journey home and became her close friend; Queen Margaret would visit Alice at her husband's manor of Wingfield during a progress through the Midlands in 1452. William, however, was to receive the brunt of the criticism for the marriage, which brought no benefit to England, as Margaret came without a dowry, and a secret clause in the marriage contract returned the conquered counties of Maine and Anjou to France.

In 1448 William was created Duke of Suffolk by Henry VI. However, while he still had the confidence of the king, the lords turned against him and his downfall soon followed. He had fallen foul of the powerful Duke of York and became the scapegoat for the ineptitude of Henry VI's policies. On 7 February 1450, the Paston Letters recorded Suffolk's impeachment, which charged that:

> William de la Pole, Duke of Suffolk, late of Ewelme, in the county of Oxford, falsely and traitorously hath imagined, compassed, purposed forethought, done and committed divers high, great, heinous, and horrible treasons against your most royal person, your commons of your realms of England and France, your duchy of Guienne and Normandy, and your whole inheritance of your county of Anjou and Maine, the estate and dignity of the same, and the universal wele and prosperity of all your true subjects.[42]

The king tried to stand by Suffolk, and refused to accept the charges of treason; he banished the Duke from the realm for five years. William de la Pole was given six weeks to set his affairs in order before leaving England on 1 May 1450. The Duke wrote a moving letter to his six-year-old son, John, full of fatherly advice and commending him to his mother, saying: 'Thirdly, in the same wise, I charge you, my dear son, always, as you're bound by the commandment of God to do, to love, to worship your lady and mother, and also that you obey always her commandments and to believe her councils and advice in all your works, the which dread not, but shall be best and truest to you. And if any other body would stir you to the contrary, to flee the counsel in any wise, for you shall find it nought and evil.'[43]

The letter is all the more poignant, as it turned out to be William de la Pole's last communication with his son. He left England on the ship *Nicholas of the Tower*, but it was intercepted by unknown persons and on 2 May, 1450, the Duke of Suffolk was forced to endure a mock trial before he was gruesomely beheaded with a rusty sword. His body was left on the beach at Dover and his head stuck on a pole beside it. He was later buried at his family's manor of Wingfield in Suffolk.

Widowed for a third and final time, Alice devoted her time and energies to protecting her son's inheritance. On 8 May she secured the keeping of all the lands belonging to her husband. However, she was still an object of derision among the malcontents; she was one of those mentioned by name in a Commons petition to have people removed from court. Henry initially acquiesced, but failed to keep his promise to banish the twenty-nine people named in the petition. Alice remained at court as one of Queen Margaret's ladies. She was with the queen at her churching on 18 November 1453, following the birth of Edward, prince of Wales. The magnificent ceremony was attended by six Duchesses, including Alice, eight countesses and seven baronesses.

Alice proved to be a formidable Duchess, pursuing her family's interests with the utmost vigour. Following her husband's death, she continued in his claims to some manors in East Anglia, which belonged to John Fastolf. The Pastons, a prominent East Anglian family who wrote a remarkable number of letters during this period, also laid claim to the lands following Fastolf's death in 1459. The dispute over Caistor Castle continued long into the next decade. In 1469, John Paston wrote to his younger brother, another John, that 'the Quene hath sent a letter unto my Lady of Suffolk the elder [Alice] desyryng theym to common [speak] with my lordis that all such matters as the Kyng wrote unto them fore mabe kept so that no defaute be founden in them, as ye may understand by youre lettre sent frome the Quene'.[44] Although Suffolk's claim on the properties had been dubious and despite the opposition of the Pastons, Alice's litigation was successful.

Alice still needed powerful allies, however, and so, following her husband's death, she soon broke her son's betrothal to the

Lancastrian, Margaret Beaufort, and turned to the House of York. In 1458, Alice negotiated John's marriage with Elizabeth, daughter of Richard, Duke of York and Cecily Neville. Her son and grandsons would become stalwarts of the Yorkist cause. Of the eleven children of John and Elizabeth, their eldest son, another John, having been named as his heir by Richard III, was killed fighting Henry VII's Lancastrian army at the Battle of Stoke Field, the final engagement of the Wars of the Roses, in 1487. He was succeeded as Duke of Suffolk by his brother, Edmund, who was executed, because of his Yorkist blood, by Henry VIII in 1513.

Alice was favoured by Edward IV, who won the throne for the Yorkists in 1461, gaining exemptions in his Acts of Resumption. She was among the more honoured guests at the sumptuous feast, hosted by Richard Neville, Earl of Warwick, for the enthronement of his brother, George Neville, as Archbishop of York. The feast was held at the Archbishop's castle of Cawood in 1465, and Alice was given a place of honour at a high table in a second chamber – a sign of distinction as opposed to a place on a secondary table in the great hall – alongside the Countess of Warwick and the new Archbishop's sisters, the Countess of Oxford, Lady Hastings and Lady Fitzhugh.[45] A further sign of trust came in 1471; following the Battle of Tewkesbury and the capture of Margaret of Anjou, it was into Alice's keeping that Edward entrusted the former queen. Margaret was held at Wallingford Castle, which was held by Alice and was close to her estate at Ewelme. The Duchess was the queen's jailer for the last four years of her life. Following Alice's death, Margaret of Anjou was ransomed by Louis XI of France, and returned to France in 1476.

Through her family inheritance and three marriages, Alice Chaucer had become an incredibly wealthy woman. She held estates in twenty-two counties; in 1454 she received an income of £1300 from three of them alone. Given that her grandfather was Geoffrey Chaucer, it is no surprise that Alice was a patron of the arts, particularly literature, including John Lydgate. An inventory of her goods, taken in 1466 during a move back to Ewelme, included many books.[46] Alice died sometime between 20 May and 9 June, 1475, aged around seventy-one. She was laid to rest in the church of St Mary the Virgin, at Ewelme, where her parents were also buried. Her magnificent tomb lies between the nave and the chapel of St John the Baptist, an effigy of Alice lies atop the tomb, with the Duchess wearing a ducal coronet and the Order of the Garter on her arm.

Alice had led a remarkable life, successfully weathering the political turmoil that claimed the life of her third husband. She, as with all the women in this chapter, was a survivor and a heroine, successfully negotiating the pitfalls and dangers of the medieval world, forging her own path to see herself and her son through. It is impossible to overestimate the dangers these women faced in their lives. As to Eleanor of Aquitaine, crusading with her first husband and encouraging her sons to rise up against her second, or simply the danger presented by the years of repeated childbirth, the travel between her lands and across the perilous English Channel, all these perils make the achievement of reaching her eighties even more remarkable. And yet, she was no retiring octogenarian, ensuring the accession of her son and arranging marriages for her grandchildren, almost to her very last breath. These women deserve to be admired, their survival and perseverance in itself making a mark on the world worthy of recognition.

Their Stories Live On

Writing this book has been an incredible experience. There are so many medieval women whose stories deserve to be told, and it has been a privilege to examine the lives of just a handful of them. The remarkable discovery I have made is that the women whose lives I have highlighted are just the tip of the iceberg. They are a small percentage of the remarkable women who helped to shape the medieval world.

They do, however, serve to highlight the depth of influence that women had over every aspect of medieval life. It is unfortunate that there is only one peasant in the book, although not surprising when you think that the chroniclers wrote little enough about noblewomen, let alone the lower strata of society. Joan of Arc's remarkable achievements could not be ignored, however. She is one of the most remarkable heroines, not only given her lowly social status, but also considering her tender years. Joan, as with many of the women, could have featured in several of the chapters, but she was put in with the fighters, because that is, in my opinion, what she deserves to be most remembered for; she revitalised the French forces and set them on the road to eventual victory in the Hundred Years War.

The story of Eleanor of Aquitaine was another that would have graced several chapters and it probably hasn't escaped anyone that her three daughters by Henry II, also made it into the book. It is a notable outcome of my research to find that so many of these women were related in some way. Mothers and daughters, sisters and cousins, all have achieved the remarkable and became heroines in their own right, and for different reasons. It may be that this serves to highlight how close-knit society was in the Middle Ages.

Today, there is more interest in the history of women than ever before. Historians such as Amy Licence, Dr Janina Ramirez and Tracy Borman are bringing the lives of women, and their contributions to history, out the shadows and into the centre of the world in which they lived. Women's history is a relatively unexplored discipline, in comparison to political or military history. This means there is still much to explore, and a lot that we do not know. Nevertheless, looking into the lives of these women is, simultaneously, illuminating, fascinating and inspiring.

With the advent of social media and the internet, there is now an abundance of blogs, groups and websites dedicated to the history of women. A large number of people now find an interest in history through historical fiction. Mention of Katherine Swynford invariably brings to mind Anya Seton's *Katherine*. And novelists, such as Elizabeth Chadwick and Anne O'Brien, are breathing life into these women once more, helping to bring medieval history – and particularly the history of medieval women – to a wider audience.

The story of individual women's lives is now being explored, demonstrating the huge impact they had, not just in the social and family sphere, but in the political as well. These women had an important role on the international stage, taking on the responsibility of peacekeepers, alliance makers and even warriors. Although Edward I's treatment of Robert the Bruce's wife and daughter was reprehensible, it does serve to highlight the importance of women in medieval politics. In holding Robert the Bruce's wife hostage, he was also holding hostage the future of Scotland and King Robert's ability to produce a son and heir to the Scottish throne.

Edward I's actions, and those of King John in holding Eleanor of Brittany, serve to demonstrate that while monks may not have acknowledged the importance of women in the medieval world, kings did. They were acutely aware of the power women wielded, in their ability to support their husbands, produce children and – when need be – rule. They were heroines.

Footnotes

1: The Medieval Ideal

1. Teresa Cole, *The Norman Conquest: William the Conqueror's Subjugation of England* pages 157–9
2. William of Malmesbury, quoted by Elizabeth van Houts in oxforddnb.com, May 2008
3. *Vita B Simonis*, col. 1219, quoted by Elizabeth van Houts in oxforddnb.com, May 2008
4. MGH, *Epistolae Selectae, Das Register Gregors VII*, ed. Erich Caspar (Berlin: Weidmann, 1920–23), ep. 1.71, p. 102–03, dated April 1074. Quoted by epistolae.ccnmtl.columbia.edu
5. P. Abrahams, editor, *Les Oeuvres Poétiques de Baudri de Bourgueil (10446–1130)*.
6. L. Couppey, 'Encore Héauville! Supplément aux notes historiques sur le prieur, conventuel d'Héauville la Hague', *Revue catholique de Normandie*, X, 1900–01, p. 348–49. Quoted by epistolae.ccnmtl.columbia.edu
7. Musset *La Reine Mathilde* p. 193, quoted by Elizabeth van Houts in oxforddnb.com, May 2008
8. *ibid*
9. Tracy Borman, *Matilda, Wife of the Conqueror, First Queen of England*, p. 205.
10. *ibid* 206.
11. William of Malmesbury, *Chronicles of the Kings of England, From the Earliest Period to the Reign of King Stephen*
12. Ordericus Vitalis, *The Ecclesiastical History of England and Normandy*
13. Peter Rex, *William the Conqueror: The Bastard of Normandy*, p. 258.
14. William Farrer and Charles Travis Clay, editors, *Early Yorkshire Charters, Volume 8: The Honour of Warenne*, p. 13. Through his mother, Isabel de Vermandois, granddaughter of Henry I of France, William de Warenne was a second cousin of Louis VII.
15. *ibid*, p. 16–17.

16. *ibid*, p. 14. Richard Brito struck his blow with the words 'Hoc habeas pro amore domini mei Willelmi fratris regis.' Quoted from *Vita S. Thomas* (*Becket Materials*, Rolls Ser., vol. iii).
17. Susan M. Johns, *Warenne, Isabel de, suo jure Countess of Surrey (d. 1203)*
18. Elizabeth Hallam, editor, *The Plantagenet Chronicles*, p. 146.
19. William Farrer and Charles Travis Clay, editors, *Early Yorkshire Charters, Volume 8: The Honour of Warenne*, p. 19.
20. *ibid*, p. 14.
21. *ibid*, p. 127.
22. Alison Weir, *Eleanor of Aquitaine, by the Wrath of God Queen of England*, p. 181.
23. *ibid*, p.228.
24. *ibid*, p. 334
25. Elizabeth Hallam, editor, *The Plantagenet Chronicles*, p. 115.
26. Douglas Boyd, *Eleanor, April Queen of Aquitaine*, p. 326.
27. Elizabeth Hallam, editor, *The Plantagenet Chronicles*, p. 115.
28. Amy Licence, *Red Roses, Blanche of Gaunt to Margaret Beaufort*, p. 30.
29. *ibid*, pp. 32–33
30. *ibid*, pp. 34
31. Anthony Goodman, *John of Gaunt: The Exercise of Princely Power in Fourteenth-Century Europe*.
32. Amy Licence, *Red Roses, Blanche of Gaunt to Margaret Beaufort*
33. Froissart, Jean, *Chronicles*, translated by G. Brereton
34. Amy Licence, *Red Roses, Blanche of Gaunt to Margaret Beaufort*
35. *ibid*. p. 75.
36. David Williamson, *Brewer's British Royalty*, p. 293.
37. Amy Licence, *Red Roses, Blanche of Gaunt to Margaret Beaufort*
38. David Williamson, *Brewer's British Royalty*, p. 293.

2: Heroines in Religion

1. *Chronicles of the Age of Chivalry* edited by Elizabeth Hallam.
2. G.W.S. Barrow, Oxforddnb.com *Margaret St Margaret. (d. 1093), Queen of Scots, consort of Malcolm III*, 2004
3. Symeon of Durham, *Vita Sanctae Margaretae Scotorum reginae, Symeonis Dunelmensis opera et collectanea*, ed. J. H. Hinde, Surtees Society, 1868.
4. Ordericus Vitalis, *The Ecclesiastical History of England and Normandy*
5. *Britain's Royal Families, the Complete Genealogy* by Alison Weir
6. *ibid*.
7. *The Anglo-Saxon Chronicle*
8. *Brewer's British Royalty* by David Williamson
9. *ibid*.
10. S.P. Thompson, Oxforddnb.com, *Mary of Blois], suo jure Countess of Boulogne (d. 1182), Princess and abbess of Romsey*, 2014.
11. *ibid*.
12. *ibid*.
13. *Eleanor of Castile: The shadow Queen* by Sara Cockerill
14. *ibid*.

15. *A Place for Our Kings: The History and Archaeology of a Mediaeval Royal Palace in the Heart of Sherwood Forest* by James Wright.
16. *Annales Sex Regum Angliae* by Nicholas Trivet, 310.
17. *ibid.*
18. *Eleanor of Castile: The shadow Queen* by Sara Cockerill.
19. Julian of Norwich, *Revelations of Divine Love.*
20. Father John Julian, *The Complete Julian of Norwich*, pp. 23–27.
21. Julian of Norwich, *Revelations of Divine Love*, Chapter 3.
22. Janina Ramirez, *Julian of Norwich, a Very Brief History*, p. 38.
23. *ibid.* pp. 10–13.
24. Hugh White, translator, *Ancrene Wisse: Guide for Anchoresses.*
25. Henrietta Leyser, *Medieval Women, A Social History of Women in England 450–1500*, Chapter 10.
26. *ibid.*
27. Julian of Norwich, *Revelations of Divine Love*, Chapter 9
28. Janina Ramirez, *Julian of Norwich, a Very Brief History*, p. 18.
29. Toni Mount, *A Year in the Life of Medieval England* p. 28.
30. *ibid.*
31. Janina Ramirez, *Julian of Norwich, a Very Brief History*, p. 19–23.
32. Felicity Riddy, *Kempe, Margery (b. c.1373, d. in or after 1438)*, Oxforddnb.com.
33. Janina Ramirez, *Julian of Norwich, a Very Brief History*, p. 19–23.
34. Margery Kempe, *The Book of Margery Kempe*, edited by S.B. Meech and H.E. Allen.

3: Mistresses

1. *Eadgifu Eddeua. the Fair the Rich. (fl. 1066), magnate* by Ann Williams, oxforddnb.com, 2004
2. *Princess Nest – The Helen of Wales* by Terry John, bluestoneWales.com.
3. *Chronicle of the Princes*, quoted on castlewales.com.
4. *Princess Nest – The Helen of Wales* by Terry John, bluestoneWales.com.
5. *Eadgifu Eddeua. the Fair the Rich. (fl. 1066), magnate* by Ann Williams, oxforddnb.com, 2004
6. '*a devil and enchantress*' the *Anonimalle Chronicle*, 153, quoted by Simon Walker in oxforddnb.com, January 2008.
7. Simon Walker in *oxforddnb.com*, January 2008.
8. Thomas of Walsingham, *Thomae Walsingham Historia Anglicana* (in part one of *Chronica Monasterii Sancti Albani*).
9. W.M. Ormrod, *English Historical Review* December 2015.
10. C. Given-Wilson, *Perrers, Alice (d. 1400/01)* (article)
11. Paul Johnson, *The Life and Times of Edward III*
12. *Gesta abbatum*, 3.228, quoted by C. Given-Wilson, *Perrers, Alice (d. 1400/01)* (article)
13. Paul Johnson, *The Life and Times of Edward III*
14. C. Given-Wilson, *Perrers, Alice (d. 1400/01)* (article)
15. *ibid.*
16. Thomas of Walsingham, *Thomae Walsingham Historia Anglicana* (in part one of *Chronica Monasterii Sancti Albani*).

17. *ibid.*

18. Jean Froissart *The Chronicles of Froissart*

19. Strachey, J editor; *Rotuli parliamentorum ut et petitiones, et placita in parliamento*, 6 vols. (1767–77)

20. C. Given-Wilson, *Perrers, Alice (d. 1400/01)* (article)

21. Nicolas, N.H. editor, *Testamenta vetusta: being illustrations from wills*, 2 vols. (1826)

4: *Scandalous Women*

1. *Magna rotuli, 2–569*, quoted in *Joan, d. 1237*, by Kate Norgate and Rev. A.D. Carr in Oxfroddnb.com, 2004.

2. *Joan, daughter of King John* by Professor Louise Wilkinson, magnacarta800th. com, 2016.

3. *Joan, d. 1237*, by Kate Norgate and Rev. A.D. Carr in Oxfroddnb.com, 2004.

4. *Brut y Tywysogyn* or *The Chronicle of the Princes: Peniarth MS 20 Version*, editor T. Jones, Cardiff 1952.

5. *Llywelyn ab Iorweth 9c. 1173–1240)* by A.D. Carr, Oxfroddnb.com, 2004.

6. finerollshenry3.org.uk/content/calendar/roll_027:

   12/119 (27 March 1228), *27 March. Reading. Concerning lands to be taken into the King's hand. Order to the sheriff of Leicestershire to take the manor of Rothley with appurtenances into the King's hand, which the King has committed to Joan, wife of L. prince of North Wales, for as long as it pleases the King, and to keep it safely until the King orders otherwise*;

   And 12/2779 (21 September 1228), *Concerning the corn of Condover. Order to the sheriff of Staffordshire and Shropshire to take into the King's hand without delay the corn of this autumn that Joan, wife of L. prince of North Wales, caused to be sown in the manor of Condover, which she had by bail of the King for as long as it pleases him, notwithstanding the King's command to him to demise that corn to her in peace.*

7. *Letters of Medieval Women* edited and translated by Anne Crawford, 2002.

8. *Brut y Tywysogyn* or *The Chronicle of the Princes: Peniarth MS 20 Version*, editor T. Jones, Cardiff 1952.

9. *Joan, Lady of Wales (c.1191–1237)*, englishmonarch.co.uk, 2004.

10. *Divorce, Medieval Welsh Style*, article by Robin Chapman Stacey, *Speculum*, Volume 77, issue 4 October 2002, University of Chicago Press.

11. Pierre Goubert, *The Course of French History*, p. 42.

12. Kathryn Warner, *Isabella of France, the Rebel Queen*, pp. 84–86

13. Pierre Goubert, *The Course of French History*, p. 42.

14. Toni Mount *A Year in the Life of Medieval England*, p. 240.

15. Jean Froissart *The Chronicles of Froissart*

16. *Holland, Thomas, Earl of Kent (c.1315–1360)* by M.M.N. Stansfield, Oxfroddnb.com, Jan. 2008.

17. Toni Mount, *A Year in the Life of Medieval England*, 240.

18. *The Life of the Black Prince by the Herald of Sir John Chandos*, edited by Mildred K. Pope.

19. Jean Froissart *The Chronicles of Froissart*

20. *The Perfect King, the Life of Edward III* by Ian Mortimer
21. Jean Froissart *The Chronicles of Froissart*
22. *The Life of the Black Prince by the Herald of Sir John Chandos*, edited by Mildred K. Pope.
23. Thomas of Walsingham, *Thomae Walsingham Historia Anglicana*
24. *ibid.*
25. *Richard, Earl of Cambridge (1385–1415)* G.L. Harriss, Oxfroddnb.com, 2004.
26. Stow, John, *The Annales of England, "The race of the Kings of Brytaine after the received opinion since Brute, &c"*, G. Bishop and T. Adams, London, 1605.
27. *Eleanor Cobham: The Duchess and her Downfall*, article by Susan Higginbotham, susanhigginbotham.com, 16 September 2013.
28. *Humphrey, Duke of Gloucester* article in *Brewer's British Royalty* by David Williamson.
29. *Eleanor Cobham: The Duchess and her Downfall*, article by Susan Higginbotham, susanhigginbotham.com, 16 September 2013.

5: The Disinherited Heroines

1. Robert B. Patterson, *Isabella, suo jure Countess of Gloucester (c.1160–1217)*, Oxforddnb.com
2. Marc Morris, *King John: Treachery, Tyranny and the Road to Magna Carta*, p. 61.
3. Ralph of Diceto, *Images of History*, 166–175
4. Robert B. Patterson, *Isabella, suo jure Countess of Gloucester (c.1160–1217)*, Oxforddnb.com
5. *ibid.*
6. Thomas of Walsingham, *Thomae Walsingham Historia Anglicana*
7. David Williamson, *Brewer's British Royalty*
8. J. R. Maddicott, *Thomas of Lancaster, second Earl of Lancaster, second Earl of Leicester, and Earl of Lincoln (c.1278–1322)*, Oxforddnb.com.
9. Kathryn Warner, *Isabella of France, the Rebel Queen.*
10. *ibid.*
11. Jean Froissart, *Chronicles*, hrionline.ac.uk/onlinefroissart
12. Charlotte M. Yonge, *History of France*
13. Sara Hanna-Black, *themortimersblog*
14. Ian Mortimer, *The Perfect King, the Life of Edward III*
15. Sara Hanna-Black, *themortimersblog*
16. Ian Mortimer, *The Perfect King, the Life of Edward III*
17. Sara Hanna-Black, *themortimersblog*
18. *ibid.*
19. David Williamson, *Brewer's British Royalty*
20. Martyn Atkins, *Jacqueline, suo jure Countess of Hainault, suo jure Countess of Holland, and suo jure Countess of Zeeland (1401–1436)* (article) Oxforddnb.com
21. John Stow, *The Annales of England, "The race of the Kings of Brytaine after the received opinion since Brute, &c"*,

6: The Pawns

1. Dan Jones, *the Plantagenets, the Kings who made England*
2. Alison Weir, *Eleanor of Aquitaine, by the Wrath of God, Queen of England*
3. *ibid.*
4. *ibid.*
5. Douglas Boyd, *Eleanor, April Queen of Aquitaine*
6. Elizabeth Hallam, editor, *The Plantagenet Chronicles*, p. 146.
7. Douglas Boyd, *Eleanor, April Queen of Aquitaine*, pp. 227–228.
8. Elizabeth Hallam, editor, *The Plantagenet Chronicles*, p. 212.
9. *ibid* p. 224.
10. Douglas Boyd, *Eleanor, April Queen of Aquitaine*, p. 321
11. *ibid.* pp. 323–4
12. H. R. Luard, editor, *Annales monastici*, 5 vols., RS, 36
13. The letter from Isabella to Henry III reads: "We do to wit that the Counts of La Marche and Eu being both dead, Sir Hugh de Lusignan was left, as it were, alone and without an heir, and his friends would not allow him to marry our daughter on account of her tender age, but counselled him to make such a marriage that he might speedily have an heir; and it was proposed that he should take a wife in France; which if he should do, all your land in Poitou and Gascony, and ours too, would be lost. We therefore, seeing the great danger that might arise if such a marriage should take place, and getting no support from your counsellors, have taken the said Hugh Count La Marche to be our lord and husband." Matthew Lewis, *Henry III, the Son of Magna Carta*, p. 68
14. finerollshenry3.co.uk
15. *Chronicle of Melrose 731–1270*, MS Cotton Faustina B ix
16. Keith Stringer, *Joan (1210–1237)* (article), Oxforddnb.com
17. *ibid.*
18. H. R. Luard, editor, *Matthaei Parisiensis, monachi sancti Albani, Chronica majora*, 7 vols., RS, 57 (1872–83)
19. finerollshenry3.co.uk, *22 HENRY III (28 October 1237–27 October 1238)*
20. H. R. Luard, editor, *Matthaei Parisiensis, monachi sancti Albani, Chronica majora*, 7 vols., RS, 57 (1872–83).
21. The Chronicle of Lanercost, 1272–1346.
22. Elizabeth Hallam, editor, *Chronicles of the Age of Chivalry*, p. 120.
23. *ibid.*
24. Marc Morris, *A Great and Terrible King, Edward I and the Forging of Britain*, p. 178
24. Jem Duducu, *Forgotten History, Unbelievable Moments from the Past*, p. 112–114.
25. *ibid.*
26. Marc Morris, *A Great and Terrible King, Edward I and the Forging of Britain*, p. 235.
27. *ibid*, p. 237.
28. *ibid*, p. 237
29. A. A. M. Duncan, *Margaret the Maid of Norway. (1282/3–1290)*, Oxforddnb.com.

7: Captive Heroines

1. Géraud, Hercule, *Ingeburge de Danemark, reine de France, 1193–1236. Mémoire de feu Hercule Géraud, couronné par l'Académie des Inscriptions et Belles-Lettres dans sa séance du 11 août 1844. Première partie.* Article

2. *ibid.*

3. Étienne de Tournai, quoted in Géraud, Hercule, *Ingeburge de Danemark, reine de France, 1193–1236. Mémoire de feu Hercule Géraud, couronné par l'Académie des Inscriptions et Belles-Lettres dans sa séance du 11 août 1844. Première partie..* Article

5. Géraud, Hercule, *Ingeburge de Danemark, reine de France, 1193–1236. Mémoire de feu Hercule Géraud, couronné par l'Académie des Inscriptions et Belles-Lettres dans sa séance du 11 août 1844. Première partie.* Article.

4. Chris Agde, *Le Triste Destin de Ingebourg de Danemark* (article); "Elle passe ses journées entières à prier, à lire, à travailler; les exercises sérieux remplissent tous ses moments".

6. "...*cette malheureuse Princesses se vit obligée, pour vivre, de vendre ou d'engager le peu qu'elle possédait et jusqu'*à ses habits..." Géraud, Hercule, *Ingeburge de Danemark, reine de France, 1193–1236. Mémoire de feu Hercule Géraud, couronné par l'Académie des Inscriptions et Belles-Lettres dans sa séance du 11 août 1844. Première partie.* Article.

7. "*... rejetée à terre comme une branche stérile et dessechée; me voilà privée de toute secours et de toute consolation.*" Géraud, Hercule, *Ingeburge de Danemark, reine de France, 1193–1236. Mémoire de feu Hercule Géraud, couronné par l'Académie des Inscriptions et Belles-Lettres dans sa séance du 11 août 1844. Première partie.* Article.

8. Anna Belfrage *Weep, Ingeborg, weep,* (article) annabelfrage.wordpress.com.

9. Chris Agde, *Le Triste Destin de Ingebourg de Danemark* (article); "Elle passe ses journées entières à prier, à lire, à travailler; les exercises sérieux remplissent tous ses moments".

10. Anonymous of Béthune paraphrased in Marc Morris, *King John: Treachery, Tyranny and the Road to Magna Carta*

11. *Brut y Tywysogyn* or *The Chronicle of the Princes: Peniarth MS 20 Version,* editor T. Jones, Cardiff 1952.

12. Thomas Asbridge, *The greatest Knight*

13. Roger of Wendover, *Roger of Wendover's Flowers of history, Comprising the history of England from the descent of the Saxons to A.D. 1235*

14. Marc Morris, *King John: Treachery, Tyranny and the Road to Magna Carta*

15. *ibid.*

16. Anonymous of Béthune quoted in Marc Morris, *King John: Treachery, Tyranny and the Road to Magna Carta*

17. *Magna Carta* British Library, transcript from bl.uk

18. Douglas Boyd, *Eleanor, April Queen of Aquitaine*

19. "*Eleanor, Princess (1184–1241)*", David Williamson, *Brewer's British Royalty*

20. *ibid.*

21. Ross, David, editor, *Sempringham Priory, Church and Holy Well,* britainexpress.com.

22. englishmonarchs.co.uk, 2004

23. *ibid.*
24. *Calendar of the Charter Rolls, 1–14, Edward III*
25. The Princess Gwenllian Society, Princessgwenllian.co.uk
26. Marc Morris, *A Great and Terrible King: Edward I and the Forging of Britain*
27. Nigel Tranter, *The Story of Scotland*, e-book
28. Fiona Watson, *Bruce, Christian (d. 1356)*, Oxforddnb.com
29. Nigel Tranter, *The Story of Scotland*, e-book.
30. *ibid.*
31. Fiona Watson, *Buchan, Isabel, Countess of Buchan (b. c.1270, d. after 1313)* Oxforddnb.com
32. Interim annalist, *Flores Historiarum*, Volume III
33. Pilling, David, *Ladies in Cages* (article)

8: Warrior Heroines

1. Marios Costambeys, 'Æthelflæd Ethelfleda. (d.918), ruler of the Mercians' *oxforddnb.com*, 2004.
2. William of Malmesbury, *The History of the Kings of England*, vol. III part I
3. Marios Costambeys, 'Æthelflæd Ethelfleda. (d.918), ruler of the Mercians' *oxforddnb.com*, 2004.
4. *The Anglo-Saxon Chronicle* quoted in *Alfred the Great* by David Sturdy
5. B-text *The Anglo-Saxon Chronicle* quoted in *Alfred the Great* by David Sturdy.
6. *ibid*
7. Texts A, B and C *Anglo-Saxon Chronicle*, sa 919.
8. Antonia Fraser, *The Warrior Queens: Boadicea's Chariot*
9. Henry, Archdeacon of Huntingdon, quoted by Marios Costambeys, *oxforddnb.com*, 2004.
10. Bryan Golding, 'Gerard de Canville (died 1214)' *oxforddnb.com*, edited 2006.
11. *The Chronicle of Richard of Devizes*
12. Marc Morris *King John*
13. Susan M. Johns 'Haie, Nicola de la (d. 1230), landowner' *oxforddnb.com* 2004.
14. Dan Jones *The Plantagenets: The Kings Who Made England*
15. *The Plantagenet Chronicles* edited by Elizabeth Hallam
16. *ibid.*
17. *Rotuli hundredonum, 1.315* quoted in Susan M. Johns 'Haie, Nicola de la (d. 1230), landowner' *oxforddnb.com* 2004 and Irene Gladwin *The Sheriff: the Man and his Office.*
18. *Historical Collections of Walter of Coventry 2.237–8*
19. David Crouch and Anthony J. Holden *History of William Marshal: Text & translation (II. 10032–end)*
20. Thomas Asbridge *The Greatest Knight*
21. *Chronicles of the Age of Chivalry* edited by Elizabeth Hallam.
22. *Annales Monastici: Annales prioratus de Dunstaplia (A.D. 1–1297) Annales monasterii de Bermundesia (A.D. 1042–1432)*
23. catherinehanley.co.uk/historical-background/nicola-de-la-haye

24. www.finerollshenry3.org.uk/content/calendar/roll_030.html#it072_008a
25. A.A.M. Duncan, *Randolph, Thomas, first Earl of Moray (d. 1332), soldier and guardian of Scotland* oxforddnb.com, 2004.
26. *The historie and cronicles of Scotland ... by Robert Lindesay of Pitscottie*, ed. A. J. G. Mackay, 3 vols, Scottish Text Society, 42–3, 60 (1899–1911)
27. Kyra Cornelius Kramer *Black Agnes and Psychological Warfare*, kyrackramer. com, 8 July 2016.
28. *The historie and cronicles of Scotland ... by Robert Lindesay of Pitscottie*, ed. A. J. G. Mackay, 3 vols, Scottish Text Society, 42–3, 60 (1899–1911)
29. Nigel Tranter, *The Story of Scotland*
30. Kyra Cornelius Kramer *Black Agnes and Psychological Warfare*, kyrackramer. com, 8 July 2016.
31. Nigel Tranter, *The Story of Scotland*
32. Fiona Watson, *Dunbar, Patrick, eighth Earl of Dunbar or of March, and Earl of Moray (1285–1369), soldier and magnate* Oxforddnb.com, January 2008.
33. Kyra Cornelius Kramer *Black Agnes and Psychological Warfare*, kyrackramer. com, 8 July 2016.
34. Nigel Tranter, *The Story of Scotland*
35. *Historia Anglicana*, quoted in Fiona Watson, *Dunbar, Patrick, eighth Earl of Dunbar or of March, and Earl of Moray (1285–1369), soldier and magnate* Oxforddnb.com, January 2008.
36. Charlotte Hodgman quoting Kelly De Vries, *Joan of Arc*, BBC History Magazine, Vol. 13, no 1, January 2012
37. Yvonne Lanhers, *Saint Joan of Arc* Britannica.com.
38. *ibid.*
39. *Letter to the English* Joan of Arc, archive.joan-of-arc/joanofarc_letter_Mar1429.html
40. Folio 68, www.british-history.ac.uk/london-letter-books/volk/pp92–105
41. Yvonne Lanhers, *Saint Joan of Arc* Britannica.com.
42. *ibid.*
43. Philip A. Mackowiak *Joan of Arc's Heresy*, blog.oup.com 30 May 2016
44. *ibid.*
45. *ibid.*
46. *ibid.*

9: Heroines Who Ruled

1. *Prominent Russians: Anna Yaroslavna* (article), russiapedia.rt.com/prominent-russians/the-ryurikovich-dynasty/anna-yaroslavna.
2. epistolae.ccnmtl.columbia.edu, *Anne of Kiev (Anna Yaroslavna)* (article). Quoted from Bauthier, 550; Hallu, 168, citing *Comptes de Suger.*
3. *Prominent Russians: Anna Yaroslavna* (article), russiapedia.rt.com/prominent-russians/the-ryurikovich-dynasty/anna-yaroslavna
4. Moniek Bloks, *Anne of Kiev, the First Female Regent of France*
5. epistolae.ccnmtl.columbia.edu, *Anne of Kiev (Anna Yaroslavna)* (article). The St Maur-les-Fosses charter reads '*annuente mea conjuge Anna et prole Philippo, Roberto ac Hugone*'.
6. epistolae.ccnmtl.columbia.edu, *Anne of Kiev (Anna Yaroslavna)* (article).

7. Letter from Pope Nicholas II to Anne of Kiev, October 1059, epistolae.ccnmtl. columbia.edu/letter/1190, translated by Ashleigh Imus.

8. Tracy Borman, *Matilda, Wife of the Conqueror, First Queen of England*, p. 107.

9. Lois L. Huneycutt, *Adela, Countess of Blois (c.1067–1137)* (article)

10. Phyllis Abrahams, *Les Oeuvres Poétiques de Baudri de Bourgueil (10446–1130)*.

11. William of Malmesbury, *Chronicles of the Kings of England, From the Earliest Period to the Reign of King Stephen*, c. 1090–1143.

12. Robert Bartlett, *England Under the Norman and Angevin Kings, 1075–1225*, p. 403.

13. Lois L. Huneycutt, *Adela, Countess of Blois (c.1067–1137)* (article)

14. William Urban, *The Teutonic Knights, a Military History*

15. Anthony Casey, *Jadwiga – Poland's Female King* (article)

16. William Urban, *The Teutonic Knights, a Military History*

17. Anthony Goodman, *Katherine (1372–1418)* (article)

18. Amy Licence, *Red Roses, Blanche of Gaunt to Margaret Beaufort*

19. Jean Froissart, *Chronicles of Froissart*

20. Fernán Pérez de Guzmán quoted by Anthony Goodman in *Katherine (1372–1418)* (article)

21. Pierre Goubert, *The Course of French History*, p. 67

22. *ibid.*

23. Abernethy, Susan, *Anne de Beaujeu, Duchess of Bourbon and Regent of France* (article)

24. In French, Louis XII said *'elle était la moins folle femme de France, car de sage il n'en était point.'*

25. *ibid.*

26. *Les Enseignements d'Anne de France, Duchesse de Bourbonnais et d'Auvergene, à sa fille Suzanne de Bourbon* translates as *The lessons of Anne of France, Duchess of Bourbon and Auvergne, to her daughter Suzanne of Bourbon*

10: *True Love*

1. Marc Morris, *A Great and Terrible King, Edward I and the Forging of Britain*

2. Sara Cockerill, *Eleanor of Castile, the Shadow Queen*

3. Marc Morris, *A Great and Terrible King, Edward I and the Forging of Britain*

4. Sara Cockerill, *Eleanor of Castile, the Shadow Queen*

5. *ibid.*

6. *ibid.*

7. *ibid.*

8. *ibid.*

9. Marc Morris, *A Great and Terrible King, Edward I and the Forging of Britain*

10. Ian Mortimer, *The Perfect King, the Life of Edward III*

11. Amy Licence, *Red Roses, Blanche of Gaunt to Margaret Beaufort*

12. Ian Mortimer, *The Perfect King, the Life of Edward III*

13. Paul Johnson, *The Life and Times of Edward III*.

14. Ian Mortimer, *The Perfect King, the Life of Edward III*

15. Nigel Tranter, *The Story of Scotland*
16. *ibid.*
17. King James I, *The Poetical Remains of James I*
18. Amy Licence, *Red Roses, Blanche of Gaunt to Margaret Beaufort*
19. *ibid.*
20. David Williamson, *Brewer's British Royalty*
21. Michael Jones, *24 Hours at Agincourt, 25 October 1415*
22. *ibid.*
23. S. J. Payling, *Cornewall, John, Baron Fanhope (d. 1443)* (article)
24. *ibid.*

11: Literary Heroines

1. *The Letters of Hildegard of Bingen*, translated by Joseph L. Baird and Radd K. Ehrman
2. *Hildegardis Bingensis, Epistolarium*, edited by Lieven Van Acker and Monika Klaes-Hachmoller
3. Quoted in *Medieval Europe 400–1500* by H.G. Koenigsberger
4. Medievalists.net, *The Herbal Cures of Hildegard von Bingen – was she right?*
5. *Hildegard von Bingen's Physica: The Complete English Translation of Her Classic Work on Health and Healing* by Priscilla Throop.
6. Quoted in Susan Signe Morrison's article, *Six Trailblazing Medieval Women*
7. *The Letters of John of Salisbury*, edited by W.J. Miller, S.J. Butler, H.E. Butler and revised by C.N.L. Brooke
8. *Heloïse, une ascendence controversée*, pierre-abelard.com
9. Peter Abelard quoted in *Scandalous Nun: Heloïse d'Argenteuil* (article), by Emma Mason
10. My translation from Abelard, who wrote: "Peu après, la jeune fille sentit qu'elle était mère, et elle me l'écrivit aussitôt avec des transports d'allégresse, me consultant sur ce qu'elle devait faire. Une nuit, pendant l'absence de son oncle, je l'enlevai, ainsi que nous en étions convenus, et je la fis immédiatement passer en Bretagne, où elle resta chez ma soeur jusqu'au jour où elle donna naissance à un fils qu'elle nomma Astrolabe." Peter Abelard, *Historia Calimatatum*
11. Quoted in *Medieval Europe 400–1500* by H.G. Koenigsberger
12. Quoted in *Scandalous Nun: Heloïse d'Argenteuil* (article), by Emma Mason
13. My translation from Abelard, who wrote: "Nous confions donc à ma soeur notre jeune enfant, et nous revenons secrètement à Paris. Quelques jours plus tard, après avoir passé une nuit à célébrer vigiles dans une église, à l'aube du matin, en présence de l'oncle d'Héloïse et de plusieurs de nos amis et des siens, nous fûmes unis par la bénédiction nuptiale." Peter Abelard, *Historia Calimatatum*
14. Translation from *The Correspondence of Heloise and Abelard and Related Writings*, translated by Mary Martin McLaughlin in epistolae.ccnmtl. columbia.edu.
15. *ibid.*
16. Peter Abelard, *Hymnarius Paraclitensis*, edited by Joseph Szöverffy
17. *The Letters of Peter the Venerable*, edited by Giles Constable

18. 'My name is Marie and I am from France', quoted in *Rethinking Marie* by Dinah Hazell

19. *Marie (fl. c.1180–c.1189)* (article) by Tony Hunt

20. *Rethinking Marie* by Dinah Hazell

21. *Marie (fl. c.1180–c.1189)* (article) by Tony Hunt

22. *The Plantagenet Chronicles* edited by Elizabeth Hallam.

23. Translated from; '*Al finement de cest escrit, Que en romanz ai treité e dit, Me numerai pur remembrance: Marie ai num, si sui de France. Put cel ester que clerc plusur Prendreient sur eus mun labur. No voil que nul sur li le die! E il fet que fol ki sei ublie!*' Taken from *Marie de France: Fables*, edited and translated by Harriet Spiegel.

24. Quoted in *Margaret (1424–1445)* (article) by M. H. Brown.

25. *ibid.*

26. *The Life and Triumphs of Christine de Pzsan* (article), faculty.msmc.edu.

27. *The Writing of Christine de Pizan* translated by Nadia Margolis, edited by Charity Cannon Willard

28. *ibid.*

29. *The Book of the City of Ladies* by Christine de Pisan, translated by Rosalind Brown-Grant

12: The Survivors

1. Jane Martindale, *Eleanor, suo jure Duchess of Aquitaine (c.1122–1204)* (article).

2. Douglas Boyd, *Eleanor, April Queen of Aquitaine*

3. *The Plantagenet Chronicles*, edited by Elizabeth Hallam.

4. Douglas Boyd, *Eleanor, April Queen of Aquitaine*

5. Mike Ashley, *The Mammoth Book of British Kings & Queens*

6. Thomas Abridge, *The greatest Knight*

7. *ibid.*

8. Douglas Boyd, *Eleanor, April Queen of Aquitaine*

9. Mary Anne Everett Green, *Lives of the Princesses of England from the Norman Conquest*, Volume 2, suggests 1395 as Joan's date of birth.

10. F. Royston Fairbank, *The Last Earl of Warenne and Surrey, and the Distribution of His Possessions* (article), *Yorkshire Archaeological Journal*

11. Langtoft quote in F. Royston Fairbank, *The Last Earl of Warenne and Surrey, and the Distribution of His Possessions* (article), *Yorkshire Archaeological Journal*

12. Dan Jones, *The Plantagenets, The Kings Who Made England*

13. *Chronicles of the Age of Chivalry*, edited by Elizabeth Hallam

14. Walter Reynolds, Archbishop of Canterbury, quoted in F. Royston Fairbank, *The Last Earl of Warenne and Surrey, and the Distribution of His Possessions* (article), *Yorkshire Archaeological Journal*

15. *ibid.*

16. Kathryn Warner, *Isabella of France: The Rebel Queen*

17. F. Royston Fairbank, *The Last Earl of Warenne and Surrey, and the Distribution of His Possessions* (article), *Yorkshire Archaeological Journal*

18. Kathryn Warner, *Isabella of France: The Rebel Queen*

19. *English Heritage Guidebook for Conisbrough Castle* by Steven Brindle and Agnieszka Sadrei

20. F. Royston Fairbank, *The Last Earl of Warenne and Surrey, and the Distribution of His Possessions* (article), *Yorkshire Archaeological Journal*

21. *ibid.*

22. Kathryn Warner, *Isabella of France: The Rebel Queen*

23. F. Royston Fairbank, *The Last Earl of Warenne and Surrey, and the Distribution of His Possessions* (article), *Yorkshire Archaeological Journal*

24. *ibid.*

25. Dan Jones, *The Plantagenets, The Kings Who Made England*

26. *ibid.*

27. Thomas of Walsingham, *Thomae Walsingham Historia Anglicana* (in part one of *Chronica Monasterii Sancti Albani*)

28. C. Rawcliffe, *The Staffords, Earls of Stafford and Dukes of Buckingham, 1394–1521*

29. Michael Jones, *24 Hours at Agincourt, 25 October 1415*

30. C. Rawcliffe, *The Staffords, Earls of Stafford and Dukes of Buckingham, 1394–1521*

31. *ibid.*

32. *ibid.*

33. Henry Summerson, *Clifford, Thomas, sixth Baron Clifford (1362/3–1391)* (article)

34. Matthew Lewis, *Richard Duke of York, King by Right*

35. Brian Wainwright, *Maud Clifford secures a good divorce settlement* (article)

36. William Shakespeare, *Henry VI, Part 3, Act 1 Scene 3*

37. *English Heritage Guidebook for Conisbrough Castle* by Steven Brindle and Agnieszka Sadrei

38. Rowena E. Archer, *Chaucer, Alice, Duchess of Suffolk (c.1404–1475)* (article).

39. *ibid.*

40. K.L. Clark, *The Nevills of Middleham: England's Most Powerful Family in the Wars of the Roses*

41. Kristie Dean, *On the Trail of the Yorks*

42. Matthew Lewis, *Richard Duke of York, King by Right*

43. K.L. Clark, *The Nevills of Middleham: England's Most Powerful Family in the Wars of the Roses*

44. David Baldwin, *Elizabeth Woodville, Mother of the Princes in the Tower*

45. K.L. Clark, *The Nevills of Middleham: England's Most Powerful Family in the Wars of the Roses*

46. Rowena E. Archer, *Chaucer, Alice, Duchess of Suffolk (c.1404–1475)* (article).

Bibliography

Primary Sources

Abelard, Peter, *Historia Calamitatum* in Betty Radice's translation in *The Letters of Abelard and Heloise*. Penguin, Harmondsworth, 1974.

Abelard, Pierre, *Historia Calimatatum* at pierre-abelard.com, 1999.

Abrahams, Phyllis, *Les Oeuvres Poétiques de Baudri de Bourgueil (10446–1130)*, Paris, Champion, 1926.

Adam of Usk, *Chronicon Adae de Usk, A.D. 1377–1421*, edited, with translation and notes, by Sir Edward Maunde Thompson, K.C.B., Oxford, Oxford University Press, 1904.

Annales Monastici: Annales prioratus de Dunstaplia (A.D. 1–1297) Annales monasterii de Bermundesia (A.D. 1042–1432) Edited by Henry Richards Luard, London, Longmans, 1866.

Berners, John Bourchier, Lord, translator and Macauley, G.C., editor, *The Froissart, Jean, Chronicles of Froissart*, London, MacMillan & Co., 1899.

Brut y Tywysogyn or *The Chronicle of the Princes: Peniarth MS 20 Version*, editor T. Jones, Cardiff 1952.

Calendar of Close Rolls, Henry V: Volume 1, 1413–1419, british-history.ac.uk.

Calendar of Close Rolls, Henry VI: Volume 1, 1422–1429, british-history.ac.uk.

Calendar of Close Rolls, Henry VI: Volume 3, 1435–1441, british-history.ac.uk.

Calendar of Close Rolls, Henry VI: Volume 4, 1441–1447, british-history.ac.uk.

Calendar of Close Rolls, Henry VI: Volume 5, 1447–1454, british-history.ac.uk.

Calendar of the Charter Rolls preserved in the Public Record Office, Vol. IV, 1–14, Edward III, AD 1327–1341, London, 1912.

Chronicle of Melrose 731–1270, MS Cotton Faustina B ix, British Library.

Chaucer, Geoffrey, *The Canterbury Tales*, edited by D. Laing Purves, MacMay, e-book, 2007.

Chaucer, Geoffrey, *The Complete Works of Geoffrey Chaucer*, edited by Thomas Thynne, Kindle edition, 2014.

Crouch, David And Anthony J. Holden, *History of William Marshal: Text & translation (II. 10032–end)* Anglo-Norman text society from Birkbeck College, 2002.

De Pizan, Christine, *The Book of the City of Ladies*, translated by Rosalind Brown-Grant, London, Penguin Books, 1999.

Dronke, Peter, *Medieval Testimonies*. Glasgow, University of Glasgow Press, 1976.

Florentii Wigorniensis monachi chronicon ex chronicis, B. Thorpe, editor, 2, English Historical Society, 10 (1849)

Bibliography

Froissart, Jean, *Chronicles*, hrionline.ac.uk/onlinefroissart

Froissart, Jean, *Chronicles*, translated by G. Brereton, London, Penguin Classics, 1968, revised edition 1978.

Gervase of Canterbury *The Deeds of Kings* edited by W. Stubbs in *The Historical Works of Gervase of Canterbury*, Rolls Series, 1880.

Henry III Fine Rolls, *finerollshenry3.org.uk*.

Hildegardis Bingensis, Epistolarium, ed. Lieven Van Acker and Monika Klaes-Hachmoller, CCCM, 91, 91a, 91b Turnhout: Brepols, 1991, 1993, 2001.

Hildegard von Bingen, *The Letters of Hildegard of Bingen*, translated by Joseph L. Baird and Radd K. Ehrman, Oxford, Oxford University Press, 1994.

John of Salisbury, *The Letters of John of Salisbury*, edited by W.J. Miller, S.J. Butler, H.E. Butler and revised by C.N.L. Brooke, London, Thomas Nelson and Sons, 1955.

Julian of Norwich, *Revelations of Divine Love*, translated by John Skinner, New York, Doubleday, 1996.

Kempe, Margery, *The Book of Margery Kempe*, edited by S.B. Meech and H.E. Allen, Early English Text Society, 1940.

King James I, *The Poetical Remains of James I*, Edinburgh, J. and E. Balfour, 1793.

Luard, H. R., editor, *Matthaei Parisiensis, monachi sancti Albani, Chronica majora*, 7 vols., RS, 57 (1872–83).

Mackay, A. J. G., editor, *The historie and cronicles of Scotland ... by Robert Lindesay of Pitscottie*, 3 vols, Scottish Text Society, 42–3, 60 (1899–1911)

Magna Carta British Library, transcript from bl.uk

Maxwell, Herbert, *The Chronicle of Lanercost, 1272–1346*, e-book.

Nicolas, N.H. editor, *Testamenta vetusta: being illustrations from wills*, 2 vols. (1826).

Ordericus Vitalis, *The Ecclesiastical History of England and Normandy*, London, H.G. Bohn, 1853.

Paris, Matthew, Robert de Reading and others, *Flores Historiarum*, Volume III, edited by Henry Richards Luard, H.M. Stat. Off., 1890.

Peter Abelard, *Hymnarius Paraclitensis*, edited by Joseph Szöverffy, Albany, Classical Folia, 1975

Peter the Venerable, *The Letters of Peter the Venerable*, edited by Giles Constable, Cambridge, MA., 2v Harvard University Press, 1967.

Pisan, Christine de, *The Book of the City of Ladies*, translated and with introduction and notes by Rosalind Brown- Grant, London, Penguin, 1999.

Pizan, Christine de, *The Writings of Christine de Pizan*, translated by Nadia Margolis, edited by Charity Cannon Willard, New York, Persea Books, 1994.

Ralph of Coggeshall *The English Chronicle* edited by J. Stevenson in *Chronicon Anglicanum*, Rolls Series 1875.

Ralph of Diceto, *Images of History*, edited by W. Stubbs in *The Historical Works of Master Ralph of Diceto*, Rolls Series 1876

Richard of Devizes *The Chronicle of Richard of Devizes: concerning the deeds of Richard the First King of England also Richard of Cirencester's Description of Britain* translated and edited by JA Giles, London, 1841.

Roger of Wendover, *Roger of Wendover's Flowers of history, Comprising the history of England from the descent of the Saxons to A.D. 1235*, Volume II, edited by J.A. Giles, London, H.G. Bohn, 1849.

Sawyer, P.H. *Anglo-Saxon charters: an annotated list and bibliography*, Royal Historical Society Guides and Handbooks (1968).

Sharpe, J, translator, *The History of the Kings of England and of his Own Times by William Malmesbury*, Seeleys, 1854.

Stow, John, *The Annales of England*, *"The race of the Kings of Brytaine after the received opinion since Brute, &c"*, London, G. Bishop and T. Adams, 1605.

Strachey, J edited; *Rotuli parliamentorum ut et petitiones, et placita in parliamento*, 6 vols. (1767–77).

Symeon of Durham, *Vita Sanctae Margaretae Scotorum reginae, Symeonis Dunelmensis opera et collectanea*, ed. J. H. Hinde, Surtees Society, 1868.

The 'Barnwell' Annals (anon.), edited by W. Stubbs in *The Historical Collections of Walter of Coventry* Rolls Series 1873.

The Letters of Hildegard of Bingen, trans. Joseph L. Baird and Radd K. Ehrman Oxford University, 1994, 1998, 2004.

The Life of the Black Prince by the Herald of Sir John Chandos, edited by Mildred K. Pope, Oxford, Clarendon Press, 1910.

The register of Henry Chichele, Archbishop of Canterbury, 1414–1443. Edited by E.F. Jacob, Oxford, Oxford University Press, 1937–47.

Thomas of Walsingham, *Thomae Walsingham Historia Anglicana* (in part one of *Chronica Monasterii Sancti Albani*) ed. HT Riley in Rolls Series 1863–4. Vol. 1.

Trivet, Nicholas, *Annales Sex Regum Angliae* edited by T. Hog, 1845.

White, Hugh, translator, *Ancrene Wisse: Guide for Anchoresses*, Penguin, Harmondsworth, 1993.

Whitelock, D & D. C. Douglas, and S. I. Tucker, eds. and trans., *The Anglo-Saxon Chronicle: a revised translation* (1961).

Willard, Charity Cannon, editor, *The Writings of Christine de Pizan*, New York, Persea Books, 1994.

William of Malmesbury, *Chronicles of the Kings of England, From the Earliest Period to the Reign of King Stephen*, c. 1090–1143, edited by John Sharpe and J.A. Giles, London, H.G. Bohn, 1847.

Secondary Sources

A History of the County of Rutland: Volume 2, London, Victoria County History, 1935.

Abernethy, Susan, *Anne de Beaujeu, Duchess of Bourbon and Regent of France*, (article) the freelancehistorywriter.com, 13 November 2015.

Abernethy, Susan, *Jacqueline, Duchess of Bavaria-Straubing, Countess of Holland, Zeeland, Hainaut and Oostervant*, (article) thefreelancehistorywriter.com, 2 December 2016

Agde, Chris, *Le Triste Destin de Ingebourg de Danemark* (article) chrisagde.free.fr/capet, 2017.

Archer, Rowena E., *Chaucer, Alice, Duchess of Suffolk (c.1404–1475)* (article), *Oxford Dictionary of National Biography*, Oxford University Press, online edition, May 2011.

Asbridge, Thomas *the Greatest Knight: The Remarkable Life of William Marshal, the Power behind Five English Thrones*, London, Simon & Schuster, 2015.

Ashley, Mike, *The Mammoth Book of British Kings & Queens* London, Robinson, 1998.

Atkins, Martyn, *Jacqueline, suo jure Countess of Hainault, suo jure Countess of Holland, and suo jure Countess of Zeeland (1401–1436)* (article) *Oxford Dictionary of National Biography*, Oxford University Press, online edition, May 2006.

Baldwin, David, *Elizabeth Woodville, Mother of the Princes in the Tower*, Stroud, Sutton Publishing, 2002.

Barrow, G.W.S., *A Kingdom in crisis: Scotland and the Maid of Norway* (article), Scottish Historical Review, 69, 1990.

Barrow, G.W.S., *Margaret [St Margaret] (d. 1093), Queen of Scots, consort of Malcolm III* (article), *Oxford Dictionary of National Biography*, Oxford University Press, online edition, 2004.

Bartlett, Robert, *England Under the Norman and Angevin Kings, 1075–1225* Oxford, Oxford University Press, 2000.

Belfrage, Anna, *Weep, Ingeborg, weep* (article), annabelfrage.wordpress.com, 29 October 2016.

Bémont, Charles, *Medieval Europe, 395–1270*, Lecturable, e-book, 2012.

Bernardini, Alex, *Madame la Grande* (article), alex-bernardini.fr 33 December 2015.

Bloks, Moniek, *Anne of Kiev, the First Female Regent of France*, (article) historyofroyalwomen.com, 10 February 2015.

Bloks, Moniek, *Ingeborg of Denmark, the Repudiated French Queen*, (article) historyofroyalwomen.com, 20 April, 2015.

Borman, Tracy, *Matilda, Wife of the Conqueror, First Queen of England*, London, Vintage Books, 2012.

Boyd, Douglas, *Eleanor, April Queen of Aquitaine*, Stroud, Sutton Publishing, 2004.

britannica.com, *Jadwiga, Queen of Poland*, (article) The Editors, 9 September 2016.

British History Online, British-history.ac.uk

Brindle, Steven and Agnieszka Sadraei, *Conisbrough Castle, English heritage Guidebook*, London, English Heritage, 2015

Brooks, Richard, *The Knight who Saved England, William Marshal and the French Invasion, 1217*, Oxford, Osprey Publishing, 2014.

Brown, M.H., *Margaret (1424–1445)* (article), *Oxford Dictionary of National Biography*, Oxford University Press, online edition, 2004.

Burghart, Alex, *Æthelflæd, Iron Lady of Mercia* (article), BBC History Magazine, Vol. 12, no. 8, August 2011.

Campbell, Bruce, *Britain 1300* (article), History Today, Volume 50 (6), June 2000.

Cannon, John, editor, *The Oxford Companion to British History*, Oxford, Oxford University Press, 1997.

Casey, Anthony, *Jadwiga – Poland's Female King*, (article) inside-poland.com, 1 July 2013.

Clark, K.L., *The Nevills of Middleham: England's Most Powerful Family in the Wars of the Roses*, Stroud, The History Press, 2016.

Cockerill, Sara, *Eleanor of Castile: The shadow Queen*, Stroud, Amberley, 2014.

Cole, Teresa *The Norman Conquest: William the Conqueror's Subjugation of England*. Stroud, Amberley, 2016.

Crawford, Anne, editor and translator, *Letters of Medieval Women*, Stroud, Sutton Publishing, 2002.

Crazypolishguy.wordpress.com, *Jadwiga: The Woman Who Became Poland's King*, (article).

Danziger, Danny and John Gillingham, *1215 The Year of magna Carta* London, Hodder & Stoughton, 2004.

Davis, William Stearns, *A History of France from the Earliest Times to the Treaty of Versailles*, Cambridge Massachusetts, The Riverside Press, 1919.

Dean, Kristie, *On the Trail of the Yorks*, Stroud, Amberley, 2016.

Devaux, Baptiste, *Anne de Beaujeu: une régent qui ne semble n'être jamais venue a Beaujeu* (article), leprogres.fr.

Dougherty, Martin J., *The Wars of the Roses, The Conflict that Inspired Game of Thrones*, London, Amber Books, 2015.

Douglas Murray, T, Editor, *Saint Joan of Arc's Trial and Condemnation* (article), Stjoan-centre.com/Trials

Duducu, Jem *Forgotten History: Unbelievable Moments from the Past* Stroud, Amberley, 2016.

Duncan, A.A.M., *Margaret the Maid of Norway] (1282/3–1290)* (article), Oxforddnb.com, 2004.

Duncan, A.A.M., *Randolph, Thomas, First Earl of Moray (d. 1332), soldier and guardian of Scotland* (article), *Oxford Dictionary of National Biography*, Oxford University Press, online edition, 2004.

Duruy, Victor, *History of the Middle Ages*, Lecturable, e-book, 2012.

Encyclopaedia Universalis, *Anne de France, dite La Dame de Beaujeu (1462–1522)* (article), universali.fr/encyclopedie, 15 September 2016.

englishmonarch.co.uk, *Gwenllian of Wales (June 1282–7 June 1337)* (article), 2004.

englishmonarch.co.uk; *Joan, Lady of Wales (c.1191–1237)* (article), 2004.

epistolae.ccnmtl.columbia.edu, *Anne of Kiev (Anna Yaroslavna)* (article).

epistolae.ccnmtl.columbia.edu, *Heloise, Abbess of the Paraclete* (article).

epistolae.ccnmtl.columbia.edu, *Hildegard of Bingen* (article).

Faculty.msmc.edu., *The Life and Triumphs of Christine de Pizan* (article)

Fairbank, F. Royston, *The Last Earl of Warenne and Surrey, and the Distribution of His Possessions,* (article) Yorkshire Archaeological Journal, Volume 19, 1907.

Farrer, William and Charles Travis Clay, editors, *Early Yorkshire Charters, Volume 8: The Honour of Warenne*, Cambridge, Cambridge University Press, 2013 edition, first published 1949.

Fraser, Antonia, *The Warrior Queens: Boadicea's Chariot,* London, George Weidenfeld & Nicolson Ltd, 1993.

Gabel, Mathias and Carlyn Iuzzolino, translators, *Jeanne d'Arc, Maid of Orleans, Deliverer of France.* London, Heineman, 1903.

Gardiner, Juliet and Neil Wenborn, Editors *History Today Companion to British History* London, Collins & Brown, 1995.

Géraud, Hercule, *Ingeburge de Danemark, reine de France, 1193–1236. Mémoire de feu Hercule Géraud, couronné par l'Académie des Inscriptions et Belles-Lettres dans sa séance du 11 août 1844. [Première partie.]* (article), Bibliothèque de l'école des chartes Année, 1845, Volume 6, Numéro 1, pp. 3–27.

Gillingham, John, *The Wars of the Roses, Peace & Conflict in 15th Century England*, London, Phoenix Press, 1988.

Given-Wilson, C, *Perrers, Alice (d. 1400/01)* (article) *Oxford Dictionary of National Biography*, Oxford University Press, online edition, January 2008.

Gladwin, Irene *The Sheriff: The Man and his Office,* Victor Gollancz, London, 1974.

Goodman, Anthony, *John of Gaunt: The Exercise of Princely Power in Fourteenth-Century Europe*, London, Routledge, 1992.

Goodman, Anthony, *Katherine (1372–1418)* (article), *Oxford Dictionary of National Biography*, Oxford University Press, online edition, 2004.

Grant, Lindy, *Eleanor of Aquitaine* (article), BBC History Magazine, August 2016.

Goubert, Pierre *The Course of French History* London, Routledge, 1991.

Green, Mary Anne Everett Green, *Lives of the Princesses of England from the Norman Conquest*, Volume 2, London, Longman, Brown, Green, Longman, & Roberts, 1857.

h2g2.com/approved_entry/A2503298, *Philippa of Lancaster (1360–1415) – A tale from the History of Portugal* (article), 15 June 2004, updated 2008.

Hallam, Elizabeth, editor, *Chronicles of the Age of Chivalry,* Twickenham, Tiger Books, 1995.

Bibliography

Hallam, Elizabeth, editor, *The Plantagenet Chronicles*, Twickenham, Tiger Books, 1995.

Hanley, Catherine, *Nichola de la Haye* (article), catherinehanley.co.uk.

Hanna-Black, Sara, *themortimersblog.wordpress.com*

Hanna-Black, Sara, *The Last Mortimers, 1330–1425*, Stroud, Amberley, not-yet-published.

Hazell, Dinah, *Rethinking Marie*, (article) sfsu.edu.

Higginbotham, Susan, *The Woodvilles, the Wars of the Roses and England's Most Infamous Family*, Stroud, The History Press, 2013.

Hilliam, David *Kings, Queens, Bones and Bastards: Who's Who in the English Monarchy from Egbert to Elizabeth II*, Stroud, The History Press, 2008 (first published 1998).

Historychannel.com.au, *Jadwiga of Poland*, (article)

Helle, K., *Norwegian foreign policy and the Maid of Norway* (article), Scottish Historical Review, 69, 1990.

Hodgman, Charlott, *Joan of Arc* (article), BBC History Magazine, Vol. 13 no 1, January 2012.

Huizinga, J. *The Waning of the Middle Ages*, 4th edition. London, The Folio Society, 2000.

Huneycutt, Lois L., *Adela, Countess of Blois (c.1067–1137)* (article), *Oxford Dictionary of National Biography*, Oxford University Press, online edition, 2004.

Hunt, Tony, *Marie (fl. c.1180–c.1189)* (article), *Oxford Dictionary of National Biography*, Oxford University Press, online edition, 2004.

James, Jeffrey, *Edward IV, Glorious Son of York*, Stroud, Amberley, 2015.

Jenner, Maureen, *Gwenllian, The Last Princess of Wales* (article), britainexpress.com.

Johnson, Paul *The Life and Times of Edward III* London, Wiedenfeld and Nicolson and Book Club Associates, 1984.

John, Terry, *Princess Nest – The Helen of Wales* (article) bluestonewales.com June 1, 2015.

Johns, Susan M., *Warenne, Isabel de, suo jure Countess of Surrey (d. 1203)* (article) *Oxford Dictionary of National Biography*, Oxford University Press, online edition, 2004.

Jones, Dan, *The Plantagenets, The Kings Who Made England*, Kindle edition, London, Harper Collins, 2013.

Jones, Michael, *24 Hours at Agincourt, 25 October 1415*, London, W.H. Allen, 2015.

Jones, Terry, *Terry Jones' Medieval Lives*, London, BBC Books, 2005.

Julian, Father John, *The Complete Julian of Norwich*, (3rd edition), Massachusetts, Paraclete Press, 2011.

Koenigsberger, H.G., *Medieval Europe 400–1500* New York, Longman, 1987.

Kramer, Kyra C., *Black Agnes and Psychological Warfare* (article), kyrackramer.com, 8 July 2016.

Laffin, John *Brassey's Battles: 3,500 Years of Conflict, Campaigns and Wars from A–Z*, London, Brassey's, 1995.

Lanhers, Yvonne, *Saint Joan of Arc* (article), Britannica.com 02/01/16.

Lewis, Matthew, *Henry III, the Son of Magna Carta*, Stroud, Amberley, 2016.

Lewis, Matthew, *Richard Duke of York, King by Right*, Stroud, Amberley, 2016.

Leyser, Henrietta, *Medieval Women, A Social History of Women in England 450–1500*, Phoenix, e-book, 2013.

Licence, Amy, *Red Roses, Blanche of Gaunt to Margaret Beaufort*, Stroud, The History Press, 2016.

Lloyd, Jean, *Christine de Pizan (b. 1365–d.1430)* (article), departments.kings.edu.

Lucraft, Jane, *Missing From History; Katherine Swynford* (article), History Today Volume 52 (5), May 2002.

Mackowiak, Philip A., *Joan of Arc's Heresy* (article), blog.oup.com, 30/05/16.

Maddicott, J.R, *Thomas of Lancaster, second Earl of Lancaster, second Earl of Leicester, and Earl of Lincoln (c.1278–1322)* (article), *Oxford Dictionary of National Biography*, Oxford University Press, online edition, January 2008.

Marlow, Joyce, *Kings & Queens of Britain*, (sixth edition) London, Artus Publishing, 1979.

Martindale, Jane, *Eleanor, suo jure Duchess of Aquitaine (c.1122–1204)* (article), *Oxford Dictionary of National Biography*, Oxford University Press, online edition, May 2006.

Mason, Emma, *Scandalous Nun: Heloïse d'Argenteuil* (article), historyextra.com 2 June 2016.

Matthew, Donald, *King Stephen*, London, Hambledon and London, 2002.

Maund, Kari *Princess Nest of Wales, Seductress of the English*, eBook edition, Stroud, The History Press, 2012.

Mcglynn, Sean, *King John and the French Invasion of England* (article), BBC History Magazine, Vol. 11, no. 6, June 2010.

Medievalists.net, *The Herbal Cures of Hildegard von Bingen – was she right?* (article), 24 July 2016.

Mews, Constant J., *The Lost Love Letters of Heloise and Abelard, Perceptions of Dialogue in Twelfth-Century France.* New York, St. Martin's Press, 1999.

Morris, Marc, *A Great and Terrible King: Edward I and the Forging of Britain*, London, Windmill Books, 2009.

Morris, Marc, *From Friendly Neighbours to Bitter Enemies* (article), BBC History Magazine, Vol. 9 no. 3, March 2008.

Morris, Marc *King John: Treachery, Tyranny and the Road to Magna Carta* London, Windmill Books, 2015.

Morris, Marc, *William I, England's Conqueror*, London, Penguin Books, 2016.

Morrison, Susan Signe, *Six Trailblazing Medieval Women* (article), historyextra. com, 2 June 2016.

Mortimer, Ian, *The Perfect King, the Life of Edward III*, Kindle edition, London, Jonathan Cape, 2006.

Mount, Toni, *A Year in the Life of Medieval England*, Stroud, Amberley, 2016.

Norgate, Kate and Rev. A.D. Carr, *Joan, d. 1237* (article), Oxfroddnb.com, 2004.

Mundy, John H., *The High Middle Ages 1150–1309*, London, The Folio Society, 1998.

Ormrod, WM; *English Historical Review* (article) December 2015.

Ormrod, WM; *The Reign of Edward III*, Stroud, Tempus, 2000.

Patterson, Robert B., *Isabella, suo jure Countess of Gloucester (c.1160–1217)* (article), *Oxford Dictionary of National Biography*, Oxford University Press, online edition, 2004.

Payling, S.J. *Cornewall, John, Baron Fanhope (d. 1443)* (article), *Oxford Dictionary of National Biography*, Oxford University Press, online edition, 2004.

Pilling, David, *Ladies in Cages* (article), facebook.com/KingEdwardI/, 28 November 2016.

Power, Eileen, *Medieval English Nunneries c. 1275–1535*, London, Cambridge University Press, 1922.

Prestwich, M., *Edward I and the Maid of Norway* (article), Scottish Historical Review, 69, 1990.

Ramirez, Janina, *Julian of Norwich, a Very Brief History*, London, SPCK Publishing, 2016.

Bibliography

Rawcliffe, C., *The Staffords, Earls of Stafford and Dukes of Buckingham, 1394–1521*, Cambridge Studies in Medieval Life and Thought, 3rd ser., 11, 1978.

Rex, Peter; *William the Conqueror, the Bastard of Normandy* (third edition) Stroud, Amberley, 2016.

Riddy, Felicity, *Kempe, Margery (b. c.1373, d. in or after 1438)* (article), *Oxford Dictionary of National Biography*, Oxford University Press, online edition, May 2009.

Ross, David *Scotland, History of a Nation*, Broxburn, Lomond Books Ltd, 2014.

Ross, David, editor, *Sempringham Priory, Church and Holy Well*, (article) britainexpress.com.

Royalwomen.tripod.com, *Jadwiga of Poland*, (article).

Russiapedia.rt.com, *Prominent Russians: Anna Yaroslavna* (article), russiapedia. rt.com/prominent-russians/the-ryurikovich-dynasty/anna-yaroslavna, 2005–2017.

Santuiste, David, *Edward IV and the Wars of the Roses*, Barnsley, S. Yorks, Pen & Sword, 2010

Seward, Desmond; *The Demon's Brood* London, Constable, 2014.

Shakespeare, William, *Henry VI, Part 3*, edited by Edward Burns, e-book, 2009.

Shoaf, Judith P., *The Lais of Marie de France* (article) users.clas.ufl.edu 1991–1996.

Southern, R.W., *The Making of the Middle Ages*, 4th edition, London, The Folio Society, 1998.

Spiegel, Harriet, editor and translator, *Marie de France: Fables*, Toronto, University of Toronto Press, 1994.

Stacey, R.C., *Divorce, Medieval Welsh Style*, (article), *Speculum*, Volume 77, issue 4 October 2002, University of Chicago Press.

Stansfield, M.M.N., *Holland, Thomas, Earl of Kent (c.1315–1360)*, Oxfroddnb. com, Jan. 2008.

Stringer, Keith, *Joan (1210–1237)* (article), *Oxford Dictionary of National Biography*, Oxford University Press, online edition, 2004.

Sturdy, David *Alfred the Great*, London, Constable, 1995.

Summerson, Henry, *Clifford, Thomas, sixth Baron Clifford (1362/3–1391)* (article), *Oxford Dictionary of National Biography*, Oxford University Press, online edition, 2008.

Swaton Parish Council, *The History of Swaton* (article), swaton.org.uk

Tallis, Nicola, *Alice Chaucer, Duchess of Suffolk* (article), nicolatallis.com, 19/08/16.

The Princess Gwenllian Society, *Gwenllian – The Facts* (article), Princessgwenllian. co.uk.

Thompson, S.P., *Mary [Mary of Blois], suo jure Countess of Boulogne (d. 1182), Princess and abbess of Romsey* (article), *Oxford Dictionary of National. Biography*, Oxford University Press, online edition, May 2014.

Throop, Priscilla, *Hildegard von Bingen's Physica: The Complete English Translation of Her Classic Work on Health and Healing*, Rochester, Vermont, Healing Arts Press, 1998.

Tranter, Nigel, *The Story of Scotland*, e-book, 4th edition, Neil Wilson Publishing, 2011.

Urban, William, *The Teutonic Knights, a Military History*, London, Greenhilll Books, 2003.

Van Houts, Elizabeth; *Matilda of Flanders (d. 1083) Queen of England, consort of William I* (article), *Oxford Dictionary of National Biography*, Oxford University Press, online edition, May 2008.

Wainwright, Brian, *Maud Clifford secures a good divorce settlement* (article), yorkistage.blogspot.co.uk, 9 March 2008

Walker, Simon, *Katherine Roelt (1350?–1403)* (article), *Oxford Dictionary of National Biography*, Oxford University Press, online edition, January 2008.

Wall, Martin, *The Anglo-Saxons in 100 Facts* Stroud, Amberley, 2016.

Wall, Martin, *The Anglo-Saxon Age, the Birth of England*, Stroud, Amberley, 2015.

Wall, Martin, *Warriors and Kings, The 1500–Year Battle for Celtic Britain*, Stroud, Amberley, 2017.

Ward, Emily Joan, *Anne of Kiev (c.1024–c.1075) and a reassessment of maternal power in the minority kingship of Philip I of France* (article), Institute of Historical Research, vol. 89, no. 245, August 2016.

Warner, Kathryn, *Isabella of France, The Rebel Queen*, Amberley, Stroud, 2016.

Watson, Fiona, *Bruce, Christian (d. 1356), Oxford Dictionary of National Biography*, Oxford University Press, online edition, 2004.

Watson, Fiona, *Buchan, Isabel, Countess of Buchan (b. c.1270, d. after 1313)* (article), *Oxford Dictionary of National Biography*, Oxford University Press, online edition, 2004.

Watson, Fiona, *Dunbar, Patrick, eighth Earl of Dunbar or of March, and Earl of Moray (1285–1369), soldier and magnate* (article), *Oxford Dictionary of National Biography*, Oxford University Press, online edition, January 2008.

Weir, Alison, *Britain's Royal Families; the Complete Genealogy* London, Pimlico, 1996 (second edition).

Weir, Alison, *Eleanor of Aquitaine; By the Wrath of God, Queen of England*, London, Jonathan Cape, 1999.

Weir, Alison, *The Wars of the Roses*, London, Jonathan Cape, 1995.

Wilkinson, Louise, *Joan, daughter of King John* (article), magnacarta800th.com. 2016.

Wilkinson, Louise *Women in Thirteenth-Century Lincolnshire* Suffolk, Boydell, 2007.

Willard, Charity Cannon, *Christine de Pizan: Her Life and Works*, New York, Persea Books, 1984.

Williamson, David *Brewer's British Royalty* London, Cassell, 1996.

Wilson, Derek, *The Plantagenets*, London, Quercus, 2011.

Woodruff, Douglas, *The Life and Times of Alfred the Great*, London, George Weidenfeld and Nocolson Ltd and Book Club Associates, 1974.

Wright, James, *A Place for Our Kings: The History and Archaeology of a Mediaeval Royal Palace in the Heart of Sherwood Forest*, London, Triskele Publishing, 2016.

Yonge, Charlotte M., *History of France*, New York, D. Appleton and Company, 1882.

Zarzeczny, Dr M., *The Woman King of Poland*, (article), historyandheadlines. com, 2013.

Index